Decisions and Organizations

James G. March

Basil Blackwell

First published 1988
First published in paperback 1989
Reprinted 1989, 1990

Basil Blackwell Ltd
108 Cowley Road, Oxford OX4 1JF, UK

Basil Blackwell, Inc.
3 Cambridge Center
Cambridge, Massachusetts 02142, USA

British Library Cataloguing in Publication Data

A CIP catalogue record for this book is available from the British Library.

Library of Congress Cataloging-in-Publication Data

March, James G.
Decisions and organizations/James G. March.
p. cm.
Collection of previously published essays.
ISBN 0-631-15812-X
ISBN 0-631-168567 (pbk.)
1. Decision-making. 2. Organization. I. Title.
HD30.23.M366 1988 87-29362
658.4′03–dc 19

Typeset in 10 on 12pt Times by Dobbie Typesetting Service, Plymouth, Devon
Printed and bound in Great Britain by Billing & Sons Ltd., Worcester.

Contents

Acknowledgements

The papers reprinted here are products of drinking wine with friends and corrupting them into conversation. Their specific contributions are recorded to some extent by references in the papers and by the fact that many of the papers are co-authored. I am grateful for the collaboration of my co-authors Vicki Baier, Michael Cohen, Richard Cyert, Edward Feigenbaum, Martha Feldman, Richard Harrison, Scott Herriott, Daniel Levinthal, Curtis Manns, James C. March, Johan Olsen, Harald Sætren, Guje Sevón, and Zur Shapira; and for the cooperation of the journals in which the papers first appeared. The financial support of various foundations and institutions on particular projects is acknowledged in the individual pieces, but I should like to emphasize the importance of the support given by the Spencer Foundation. Blame for the present volume lies with Tony Sweeney, who conceived the idea, and Carol Busia, who put it all together.

The contributions of others accumulate, however, and these papers cover a span of more than thirty years. Consequently, I should like to take this opportunity to acknowledge my debts to four groups of associates. The first group is a group of colleagues whom I have long known, admired and read with particular profit: Kenneth Arrow, Robert Dahl, Jon Elster, Alexander George, Albert Hirschman, Harold Leavitt, Charles Lindblom, Martin Lipset, Robert Merton, John Meyer, Charles Perrow, Jeffrey Pfeffer, Richard Scott, Herbert Simon, Arthur Stinchcombe, Amos Tversky, Karl Weick, Harrison White and Sidney Winter.

The second group is a group of Scandinavians who have contributed greatly, not only to extending my appreciation of organizations but also to making my life richer: Flemming Agersnap, Torben Agersnap, Lennart Arvedsen, Torben Beck-Jørgensen, Ingmar Björkman, Finn Borum, Berit Bratbak, Nils Brunsson, Søren Christensen, Morten Egeberg, Harald Enderud, Lars Engwall, Arent Greve, Chris Gudnason, Ingemund Hägg, Bo Hedberg, Gudmund Hernes, Helga Hernes, Gull-May Holst, Knut Jacobsen, Bengt Jacobsson, Finn Junge-Jensen, Birgitte Knudsen, Kristian Kreiner,

Per Lægreid, Janne Larsen, Helge Larsen, Johan Olsen, Dick Ramstrom, Torger Reve, Kåre Rommetveit, Jens Ove Riis, Paul Roness, Kjell-Arne Røvik, Harald Sætren, Majken Schulz, Janne Seeman, Guje Sevón, Jesper Sørensen, Per Stava, Jesper Strandgaard, Risto Tainio and Bengt-Arne Vedin.

The third group is a group of former doctoral and post-doctoral students of mine. I cannot claim them, but they can claim me. They include Svein Andersen, David Anderson, Jonathan Aronson, Elaine Backman, Vicki Eaton Baier, James Barr, Jerry Beasley, Charles Bonini, Anthony Bower, Ross Boylan, David Brereton, Warren Brown, Alan Campbell, Hanoria Casey, Ellen Chaffee, Geoffrey Clarkson, Carol Clawson, Kalman Cohen, Michael Cohen, Rey Contreras, Dwight Crane, Patrick Crecine, James Crotty, John Cumpsty, Larry Cuban, John Curry, Bryan Delaney, William Dill, Julia Dilova, Elaine Draper, Carla Edlefson, George Ekker, Omar El Sawy, Carson Eoyang, Suzanne Estler, Edward Feigenbaum, John Feilders, Julian Feldman, Martha Feldman, Tammy Feldman, Fernando García-León, Mary Garrett, Donald Gerwin, James Glenn, Jane Hannaway, Elisabeth Hansot, Peter Harris, Richard Harrison, Scott Herriott, Dean Hubbard, Herschel Kanter, Alice Kaplan, David Klahr, Kenneth Knight, Lena Kolarska, Thomas Kosnik, Theresa Lant, Daniel Levinthal, Barbara Levitt, Raymond Levitt, Ferdinand Levy, Arie Lewin, Pertti Lounamaa, Mary Ann Maguire, Curtis Manns, Gloria Marshall, Lynn Mather, Timothy McGuire, William McWhinney, Debra Meyerson, Stephen Mezias, Anne Miner, Brian Mittman, Chadwick Moore, Dale Mortenson, Patrick Murphy, Alan Patz, John Payne, Vance Peterson, Lawrence Pinfield, Stanley Pogrow, Louis Pondy, William Pounds, Lorraine Prinsky, Daniel Quirici, Amylou Reyes, Allyn Romanow, Jeffrey Roughgarden, J. Rounds, Stephen Rowley, Kaye Schoonhoven, Jitendra Singh, Sim Sitkin, Peggy Smith, Peer Soelberg, Lee Sproull, William Starbuck, Nelly Stromquist, Charles Sullivan, Stephen Swerdlick, Michal Tamuz, Theodore Van Wormer, Dale Weigel, Stephen Weiner, Andrew Whinston, Gail Whitacre, Matthew Willard, Oliver Williamson, David Wolf, Wayne Wormley, Jo Zettler and Stanley Ziontz.

The fourth group is a group of secretaries who have given intelligence, sanity, and imagination to the ordinary life of academe: Evelyn Adams, Julia Ball, Barbara Beuche, Ethel Blank, Donna Dill, Jackie Fry, Marsha Mavis, Carolyn Nattress and Mary Tomkinson.

If despite this impressive array of teachers I have failed to extract a good idea or two, the fault lies with me – or perhaps with the wine.

James G. March
Stanford, California

Introduction: A Chronicle of Speculations About Decision-Making in Organizations

James G. March

A Prologue

This is a story of several decades of speculations about organizational decision-making, a chronology of sorts. The story is fiction in at least two respects. First, it is organized around one person's work, and life is not. Second, it does not describe how the speculations actually evolved, but rather how they might be imagined to have evolved in a more orderly world. Unlike the former, the latter fiction may be defensible. A record of research can be written better as an interpretation of an incomplete tapestry of ideas than as a description of the curious chaos of its weaving.

The background is a simple set of ideas that had become the received doctrine about decision-making by 1950. Although they have been modified substantially as a result of research since that time, these ideas continue to shape the questions asked in empirical and theoretical studies of individual and organizational choice. They portray decision-making as intentional, consequential, and optimizing. That is, they assume that decisions are based on preferences (e.g., wants, needs, values, goals, interests, subjective utilities) and expectations about outcomes associated with different alternative

This chapter is based on a paper originally prepared for presentation at the Exxon lecture series on decision-making, Northwestern University, 24 October, 1986. The research has been supported by grants from the Spencer Foundation, the Mellon Foundation, and the Stanford Graduate School of Business. It has benefited from a large number of collaborators, some of whom, but not all, are listed in the references. I should acknowledge particularly my debt to Johan P. Olsen.

actions. And they assume that the best possible alternative (in terms of its consequences for a decision-maker's preferences) is chosen.

These canons of choice, found most purely in statistical decision theory and microeconomic theory, and often somewhat sullied to deal with specific cases, underlie a substantial share of the descriptive theories of modern social science. Everyday and cataclysmic events are interpreted as happening because decision-makers with the resources to make them happen expect them to lead to better consequences (as measured by the decision-maker's preferences) than will other alternatives. The ideas also are the basis for modern prescriptions for intelligent choice. A good choice from this perspective is one that considers alternatives in terms of their outcomes, normally in the form of a probability distribution over the possible consequences, conditional on a particular choice, and chooses that alternative that has the highest expected utility. Improving the quality of decision-making, in these terms, involves inducing decision-makers to follow such precepts and providing analytical aids to assist them in their calculations.

Such a theory of choice has a strong claim on scientific enthusiasm: It has been used to predict important elements of aggregate human behavior and to improve the performance of individuals and organizations; it has an axiomatic base and theoretical structure of elegance and grace; and it celebrates a view of human capacities that reinforces and extends dominant Western ideologies glorifying the role of reason in human affairs. Although decision theory has some widely-recognized problems, it has become a modern classic of truth, beauty, and justice. And although there are contending religions, it is the established church of social science.

Students of organizational decision-making are members of a deviant sect within the same church. Their challenges to dominant doctrines are in some respects fundamental, but there is a persistent symbiosis between their ideas and more doctrinaire conceptions of choice. Even while rejecting important features of the theory, behavioral speculations about decision-making in organizations, for the most part, treat the basic framework of decision theory as compelling. And although organizational theorists are outcasts from the church, ideas consistent with many of their criticisms have found their way into established dogma. As a result, the recent history of the relation between the bishops of choice theory and the heretics of organization theory is a story of disagreements that have, for the most part, not led to a decisive schism but rather to a record of tension and accommodation (March, 1965; 1982; March and Sevón, 1987).

This chapter examines a semi-chronology of some of these heresies. The discussion is organized around four broad challenges to classical decision theory: First, a set of ideas emphasizing the importance of attention to decision-making. Second, an approach to conflicting interests in organizations that focuses on attention buffers to conflict. Third, a conception of organizational action as involving the following of rules that adapt to experience, rather than anticipatory choice. Fourth, a concern with the implications for decision-making of ambiguity about preferences, technology, and history. The ordering of the ideas is not entirely arbitrary. Some ideas mostly preceded other ideas. The ordering is not a strict chronology, however, and a more proper history would examine the ways in which the ideas evade conceptions of sequential development.

The Allocation of Attention

One of the oldest behavioral speculations about decision-making in organizations is that time and attention are scarce resources. Neither all alternatives nor all the consequences of any one of them can be known (March and Simon, 1958). Nor can organizations attend to all of their goals simultaneously (Cyert and March, 1963). Awareness of limitations on attention has led to concern for making the costs of obtaining information an explicit part of the structure of decision problems, and to the development of various forms of information and transaction cost economics that comprise a large part of contemporary microeconomic theory. Students of organizations, however, have generally been less interested in treating observed anomalies in organizational behavior in terms of information costs than in developing a behavioral theory of attention allocation. That interest leads them to see the organization of attention as a central process out of which decisions arise, rather than simply one aspect of the cost structure (March and Simon, 1958; March and Olsen, 1976). Since only a few alternatives, consequences, and goals can be considered simultaneously, actions are determined less by choices among alternatives than by decisions with respect to search.

Behavioral theories of organizational search are built on two little ideas that have proven remarkably durable. The first idea is that success is less a variable than a state (March and Simon, 1958; Cyert and March, 1963). That is, organizations distinguish rather sharply between meeting a target (success) and not meeting it (failure). They do not distinguish nearly so sharply between various levels of success or failure. In a sense, this suggests a step-function utility; and the idea of satisficing as reflecting a simplification utilities or a decision-rule was common in initial treatments (March and Simon, 1958). However, in theories of organizational decision-making, a target, or aspiration level, is not so much a step-function preference as it is a trigger for search. Organizations devote more attention to activities that are failing to meet targets than they do to activities that are meeting targets (March and Simon, 1958; Cyert and March, 1963). This squeaky wheel conception of attention is the second little idea in organizational theories of search. In periods and domains of success, search is reduced. In periods and domains of failure, search is increased. If an existing alternative is not good enough, search is undertaken for another one. An organization begins with a target and searches until it finds an alternative that meets that target. Search for new alternatives continues until a satisfactory alternative is discovered or created (Cyert and March, 1956). Thus, alternatives are not compared with each other so much as they are reviewed sequentially and accepted or rejected on the basis of target aspirations for their consequences (March and Simon, 1958; Cyert, Dill and March, 1958; Cyert and March, 1963).

This simple theory of search has been used to illuminate two broad kinds of phenomena in organizational decision-making. The first is the way in which an organization directs energies among its various activities and goals. Organizations vary their search efforts in response to patterns of success and failure in their performances or expectations (Cyert, Feigenbaum and March, 1959; Cyert, March and Moore, 1962; Manns and March, 1978). For example, when faced with risky alternatives, managers do not simply assess risk as part of a package of exogenously determined attributes, but actively seek to redefine alternatives, looking for options that retain the opportunities but eliminate the dangers (March and Shapira, 1987). Such behavior fits naturally into a theory that sees choice as driven by attention allocation, less naturally into a theory that sees choice as driven by explicit optimization.

The second set of phenomena illuminated by such a theory of search involves organizational slack, i.e., resources and effort directed toward activities that cannot be justified easily in terms of their immediate contribution to organizational objectives. Slack increases during periods of success and declines during periods of failure (March and Simon, 1958; Cyert, Feigenbaum and March, 1959; Cyert and March, 1963). Early theories of slack saw it primarily as a form of waste or as an incompletely rationalized reallocation of resources to subunits or individuals (March and Simon, 1958). But it was also pictured as an emergency reservoir of unused performance capabilities. By providing an inventory of unexploited efficiencies, slack serves to smooth performance in the face of a variable environment, a property not entirely lacking in organizational intelligence (March, 1981b). Subsequently, it has been observed that slack is also associated with changes in patterns of control in organizations and that activities stimulated by slack can be interpreted as forms of search. Slack search proceeds without the explicit organizational targets that distinguish problem-oriented search (Cyert and March, 1963; March, 1981b). Thus, it is less likely to solve immediate problems, more likely to be directed to subunit or individual objectives, and more likely to discover distinctively new alternatives. The distinction between slack search and problem-oriented search is at the base of several efforts to understand innovation in organizations and to explore the conditions under which different kinds of innovation are associated with failure or success (March, 1981b; Levinthal and March, 1981).

Limiting a theory of organizational search to search that is stimulated either by problems (problemistic search) or by the relaxation of organizational controls (slack search), however, underestimates the contribution of the market in alternatives and information to attention allocation. Although problems search for solutions, solutions also search for problems for which they might be imagined to be the solution (Cyert and March, 1963; March and Olsen, 1976; March, 1981b). Organizational discoveries, thus, are related not only to an organization's performance and aspirations, but also to the successes and failures of solution mongers in meeting their own targets. In such a conception, solutions for one organization are generated by the existence of problems in another; and a theory of organizational attention and search becomes a theory of a system of interacting organizations, rather than a single organization responding to an inert environment.

Conflict in Organizations

Some early treatments of organizational decision-making, particularly in economics, viewed organizations as actors possessing attributes commonly assigned to single individuals, particularly a coherent, well-defined set of preferences. But for the most part, decision-making in organizations has been seen as involving multiple actors with inconsistent preferences, thus a political system (Cyert and March, 1959; March, 1962a, 1962b). On the one hand this leads to some classical issues in evaluating alternative institutions for decision-making in the absence of agreement on objectives. Contemporary work on comparative institutions, both in economics and in political science, tends to focus on solving the problems of aggregation, the merging of prior individual preferences into the collective choice having favorable properties (e.g., with respect to reflecting Pareto-preferred solutions). The classical political institution for such a task is a system of elected representatives making bargains in the context of a representation function (Levitan and March, 1957; March 1958). The classical economic instrument for solving such problems is a contract and its associated incentives for inducing mutually beneficial behavior. Recent treatments, in economics as well as other social sciences, are substantially more sensitive to the problems of conflict than were some previous discussions of the employment contract, recognizing the difficulty of designing incentive schemes for strategic agents that lead them to behave in ways compatible with the wishes of principals, particularly where information is not completely shared. Students of organizations, like classical political philosophers, are inclined to augment this focus on representative systems and bilateral contracts between self-interested actors with an emphasis on institutions of integration that use processes of choice to develop shared preferences or senses of civic and bureaucratic virtue (March and Olsen, 1984; 1987), or to manage the salience of potential conflicts (March and Simon, 1958).

This search for appropriate institutions from a prescriptive point of view has been paralleled by a search for descriptive models of decision-making in conflict systems. Initially, these models emphasized the familiar mechanisms of classical theories of collective choice: power and exchange. Problems in the measurement of power in an organizational or social setting have been examined at some length (March, 1956a; 1957), and have been recognized to involve not only difficulties in measurement but also more profound inadequacies in model specification (March, 1966). Power has proven to be a disappointing concept. It tends to become a tautological label for the unexplained variance in a decision situation, or as a somewhat more political way of refering to differences in resources (endowments) in a system or bargaining and exchange (March, 1970).

The idea that individuals and groups within an organization use their resources, including their control over information, as leverage for pursuing their own interests has proven more useful as a way of framing organizational problems of conflict of interest. It has led to an interest in the ways in which the interests of different organizational participants fit together (March, 1954; 1955; 1980), and in the role of misrepresentation of information (lying) in organizations (March, 1978b; 1981a). Although it is by no means clear that organizational participants always lie when it would be in their immediate self-interest to do so; self-interested manipulation of information is a palpable feature of organizational life. The lack of innocence in organizational information is potentially important. For example, most standard procedures for statistical estimation implicitly assume innocent data, and it has been suggested that one reason experienced organizational participants do not follow such procedures is that they recognize the inadequacies of standard sampling theory in dealing with information provided by strategic actors (March, 1987a).

If strategic behavior is not only common but commonly anticipated, an adequate theory of information in organizations must deal with both the reality of lying (and other strategic action) and the likelihood of its anticipation. This concern for the equilibria of systems of anticipated reactions has made game theory an attractive vehicle for examining the interplay of known liars. In a more behavioral tradition, one early experiment of a very simple estimation problem under partial conflict of interest showed that counter-biases tended to correct for biases (Cyert, March and Starbuck, 1961), a result that has secured some support in more recent studies. But a more general treatment of the problem involves concepts such as trust and reputation that are familiar to behavioral students of organizations and have become a significant concern to modern game-theoretic treatments of strategic information (March, 1981a).

Students of conflict of interest in organizations, however, have also highlighted a somewhat different way in which organizations make decisions in the face of disparate individual and sub-unit goals. A conspicuous feature of standard theories of conflict is the assumption that all competing interests, desires, goals, and preferences in an organization are evoked at the same time and in the same place. Empirical observations of organizations, on the other hand, indicate that attention buffers in organizations limit the simultaneous salience of conflicting demands and the responsiveness of organizations to apparent power (March and Romelaer, 1976). Those buffers are the consequences of three standard features of organizational life. The first is departmentalization and the division of labor (March, 1953; March and Olsen, 1976). Hierarchical organizational structures narrow the audience for any particular decision process, and thereby restrict the realizations of potential conflict across divisions.

The second buffer arises from the limitations on attention imposed by scarcities of time and energy (Cyert and March, 1963; March and Olsen, 1976). Not everything can be attended by everyone. Attention is focused on current problems (currently evoked goals). Action taken to solve current problems produces new problems with respect to other (conflicting) goals, which are then activated. But by then, the individuals or groups who share the first set of concerns are likely to be no longer active. Thus, competing objectives can be addressed sequentially, and conflicts that would threaten a coalition if they were simultaneously salient are buffered from each other.

The third buffer that shields an organization from having to make latent conflict manifest is organizational slack. Excess resources reduce the likelihood that inconsistent demands will be triggered by simultaneous failures to meet targets (Cohen and March, 1974; 1986; March and Olsen, 1976). They reduce the need for joint decision-making (March and Simon, 1958). Large in-process inventories limit the occasions for conflict between producing and consuming units. Large uncommited resources reduce the risk of facing multiple budget demands that are, in total, impossible to meet (Cyert and March, 1963).

The buffers that make attention to conflicting pressures sequential rather than simultaneous result in organizational phenomena that are often viewed as perverse or inefficient. Organizations solve problems in one part of their domain by creating problems in another, which in turn are solved by creating problems in the first (or another) domain (Cyert and March, 1963). They set policies that they do not subsequently implement (March and Olsen, 1976; Baier, March and Sætren, 1986). They are tolerant of substantial inconsistencies among the actions of different subunits, and they allow the elaboration of multiple duplicative resources and activities (Cohen and March, 1974; 1986; March and Olsen, 1976). These apparently peculiar processes, however, cannot be trivially eliminated. Despite conventional modern ideologies advocating the confrontation and resolution of conflict, organizational experience with conflict indicates that institutions that would otherwise be seriously threatened by internal inconsistencies are able to sustain themselves for long periods by buffering inconsistent demands from each other. And this is possible, primarily because a fundamental feature of organizations is that not everything can be attended at once.

Adaptive Rules

Much organizational behavior, including choice behavior, involves rule-following more than calculation of consequences (March and Simon, 1958; Cyert and March, 1960; Cyert, March and Moore, 1962; Cyert and March, 1963). The logic of rule-following is one of appropriate, rather than optimal, behavior (March, 1981a). Organizations have standard operating procedures, some formally specified and less formal but nonetheless observed. Organizations use employees who are members of professions or who have learned crafts that specify proper procedures. Even where strong elements of consequential decision-making are observed, there are symptoms that the procedures are followed because they have been learned as appropriate in a particular situation or as part of a particular role, rather than because they reflect a deeper commitment to rational choice as a basis for action (March, 1978a; March and Olsen, 1983).

Recognition that rule-following characterizes much of the behavior in organizations directs attention to the processes by which rules are created and changed (March, 1981b; Levitt and March, 1988). The central presumption of most students of organizations is that rules encode experience, that they reflect but normally do not record the lessons of history (March, 1981b, March and Olsen, 1984). To see decisions as driven by rules, and rules as reflecting history, is to argue that a theory of anticipatory, consequential choice will be inadequate to describe many decision situations in organizations. In contrast to the way consequential decision processes look forward in terms of expectations about the future (Cyert and March, 1955), history dependent processes look backward to experience.

Consequential processes of decision-making match contemporaneous desires and actions; history dependent processes are independent of subjective preferences (at least at the time of action).

Most treatments of history dependent processes in the study of organizational decision-making involve either models of variation and selection, as found in population ecology, or models of direct and vicarious experiential learning, as found in theories of organizational learning and imitation (March and Olsen, 1975; March, 1981b; Levinthal and March, 1981; Herriott, Levinthal and March, 1985; Lounamaa and March, 1987). As instruments of intelligence, such processes have the advantage of summarizing the implications of irretrievable past events experienced by many different individuals and groups. As a result, it has occasionally been argued that history-dependent processes of selection and learning assure that surviving rules and organizational forms will have properties of optimality, that inferior rules will be eliminated or transformed, leaving the remaining rules as implicit solutions to optimization problems that are not explicitly solved nor solvable by current rule-followers. Such arguments have been used both to support theories of rational choice in the face of the observation that they posit unrealistic capabilities on the part of decision-makers and to sustain the proposition that effective organizations will be those that learn relatively quickly and relatively precisely.

More careful work on history-dependent processes suggests that they do not reliably lead either to a unique equilibrium or to optimal decisions (March and Olsen, 1975; 1984; March, 1987a). They have the disadvantage of assuming, but not assuring, a fit between the situation in which a rule is applied and the situation in which it has developed, thus of being insensitive to changes in either the environment or the preferences of rule followers (March, 1981b; March and Olsen, 1984). The processes often have multiple equilibria, often seem to be relatively slow compared with the rate of change in the environment, and under some characteristic circumstances trap an adaptive system in behavior rather far from the best (Levinthal and March, 1981; Herriott, Levinthal and March, 1985; Lounamaa and March, 1987).

The work can be illustrated by models of experiential learning in organizations. Several analyses of learning in organizations suggest that experiential learning often leads to intelligent actions, but that it is not guaranteed to do so (March and Olsen, 1975; Herriott, Levinthal and March, 1985). For example, organizations can be described as learning along two dimensions: First, they learn what allocations, strategies, or technologies to use. They come to pursue allocations, strategies, and technologies that have led to success in the past, tend to avoid those that have led to failure (Cyert and March, 1963; Lave and March, 1975).

Second, they learn competence. They become better at things they do often, lose competence at things they do infrequently (Levinthal and March, 1981; Herriott, Levinthal and March, 1985). Within such a framework, it has been shown that learning organizations can rather easily become fixated on sub-optimal allocations, strategies, or technologies. These models show how false learning can lead to actions that compound an error rather than correct it (Lave and March, 1975; Levintnal and March, 1981; Herriott, Levinthal and March, 1985). They indicate that even in a single organization operating within an exogenous environment, rapid learning is frequently a poor learning strategy. Rapid learning tends to overreact to noise and to foreclose the experimentation necessary for discovering good alternatives (Levinthal and March, 1981; Herriott, Levinthal and March, 1985; Lounamaa and March, 1987). When the analysis is extended to an environment of learning organizations, the complications of learning become more profound and the intelligence of rapid learning even more questionable (Herriott, Levinthal and March, 1985; Lounamaa and March, 1987).

These effects are moderated somewhat if experiential knowledge is pooled among a group of organizations through diffusion. Diffusion of experiential knowledge increases the sharing of experience, and average performance of organizations that share knowledge tends to be better than that of isolated learning organizations (Herriott, Levinthal and March, 1985). However, diffusion is a mixed blessing in the long run. As organizations become similar in their choices, their experiences tend to become similar, the information gained from the learning of one tends to become redundant with the learning gained from the learning of the others, and variation among organizations is reduced (Herriott, Levinthal and March, 1985). As a result, profiting from the experience of others appears to be a strategy that is often more sensible from the point of view of any one organization than it is from the point of view of the family of organizations (e.g., an industry or society) unless it is combined with some measures that assure continued experimentation, or foolishness (March, 1971; 1981b).

Such problems in identifying intelligent actions within complex ecologies become more obvious as we explore the development of strategies (whether learned or calculated) within competing organizations containing several levels existing over long periods of time. What is optimal in the short run is not necessarily optimal in the long run, so it is quite possible that strategies permitting an organization to thrive in its maturity make it unlikely that it will reach that stage (March, 1981b; Levinthal and March, 1981). What is optimal for a subunit is not necessarily optimal for the organization (March, 1955; 1980). What is optimal for each organization in a family of organizations may not be optimal for the family viewed as a renewable collection (March, 1956b; 1956c; 1981b; 1988). These complications have led to considerable diminution in our confidence in simple models for assessing the intelligence of alternative organizational actions.

Models of experiential learning treat success as rewarding and failure as punishing. In the tradition of earlier studies of organizations, success and failure are differentiated by a target or aspiration level. The sharpness of the distinction has consequences (Levinthal and March, 1981), but even greater consequences follow from the fact that the aspirations adapt to experience, generally rising with success and falling with failure – though not necessarily at the same rate (March and Simon, 1958; Cyert, Feigenbaum and March, 1959; Cyert and March, 1963) Aspirations also adapt to the experience of others within a reference group (Cyert and March, 1963; Herriott, Levinthal and March, 1985). These relations between aspirations and past experience have long been noted. Their importance has only gradually been recognized.

Aspirations that adapt strictly to the experience of the single organization change the original slack/search model. Slack adjustment and aspiration adaptation are, in effect, alternative mechanisms for bringing organizational goals and organizational performance together. When aspirations change in the direction of performance, parallel fluctuations in organizational slack are reduced (and vice versa) (March and Sevón, 1987). Adaptive aspirations also have consequences for risk taking in organizations. Risk taking is sensitive to the difference between performance and aspirations. A context of moderate failure leads to greater risk taking than a context of moderate success (March and Shapira, 1982; 1987; March, 1988). This variation in risk taking is usually discussed in terms of its contribution to improving the likelihood of survival (March, 1981b). Such a risk strategy protects survival; but because survivors become risk averse, the strategy limits the aggregate performance of the population of survivors. Thus, it may not be attractive to a family of organizations. However, it has been shown that variable risk taking, when combined with an appropriately adaptive aspiration, leads not only to a higher survival rate but also to higher average performance of survivors than is achieved with a fixed risk preference of the same scale (March, 1988).

Finally, adaptive aspirations have implications for understanding organizational learning. If there are modest fluctuations over time (due either to noise or to exogenous shocks) in the potential of the environment, rapid adjustment of an organization's aspirations to its own achievements tends to produce a sequence of successes and failures that is independent of the strategies chosen. Thus, it leads to high rates of experimentation but little effective learning (Levinthal and March, 1981; Herriott, Levinthal and March, 1985). On the other hand, if aspirations diffuse through a population of organizations, targets tend to become more similar across organizations than do achievements. As a result, organizations tend to have either long strings of subjective successes or long strings of subjective failures. Either kind of experience produces superstitious learning (Herriott, Levinthal and March, 1985). Organizations that are persistently successful tend to become fixated on one strategy or another, independent of their comparative values. Organizations that are persistently unsuccessful tend to keep shifting strategies (Lave and March, 1975).

Decision-making under Ambiguity

Classical models of choice and their modern derivatives ordinarily recognize two major kinds of complications in making decisions. The first is the fact that although the possible outcomes due to nature are known, it is not known which of these possibilities will be realized. Consequences can be anticipated only up to a probability distribution. This complication has led to considerable elaboration of procedures for dealing with single-person decision-making under risk. The second major complication is the fact that some consequences depend on the action of other strategic actors (who are simultaneously aware of the interdependence). This complication has led to considerable elaboration of game theory. Students of organizational decision-making have profited from, and contributed to, speculations about the consequences of these two classical problems in choice, but they have added several others that have come collectively to be called the problem of ambiguity.

The first ambiguity is an *ambiguity about preferences*. Within decision theory, preferences are treated as important but unproblematic. A decision-maker is assumed to have preferences that are consistent, stable, and exogenous to the choice process. Observations of organizations suggest that preferences are often far from consistent, stable, or exogenous (Feigenbaum and March, 1960; Cohen and March, 1974; 1986; March, 1978b). Indeed, organizations are frequently criticized for their inabilities to exhibit such preferences. The criticism is sometimes articulated in terms of implementation problems, although some of the more conspicuous studies of implementation failures seem to exaggerate the probable clarity of policy maker intentions (Baier, March and Sætren, 1986). More generally, organizational preferences change, partly as a result of exogenous pressures but also partly as a result of the actions they control. Aspiration levels adapt to experience, and the dimensions of desires are transformed through the experience of deciding among actions, implementing them, and observing their consequences (March, 1978b).

The second ambiguity is an *ambiguity about relevance*. In classical discussions of decision-making in organizations, a logic of causality connects policies to activities, means to ends, solutions to problems, and actions in one part of an organization to actions in another part. All of these linkages are seen as driven by a logic of causal connection. Actual events in organizations appear to be much less tightly coupled (March 1978a). Often there appear to be deep ambiguities in the causal linkages among the various activities of an organization, between problems and their 'solutions', and between how managers act and how they talk (Cohen and March, 1974; 1986; March and Olsen, 1976; March, 1984a). The garbage can model of organizational decision-making is one effort to define an alternative order in terms of which processes might be understood (Cohen, March and Olsen, 1972; March and Olsen, 1976). In a garbage can model, problems, solutions, and decision-makers are connected less by their causal relevance than by their simultaneity (March and Olsen, 1986). It is not a system of disorder, but it appears disorderly when considered within a standard means-end frame.

The third ambiguity is an *ambiguity about history*. Particularly within experiential learning models, but also in anticipatory models in so far as they use history as a basis for expectations about the future, the clarity of history is vital. Yet, history is clearly and notoriously ambiguous (Cohen and March, 1974; 1986; March and Olsen, 1975; 1976). For example, ambiguities about historical causality lie at the heart of difficulties with the concept of power in studies of social institutions (March, 1956a; 1957; 1966). Students of organizations have been particularly interested in the possibilities for, and consequences of, misunderstanding ambiguous experience (March and Cangelosi, 1966; March, 1974a; 1987a). One reflection of this interest is found in discussions of incomplete learning cycles. A complete learning cycle is one in which individual cognitions and preferences affect individual actions, which affect organizational choices, which affect environmental responses, which affect individual cognitions and preferences (March and Olsen, 1975). Although the ambiguities of history compromise the linkages, organizations continue to 'learn' as though the cycle were complete. As a result, a theory of organizational learning has to comprehend both the ways in which ambiguity affects the cycle and the dynamics of learning under such conditions (Cyert and March, 1963; March and Olsen, 1975; Herriott, Levinthal and March, 1985).

Recent interest in the confusions of history in organizations has focused especially on the ways in which well-known human biases in inference and attribution are observed, and facilitated, by the structure of organizations and the ways in which they make decisions (March and Shapira, 1982). Organizational arrangements confound the interpretation of history most clearly through systems of hierarchical promotion, with their powerful potential for superstitious learning on the part of successful managers and their biographers (Cohen and March, 1974; 1986; March, 1978a; 1987b). Although it is not always easy to distinguish observed patterns of mobility from those that would be observed if there were only modest differences among managers (March and March, 1977; 1978; March, 1978a), a system of hierarchical promotion yields top managers who are relatively confident of their own control over their destinies (Cohen and March, 1974; 1986; March and Shapira, 1987) and the appropriateness of their positions and rewards (March, 1984b).

The fourth ambiguity is an *ambiguity about interpretation*. Thinking about life in terms of choice introduces systematic bias into interpretations of decision processes (March, 1973). The fundamental presumption of virtually all theories of decision-making is that decision processes are organized around the making of decisions and understandable in terms of decision outcomes (March and Olsen, 1976; March, 1981a). Thus, information is seen as clarifying decision outcomes; participants in the process are seen as primarily concerned with influencing substantive decisions; the activities surrounding the making of decisions are interpreted in terms of the decisions that are made. Observations of organizations suggest that these presumptions may be misleading. Although information is used in making decisions, the gathering and citing of information is often better understood as symbolic action (Feldman and March, 1981; March and Sevón, 1984). Although participants care about outcomes, they also often care about the symbolic meaning of the process and the outcome (March, 1956d; March and Olsen, 1976; 1983). Although participants come and go partly as a function of the importance of the issues involved, they also enter the decision arena and leave it as a function of the rest of their lives within which any particular organizational decision often is relatively unimportant (March and Olsen, 1976; March and Romelaer, 1976). In short, decision-making is a highly contextual, sacred activity, surrounded by myth and ritual, and as much concerned with the interpretative order as with the specifics of particular choices (March and Olsen, 1983; 1984; March and Sevón, 1984).

Understanding these ambiguities is necessary not only for understanding and predicting organizational choice behavior, but also for improving it (Cohen and March, 1974; 1986; March 1978a; 1978b; 1984a). On the one hand, intelligent tactics within ambiguous worlds require an understanding of ambiguity even by a decision-maker who is endowed with unambiguous goals and a clear comprehension of history. Successful tactics for the Machiavellian actor in an ambiguous world call for the exploitation of garbage cans and incomplete learning cycles in the name of rationality (Cohen and March, 1974; 1986). They recognize the implications of superstitious learning for managerial motivation and education (March and March, 1977; March, 1978a; 1984a; 1987b). They include procedures for dealing with decision disappointment and biases in inference (March and Shapira, 1982; Harrison and March, 1984). They involve developing a culture of interpretation that organizes the actions of others and provides cultural support for desired actions (March and Olsen, 1983; 1987).

Such strategies are characteristically ways in which clever people can exploit ambiguity for unambiguous ends. Prescriptive discussions of ambiguity go beyond such tactics, however. It is argued that ambiguity is not only a fact of life, thus a necessary context for action by rational actors, but also often a normatively attractive state. The argument is that ambiguity about preferences allows goals to develop through experience (March, 1971; 1978b; Cohen and March, 1974; 1986). Ambiguity about relevance allows relevance to be explored (March and Olsen, 1976; 1986). Ambiguity about history facilitates motivation to cope with it (March, 1974b; 1975; 1987b). Ambiguity about interpretation allows communication to evoke more than a communicator knows (March and Sevón, 1984; March, 1987a). At a more general level, it is argued that the development of meaning through myth, ritual, and the elaboration of cultural symbols is a major part of modern organizational life. Interpretation, not choice, is what is distinctively human (March and Olsen, 1983; 1984; March and Sevón, 1984; March, 1987a).

An Epilogue

If scientific progress is measured by simplification, this is a story of retrogression. From a simple perspective of anticipatory, consequential, rational choice, we have gone first to a recognition of the limitations on rationality, then to concern for internal conflict, then to history dependent conceptions of human action, and finally to an awareness of the profound ambiguities surrounding action in organizations. Although decision-making as it occurs in organizations can probably be better understood and improved through these speculations, the speculations force us to less simple formulations. Life has proven to be more complicated than our earlier mythologies of it.

The research has been on organizational decision-making, and the speculations are about that domain; but they highlight a few issues that transcend the study of organizations or decision-making. These issues are particularly significant for understanding research on behavior that might be interpreted as being intentional or functional, thus as being understandable in terms of its consequences. Studies of decision-making in organizations are natural contexts for examining the limitations of consequential logics as bases for the interpretation of human action. The meta-theoretical issues that differentiate speculations about decisions in organizations from more classical ideas about choice are broad ones that permeate the social and behavioral sciences; and it is possible that some of the speculations that have arisen within the relatively limited context of modern hierarchical organizations as they make decisions may have implications for other speculative endeavors.

1. The question of *historical efficiency*. Many theories in a consequential tradition treat outcomes as a functionally necessary consequence of environmental conditions (at equilibrium). They assume that the processes of history are efficient in driving organizations to unique equilibria relatively quickly. As a result, such theories are relatively uninterested in time paths to equilibria or in the details of historical development. They are substantially indifferent to understanding the processes or mechanisms that translate environmental imperatives into action. The traditions of organizational decision research, on the other hand, are traditions of understanding the mechanisms by which outcomes are realized, even when correct predictions can be made without such understanding. And those traditions embrace the proposition that history is often inefficient in the sense that it has multiple equilibria and moves toward those equilibria relatively slowly.
2. The question of *ecological complexity*. Many theories of strategic action assume that strategies of decision-making that are intelligent for a single actor in an ecologically simple world will also prove to be intelligent in a complex ecology involving many actors making choices simultaneously. In effect, a complex world of intelligent action is assumed to be decomposable into numerous simple worlds whose interactions can be ignored. In a structure of nested interactive learning institutions, such a decomposition assumption is likely to be implausible. The problems include, but go beyond the interactions considered within n-person game theory. Studies of organizational decision-making suggest that the environmental context of human behavior is relatively complex, thus that determining intelligent action in a particular case is difficult, and many apparently attractive strategies will prove to be less attractive with deeper analysis or longer experience.
3. The question of *preferences*. Many contemporary theories of human behavior and human institutions assume that preferences are important to action, that choice is driven by human desires, wants, interests, values, goals, or subjective utilities; and that intelligence requires such a linkage. At the same time, the creation and modification of those preferences are typically treated as being incomprehensibly subjective, thus beyond the realm of either descriptive or prescriptive theories. In effect, we have

theories of willful and intentional action without a theory of will or intention. Theories of organizational decision-making are different in two respects. On the one hand, many elements of a theory of organizational decision-making are devoid of explicit preferences. Choices are made by following rules and roles and criteria of appropriateness, rather than by a calculation of expected consequences. On the other hand, decision-making is seen as a primary arena for the molding of preferences as well as acting on them. As a result, preferences become endogenous to a theory of choice.

4. The question of *coherence*. The idea of coherence is central to modern thinking about human existence. Individuals are seen as seeking and securing coherence in attitudes and between attitudes and action; institutions are seen as coherent assemblages of tasks and activities; intra-individual and inter-individual conflict is seen as moving toward resolution; health in individuals and institutions is associated with internal integration. Observations in organizations, on the other hand, suggest enduring incoherence. Although there are pressures and processes leading to coherence in organizations and action in organizations are in some ways impressively coordinated, the apparent coherence is produced less by resolving inconsistencies than by obscuring them. By limiting attention at any one time to a relatively small number of problems, values, participants, and constraints, organizations maintain an ideology of consistency within a reality of contradictions and dualities among actions and beliefs.

5. The question of *meaning*. Theories of intentional action generally build on ideas of comprehension mediated by language. These comprehensions are treated as substantially self-evident. The terms of reference of choice are taken as given and imposed on decision makers by the logic of the choice situation. Within the tradition of organizational decision research, on the other hand, all human behaviors, including the making of choices and learning from experience, are seen as embedded in interpretive systems to which they contribute and from which they draw meaning. It is through understanding these contributions to the interpretive order that the institutions of society can be understood.

At the outset, organization theorists were described as a deviant sect in the church of rational choice. Like many deviants, they simultaneously treasure their heretical status and labor to convert the faithful. In the latter mode, they cannot avoid noting the substantial extent to which the speculative heresies of students of organizational decision-making have achieved respectability in the catechism of the mother church. In the former mode, they observe, with an unreconciled mixture of dismay and gratification, the extent to which the bishops continue to sustain and reproduce their orthodoxies, leaving to the deviants the gratifications of savoring and elaborating their heresies.

References

Baier, V. E., March, J. G., and Sætren, H. (1986) Implementation and Ambiguity, *Scandinavian Journal of Management Studies*, 2: 197–212.

Cohen, M. D., and March, J. G. (1974) *Leadership and Ambiguity: The American College President*. New York, NY: McGraw-Hill.

Cohen, M. D., and March, J. G. (1986) *Leadership and Ambiguity*, 2nd ed. Boston, MA: Harvard Business School Press.

Cohen, M. D., March, J. G., and Olsen, J. P. (1972) A Garbage Can Model of Organizational Choice, *Administrative Science Quarterly*, 17: 1–25.

Cyert, R. M., Dill, W. R., and March, J. G. (1958) The Role of Expectations in Business Decision-Making, *Administrative Science Quarterly*, 3: 309–40.

Cyert, R. M., Feigenbaum, E. A., and March, J. G. (1959) Models in a Behavioral Theory of the Firm, *Behavioral Science*, 4: 81–95.

Cyert, R. M., and March, J. G. (1955) Organizational Structure and Pricing Behavior in an Oligopolistic Market, *American Economic Review*, 45: 129–39.

Cyert, R. M., and March, J. G., (1956) Organizational Factors in the Theory of Oligopoly, *Quarterly Journal of Economics*, 70: 44–64.

Cyert, R. M., and March, J. G., (1959) A Behavioral Theory of Organizational Objectives, in M. Haire (ed.), *Modern Organization Theory*. New York, NY: Wiley, pp. 76–90.

Cyert, R. M., and March, J. G., (1960) Business Operating Procedures, in B. von Haller Gilmer (ed.), *Industrial Psychology*. New York, NY: McGraw-Hill, pp. 67–87.

Cyert, R. M., and March, J. G., (1963) *A Behavioral Theory of the Firm*. Englewood Cliffs, NJ: Prentice-Hall.

Cyert, R. M., March, J. G., and Moore, C. G. (1962) A Model of Retail Ordering and Pricing Behavior by a Department Store, in R. Frank, A. A. Kuehn, W. Massy (eds), *Quantitative Techniques in Marketing Analysis*. Homewood, IL: Irwin, pp. 502–22.

Cyert, R. M., March, J. G., and Starbuck, W. H. (1961) Two Experiments on Organizational Estimation under Conflict of Interest, *Management Science*, 7: 254–64.

Feigenbaum, E. A., and March, J. G. (1960) Latent Motives, Group Discussion, and the 'Quality' of Group Decisions in a Non-objective Decision Problem, *Sociometry*, 23: 50–6.

Feldman, M. S., and March, J. G. (1981) Information in Organizations as Signal and Symbol, *Administrative Science Quarterly*, 26: 171–86.

Harrison, J. R., and March, J. G. (1984) Decision Making and Post-Decision Surprises, *Administrative Science Quarterly*, 29: 26–42.

Herriott, S. R., Levinthal, D., and March, J. G. (1985) Learning from Experience in Organizations, *American Economic Review*, 75: 298–302.

Lave, C. A., and March, J. G. (1975) *An introduction to Models in the Social Sciences*. Philadelphia: Harper and Row.

Levinthal, D., and March, J. G. (1981) A Model of Adaptive Organizational Search, *Journal of Economic Behavior and Organization*, 2: 307–33.

Levitan, R. E., and March, J. G. (1957) A Set of Necessary, Sufficient, and Independent Conditions for Proportional Representation (abstract), and *Econometrica*, 25: 361–2.

Levitt, B., and March, J. G. (1988) Organizational Learning, *Annual Review of Sociology*, 14: forthcoming.

Lounamaa, P. H., and March, J. G. (1987) Adaptive Coordination of a Learning Team, *Management Science*, 33: 107–23.

Manns, C. L., and March, J. G. (1978) Financial Adversity, Internal Competition, and Curricular Change in a University, *Administrative Science Quarterly*, 23: 541–52.

March, J. C., and March, J. G. (1977) Almost Random Careers: The Wisconsin School Superintendency, 1940–1972, *Administrative Science Quarterly*, 22: 307–409.

March, J. C., and March, J. G. (1978) Performance Sampling in Social Matches, *Administrative Science Quarterly*, 23: 434–53.

March, J. G. (1953) Husband-Wife Interaction over Political Issues, *Public Opinion Quarterly*, 17: 461–70.

March, J. G. (1954) Group Norms and the Active Minority, *American Sociological Review*, 19: 733–41.

March, J. G. (1955) Group Autonomy and Internal Group Control, *Social Forces*, 33: 322–6.

March, J. G. (1956a) An Introduction to the Theory and Measurement of Influence, *American Political Science Review*, 49: 431–51.

March, J. G. (1956b) Sociological Jurisprudence Revisited, *Stanford Law Review*, 8: 499–534.

March, J. G. (1956c) Reply, *Stanford Law Review*, 8: 772–3.

March, J. G. (1956d) Influence Measurement in Experimental and Semi-Experimental Groups, *Sociometry*, 19: 260–71.

March, J. G. (1957) Measurement Concepts in the Theory of Influence, *Journal of Politics*, 19: 202–26.

March, J. G. (1958) Party Legislative Representation as a Function of Election Results, *Public Opinion Quarterly*, 21: 521–42.

March, J. G. (1962a) Some Observations on Political Theory, in L. K. Caldwell (ed.), *New Viewpoints on Politics and Public Affairs*. Bloomington, IN: University of Indiana Press, pp. 121–39.

March, J. G. (1962b) The Business Firm as a Political Coalition, *Journal of Politics*, 24: 662–78.

March, J. G., (ed.) (1965) *Handbook of Organizations*. Chicago, IL: Rand McNally.

March, J. G. (1966) The Power of Power, in D. Easton (ed.), *Varieties of Political Theory*. Englewood Cliffs, NJ: Prentice-Hall, pp. 39–70.

March, J. G. (1970) Politics and the City, in W. Gorham (ed.), *Urban Processes as Viewed by the Social Sciences*. Washington, DC: The Urban Institute, pp. 21–37.

March, J. G. (1971) The Technology of Foolishness, *Civiløkonomen* (Copenhagen), 18(4): 4–12.

March, J. G. (1973) Model Bias in Social Action, *Review of Educational Research* 42: 413–29.

March, J. G. (1974a) Analytical Skills and the University Training of Educational Administrators, *Journal of Educational Administration,* 7: 17–44.

March, J. G. (1974b) Competence and Commitment in Educational Administration, in L. B. Mayhew (ed.), *Educational Leadership and Declining Enrollments.* Berkeley, CA: McCutchan, pp. 131–41.

March, J. G. (1975) Education and the Pursuit of Optimism, *Texas Tech Journal of Education,* 2: 5–16.

March, J. G. (1978a) American Public School Administration: A Short Analysis, *School Review,* 82: 217–50.

March, J. G. (1978b) Bounded Rationality, Ambiguity, and the Engineering of Choice, *Bell Journal of Economics,* 9: 587–608.

March, J. G. (1980) *Autonomy as a Factor in Group Organization: A Study in Politics.* New York, NY: Arno Press.

March, J. G. (1981a) Decisions in Organizations and Theories of Choice, in A. Van de Ven and W. Joyce (eds), *Assessing Organizational Design and Performance.* New York, NY: Wiley Interscience, pp. 205–44.

March, J. G. (1981b) Footnotes to Organizational Change, *Administrative Science Quarterly,* 26: 563–77.

March, J. G. (1982) Theories of Choice and Making Decisions, *Transaction/SOCIETY,* 21: 29–39.

March, J. G. (1984a) How We Talk and How We Act: Administrative Theory and Administrative Life, in T. J. Sergiovanni and J. E. Corbally (eds), *Leadership and Organization Culture.* Urbana, IL: University of Illinois Press, pp. 18–35.

March, J. G. (1984b) Notes on Ambiguity and Executive Compensation, *Scandinavian Journal of Management Studies,* 1: 53–64.

March, J. G. (1987a) Ambiguity and Accounting: The Elusive Link between Information and Decision Making, *Accounting, Organizations, and Society,* forthcoming, 1987.

March, J. G. (1987b) Mundane Organizations and Heroic Leaders, in L. Mayhew and F. León García (eds), *Seminarios Sobre Administración Universitaria.* Mexicali, México: Centro de Enseñanza Técnica y Superiór.

March, J. G. (1988) Variable Risk Preferences and Adaptive Aspirations, *Journal of Economic Behavior and Organizations,* 9: forthcoming.

March, J. G., and Cangelosi, V. E. (1966) An Experiment in Model Building, *Behavioral Science* 11: 71–5.

March, J. G., and Olsen, J. P. (1975) The Uncertainty of the Past: Organizational Learning Under Ambiguity, *European Journal of Political Research,* 3: 147–71.

March, J. G., and Olsen, J. P. (1976) *Ambiguity and Choice in Organizations.* Bergen, Norway: Universitetsforlaget.

March, J. G., and Olsen, J. P. (1983) Organizing Political Life: What Administrative Reorganization Tells Us about Governing, *American Political Science Review,* 77: 281–96.

March, J. G., and Olsen, J. P. (1984) The New Institutionalism: Organizational Factors in Political Life, *American Political Science Review,* 78: 734–49.

March, J. G., and Olsen, J. P. (1986) Garbage Can Models of Decision Making in Organizations, in J. G. March and R. Weissinger-Baylon (eds), *Ambiguity and Command: Organizational Perspectives on Military Decision Making.* Cambridge, MA: Ballinger, pp. 11–35.

March, J. G., and Olsen, J. P. (1987) Popular Sovereignty and the Search for Appropriate Institutions, *Journal of Public Policy*, forthcoming.

March, J. G., and Romelaer, P. (1976) Position and Presence in the Drift of Decisions in J. G. March and J. P. Olsen, *Ambiguity and Choice in Organizations.* Bergen, Norway: Universitetsforlaget, pp. 251–275.

March, J. G., and Sevón, G. (1984) Gossip, Information, and Decision-Making, in L. S. Sproull and J. P. Crecine (eds), *Advances in Information Processing in Organizations,* Vol. I. Greenwich, CT: JAI Press, pp. 95–107.

March, J. G., and Sevón, G. (1987) Behavioral Perspectives on Theories of the Firm, in W. F. van Raaij, G. M. van Veldhoven, and K–E. Wärneryd (eds), *Handbook of Economic Psychology.* Amsterdam: North-Holland.

March, J. G., and Shapira, Z. (1982) Behavioral Decision Theory and Organizational Decision Theory, in G. Ungson and D. Braunstein (eds), *Decision Making: An Interdisciplinary Inquiry.* Boston, MA: Kent Publishing Company, pp. 92–115.

March, J. G., and Shapira, Z. (1987) Managerial Perspectives on Risk and Risk Taking, *Management Science,* forthcoming.

March, J. G., and Simon, H. A. (1958) *Organizations.* New York, NY: Wiley.

Part I
The Allocation of Attention

1

Organizational Structure and Pricing Behavior in an Oligopolistic Market

R. M. Cyert and J. G. March

One of the most common propositions in the literature of organization theory is that a change in organizational structure results in a change in operative organization goals.[1] To the extent that this is true, it should be possible to develop a model that specifies a meaningful relationship between significant characteristics of organizational structure and some important attributes of organizational behavior.[2]

The theory of price determination in an oligopolistic market situation is generally unsatisfactory to economists.[3] Typically, neither the level of

1 See, for example, E. Dale, *Planning and Developing the Company Organization Structure,* AMA Research Report No. 20 (New York, 1952), pp. 23–38; H. A. Simon, D. W. Smithburg, V. A. Thompson, *Public Administration* (New York, 1950), pp. 136, 168–72. For a study of a specific example, see H. A. Simon, Birth of an Organization: The Economic Cooperation Administration. *Public Administration Review,* Autumn 1953, XIII, 227–36.

2 For a general discussion of the application of organizational theory to the economic theory of the firm, see A. G. Papandreou, Some Basic Problems in the Theory of the Firm, in B. F. Haley, (ed.), *A Survey of Contemporary Economics*, Vol. 2 (Homewood, Illinois, 1952). The present paper may be reviewed as an attempt to meet the comments of E. S. Mason, *ibid*, pp. 221–2, with reference to the need for specific theoretical examples of how the addition of organization theory variables contributes to the explanation of firm behavior.

3 See K. N. Rothschild, Price Theory and Oligopoly. *Economic Journal*, September 1947, LVII, 299–320.

This paper was first published in the *American Economic Review*, XLV, March 1955. It is based in part on work done under a grant made to the Carnegie Institute of Technology by the Ford Foundation for the study of organization theory. The authors, who are, respectively, assistant professor of economics and senior research fellow in administration at the Carnegie Institute of Technology, Pittsburgh, wish to express their thanks to their colleagues on the faculty of the Graduate School of Industrial Administration and to Professor James W. Fesler for their helpful comments on an earlier draft.

price nor price changes can be explained. The tendency of oligopolistic firms to change price relatively infrequently in comparison with firms in competitive markets has frequently been noted.[4] While it is not maintained here that organization theory can provide the whole, or even the major answer, it is the purpose of this paper to indicate some of the ways in which such theory can be brought to bear on the problem of the price behavior of a firm in an oligopoly market.

Since 'organizational structure' and 'price behavior' are ambiguous terms, they are defined in section I. In addition, the development of the model requires the specification of a series of functional relations between organizational features and pricing behavior. This is done in section II. In section III, an example of two ideal-type organization models, which under our hypotheses will exhibit distinctively different price behavior, is presented, and the implications of the paper are illustrated by an application to a classical problem in economic theory. Finally, in section IV, a program for empirical analysis is indicated.

Definition of Variables

The approach taken here should not be viewed as challenging the basic variables that have been treated as price determinants in economic theory. For firms operating in a perfectly competitive market, for example, nothing discussed in this paper has much relevance. The position taken is that the firm's perception of the market and the firm's perception of its capabilities for action are both affected by its own organizational structure. Given significantly different organizational structures, two firms facing the same external market and using the same set of variables in decision-making will exhibit substantial differences in price behavior.

Price behavior is defined in terms of three characteristics:

1 frequency of price change is measured as the number of changes per time unit;[5]
2 magnitude of price change is measured for any given change by the ratio of the amount of change (i.e., the absolute difference between the old and the new prices) to the old price;
3 direction of price change can be positive or negative, measured with respect to the last previous price.

---

4 P. Sweezy, Demand under Conditions of Oligopoly. *Journal Political Economy,* August 1939, XLVII, 568–73. See also, G. J. Stigler, 'The Kinky Oligopoly Demand Curve and Rigid Prices,' *Journal Political Economy,* October 1947, LV, 432–49.

5 In the present analysis, the primary interest is in the organizational effect on price behavior of firms operating in the same market. The restriction to firms operating in the same

Organization structure is defined in terms of two characteristics:

1 The communication pattern of the organization. Pricing decisions are assumed to be based upon expectations concerning future sales, costs, and competitors' behavior. One of the functions of the organization of the firm is to provide information upon which such expectations can be based, and the design of informational channels by means of which such information reaches the decision-makers comprises the communication pattern of the firm.[6]

Primary interest is in the relay points in a communication chain. A relay point is a 'message center' which receives, decodes, encodes, and then retransmits an item of information.[7] Relay points can be distinguished by the number of major variables (e.g., cost) about which they transmit information. This distinction is hypothesized to have important consequences for the amount of bias introduced at a particular relay point. Bias is defined to occur if any information is eliminated, modified, or added before a message is retransmitted. The character of control over a relay point is hypothesized to be decisive for the direction of the bias introduced, as is indicated more explicitly below.

The communication pattern of the organization is described by the nature of four different communication chains within the organization: the communication chains for demand information, for cost information, for information on competitors' behavior, and for information on firm policy. The nature of a given communication chain is determined by: (a) the number of relay points in the chain; (b) their character; and (c) their order. The number of relay points in a communication chain is represented by a nonnegative integer. The character of a relay point is determined by the type of information transmitted through it. If a relay point transmits only one type of information, it is defined to have the characteristic of that information. If information relating to more than one variable is transmitted by a relay point, the character of the relay point is determined by the relative

in the same market is made in order to hold constant the restraints imposed by market forces upon the frequency of price changes. Since the stringency of such restraints varies from one market to another, a comparison across markets of the organizational effect upon frequency of price change could not be made without the introduction of some concept of 'opportunities for change'.

6 Obviously, the relevant communication channels are those actually in use – not necessarily simply those specified by formal organization rules. There is no reason to believe that such insistence creates insuperable observational difficulties. See K. Davies, A Method of Studying Communication Patterns in Organizations. *Pers. Psychology,* Autumn 1953, VI, 301–12; A. H. Rubenstein, Problems in the Measurement of Interpersonal Communication in an Ongoing Situation. *Sociometry,* February 1953, XVI, 78–100.

7 See C. E. Shannon, *The Mathematical Theory of Communication* (Urbana, 1949).

frequency over time of incoming communications concerning the different variables. Thus, if most of the messages received relate to cost information, the relay point is considered to be a 'cost' relay. The ordering of relay points is specified to distinguish, for example, a communication chain for competitors' behavior in which information on competitors passes through a 'demand' relay point and subsequently through a 'cost' relay prior to reaching the decision-making unit from a similar chain in which the ordering of 'cost' and 'demand' relay points is reversed.

2 The size of the decision-making unit in the organization is measured by the number of individuals in the decision-making unit for each of whom it is correct to say that there is no more influential person in the unit. Thus, if the decision-making unit for a pricing decision is a committee of four in which two committee members are dominant over the other two but equal in power with respect to each other, the size of the decision-making unit is 2. The problem of identifying the distinguishing power differentials within the formal decision-making unit is susceptible to solution by the application of social-psychological techniques of influence measurement to the decision-making activities of the unit under investigation.[8] For example, one method for defining power relations that has been used successfully consists in an analysis of the remarks made during decision-making conferences.[9] The variable, therefore, is operationally defined although one should not expect the analysis in any given case to be simple. Under certain conditions, distinctive pricing consequences are seen as arising from critical differences in the size of the decision-making unit. These hypotheses are found below.

Functional Relations

Demand, cost, and competitors' behavior have been the standard variables of most oligopoly models since Cournot. This paper makes no attempt to deviate from that tradition. On the contrary, the goal is to augment oligopoly theory by introducing into it some fundamental propositions of the theory of organizational behavior. Two modifications of traditional oligopoly models are suggested by such theory. The first is recognition

8 For some examples of influence measures, see C. I. Hovland, I. L. Janis, H. H. Kelley, *Communication and Persuasion* (New Haven, 1953); R. Lippitt, N. Polansky, S. Rosen, The Dynamics of Power. *Human Rel.*, February 1952, V, 37–64.

9 J. G. March, Husband–Wife Interaction over Political Issues, *Public Opinion Quarterly*, Winter, 1953–4, XVII, 461–70; T. M. Mills, Power Relations in Three-Person Groups. *Am. Soc. Rev.*, Aug. 1953, XVIII, 351–57; F. L. Strodtbeck, Husband–Wife Interaction over Revealed Differences. *Am. Soc. Rev.*, August 1951, XVI, 468–73.

of the fact that the values of the relevant variables actually used within the firm for establishing price are functions both of data drawn from the real world and of the organizational structure through which those data are transmitted to the decision-making unit; the second is similar recognition of the fact that the method by which perceived information on the relevant variables is translated into pricing decisions is a function of the decision-making unit's perception of, and adherence to, official firm policy.

Official firm policy, in the sense in which it is used here, consists in a specific set of constraints placed by the holders of legitimate authority in the firm upon the pursuit of organizational goals by their subordinates. A series of hypotheses with respect to the relative dependence of a pricing decision upon official firm policy, given the size of the decision-making unit, is made. The mechanisms involved are also specified.

1 Decisions by a group will, in general, be more dependent upon firm policy than will decisions by an individual. The proposition is deduced from the theory of group norms and reference-group behavior.[10] There is a reasonable amount of evidence to support the prediction that an individual with an attitude at variance with his perception of the group's attitude will tend (according to the relevance of the group for the satisfaction of individual goals) to adjust his 'public' position to conform to the position he expects the group to take.[11] Such behavior may be exhibited even in the limiting case where all members hold a position at variance with their common perceptions of the group standard.[12] Thus, even if every member of the decision-making group is 'cost-minded', if each believes all of the others to be 'sales-minded', the decision will tend to be a sales-minded one. Since in the absence of contradictory evidence, each member of the group can be assumed to believe all other members of the group to be in agreement with firm policy, the operation of group norms serves to enforce conformity to that policy.

10 A reference group for a given individual consists in those other individuals with whom he perceives himself sharing common evaluative criteria for judging an attitudinal position. The literature on reference-group theory is fairly extensive. For example, see T. M. Newcomb, *Social Psychology* (New York, 1950), chapter 14, pp. 220–32; R. K. Merton and A. S. Kitt, Contributions to the Theory of Reference Group Behavior, in Merton and P. F. Lazarsfeld, (eds), *Continuities in Social Research, Studies in the Scope and Method of 'The American Soldier'* (Glencoe, 1950). The theory of group norms is less well developed. See S. A. Stouffer, An Analysis of Conflicting Social Norms. *Am. Soc. Rev.*, December 1949, XIV, 707–17; J. G. March, Group Norms and the Active Minority. *Am. Soc. Rev.*, December 1954, XIX, No. 6.

11 For example, see R. L. Gorden, Interaction Between Attitude and the Definition of the Situation in the Expression of Opinion. *Am. Soc. Rev.*, February 1952, XVII, 50–8; M. Sherif, A Study of Some Social Factors in Perception. *Archiv. Psychol.* (1935), No. 187.

12 On this point, see H. A. Simon, Notes on the Observation and Measurement of Political Power. *Jour. Pol.*, November 1953, XV, 500–16, especially 510–11.

From this it should be clear that when a relationship is predicted between the size of the decision-making unit and the extent to which decisions will be independent of official firm policy, the assumption is made that reference groups (e.g., Board of Directors, professional associations) other than the pricing unit itself can be ignored. Such an assumption is based on a prediction that all decision-making units, whether composed of an individual or a group, will be subject to the same outside pressures; but only the members of a group unit will have the additional pressure of internal group norms.[13]

2 If a decision contrary to firm policy is reached by a decision-making unit, it will be more stable if made by a group than if made by an individual. This follows from the premises of the preceding hypothesis. A group provides the individual with a defense against outside pressures and simultaneously exerts a pressure toward intragroup conformity upon him.[14] The group will ordinarily be less effective in enforcing a 'revolutionary' decision than in enforcing an 'ideologically sound' decision. This stems from the prediction that the latter type of decision will ordinarily create fewer cross-pressures than the former.[15]

With respect to the communication-structure variable, two hypotheses of perceptual bias are made:

1 As the length of the communication chain is increased, factors are introduced that have the effect of inhibiting change. The temporal bias introduced by the change in conditions during the interval from the original transmission of the information to its final receipt by the decision-making unit is represented as a function of the number of relay points through which the information must pass. Clearly, this is only an approximation. The significance of variations in transmission speed among the relay points (e.g., cost data travels more rapidly through cost channels than through demand channels) is neither denied nor introduced into the system, except implicitly in the statement of the second bias below.

The consequences of the temporal bias for the frequency of price adjustments stem both from the fact that one never 'catches up' with

13 Otherwise, it might be argued that where a pricing decision is made by a single individual, he will act with the originators of firm policy as a referent, and that, therefore, the test of the mechanism posited here would be vitiated by this restraint upon his 'independence'.

14 For a general introduction to the study of group pressures, see L. Festinger, S. Schachter, K. Back, *Social Pressures in Informal Groups* (New York, 1950); D. Cartwright and A. Zander, *Group Dynamics: Research and Theory* (Evanston, 1953), Part 3.

15 For discussions of the consequences of cross-pressures, see L. M. Killian, The Significance of Multiple-Group Membership in Disaster. *Am. Jour. Soc.,* January 1952, LVII, 309–14; L. Festinger, The Role of Group Belongingness in a Voting Situation. *Human Relations*, November 1947, I, 154–80; A. H. Leighton, *The Governing of Men* (Princeton, 1945).

current information and also from the attempts of members of the organization to adjust for the bias by means of forecasts (e.g., 'What will the situation be by the time this information reaches the decision-maker?'). It is hypothesized that both major consequences of the time-lag in communication serve to introduce into the premises of the pricing decision a bias against change. Note that this bias operates not only in the communication of, for example, cost information upward but also in the communication of firm-policy information downward.

2 The character of the communication chain introduces a bias into the information transmitted to the decision-making unit. The form of the bias is a tendency for a relay point to de-emphasize information inconsistent with the information with which it is primarily concerned. For example, let us make the assumption that the size of the market is consistently overestimated by sales departments and costs are consistently overestimated by accounting departments.[16] Let us further assume that overestimation of demand results in an aggressive price policy (i.e., frequent price changes, price-leadership), overestimation of cost in a passive price policy (i.e., infrequent changes, price-following). Under these assumptions, the firm's reaction to the behavior of others will be related to the number of biasing relay points through which cost data must pass relative to the number for demand data. In particular, it is predicted that the communication of demand data through a cost relay point will tend to produce a passive price policy, and the communication of cost data through a demand relay point an aggressive price policy. Similar deductions can be made with reference to communications downward regarding firm policy.

If the organization is stable, it is expected that the biasing of information will be reinforced by a learning phenomenon, resulting in a gradual lowering of the level in the communication hierarchy at which consistently suppressed information is filtered out of the communicated message. Thus, for example, if a given relay point has been transmitting information on the potential market but finds that this information is never retransmitted by the next relay point, and if there are no alternative channels of communication, the transmission of information on the potential market will tend to cease at the lower level.

Two Extreme Models

It is now possible to present two models that arise as antitheses from the propositions advanced above:[17]

16 See C. C. Saxton, *The Economics of Price Determination* (London, 1942), p. 148.

17 It should be clear that these are only two out of a large number of permutations and combinations of organizational features that might be defined.

1 A model of a firm in which price changes tend to be infrequent and reaction to competitors primarily passive might have the following organizational characteristics:

(a) Price is determined by a committee of equals.
(b) Communication chains between the decision-making unit and the primary sources of information are long (both upward and downward).
(c) The unit making the actual price decisions does not have the responsibility for establishing the criteria for price decisions (i.e., the decision-making unit is decentralized and is subject to dicta from above with respect to price policy).
(d) Demand information is channeled through a cost relay point.
(e) Firm policy information is channeled through a cost relay point.
(f) Information on competitors is channeled through a cost relay point.

2 A model of a firm in which price changes tend to be frequent and reaction to competitors tends to take the form of price-leadership might have the following organizational characteristics:

(a) Price is determined by an individual.
(b) Communication chains between the decision-making unit and the primary sources of information are short (both upward and downward).
(c) The decision-maker for specific price decisions also has the responsibility for establishing the criteria for price decision (i.e., the decision-making unit is centralized).
(d) Cost information is channeled through a demand relay point.
(e) Firm policy information is channeled through a demand relay point.[18]
(f) Information on competitors is channeled through a demand relay point.

In order to make explicit the implications found here for the analysis of the behavior of the firm, consider the predicted behavior in a classic duopoly situation of firms possessing the characteristics listed above. The Cournot duopoly model is taken for purposes of illustration.[19]

Let there be two duopolists in the market. Assume that Firm 1 has the organizational characteristics of the first model above, Firm 2 the

18 Strictly speaking, if '(c)' holds, there are no channels of firm-policy information since firm policy is made by the decision-maker; but in so far as one deals with approximations to the model, '(e)' becomes relevant.

19 See *Recherches sur les Principes Mathematiques de la Theorie des Richesses* (Paris, 1838), chapter 7. English translation: N. Bacon (trans.) *Researches into the Mathematical Principles of Wealth* (New York, 1897).

organizational characteristics of the second model above. Following Cournot, let there be no costs.

The market demand function is defined to be:

$$p = 25 - \frac{x_1 + x_2}{3}$$

where p = price
x_1 = output of Firm 1
x_2 = output of Firm 2.

It is further specified that each duopolist expects no reaction on the part of the other in response to a change in output:

$$\frac{dx_1}{dx_2} = \frac{dx_2}{dx_1} = 0 \text{ (conjectural variation terms).}$$

The Cournot market solution is reached by setting marginal revenue for each duopolist equal to zero (i.e., the point of optimal production under the assumption of no costs) and solving the resulting equations.

$$px_1 = 25x_1 - x_1 \frac{(x_1 + x_2)}{3} \tag{1}$$

$$\frac{dpx_1}{dx_1} = 25 - \frac{2x_1}{3} - \frac{x_2}{3} - \frac{x_1}{3} \quad \frac{dx_2}{dx_I} = 0 \tag{2}$$

$$x_1 = \frac{75}{2} - \frac{x_2}{2} \tag{3}$$

Similarly

$$x_2 = \frac{75}{2} - \frac{x_1}{2}. \tag{4}$$

And thus,

$$\begin{aligned} x_1 &= 25 \\ x_2 &= 25 \\ p &= 8.33. \end{aligned} \tag{5}$$

To explore some of the implications of this paper, assume that in the market specified above, Firm 1 and Firm 2 have reached the equilibrium point specified by the Cournot solution and are both producing 25 units. Next, assume that the market demand increases, such that

$$p = 30 - \frac{x_1 + x_2}{3}.$$

Under the assumptions previously outlined, it is predicted that Firm 1 will tend (a) to be slow in changing its perception of the market demand, (b) to underestimate demand when its perception does change, and (c) to give a positive value to the conjectural variation term. Thus, Firm 1 might have expectations with regard to the market demand function and the conjectural variation term as follows:

$$p = 25 - \frac{x_1 + x_2}{3}$$

$$\frac{dx_2}{dx_1} = 1.$$

Similarly, it is predicted that Firm 2 will tend (a) to change its perception of market demand quickly, (b) to overestimate demand, (c) to give a value of zero to the conjectural variation term. Thus Firm 2 might have the following estimates of key information:

$$p = 100 - x_1 - x_2$$

$$\frac{dx_1}{dx_2} = 0.$$

Under these conditions, the market solution deviates significantly from the standard Cournot solution.

$$x_1 = 10$$
$$x_2 = 45$$
$$p = 11.67.$$

The effect is to make Firm 2 dominant in the market.

Note that the solution above will be stable only if the new production level and the resultant profits are acceptable to the dominant control groups of the two firms. If, for example, the control groups of Firm 1 are not satisfied, they may demand a reorganization of the firm. Specifically, they may insist that its organizational structure be more like that of Firm 2. Such a reorganization would have obvious consequences for the estimation of demand, etc., with a resultant impact upon the market. In point of fact, it is possible to specify a set of values for organizational structure and the aspiration level of control groups such that a market which has, under standard economic analysis, a given equilibrium point has, with the addition of the organizational factors, either a different equilibrium point or no stable equilibrium at all.

Program for Empirical Analysis

In this paper a framework has been presented for dealing with certain variables which have not previously been formally introduced into oligopoly theory by economists but which, nevertheless, seem to be significant. That framework, and the hypotheses suggested, have been based explicitly upon a substantial body of empirical research previously reported in the literature of economics and the other social sciences. However, further refinement and testing of the hypotheses advanced here depends upon research specifically directed toward that end. While it is not the intention here to indicate in detail the types of empirical study that are being used to test the theoretical structure proposed above, some indication of the research program may be desirable.

Three stages of research are projected. On the basis of the framework outlined above, a myriad of models could be constructed by imputing values to the variables and by taking various combinations and permutations of these variables. Consequently, it seems clear that the most economical first step to be taken is a study within the theoretical framework defined in this paper of a number of firms in oligopolistic markets, with the goal of determining the patterns most commonly observed in the organizational variables specified above. Secondly, with constraints thus imposed upon the organizational variables, it will be possible to approximate more accurately the quantitative relationships existing. At this point, it is believed that the facilities of the laboratory can be exploited, since it is possible in the laboratory to study the effects of a single variable (or pair of variables, etc.) while holding others constant.[20] Such manipulation

20 In general, economists have not utilized laboratory studies to validate propositions concerning firm behavior to the same extent that students of the other social sciences have. On the basis of the experience of social psychologists in the use of the laboratory for the observation of organizational phenomena, it seems possible to utilize such techniques for the study of pricing behavior. For example, Harold Guetzkow, of the Carnegie Institute of Technology, has recently developed a laboratory design for testing certain propositions in organization theory. In his design, individual participants assume roles in sales and production departments in a firm and attempt to maximize firm profits in an experimentally standardized environment. Tests are made of the differences in profitability associated with differing organizational structures. It is anticipated that such a design can be modified, or a new design of this type developed, to provide experimental tests for the hypotheses relating pricing behavior and the organizational characteristics discussed in this paper.

is ordinarily impossible in the study of existing organizations, although under some conditions environmental circumstances may, in essence, duplicate an experimental situation by providing examples of all possible combinations of values for the variables under examination. The advantages of the laboratory stem from the opportunity to guarantee such examples. Finally, on the basis of the clarification provided by the laboratory results and the preliminary field study, a set of hypotheses appropriate to actual situations will be made. These hypotheses will be in the form of specific predictions of the dimensions of price behavior listed above and will be tested systematically against actual organizational and market data. In this fashion, the hypotheses generated will be accepted or rejected and a further refinement of oligopoly theory will be feasible.

2

Models in a Behavioral Theory of the Firm

R. M. Cyert, E. A. Feigenbaum, and J. G. March

Abstract

How do business organizations make decisions? What process do they follow in deciding how much to produce? And at what price? A behavioral theory of the firm is here explored. Using a specific type of duopoly, a model is written explicitly as a computer program to deal with the complex theory implicit in the process by which businesses make decisions. This model highlights our need for more empirical observations of organizational decision-making.

Recent attempts to develop a behavioral theory of the firm have focused particularly on the internal characteristics of a business firm as a decision-making organization. They have used the rough framework of both the theory of competitive pricing and the modern efforts to extend that theory to situations of imperfect competition such as the case of oligopoly and duopoly where only a few, or possibly only two, firms supply a given market. They have, however, gone further in introducing as an important part of the theory the process by which business organizations make decisions. Since business firms are organizations, it has seemed reasonable *a priori* to assume that a theory of business behavior ought not to treat them as individual decision-makers. (Alt, 1949; Bushaw and Clower, 1957;

This chapter was first published in *Behavioral Science*, Vol. 4, No. 2, April 1959. It is based on research supported by grants made by the Graduate School of Industrial Administration, Carnegie Institute of Technology, from the School's research funds and from funds provided by the Ford Foundation for the study of organizational behavior. The authors owe a considerable debt to a large group of colleagues and students for their comments on the general approach and specific models presented here.

Chamberlin, 1946; Cooper, 1951; Cyert and March, 1955; Cyert and March, 1956; Gordon, 1948; Papandreou, 1952; Weintraub, 1942).

Two major obstacles to the acceptance of such a theory of pricing are obvious. First, it must be shown that the theory is at least as good as other existing theories in its ability to predict firm behavior (Friedman, 1953). Convincing demonstrations on either side of this point are not available. In our judgment, a major portion of the effort in the next decade of research on pricing should be directed to answering this question (or to making it irrelevant). But we do not propose to discuss the point in detail here. Second, a way must be found to deal with the complex theory implicit in the decision-making process approach. A major problem perceived by those sympathetic to a behavioral theory has been the lack of a methodology suitable for handling the kinds of complexities that seemed to be needed (Koopmans, 1957). It is to this problem and to the development of a specific model to which we address ourselves in this paper.

We show that a relatively complex model of the firm as a decision-making organization can be developed and used to yield economically relevant and testable predictions of business behavior. The methodology involved is computer simulation. The model is one of a specific type of duopoly. As a rough test of resonableness, we compare the predictions of the model with actual data. Our hope is that the model will illustrate the promise of simulation as a technique of model building in economic theory and the behavioral sciences in general and at the same time demonstrate a general method for examining many of the concepts previously discussed in more abstract terms.

The Decision-Making Process

Recent theories of organizational behavior have emphasized several important characteristics of the decision-making process that are dealt with awkwardly in the theory of the firm. First, organizational decisions depend on information, estimates, and expectations that ordinarily differ appreciably from reality. These organizational perceptions are influenced by some characteristics of the organization and its procedures. The procedures provide concrete estimates – if not necessarily accurate ones (Cyert and March, 1955). Second, organizations consider only a limited number of decision alternatives. The set of alternatives considered depends on some features of organizational structure and on the locus of search responsibility in the organization. This dependence seems to be particularly conspicuous in such planning processes as budgeting and price–output determination (Alt, 1949). Finally, organizations vary with respect to the amount of resources they devote to organizational goals on the one hand and suborganizational and individual goals on the other. In particular, conflict and partial conflict of interests is a feature of most organizations and under some conditions organizations develop substantial internal slack susceptible to reduction under external pressure (Cyert and March, 1956).

The concept of organizational or internal slack is used to describe a situation within an organization in which individual energies potentially utilizable for the achievement of organizational goals are permitted to be diverted. The form of the slack may vary from a labor force not working at its full capability to overly large departmental budgets. The extent and regularity with which the organization meets its goals, especially the profit goal, will affect the amount of internal slack.

Our objective is to show how the general attributes of decision-making, some of which have been described above, can be introduced into a behavioral theory of the firm. Although our elaboration is an obvious abstraction of the details of procedures used in a complex organization, each of the processes specified can serve as headings for a further set of subprocesses. We have specified a decision process that involves nine distinct steps:

1 *Forecast competitors' behavior*. The fact that firms assume something about the reactions of their rivals is, of course, incorporated in any theory of oligopoly. Our approach is to build into the model some propositions about the ways in which organizations gain, analyze, and communicate information on competitors. The concept of organizational learning, a process by which expectations of competitors' behavior are modified on the basis of experience, is a major element in this formulation.

2 *Forecast demand*. We have attempted to build a model that can encompass descriptions of the process by which the demand curve (the relationship between the price of the product and the quantity which can be sold at that price) is estimated in the firm. In this manner, we are able to introduce organizational biases in estimation and allow for differences among firms in the way in which they adjust their current estimates on the basis of experience.

3 *Estimate costs*. We do not assume, as in the theory of the firm of economics, that the firm has achieved the optimum combination of resources and the lowest cost per unit of output for any given size plant. We believe it is necessary to introduce the factors that actually affect the firm's costs, estimated as well as achieved.

4 *Specify objectives*. As has been noted above, organizational 'objectives' may enter at two distinct points and perform two quite distinct functions. First, in this step they consist in goals the organization wishes to achieve and which it uses to determine whether it has at least one viable plan (see step 5). There is no requirement that the objectives be co-measurable since they enter as separate constraints all of which 'must' be satisfied. Thus, we expect to be able to include profit goals, share of

the market goals, production goals, etc. (Simon, 1955). Second, the objectives may be used as decision criteria in step 9. As will become clear below, the fact that objectives serve this twin function rather than the single (decision-rule) function commonly assigned to them is of major importance to the theory.

The order of steps 1, 2, 3, and 4 is irrelevant in the present formulation. We assume that a firm performs such computations more or less simultaneously and that all are substantially completed before any further action is taken. Since the subsequent steps are all contingent, the order in which they are performed may have considerable effect on the decisions reached. This is particularly true with respect to the order of steps 6, 7, and 8. Thus, one of the structural characteristics of a specific model is the order of the steps.

5 *Evaluate plan*. On the basis of the estimates of 1, 2, and 3 alternatives are examined to see whether there is at least one alternative that satisfies the objectives defined by 4. If there is, we transfer immediately to 9 and a decision. If there is not, however, we go on to step 6. This evaluation represents a key step in the planning process that is ignored in a model that uses objectives solely as the decision-rule. Certain organizational phenomena (e.g., organizational slack) increase in importance because of the contingent consequences of this step.

6 *Re-examine costs.* We specify that the failure to find a viable plan initially results in the re-examination of estimates. Although we list the re-examination of costs first here, the order is dependent on some features of the organization and will vary from firm to firm.[1] An important feature of organizations is the extent to which a firm is able to 'discover' under the pressure of unsatisfactory preliminary plans 'cost savings' that could not be found otherwise. In fact, we believe it is only under such pressure that firms begin to approach an optimum combination of resources. With the revised estimate of costs, step 5 occurs again. If an acceptable plan is possible with the new estimates, the decision-rule is applied. Otherwise, step 7.

7 *Re-examine demand.* As in the case of cost, demand is reviewed to see whether a somewhat more favorable demand picture cannot be obtained. This might reflect simple optimism or a consideration of new methods for influencing demand (e.g., an additional advertising effort). In either case, we expect organizations to revise demand estimates under some conditions and different organizations to revise them in different ways. Evaluation 5 occurs again with the revised estimates.

1 Although we have identified these re-evaluations in terms of strict sequence, an alternative interpretation can be made in terms of intensity of search.

8 Re-examine objectives. Where plans are unfavorable, we expect a tendency to revise objectives downward. The rate and extent of change we can attempt to predict. As before, evaluation 5 is made with the revised objectives.

9 Select alternative. The organization requires a mechanism (a) for generating alternatives to consider and (b) for choosing among those generated. The method by which alternatives are generated is of considerable importance since it affects the order in which they are evaluated. Typically, the procedures involved place a high premium on alternatives that are 'similar' to alternatives chosen in the recent past by the firm or by other firms of which it is aware. If alternatives are generated strictly sequentially, the choice phase is quite simple: choose the first alternative that falls in the estimate space, that is the set of positions determined by the estimated demand and estimated cost curves. If more than one alternative is generated at a time, a more complicated choice process is required. For example, at this point maximization rules may be applied to select from among the evoked alternatives. In addition, this step defines a decision-rule for the situation in which there are no acceptable alternatives (even after all re-examination of estimates).

There are two important observations to be made about a theory having these general characteristics. First, as we increase the emphasis on describing in some detail the actual process by which the firm makes price and output decisions, we decrease the relevance of one of the major debates in the theory of the firm. Whether the firm maximizes, 'satisfices',[2] or just tries to survive is not the main issue (if indeed it is an issue at all). The emphasis on the process of making decisions in an organization obviates the need for the simple decision-rules and simple models implicit in much of that controversy.

The second point is a related one. Conventional mathematics is a somewhat awkward tool for developing the implications of a theory such as the one described here. It is no accident, therefore, that interest in detailed process models has grown with the development of the digital computer. Computer simulation is well suited to the complexities that are introduced when internal firm variables are utilized in the theory. The significance of simulation for business behavior has been explored vigorously in the so-called 'business games' developed as business training devices; their potential for economic theory is at least as great.

2 'The key to the simplification of the choice process in both cases is the replacement of the goal of *maximizing* with the goal of *satisficing*, of finding a course of action that is "good enough".' (Simon, 1957, pp. 204–5).

A Specific Duopoly Model

The theoretical framework we have outlined in the preceding section can be viewed as an executive program for organizational decisions. That is, we conceive of any large scale oligopolistic business organization as pursuing the steps indicated. A change in decision must (within the theory) be explained in terms of some change in one of the processes specified. As we have noted above, such a conception of the theory seems to suggest a computer-simulation model rather than treatment in mathematical form (Cyert, Simon and Trow, 1956). The rationale, of course, remains the same. We wish to explore the implications of the model.

The intention has been to construct a plausible set of estimation and decision-rules for different types of organizations, and to simulate on a computer the behavior of these firms over time. When we attempt to develop models exhibiting the process characteristics we have discussed above, it becomes clear that our knowledge of how actual firms do, in fact, estimate demand, cost, etc., is discouragingly small. We know with reasonable confidence some of the things that many firms do but at a number of points in the model we can make only educated guesses. Moreover, what knowledge we have (or think we have) tends to be qualitative in nature in situations where it would be desirable to be quantitative.

Because of these considerations, the models of firms with which we will deal here should be viewed as tentative approximations. They contain substantial elements of arbitrariness and unrealistic characterizations. For example, we believe that each of the models as it stands almost certainly exaggerates the computational precision of organizational decision-making. In general, we have not attempted to introduce all of the revisions we consider likely at this time primarily because we wish to examine whether some major revisions produce results which reasonably approximate observed phenomena.

The model is developed for a duopoly situation. The product is homogeneous and, therefore, only one price exists in the market. The major decision that each of the two firms makes is an output decision. In making this decision the firm must estimate the market price for varying outputs. When the output is sold, however, the actual selling price will be determined by the market. No discrepancy between output and sales in assumed, and thus no inventory problem exists in the model.

We assume a duopoly composed of an ex-monopolist and a firm developed by former members of the established firm. We shall call the latter, 'the splinter', and the former, 'the ex-monopolist' or, for brevity, 'monopolist'. Such a specific case is taken so that some rough assumptions can be made about appropriate functions for the various processes in the model. The assumptions are gross; but it is only through some such rough model that a start can be made. To demonstrate that the model as a whole has some reasonable empirical base, we will compare certain outcomes of the model with data from the *can industry*, where approximately the same initial conditions hold.

We can describe the specific model at several levels of detail. In table 2.1 the skeleton of the model is indicated – the 'flow diagrams' of the decision-making process. This will permit a quick comparison of the two firms. In the remainder of this section of the paper we will attempt to provide

Table 2.1 Process model for output decision of firm

(1) Forecast: Competitors' reactions	Compute conjectural variation term for period *t* as a function of actual reactions observed in the past
(2) Forecast: Demand	Keep slope of perceived demand curve constant but pass it through the last realized point in the market
(3) Estimate: Average unit costs	Cost curve for this period is the same as for last period. If profit goal has been achieved two successive times, average unit costs increase
(4) Specify objectives: Profit goal	Specify profit goal as a function of the actual profits achieved over past periods
(5) Evaluate:	Evaluate alternatives within the estimate space. If an alternative which meets goal is available, go to (9) if not, go to (6)
(6) Re-examine: Cost estimate	Search yields a cost reduction. Go to (5). If after evaluation there, decision can be made, go to (9). If not, go to (7)
(7) Re-examine: Demand estimate	Estimate of demand increased after search. Go to (5). If after evaluation, decision can be made, go to (9). If not, go to (8)
(8) Re-examine: Profit goal	Reduce profit goal to a level consistent with best alternative in the estimate space as modified after (6) and (7)
(9) Decide: Set output	Selection of alternative in original estimate space to meet original goal, in modified estimate space to meet original goal, or in modified estimate space to meet lowered goal

somewhat greater detail (and rationale) for the specific decision and estimating rules used.[3]

The decision-making process postulated by the theory begins with a 'forecast' phase (in which competitor's reaction, demand, and costs are estimated) and a goal specification phase (in which a profit goal is established). An evaluation phase follows, in which an effort is made to find the 'best' alternative given the forecasts. If this 'best' alternative is inconsistent with the profit goal, a re-examination phase ensues, in which an effort is made to revise cost and demand esimates. If re-examination fails to yield a new best alternative consistent with the profit goal, the immediate profit goal is abandoned in favor of 'doing the best possible under the circumstances'. The specific details of the models follow this framework.

Forecasting a Competitor's Behavior

The model being analyzed in the paper assumes two firms in the market (a duopoly). As a result one of the significant variables in the decision on the quantity of output to produce for each firm becomes an estimate of the rival firm's output. For example, assume the monopolist in period (t) is considering a change in output from period ($t-1$). At the same time the monopolist makes an estimate of the change the splinter will make. At the end of period t the monopolist can look back and determine the amount of change the splinter made in relation to his own change. The ratio of changes can be expressed as follows:

$$V_{m,t} = \frac{Q_{s,t} - Q_{s,t-1}}{Q_{m,t} - Q_{m,t-1}}$$

where $V_{m,t}$ = the change in the splinter's output during period t as a percentage of the monopolist's output change during period t.

$Q_{s,t} - Q_{s,t-1}$ = the actual change in the splinter's output during period t.

$Q_{m,t} - Q_{m,t-1}$ = the actual change in the monopolist's output during period t.

In the same way we have for the splinter the following:

$$V_{s,t} = \frac{Q_{m,t} - Q_{m,t-1}}{Q_{s,t} - Q_{s,t-1}} = \frac{1}{V_{m,t}}$$

The Ex-monopolist

When the monopolist in period t is planning his output, he must make an estimate of his rival's output, as noted above. In order to make this estimate

3 The computer program, developed in the IT language for the IBM 650 computer, can be obtained from the authors.

we assume that the monopolist first makes an estimate of the percentage change in the splinter's output in relation to his own change, that is, an estimate of $V_{m,t}$. We have assumed that the monopolist will make this estimate on the basis of the splinter's behavior over the past three time periods. More specifically we have assumed that the monopolist's estimate is based on a weighted average, as follows:

$$V'_{m,t} = V_{m,t-1} + \tfrac{1}{7}[4(V_{m,t-1} - V_{m,t-2}) + 2(V_{m,t-2} - V_{m,t-3}) + (V_{m,t-3} - V_{m,t-4})]$$

Where $V'_{m,t}$ = the monopolist's estimate of the change in the splinter's output during period t as a percentage of the monopolist's output change during period t, that is, an estimate of $V_{m,t}$.

Note that $(V'_{m,t})\cdot(Q_{m,t} - Q_{m,t} - Q_{m,t-1})$ is the monopolist's estimate of the splinter's change in output, $Q_{s,t} - Q_{s,t-1}$.

The Splinter

We would expect the splinter firm to be more responsive to recent shifts in its competitor's behavior and less attentive to ancient history than the monopolist, both because it is more inclined to consider the monopolist a key part of its environment and because it will generally have less computational capacity as an organization to process and update the information necessary to deal with more complicated rules. Our assumption is that the splinter will simply use the information from the last two periods. Thus $V'_{s,t} = V_{s,t-1} + (V_{s,t-1} - V_{s,t-2})$.[4] In the same manner as above $(V'_{s,t})\cdot(Q_{s,t} - Q_{s,t-1})$ is the splinter's estimate of the monopolist's change in output, $Q_{m,t} - Q_{m,t-1}$.

Forecasting Demand

We assume that the actual market demand curve is linear. That is, we assume the market price to be a linear function of the total output offered by the two firms together. We also assume that the firms forecast a linear market demand curve (quite different, perhaps, from the actual demand curve). There has been considerable discussion in the economics literature of the frequent discrepancy between the 'imagined' demand curve and the actual demand curve (Weintraub, 1942), and it is this concept that is incorporated in the model. The values of the parameters of the 'imagined'

4 Obviously we do not maintain that the form and parameters of these 'learning' functions are empirically validated. The functions are somewhat arbitrary but we hope not unreasonable.

demand curve are based on rough inferences from the nature of the firms involved.

The Ex-monopolist

We assume that, because of its past history of dominance and monopoly, the ex-monopolist will be over pessimistic with respect to the quantity which it can sell at lower prices, i.e., we assume the initial perception of the demand curve will have a somewhat greater slope than the actual market demand curve. On the assumption that information about actual demand is used to improve its estimate, we assume that the ex-monopolist changes its demand estimate on the basis of experience in the market. The firm assumes that its estimate of the slope of the demand curve is correct and it 'repositions' its previous estimate to pass through the observed demand point.

The Splinter

We posit that the splinter firm will initially be optimistic with respect to the quantity which it can sell at low prices. That is, the initial slope (absolute value) of its demand curve will be somewhat less than that of the actual market demand curve. Secondly, we assume that initially the splinter firm perceives demand as increasing over time. Thus, until demand shows a down turn, the splinter firm estimates its demand to be 5 per cent greater than that found by repositioning its perceived demand through the last point observed in the marketplace.

Estimating Costs

In the process for forecasting and realizing costs, we do not make the assumption that the firm has achieved optimum costs. We assume, rather, that the firm has a simplified estimate of its average cost curve, that is, the curve expressing cost as a function of output. It is horizontal over most of the range of possible outputs; at high and low outputs (relative to capacity) costs are perceived to be somewhat higher.

Further, we make the assumption that these cost estimates are 'self-confirming', i.e., the estimated costs will, in fact, become the actual per-unit cost (Cyert and March, 1956). The concept of organizational slack as it affects costs is introduced at this point. Average unit cost for the present period is estimated to be the same as last period, but if the profit goal of the firm has been achieved for two consecutive time periods, then costs are estimated to be 5 per cent higher than 'last time'.

The specific values for costs are arbitrary. The general shape of the cost curves has been discussed in detail in the literature and studied empirically (Dean, 1951). The concept of organization slack has some important implications for the theory of the firm and has been defined earlier.

The Ex-monopolist

The monopolist's initial average unit cost is assumed to be $800 per unit in the range of outputs from 10 per cent to 90 per cent of capacity. Below 10 per cent and above 90 per cent the initial average unit cost is assumed to be $900.

The Splinter

It is assumed that the competitor will have somewhat lower initial costs. This is because its plant and equipment will tend to be newer and its production methods more modern. Specifically, initial average costs are $760 in the range of outputs from 10 per cent to 90 per cent of capacity. Below 10 per cent and above 90 per cent costs are assumed to average $870 per unit produced.

Specifying Objectives

The multiplicity of organizational objectives is a fact with which we hope to deal in later revisions of the present models. For the present, however, we have limited ourselves to a single objective defined in terms of profit. In this model the function of the profit objective is to restrict or encourage search as well as to determine the decision. If given the estimates of competitors, demand, and cost, there exists a production level that will provide a profit that is satisfactory, we assume the firm will adopt such a course. If there is more than one satisfactory alternative, the firm will adopt that quantity level that maximizes profit. Whether even such a restricted maximization procedure is appropriate is a subject for further research.

The Ex-monopolist

We assume that the monopolist, because of its size, its substantial computational ability, and its established procedures for dealing with a stable rather than a highly unstable environment, will tend to maintain a relatively stable profit objective. We assume that the objective will be the moving average of the realized profit over the last ten time periods.

Initially, of course, the monopolist will seek to maintain the profit level achieved during its monopoly.

The Splinter

The splinter firm will presumably be (for reasons indicated earlier) inclined to consider a somewhat shorter period of past experience. We assume that the profit objective of the splinter will be the average of experienced profit over the past five time periods and that the initial profit objective will be linked to the experience of the monopolist and the relative capacities of the two. Thus, we specify that the initial profit objectives of the two firms will be proportional to their initial capacities.

Re-examination of Costs

We assume that when the original forecasts define a satisfactory plan there will be no further examination of them. If, however, such a plan is not obtained, we assume an effort to achieve a satisfactory plan in the first instance by reviewing estimates and finally by revising objectives. We assume that cost estimates are reviewed before demand estimates and that the latter are only re-examined if a satisfactory plan cannot be developed by the revision of the former. The re-evaluation of costs is a search for methods of accomplishing objectives at lower cost than appeared possible under less pressure. We believe this ability to revise estimates when forced to do so is characteristic of organizational decision-making. It is, of course, closely related to the organizational slack concept previously introduced. In general, we have argued that an organization can ordinarily find possible cost reduction if forced to do so and that the amount of the reductions will be a function of the amount of slack in the organization.

It is assumed that the re-examination of costs under the pressure of trying to meet objectives enables each of the organizations to move in the direction of the 'real' minimum cost point. For purposes of this model it is assumed that both firms reduce costs 10 per cent of the difference between their estimated average unit costs and the 'real' minimum.

Re-examination of Demand

The re-evaluation of demand serves the same function as the re-evaluation of costs above. In the present models it occurs only if the re-evaluation of costs is not adequate to define an acceptable plan. It consists in revising upward the expectations of market demand. The reasoning is that some new alternative is selected which the firm believes will increase its demand.

The new approach may be changed advertising procedure, a scheme to work salesmen harder, or some other alternative which leads the firm to an increase in optimism. In any event, it is felt the more experienced firm will take a slightly less sanguine view of what is possible. As in the case of estimating demand, we assume that all firms persist in seeing a linear demand curve and that no changes are made in the perceived slope of that curve.

The Ex-monopolist

As a result of the re-examination of demand estimates, it is assumed that this firm revises its estimates of demand upward by 10 per cent.

The Splinter

The assumption here is that the upward revision of demand is 15 per cent.

Re-examination of Objectives

Because our decision-rule is one that maximizes among the available alternatives and our rule for specifying objectives depends only on outcomes, the re-evaluation of objectives does not, in fact, enter into our present models in a way that influences behavior. The procedure can be interpreted as adjusting aspirations to the 'best possible under the circumstances'. If our decision-rule were different or if we made (as we might prefer in future revisions) objectives at one time period a function of both outcomes and previous objectives, the re-evaluation of objectives would become important to the decision process.

Decision

We have specified that the organization will follow traditional economic rules for maximization with respect to its perception of costs, demand, and competitor's behavior. The specific alternatives selected, of course, depend on the point at which this step is invoked (i.e., how many re-evaluation steps are used before an acceptable plan is identified). The output decision is constrained in two ways: (1) a firm cannot produce, in any time period, beyond its present capacity. Both models allow for change in plant capacity over time. The process by which capacity changes is the same for both firms. If profit goals have been met for two successive periods and production is above 90 per cent of capacity, then capacity

Table 2.2 Initial and structural conditions for models exhibited in table 2.3

Initial market demand (unknown to firms)		$p = 2000 - q$
Initial perception of demand schedule by ex-monopolist		$p = 2200 - 3q$
Initial perception of demand schedule by splinter		$p = 1800 = q$
Ex-monopolist's average unit cost	$0.1q_{MAX,M} < q_M < 0.9q_{MAX,M}$	800
	$q_M > 0.9, q_M < 0.1$	900
Splinter average unit cost	$0.1q_{MAX,S} < q_S < 0.9q_{MAX,S}$	760
	$q_S > 0.9,\ q_S < 0.1$	870
'Real' minimum average unit cost		700
Ex-monopolist's capacity		400
Splinter's capacity		50
Market quantity		223
Market price		1500
Ex-monopolist's profit goal		163,100
Splinter's profit goal		20,387
Conjectural variations ($V'_{m,t}$ and $V'_{s,t}$)		All zero initially
Splinter's over-optimism of demand in forecast phase		5%
% Splinter raises demand forecast upon re-examination		15%
% Ex-monopolist raises demand forecast upon re-examination		10%
Cost reduction achieved in *M*'s and *S*'s search for lower costs		10% of costs above 'real' min. av. unit cost
% Cost rise attributable to increase in 'internal slack'		5%
% Actual demand schedule shifts to right each time period		8%
Constraint on changing output from that of the last period		±25%
% of capacity at which firm must be producing before it may expand (subject to other conditions)		90%
% change in capacity, when expansion occurs		20%

Table 2.3 Values of selected variables at two-period intervals

	I	*III*	*V*	*VII*	*IX*	*XI*	*XIII*	*XV*
Market								
Price	1,420	1,710	2,196	2,763	3,283	3,927	4,430	4,942
Output	290	311	262	205	209	195	303	466
Ex-Monopolist								
Aspiration level	163,100	165,671	169,631	176,800	173,221	178,385	203,693	246,746
Conjectural variations	0	0	0.74	−22.4	1.09	0.74	0.26	0.35
Costs (AUC)	826	813	881	994	1,041	1,106	1,219	1,344
Output	240	251	206	153	161	150	233	363
Number of re-examination steps	2	0	0	3	0	0	0	0
Competitor								
Aspiration level	20,387	27,107	31,448	39,763	46,218	39,684	54,245	79,060
Conjectural variations	0	0	9.2	−1.78	−6.58	8.72	3.39	3.96
Costs (AUC)	760	798	865	954	1,023	1,057	1,166	1,285
Output	50	60	56	52	48	45	70	103
Number of re-examination steps	0	0	0	3	3	0	0	0
Profit Ratio								
Competitors' profits ÷ monopolists' profits	0.19	0.21	0.26	0.34	0.30	0.30	0.30	0.28
Share of Market								
Competitors' output ÷ total output	0.17	0.19	0.21	0.25	0.23	0.23	0.23	0.22

Table 2.3 *(continued)*

	XVII	*XIX*	*XXI*	*XXIII*	*XXV*	*XXVII*	*XXIX*	*XXXI*
Market								
Price	5,425	3,722	2,785	2,573	2,229	1,719	2,286	2,970
Output	713	914	855	534	360	335	250	140
Ex-Monopolist								
Aspiration level	319,561	348,006	247,445	182,580	157,664	148,648	154,010	158,120
Conjectural variations	0.28	0.30	−0.38	0.05	0.64	−1.07	28.4	−1.40
Costs (AUC)	1,482	1,634	1,801	1,986	2,085	1,710	1,609	1,436
Output	566	703	658	369	207	193	143	80
Number of re-examination steps	0	0	0	0	1	3	0	3
Competitor								
Aspiration level	113,595	121,973	86,083	60,742	37,977	19,272	28,402	37,123
Conjectural variations	4.76	3.91	6.3	−17.1	2.21	−0.32	2.43	50.7
Costs (AUC)	1,417	1,562	1,623	1,790	1,853	1,821	1,608	1,669
Output	147	211	197	165	153	142	107	60
Number of re-examination steps	0	0	0	3	0	1	0	0
Profit Ratio								
Competitor's profit ÷ monopolist's profit	0.26	0.30	0.34	0.68	0.98	0.74	0.75	0.64
Share of Market								
Competitor's output ÷ total output	0.21	0.23	0.23	0.31	0.43	0.42	0.43	0.43

Table 2.3 *(continued)*

	XXXIII	*XXXV*	*XXXVII*	*XXXIX*	*XLI*	*XLIII*	*XLV*
Market							
Price	3,355	3,742	4,099	4,546	5,463	6,730	7,294
Output	218	340	529	735	777	727	1,126
Ex-monopolist							
Aspiration level	159,060	179,859	203,892	239,045	280,940	260,051	340,745
Conjectural variations	0.85	0.95	0.96	0.65	3.77	1.91	1.35
Costs (AUC)	1,363	1,502	1,656	1,826	2,013	2,071	2,283
Output	125	195	303	432	342	320	500
Number of re-examination steps	0	0	0	0	0	0	0
Competitor							
Aspiration level	38,627	53,005	77,001	109,136	164,566	266,512	396,911
Conjectural variations	1.32	1.31	1.32	2.3	−0.8	3.16	0.79
Costs (AUC)	1,840	2,029	2,237	2,466	2,719	2,771	3,055
Output	93	145	226	303	435	407	626
Number of re-examination steps	0	0	0	0	0	0	0
Profit Ratio							
Competitor's profit ÷ monopolist's profit	0.49	0.49	0.49	0.47	0.90	0.97	0.95
Share of market							
Competitor's output ÷ total output	0.43	0.43	0.43	0.41	0.56	0.56	0.56

increases 20 per cent; (2) a firm cannot change its output from one time period to the next more than ±25 per cent. The rationale behind the latter assumption is that neither large cutbacks nor large advances in production are possible in the very short run, there being large organization problems connected with either.

The various initial conditions specified above are summarized in table 2.2, along with the other initial conditions required to program the models.

Results of the Duopoly Model

We have now described a decision-making model of a large ex-monopolist and a splinter competitor. In order to present some detail of the behavior that is generated by the interacting models, we have reproduced in table 2.3 the values of the critical variables on each of the major decision and output factors.[5] By following this chart over time, one can determine the time path of such variables as cost, conjectural variation, and output for both of the firms. More than any one thing, a careful study of this table will give a feeling for the major characteristics of the behavioral theory we have described.

In addition, we have compared the share of market and profit ratio results with actual data generated from the competition between American Can Company and its splinter competitor, Continental Can Company, over the period from 1913 to 1956. These comparisons are indicated in figures 2.1 and 2.2.[6] In general, we feel that the fit of the behavioral model to the data is rather surprisingly good, although we do not regard this fit as validating the approach.[7]

5 Market demand was varied in the following way: (1) The slope of the demand curve was held constant. (2) At each time period the intercept, I_t, was set equal to aI_{t-1}. The value of '*a*' was 1.08 for periods 1–16, 0.90 for periods 17–20, 1.00 for periods 21–26, and 1.08 for periods 27–43.

6 One of the parameters in the model is the length of time involved in a single cycle. In comparing the output of the model with the American–Continental data, this parameter was set at 12 months.

7 It should be clear that the validity of the approach presented in this paper is not conclusively demonstrated by the goodness of fit to the can industry data. We have indicated that under the appropriate assumptions, models of firm decision processes can be specified that yield predictions approximating some observed results. However, the situation is one in which there are ample degrees of freedom in the specification of parameters to enable a number of time series to be approximated. Although in this case we have reduced the number of free parameters substantially by specifying most of them *a priori*, the problems of identification faced by any complex model are faced by this one and will have to be solved. The general methodology for testing models that take the form of computer programs remains to be developed.

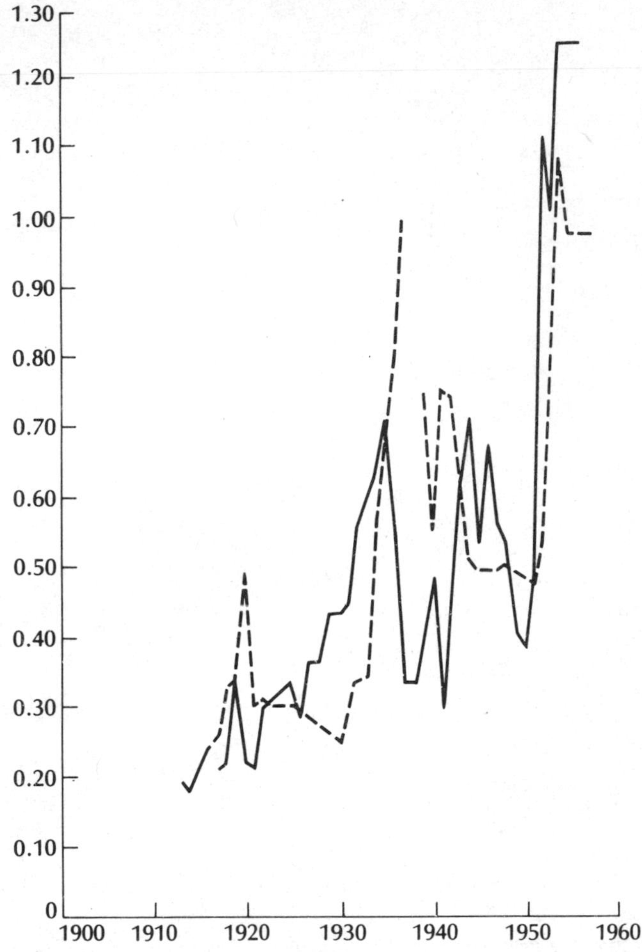

Key

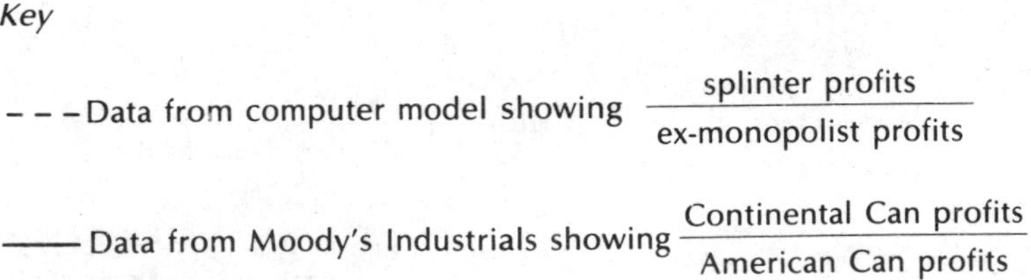

Fig. 2.1 Comparison of share of market data

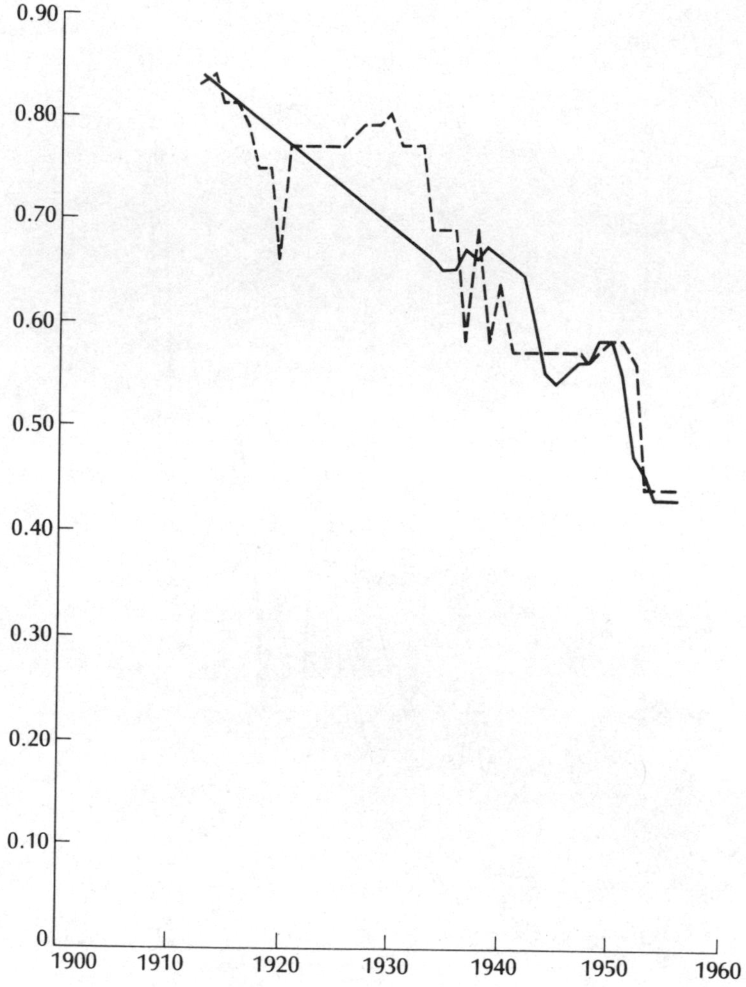

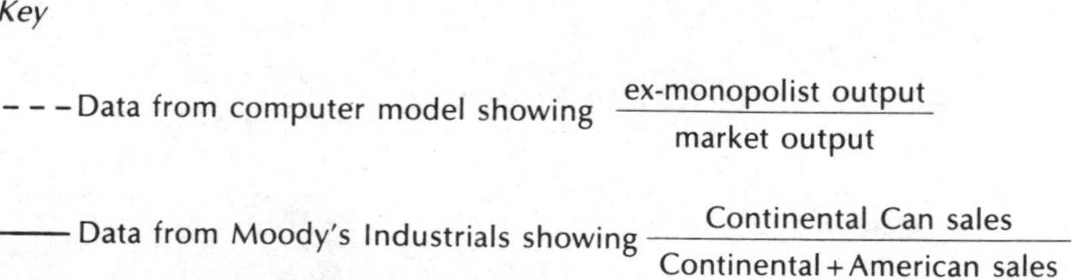

Fig. 2.2 Comparison of profit-ratio data

It should be noted that the results in period XLV do not necessarily represent an equilibrium position. By allowing the firms to continue to make decisions, changes in output as well as changes in share of market would result. One of the reasons for the expected change is the demand curve is shifting upward. Another, and more interesting reason, is that no changes have been made within the organizations. In particular, the splinter firm by period XLV is a mature firm, but the model has it behaving as a new, young firm. One of our future aims is to build in the effect on organization, and hence on decision-making, of growth and maturity of the organization.

An examination of table 2.3 indicates that the re-examination phase of the decision-making process was not used frequently by either firm. This characteristic is the result of a demand function that is increasing over most of the periods.

Whether this stems also from an inadequacy in the model's description of organizational goal-setting or is a characteristic of the real world of business decision-making is a question that can be answered only by empirical research.

Discussion

One of the primary points that has been stressed here is the importance of the decision-making process for the theory of the firm. The implication of this position is that the decisions studied by conventional theory can be better understood when variables relating to the internal operation of a business firm are added to the theory. Accordingly, we would hope that such a theory would not only lead to improved prediction on the usual questions but would also facilitate the investigation of other important problems, e.g., allocation of resources within the firm.

The theory we have used differs from conventional theory in six important respects:

1 The models are built on a description of the decision-making process. That is, they specify organizations that evaluate competitors, costs, and demand in the light of their own objectives and (if necessary) re-examine each of these to arrive at a decision.
2 The models depend on a theory of search as well as a theory of choice. They specify under what conditions search will be intensified (e.g., when a satisfactory alternative is not available). They also specify the direction in which search is undertaken. In general, we predict that a firm will look first for new alternatives or new information in the area it views as

most under its control. Thus, in the present models we have made the specific prediction that cost estimates will be re-examined first, demand estimates second, and organizational objectives third.

3 The models describe organizations in which objectives change over time as a result of experience. Goals are not taken as given initially and fixed thereafter. They change as the organization observes its success (or lack of it) in the market. In these models the profit objective at a given time is an average of achieved profit over a number of past periods. The number of past periods considered by the firm varies from firm to firm.

4 Similarly, the models describe organizations that adjust forecasts on the basis of experience. Organizational learning occurs as a result of observations of actual competitors' behavior, actual market demand, and actual costs. Each of the organizations we have used readjusts its perceptions on the basis of such learning. The learning rules used are quite simple. This is both because simple rules are easier to handle than complex rules and because we expect the true rules to be susceptible to close approximation by simple ones.

5 The models introduce organizational biases in making estimates. For a variety of reasons we expect some organizations to be more conservative with respect to cost estimates than other organizations, some organizations to be more optimistic with respect to demand than others, some organizations to be more attentive to and perceptive of changes in competitors' plans than others. As we develop more detailed submodels of the estimation process, these factors will be increasingly obvious. In the present models we have not attempted to develop such submodels but have simply predicted the outcome of the estimation process in different firms.

6 The models all introduce features of 'organizational slack'. That is, we expect that over a period of time during which an organization is achieving its goals a certain amount of the resources of the organization are funneled into the satisfaction of individual and subgroup objectives. This slack then becomes a reservoir of potential economies when satisfactory plans are more difficult to develop.

In order to deal with these revisions, the models have been written explicitly as computer programs. Such treatment has two major values. First, simulation permits the introduction of process variables. The language of the computer is such that many of the phenomena of business behavior that do not fit into classical models can be considered without excessive artificiality. Entering naturally into the model are cost and demand perceptions within the firm in relation to such factors as age of firm, organizational structure, background of executives, and phase of the business cycle; information handling within the firm and its relation to the communication structure, training, and reward system in the organization; and the effects of organizational success and failure on organizational goals and organizational slack.

Secondly, simulation easily generates data on the time path of outputs, prices, etc. For that large class of economic problems in which equilibrium theory is either irrelevant or relatively uninteresting, computer methodology provides a major alternative to the mathematics of comparative statics.

At the same time the models highlight our need for more empirical observations of organizational decision-making. Each of the major steps outlined in the program defines an area for research on business behavior. How do organizations predict the behavior of competitors? How do they estimate demand and costs? What determines organizational planning objectives? In the models we have specified we have introduced empirical assumptions for such things as organizational learning and changes in organizational aspiration levels. We have ignored several factors we consider quite important (e.g., informational biases stemming from variations in the communication structure). In the final development of the model these relationships must be defined from observable characteristics of business organizations.

We see three major directions for further research. First, we would hope that further attempts will be made to compare the results of the models with observable data. In these studies it will be possible to change such variables as have been indicated above and others that appear to be important in the model. Second, we need a great deal of work in actual organizations identifying the decision procedures used in such things as output decisions. Field research on organizations has frequently been extremely time-consuming and costly relative to the results it has produced, but we believe that research focused on the questions raised by the model is both necessary and feasible. Third, there is room for substantial basic research in the laboratory on human decision-making under the conditions found in business organizations. Many of the major propositions in organization theory depend on evidence generated by studies in the laboratory and many of the mechanisms with which we have dealt can be profitably introduced into controlled experiments.

References

Alt, R. M. (1949) The internal organization of the firm and price formation: An illustrative case. *Quarterly Journal Economics*, 58: 92–110.

Bushaw, D. W., and Clower, R. W. (1957) *Introduction to mathematical economics*. Homewood, Illinois: R. D. Irwin, Inc., pp. 176–190.

Chamberlin, E. H. (1946) *The Theory of Monopolistic Competition*. Cambridge: Harvard University Press, 5th edn, pp. 30–55, 117–29, 165–71.

Cooper, W. W. (1951) A proposal for extending the theory of the firm. *Quarterly Journal Economics,* 65: 87–109.

Cyert, R. M., and March, J. G. (1955) Organizational structure and pricing behavior in an oligopolistic market. *American Economical Review,* 45: 129–139.

Cyert, R. M., and March, J. G. (1956) Organizational factors in the theory of oligopoly. *Quarterly Journal Economics,* 70: 44–64.

Cyert, R. M., Simon, H. A., and Trow, D. B. (1956) Observation of a business decision. *J. of Business,* 29: 237–248.

Dean, Joel. (1951) *Managerial Economics.* New York: Prentice-Hall, pp. 292–6.

Friedman, Milton. (1953) *Essays in Positive Economics.* Chicago: University of Chicago Press, pp. 14–15.

Gordon, R. A. (1948) Short-period price determination. *American Economic Review,* 38: 265–68.

Koopmans, T. C. (1957) *Three Essays on the State of Economic Science.* New York: McGraw-Hill, Inc., pp. 208–217.

Papandreou, A. G. (1952) Some basic problems in the theory of the firm. In B. F. Haley (ed.) *A survey of Contemporary Economics,* Homewood, Illinois: R. D. Irwin, Inc., vol. 2.

Simon, H. A. (1955) A behavioral model of rational choice. *Quarterly Journal Economics,* 69: 99–118.

Simon, H. A. (1957) *Models of Man.* New York: John Wiley Co., pp. 204–5.

Weintraub, S. (1942) Monopoly equilibrium and anticipated demand. *Journal Political Economy,* 50: 427–34.

3

Financial Adversity, Internal Competition, and Curriculum Change in a University

Curtis L. Manns and James G. March

Abstract

Records at Stanford University were used to explore the relation between changes in the curriculum and financial adversity. Two hypotheses were derived from a model of universities as adaptive organizations with departments competing for resources. To test the hypotheses, changes in eight attributes of the curriculum were studied. The data show that university curriculum responded to changes in financial conditions and that departments of stronger research reputation were less responsive than departments of weaker reputation.

Basic Ideas

This paper reports a study of curriculum change in an American university. We examine a set of hypotheses about institutional response to adversity, treating change in the curriculum as one of several ways in which a university might react to financial adversity. The hypotheses were derived from standard organizational treatments of adaptive organizations, and college organizations were seen as responding to environmental change in ways similar to business firms (Cyert and March, 1963; Bower, 1970;

This paper first appeared in *Administrative Science Quarterly*, vol. 23, December 1978. The authors owe particular debts to Sally Mahoney for making much of the raw data available to them, Mark Barnett for developing and executing the procedures by which the data were organized into a computer file, and to William F. Miller and Stephen S. Weiner for their comments on the study.

Carter, 1971; Williamson, 1975) or public bureacracies (Lindblom, 1959; Crecine, 1969; Allison, 1971; Steinbruner, 1975; Wildavsky, 1975).

Rising costs, declining resources, and disappearing clientele were key elements of American university environment in the early 1970s (Cheit, 1971; O'Neill, 1971; Rubin, 1977). The problems of dealing with this environment have formed a substantial part of the literature addressed to university administrators in recent years (Bowen and Douglass, 1971; Carnegie Commission, 1972; Cyert, 1975). Administrative efforts to reduce costs and improve efficiency have been notable at most universities. It is less obvious, however, that the curriculum at major universities will also respond to such adversity. Particularly at stronger institutions, curriculum is more the prerogative of individual faculty members and collective faculty institutions than the responsibility of administrative officers (Cohen and March, 1974). It is not clear that faculty groups can, or will, respond to the university's financial adversity. The ways students move through college and receive degrees, the nature of their instruction, the options they have, the credits they accrue, the grades they receive, the accessibility of faculty and courses are central to the university and seem resistant to coordinated change.

The basic theoretical ideas are simple and well-known (March and Simon, 1958; Cyert and March, 1963; Radner, 1975; Steinbruner, 1975). Organizations are assumed to have various independent, aspiration-level goals. For example, a business firm might have a profit goal, sales goal, share-of-market goal, stock price goal. Performance with respect to each goal is compared with the aspiration level. If performance exceeds the goal, the result is organizational slack and rising aspirations. Slack includes 'payments' to coalition members in excess of the payments needed to keep them in the coalition. It may take the form of expenditures for managerial comfort, lighter workloads or reduced supervision, or unexploited opportunities (Cyert and March, 1963). The organization relaxes and reduces the level of search; but, at the same time, aspirations rise. Conversely, if performance fails to meet aspirations, the organization responds by reducing slack, and aspirations fall.

Taken together, these phenomena tend to keep performance and goals together. Slack and changes in aspiration levels are smoothing devices by which relatively large variations in external conditions are transformed into relatively small variations in subjective success. Slack also serves to reduce conflict among subunits. As a result, fluctuations in the external environment produce predictable patterns of organizational responses. During periods of rising external resources and opportunities, slack and aspiration levels rise; internal competition declines. During periods of decreasing resources, slack and aspirations decline; internal competition increases (March and Simon, 1958).

These general ideas about organizational response to environmental change suggest some ideas about how university curriculum adjusts to financial adversity. University departments earn 'profit' (or departmental slack) by increasing the difference between their revenue, which is approximately the budget of the department, and faculty effort in research and teaching. The economizing problem of a department arises from the fact that there is often some positive connection between the amount of effort (for example, the number of students taught) and the amount of resources received.

Cohen and March (1974) proposed a basic model for operating budget allocation that can be adapted for our purposes. According to their analysis, a fundamental mechanism for matching external pressures on the university with internal allocations is the enrollment market. The university (and departments within it) must maintain demand for enrollment in order to secure resources to meet the demand. The mechanism sometimes operates directly through student charges, sometimes indirectly through taxes and legislative subsidies. The effects of the enrollment market may be dampened by strong student demand or by the availability of resources that are not dependent on enrollment. When the economic environment becomes more severe, departments need to increase effort or efficiency in order to maintain revenue. One way of doing this is to change the curriculum.

Competition for resources through the enrollment market invites curriculum competition among departments. The salience of the invitation, however, depends on the extent to which resources are scarce and on the vulnerability of the department to the market. A department will be more likely to seek curriculum attractiveness in hard times; and a department that is able to use a strong research reputation to secure outside funds, student interest, and administrative favor is less dependent on maintaining an attractive curriculum in order to compete for resources (Salancik and Pfeffer, 1974).

Such ideas appear to be consistent with previous research on organizations generally and to make a certain amount of sense. It is possible, however, that the loose coupling and ordinary bureaucratic complexities of education make such fluctuations in slack and search irrelevant for the curriculum (Weick, 1976; Meyer and Rowan, 1977a, 1977b; March, 1978). It is possible that the political character of the decision process or the social structure of universities may make such adaptation imperceptible (March and Olsen, 1976). It is possible that academic organizations absorb variations in environmental conditions without modifying teaching and research activities.

Reactions of universities to financial adversity have emphasized efforts to find ways of reducing costs without making significant changes in the education offered. For example, universities have attempted to increase the number of contact hours for faculty, reduce staff costs, and eliminate or curtail services that are marginal to teaching and research activities. The possibility that adversity would also produce modifications in the curriculum that are less directly connected to the costs of education is clear in the Cohen and March (1974) argument. They describe some modifications of the curriculum intended to stimulate demand as well as some intended to reduce costs; but, as they point out, the procedures for changing the curriculum to stimulate demand are more decentralized in most universities than are those for reducing costs. This is particularly true in institutions with strong traditions of excellence and faculty control over the curriculum.

As a result, it may be useful to ask whether a detailed examination of curriculum drift in a major university shows movement that is consistent with the idea of organizational adaptation. The present paper reports an attempt to look at archival data on small shifts in the apparent attractiveness of the curriculum. The study emphasized those attributes of the curriculum that affected primarily the demand for courses rather than their costs. The question was whether such changes were connected systematically to changes in the severity of the financial environment. The study focused on two hypotheses:

Hypothesis 1: Departmental efforts to increase the attractiveness of the curriculum will be greater in times of financial adversity than in times of prosperity.
Hypothesis 2: Efforts to increase the attractiveness of the curriculum in time of adversity will be less in departments with strong research reputations than in departments with weaker reputations.

The hypotheses can be used to compare three alternative ideas about the response of a university to financial adversity. The first idea assumes that the curriculum changes as a function of educational processes that are not affected systematically by variations in the economic conditions facing the university. The second idea assumes that the curriculum changes as a university-wide response to environmental scarcity; variations in curriculum reflect variations in the environment, but they are not systematically related to departmental characteristics. The third idea assumes that the curriculum changes as a consequence of departmental competition for resources; some departments are more dependent on the enrollment market than others, and thus are more likely to make curriculum changes in times of adversity. If the first idea were correct, both of the hypotheses should be disconfirmed; if the second idea were correct, the first hypothesis should be confirmed, but not the second; if the third idea were correct, both hypotheses should be confirmed.

Data and Analysis

The study was made at Stanford University. Stanford provided a reasonable setting for examining the hypotheses. It had experienced a perceptible increase in financial stress; it had a relatively large number of departments varying in research reputation; it had unusually good records and administrative officers sympathetic to analytical explorations in those records. Nevertheless, the study ran some risk of failing to confirm the hypotheses even though they might be supported by data from other universities. Stanford, by comparison with the general population of American colleges and universities, is likely to be relatively less sensitive to the enrollment market because of student demand for admission; and Stanford faculty maintain considerable collective and individual control over the curriculum.

The data used in the study were secured from official records and publications of the university. These included grading sheets submitted to the registrar of the university by the faculty, computer tape records of the registrar, files and tapes maintained by the academic planning office, and university catalogues. Four academic years were considered. The first two (1964 and 1966) represent a period of relative plenty in the university, the second two (1971 and 1973) a period of relative stringency. Values on each of eight variables were recorded for each of the four years for 30 departments (table 3.1) that existed from 1964 to 1973 in the School of Humanities and Sciences and the School of Engineering. Graduate professional schools of business, education, law, and medicine were excluded, as well as a few departments that were eliminated or created in the interim between 1964 and 1973, and a few small departments having only graduate programs. The basic question asked about each department with respect to each variable was whether departmental responsiveness (i.e., change in the curriculum in the predicted direction) was greater between 1971 and 1973 than it was between 1964 and 1966.

It was easy to establish that several elements of the curriculum closely linked to the cost of instruction changed systematically over this period. For example, in 24 of the 30 departments the number of undergraduate courses offered per faculty member increased more between 1971 and 1973 than it did between 1964 and 1966. Similar results can be obtained for other cost-related measures of curriculum responsiveness. The interest here, however, was in exploring whether a similar trend could be detected in curriculum attributes having only minor and indirect cost effects. The attributes chosen were related to the amount of variety offered in the curriculum, the attractiveness of course packaging or advertising, the accessibility of courses to students, and direct course benefits to students.

Attributes measuring curriculum content would have been useful additions, but good records on course content were not available.

Variables

In selecting the variables, four criteria were used:

1 They should have only modest cost effects.
2 They should be plausibly connected to responsiveness; that is, it should be possible to make a prediction about the direction of change in the variables under the assumption that the basic hypotheses of the study were correct.
3 They should be independent; that is, the specific indices should involve different numbers and should not be constrained by the measurement procedures to correlate with each other.
4 The direction of movement for most departments should be unambiguous; that is, it should be true for each variable that at least 90 per cent of the departments were either more or less responsive between 1971 and 1973 (not tied).

On the basis of these criteria, eight variables were identified. Variables 1 and 2 measured some aspects of variety in course offerings; variables 3 and 4 measured some aspects of course packaging or advertising; variables 5 and 6 measured some aspects of course accessibility to students; and variables 7 and 8 measured some aspects of course benefits provided to students.

1 *Variance in course enrollment*. The enrollment recorded on the official grade sheets of the university was determined for each course in the university. Course enrollment was not identical with class size, though it was much closer to that than would be true at a larger university. Some courses had lecture/section or lecture/ laboratory formats, but instances in which the same course was divided into several lecture classes were very few. The variance across course enrollment was computed for each department each year and was treated as an index of one form of variety in course opportunities for students.

2 *Variance in average units earned in courses*. Students receive units (credits) toward graduation in each course successfully completed. The number of units earned by each student in each course was taken from the official grade sheets. The mean number of units for each course was computed, and the variance of those means was computed for each department each year. This variance was treated as an index of a second kind of variety in course opportunities for students.

3 *Length of course descriptions in the catalogue*. Each course is described in the university catalogue. Although university rules and tradition impose some restrictions on length, descriptions vary in length.

The number of print characters used by each department to describe its courses each year was estimated by counting lines of print and converting to characters (to correct for changes in type characteristics from one year to another). The mean length of a catalogue description was computed by dividing the total departmental characters by the number of courses listed. It was assumed that an increase in the average length of description increased the average market attractiveness of courses.

4 *Proportion of undergraduate courses taught by full professors.* The instructor for each undergraduate course was determined from the official grade sheets. The instructor's rank was determined from university catalogues and rosters maintained by the university planning office. The proportion of undergraduate courses taught by full professors was computed for each department each year. It was assumed that an increase in this proportion increased the market attractiveness of departmental course offerings.

5 *Proportion of courses given at non-competitive times.* Courses tend to be concentrated in the mornings (nine to twelve) of Monday, Wednesday, and Friday. Each course listed in the catalogue as being offered at times that included at least two of those nine busiest hours was classified as being given at a competitive time. The proportion of courses given at non-competitive times was calculated for each department each year. It was assumed that an increase in the proportion of courses scheduled at non-competitive times increased the average accessibility of a department's courses.

6 *Proportion of courses not requiring a prerequisite.* Admission to some courses is restricted to students meeting certain prerequisites (usually in the form of prior courses). Each course listed in the catalogue as having prerequisites was classified as being restricted. The proportion of courses without restrictions was computed for each department each year. It was assumed that an increase in the proportion of unrestricted courses increased the average accessibility of a department's courses.

7 *Average number of units earned in courses.* The number of units earned by each student in each course was taken from official grade sheets (see variable 2). It was assumed that an increase in the average unit value earned in courses increased the benefits provided to students by a department.

8 *Average grade earned in courses.* The grade received by each student in each course was taken from official grade sheets. A 13-point scale (including minuses and pluses) was used; pass/fail grades were excluded. The mean grade for each course was computed. From this the average of the mean course grade was computed for each department each year. It was assumed that an increase in the average grade earned in a course increased the benefits provided to students by a department.

Implicit in the analysis is the expectation that a department that is more responsive will be more likely to increase variety in course size, variety in units earned in courses, average length of course descriptions, and so on. These actions were seen as eight independent, equally likely alternative responses. We assumed that observed variations in the use of the eight responses were random fluctuations in a process in which the probability of a positive response was the same on each variable for any given department, but varied from one department to the other. In the absence of either any prior basis for predicting differences or any clear posterior pattern, we assume variations across variables are random fluctuations. Although such an assumption cannot be rejected at the 10 per cent level of significance on the basis of the present results, it might nonetheless be viewed as problematic. Elaboration of possible explanations for possible (real) variation is foregone here.

The specific predictions made here with respect to the direction of movement in the eight variables seem plausible, but they are not uniquely so. For example, it seems reasonable to treat increasing variety in courses as a way of improving competitive position, but the variance is not necessarily the only measure of that variety. Although longer course descriptions and more full professors teaching classes seem sensibly to reflect marketing improvements, it is possible that they do not. Scheduling courses at non-competitve times may seem a reasonable strategy, but it is possible that times are competitive precisely because that is when students want to take classes. Moreover, if some departments lengthen course descriptions in an effort to improve their attractiveness and other departments for the same reason shorten course descriptions, neither prediction will be supported strongly, even though the theory correctly specifies the true underlying mechanism. Although these problems are notable, they should not be exaggerated. The eight variables meet the criteria established, and the predictions about the direction of movement were made *a priori*.

Results

Table 3.1 shows for each department and each variable whether that department showed greater responsiveness under conditions of adversity (1971 and 1973) than under conditions of relative prosperity (1964 and 1966).

If a department was more responsive on a variable between 1971 and 1973 than between 1964 and 1966, the entry in the table is '1'; if it was less responsive on a variable between 1971 and 1973 than between 1964 and 1966, the entry in the table is '0'; if there was no difference, the entry in the table is '1/2'.

The data were reduced to table 3.1 through the following procedures. The raw data were tabulated and computed for each variable, each department, and each year, and recorded in a $30 \times 8 \times 4$ array, V. An entry in the array, $v_{i,j,k}$, showed a value for the ith department, jth curriculum variable, and kth year ($i = 1,30$; $j = 1,8$; $k = 1964, 1966, 1971, 1973$). From the V-array a $30 \times 8 \times 2$ change array, C was constructed. This array showed the difference between the values in the second and first years (i.e., 1964 and 1966, 1971 and 1973). Thus, an entry, $c_{i,j,k}$, in this array showed the changes that took place in the ith department and the jth variable during the kth time period. Since the different variables have quite different dimensions, $c_{i,j,k}$ was expressed as relative change ranging from $+1$ to -1 by dividing the algebraic difference between the second and first years by their sum. A relative change array, D, was obtained by subtracting the change in the 1960s from the change in the 1970s, and was a 30×8 array that expressed the difference between the change in the 1970s and the change in the 1960s as a number that could vary from $+2$ to -2. A 30×8 sign array, S (reproduced in table 3.1), was constructed from D by attending only to the signs of the differences.

These procedures reduced the information content of the data. The reduction is intended. The focus is on simple measures of the direction of change and low-power, non-parametric tests. The arguments for using such procedures are uncomplicated. The basic statistic computed for each department and each curricular variable is a reasonable measure of the extent to which a department modified its curriculum in the predicted direction more in the 1970s than it did in the 1960s; but the statistic has no known sampling characteristics. Moreover, it seems reasonable to reflect in the analysis no more precision than is reflected in the theory. The theory predicts the sign of the differences and some rough variations in their magnitude. The analysis focuses on the same level of precision. The simplicity of the scores and the analysis, however, should not conceal the large data base on which table 3.1 is based.

The row totals in table 3.1 are scores of departments. High scores indicate a department that was relatively responsive to adversity in the predicted direction; low scores indicate a department that was less responsive. Similarly, column totals are the scores of curriculum variables. High scores indicate a specific response that was used by relatively many departments; low scores indicate a response that was used by relatively few. All of these measures are measures of relative change. They gauge whether responses between 1971 and 1973 were more in the direction of making curriculum attractive than they were between 1964 and 1966. For example, the results with respect to mean course grade may seem surprising in the light of the widely-reported 'grade inflation' in American colleges and universities. In fact, 25 of the 30 departments showed an increase in

Table 3.1 Responsiveness of 30 academic departments in eight curriculum variables in times of financial adversity (1971 and 1973), compared with times of prosperity (1964 and 1966)[a]

	Department	Responsiveness variable 1	2	3	4	5	6	7	8	Departmental scores
1	Aeronautics and astronautics	0	0	0	1	1	0	0	0	2
2	Chemical engineering	1	1	1	0	1	1	1	1	7
3	Civil engineering	0	0	0	1	1	1	0	1	4
4	Electrical engineering	0	0	0	0	1	1	0	0	2
5	Industrial engineering	1	1	0	1	1	0	1	1	6
6	Materials science and engineering	0	0	0	0	1	1	0	0	2
7	Mechanical engineering	1	1	0	1	0	1	1	1	6
8	Applied physics	1	1	1	1	0	0	1	½	5.5
9	Anthropology	1	1	1	1	0	1	1	0	6
10	Art	0	1	1	0	½	0	1	0	3.5
11	Asian studies	1	1	0	1	1	1	1	1	7
12	Biology	1	0	0	1	1	0	0	1	4
13	Chemistry	1	1	1	1	1	1	1	1	8
14	Classics	1	1	0	0	1	0	1	1	5
15	Communication	1	1	0	0	1	1	0	1	5
16	Economics	1	1	1	1	0	0	1	0	5
17	English	0	0	1	1	1	0	1	0	4
18	History	1	1	1	0	½	0	0	0	3.5
19	Humanities specials	1	1	0	0	1	0	0	1	4
20	Mathematics	1	0	1	1	0	0	1	0	4
21	French and Italian	0	1	0	1	1	1	1	0	5
22	Music	1	1	1	1	½	0	0	1	5.5
23	Philosophy	1	1	0	1	1	0	1	0	5
24	Physics	0	0	0	1	1	0	0	1	3
25	Political science	1	1	1	0	1	1	0	1	6
26	Psychology	0	0	0	1	0	1	0	1	3
27	Sociology	0	0	1	1	1	0	0	1	4
28	Drama	1	1	1	1	0	0	0	0	4
29	Statistics	1	1	0	1	1	1	0	1	6
30	Computer science	1	1	0	1	0	0	1	0	4
	Variable scores	20	20	13	21	20.5	13	15	16.5	139

[a]0 = department less responsive to variable between 1971 and 1973 than between 1964 and 1966; 1 = department more responsive; ½ = no difference.

average grades between 1971 and 1973. Those increases were, however, often less than the increases in the same departments between 1964 and 1966. Departments and professors who wanted to raise the average grade in course during the 1970s period could not easily match the magnitude of the earlier increases. Only those departments for which grade inflation was greater in the 1970s were recorded positively on this variable.

These data can be used to test the two hypotheses. Changes in the curriculum in the direction predicted by Hypothesis 1 are indicated by '1's in table 3.1. If adversity did not affect changes in curriculum in these departments, we would expect that the cell entries in the table would sum to about 120. The observed number is 139, significantly greater than would be expected by chance ($p < .01$). Departments at Stanford responded to adversity as predicted by Hypothesis 1.

For Hypothesis 2, departments were ranked using two standard rankings, Carter (1966) and Roose and Andersen (1970). Eighteen departments were ranked on one or both of these rankings, and 16 were ranked on both. The other 12 departments were in fields that were not ranked, that is, none of them were unranked departments in a field for which there were rankings. As a result, 18 departments could be used for this part of the analysis. Departments were ordered on the basis of the mean of their reputational rankings. Ties were resolved by weighting the more recent (1970) ranking slightly more than the earlier one. Such a procedure treats a national ranking in one field as equivalent to the same rank position in another field, but this appears to be approximately what is done when a university or a student evaluates the relative distinction of its departments. Similarly, departments were ordered in terms of their responsiveness scores. The hypothesis was that the two orderings were not independent, but that departments that were relatively high in national reputation would be relatively low in curriculum responsiveness. Figure 3.1 shows the results. Although there are two clear outliers (departments 7 and 13), the null hypothesis that the two rankings are either independent or related in the opposite way can be rejected at the 0.05 level of significance. The test of significance is based on the sample distribution function and was developed by Blum, Kiefer, and Rosenblatt (1961). The value of B is 6176/1889568. Departments with stronger academic reputations made significantly fewer curriculum responses to adversity than departments with weaker reputations.

Discussion

Three alternative ideas about collegiate curriculum change were suggested. The present data reveal that under conditions of relative adversity Stanford

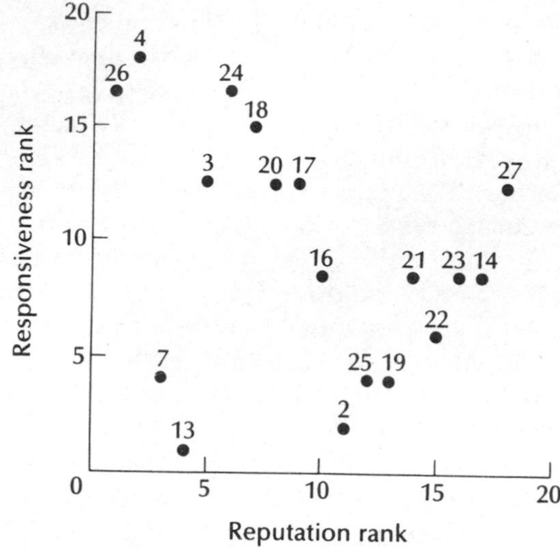

Fig. 3.1 Relation between responsiveness (rank) and reputation (rank)[a] for 18 academic departments (see table 3.1 for number code)
[a]Both ranks run from 1 (high) to 18 (low)

departments tended to increase variety in course offerings, provide more attractive packaging, make courses more accessible, and increase course benefits to a greater extent than the same department did during conditions of relative financial plenty. Departments with strong academic reputations were less likely to change than those with weaker reputations. The data support the third idea better than they do the first two. Undoubtedly, the faculty tried to develop a good curriculum that was responsive to the needs of students and the society, but those efforts appeared to be affected significantly by economic conditions and departmental reputation.

The effects were not dramatic. Without the relatively large data base on which the study was built, they might not have been easily detected. Stanford curricula were not determined completely by the problems of adjusting to adversity. The impact of competition for resources may indeed have been less than what was believed by some students, faculty, and administrators, but the impact apparently was real. Since the data are based on the fine structure of the curriculum as revealed by archival records, they may represent more persuasive evidence than the observations of participants in the process.

It might be speculated that observed differences in reputations among departments mask some other underlying variable more directly connected with departmental subject matter. Attitudes toward administrators, students, or change might vary from one discipline to another. These differences would then be reflected in different responsiveness in financial adversity. Or it might be speculated that disciplines with certain kinds of students (e.g., males) would be systematically both more highly rated and less responsive because of their clientele. At least in this case, the data do not support any obvious hypothesis related to subject matter. There are almost no differences in mean and median responsiveness scores when departments were grouped into four broad categories: engineering, science, social science, humanities. In general, inspection of the data suggests considerable difficulty in formulating a simple counter-hypothesis that depends on subject matter. The eight most responsive departments included: chemical engineering, industrial engineering, mechanical engineering, anthropology, Asian studies, chemistry, political science, and statistics. The seven least responsive departments included: aeronautics and astronautics, electrical engineering, materials science and engineering, art, history, physics, and psychology. It is not easy to propose a way of sorting those 15 departments into those two groups on the basis of their subject matter.

The fact that departments change curriculum under conditions of adversity and that departments with stronger reputations respond less supports the Cohen and March model, but the support should not be exaggerated. We have suggested that reputation made a difference because it provided alternative financial opportunities, alternative bases for attracting students, and alternative sources of power for bargaining with administrators. Departments with strong reputations were seen as less dependent on curriculum responses to economic adversity. Such an interpretation is reasonable, and the data seem to support it. But there are alternative interpretations of the same result. For example, it is possible that strong departments already have unusually attractive programs and are unable to make significant improvements, while there is more room for improvement in weaker departments. More generally, it seems likely that variations in responsiveness are not entirely the semirational consequences of departmental competition for resources suggested by the model. Academia has traditions about change. Although one can control somewhat for variations in such traditions by considering relative change within departments, one cannot entirely control for them. There may be structural features of departments that encourage, or inhibit, responsiveness (Fox, Pate and Pondy, 1976). The curriculum and the various practices that it summarizes are also symbols of different importance in different departments, protected with varying degrees of internal cohesiveness.

Nevertheless, at a highly prestigious university that is relatively strong financially, with a tradition of decentralized faculty control over the curriculum, changes in the curriculum were influenced by changes in economic adversity in a subtle, but detectable way. However diffuse the procedures by which a university increased the variety in course offerings, improved the packaging and advertising for courses, made courses more accessible, and increased direct student benefits from courses, those procedures, at least in this case, seemed to move more in the direction of trying to stimulate demand during the 1970s than they did during the 1960s. However intricate and delicate the ways in which different departments compete with each other for scarce resources, strong departments generally exhibited fewer efforts to increase curriculum attractiveness in response to declining university resources than weaker departments. The results are neither surprising nor extraordinary, but the collection of small decisions and actions involved drifted in a way that conformed to ideas drawn from theories of organizations.

References

Allison, Graham T. (1971) *Essence of Decision: Explaining the Cuban Missile Crisis*. Boston: Little, Brown.

Blum, J. R., Kiefer, J., and Rosenblatt, M. (1961) Distribution free tests of independence based on the sample distribution function. *Annals of Mathematical Statistics*, 32: 485–98.

Bosen, Howard R., and Douglass, Gordon K. (1971) *Efficiency in Liberal Education: a Study of Comparative Instructional Costs for Different Ways of Organizing Teaching–Learning in a Liberal Arts College*. New York: McGraw-Hill.

Bower, Joseph L. (1970) *Managing the Resource Allocation Process: a Study of Corporate Planning and Investment*, Boston: Harvard Graduate School of Business Administration.

Carnegie Commission on Higher Education (1972) *The More Effective Use of Resources: an Imperative for Higher Education*. Berkeley, CA: Carnegie Commission.

Carter, E. Eugene (1971) The behavioral theory of the firm and top-level corporate decisions. *Administrative Science Quarterly*, 16: 413–29.

Cheit, Earl F. (1971) *The New Depression in Higher Education: a Study of 41 Colleges and Universities*. New York: McGraw-Hill.

Cohen, Michael D., and March, James G. (1974) *Leadership and Ambiguity. The American College President*. New York: McGraw-Hill.

Crecine, John P. (1969) *Governmental Problem Solving: a Computer Simulation of Municipal Budgeting*. Chicago: Rand McNally.

Cyert, Richard M. (1975) *The Management of Non-profit Organizations*. Lexington, MA: Heath.

Cyert, Richard M., and March, James G. (1963) *A Behavioral Theory of the Firm*. Englewood Cliffs, NJ: Prentice-Hall.

Fox, Frederick, V., Pate, Larry E. and Pondy, Louis R. (1976) Designing organizations to be responsive to their clients. In Ralph Kilmann, Louis R. Pondy, and Dennis Slevin (eds), *The Management of Organization Design*, vol. 1: 53–72. New York: Elsevier North-Holland.

Lindblom, Charles E. (1959) The science of muddling through. *Public Administration Review*, 19: 79–88.

March, James G. (1978) American public school administration: a short analysis. *School Review*, 86: 217–250.

March, James G., and Olsen, Johan P. (1976) *Ambiguity and Choice in Organizations*. Bergen, Norway: Universitetsforlaget.

March, James G., and Simon, Herbert A. (1958) *Organizations*. New York: Wiley.

Meyer, John W., and Rowan, Brian (1977a) Notes on the structure of educational organizations. In Marshall W. Meyer and associates, *Environments and Organizations: Theoretical and Empirical Perspectives*, San Francisco: Jossey-Bass, pp. 78–109.

Meyer, John W. and Rowan, Brian (1977b) Institutionalized organizations: formal structure as myth and ceremony. *American Journal of Sociology*, 83: 340–63.

O'Neill, June A. (1971) *Resource Use in Higher Education: Trends in Outputs and Inputs, 1930–1967*. Berkeley, CA: Carnegie Commission.

Radner, Roy (1975) A behavioral model of cost reduction. *Bell Journal of Economics*, 6: 196–215.

Roose, Kenneth D., and Anderson, Charles J. (1970) *A Rating of Graduate Programs*. Washington: American Council on Education.

Rubin, Irene (1977) Universities in stress: decision-making under conditions of reduced resources. *Social Science Quarterly*, 58: 242–54.

Salancik, Gerald R., and Pfeffer, Jeffrey (1974) The bases and use of power in organizational decision-making: the case of a university. *Administrative Science Quarterly*, 19: 453–473.

Steinbruner, John D. (1975) *The Cybernetic Theory of Decision: New Dimensions of Political Analysis*. Princeton, NJ: Princeton University Press.

Weick, Karl E. (1976) Educational organizations as loosely coupled systems. *Administrative Science Quarterly*, 21: 1–18.

Wildavsky, Aaron (1975) *Budgeting: a Comparative Theory of Budgetary Processes*. Boston: Little, Brown.

Williamson, Oliver, E. (1975) *Markets and Hierarchies, Analysis and Anti-trust implications: a Study in the Economics of Interest Organization*. New York: Free Press.

4

Managerial Perspectives on Risk and Risk-taking

James G. March and Zur Shapira

Abstract

This paper explores the relation between decision theoretic conceptions of risk and the conceptions held by executives. It considers recent studies of attitudes and behavior among managers against the background of conceptions of risk derived from theories of choice. We conclude that managers take risks and exhibit risk-preferences, but the processes that generate those observables are somewhat removed from the classical processes of choosing from among alternative actions in terms of the mean (expected value) and variance (risk) of the probability distributions over possible outcomes. We identify three major ways in which the conceptions of risk and risk-taking held by these managers lead to orientations to risk that are different from what might be expected from a decision theory perspective: Managers are quite insensitive to estimates of the probabilities of possible outcomes; their decisions are particularly affected by the way their attention is focused on critical performance targets; and they make a sharp distinction between taking risks and gambling. These differences, along with closely related observations drawn from other studies of individual and organizational choice, indicate that the behavioral phenomenon of risk-taking in organizational settings will be imperfectly understood within a classical conception of risk.

This paper was first published in *Management Science*, vol. 33 (1987). The research was supported by grants from the Recanati Foundation, the Russell Sage Foundation, the Spencer Foundation, and the Stanford Graduate School of Business. The authors are especially grateful for the support of Marshall Robinson, as well as for the assistance of Julia Ball and the comments of Elaine Draper and Dan Galai.

Risk as a Factor in Decision-Making

The importance of risk to decision-making is attested by its position in decision theory (Allais, 1953; Arrow, 1965), by its standing in managerial ideology (Peters and Waterman, 1982), and by the burgeoning interest in risk assessment and management (Crouch and Wilson, 1982). However, empirical investigations of decision-making in organizations have not generally focused directly on the conceptions of risk and risk-taking held by managers (March, 1981a); and empirical investigations of risk in decision-making have not generally focused on managerial behavior (Vlek and Stallen, 1980; Schoemaker, 1980; 1982; Slovic, Fischhoff, and Lichtenstein, 1982). As a result, the relation between decision theoretic conceptions of risk and conceptions of risk held by managers remains relatively murky.

The Definition of Risk

In classical decision theory, risk is most commonly conceived as reflecting variation in the distribution of possible outcomes, their likelihoods, and their subjective values. Risk is measured either by non-linearities in the revealed utility for money or by the variance of the probability distribution of possible gains and losses associated with a particular alternative (Pratt, 1964; Arrow, 1965). In the latter formulation, a risky alternative is one for which the variance is large; and risk is one of the attributes which, along with the expected value of the alternative, are used in evaluating alternative gambles. The idea of risk is embedded, of course, in the larger idea of choice as affected by the expected return of an alternative. Virtually all theories of choice assume that decision-makers prefer larger expected returns to smaller ones, provided all other factors (e.g., risk) are constant (Lindley, 1971). In general, they also assume that decision-makers prefer smaller risks to larger ones, provided other factors (e.g., expected value) are constant (Arrow, 1965). Thus, expected value is assumed to be positively associated, and risk is assumed to be negatively associated, with the attractiveness of an alternative.

Finding a satisfactory empirical definition of risk within this rudimentary framework has proven difficult. Simple measures of mean and variance lead to empirical observations that can be interpreted as being off the mean-variance frontier. This has led to efforts to develop modified conceptions of risk, particularly in studies of financial markets. Early criticisms of variance definitions of risk (Markowitz, 1952) as confounding downside risk with upside opportunities led to a number of efforts to develop models based on the semi-variance (Fishburn, 1977; Coombs, 1983). Both variance and semi-variance ideas of risk, however, have been shown to be inconsistent with von Neumann axioms except under rather narrow conditions (Levy and Markowitz, 1979; Levy and Sarnat, 1984); and this result has stimulated efforts to estimate risk and risk-preference from observed prices. This procedure is essentially the approach of much of the contemporary literature on risk in financial markets. One example is the capital asset pricing model that has become one standard approach to financial analysis (Sharpe, 1964; 1977). It defines the degree to which a given portfolio covaries with the market portfolio as the systematic risk. The residual (in a regression sense) is defined as non-systematic or specific risk. These elaborations have contributed substantially to the understanding of financial markets, but the risk-return implications of the model have not always found empirical support (Gibbons, 1982).

There are numerous additional complications with decision theoretic conceptions of risk when they are taken as descriptions of the actual processes underlying choice behavior. There are suggestions, for example, that individuals tend to ignore possible events that are very unlikely or very remote, regardless of their consequences (Kunreuther, 1976). There are suggestions that individuals look at only a few possible outcomes rather than the whole distribution, and measure variation with respect to those few points (Boussard and Petit, 1967; Alderfer and Bierman, 1970); and that they are more comfortable with verbal characterizations of risk than with numerical characterizations even though the translation of verbal expressions of risk into numerical form shows high variability and context dependence (Kahneman and Tversky, 1982). There are suggestions that the likelihoods of outcomes and their values enter into calculations of risk independently, rather than as their products (Slovic, Fischhoff and Lichtenstein, 1977). Such ideas seem to indicate that the ways in which human decision-makers define risk may differ significantly from the definitions of risk in the theoretical literature, and that different individuals will see the same situation in quite different ways (Budescu and Wallsten, 1985).

Attitudes toward Risk

Early treatments by Pratt (1964), Arrow (1965) and others, as well as more recent work (Ross, 1981), assumed that individual human decision-makers are risk-averse, that is, that when faced with one alternative having a given outcome with certainty, and a second alternative which is a gamble but has the same expected value as the first, an individual will choose the certain outcome rather than the gamble. Thus, it follows that decision-makers would normally have to be compensated for variability in possible outcomes; and the greater the return on investment that is observed in a situation, the greater should be the variance involved. Levy and Sarnat

(1984) studied 25 years of investments in mutual funds and discovered that investors were averse to the variance of returns. It is not certain, however, that managers believe that risk and return are positively correlated. Some studies of mergers (Brenner and Shapira, 1983; Mueller, 1969) suggest that this is not the case. Moreover, the aggregate data yield ambiguous results. Bowman (1980) has shown a negative relation between traditional risk (i.e., simple variance) and average return across industries.

Attitudes toward risk are usually pictured as stable properties of individuals, perhaps related to aspects of personality development or culture (Douglas and Wildavsky, 1982); and efforts have been made to associate risk-preference with dimensions of personality, such as achievement motivation (McClelland, 1961; Atkinson, 1964; Kogan and Wallach, 1964). Global differences between presumed risk-takers and others within a culture or job have, however, remained relatively elusive. For example, Brockhaus (1980) attempted to study the risk-taking propensities of entrepreneurs. The individuals who quit their managerial jobs and became owners of business or managers of business ventures were compared to regular managers. Using the choice dilemma questionnaire of Kogan and Wallach (1964), he found no differences in risk-propensity among the different groups.

It is possible that risk-preference is partly a stable feature of individual personality, but a number of variable factors such as mood (Hastorf and Isen, 1982), feelings (Johnson and Tversky, 1983), and the way in which problems are framed (Tversky and Kahneman, 1974) also appear to affect perception of and attitudes toward risk. In particular, Kahneman and Tversky (1979) have observed that when dealing with a risky alternative whose possible outcomes are generally good (e.g., positive monetary outcomes), human subjects appear to be risk-averse; but if they are dealing with a risky alternative whose possible outcomes are generally poor, human subjects tend to be risk-seeking. This pattern of context dependence is familiar to students of risk-taking by animals (Kamil and Roitblat, 1985), individuals (Griffith, 1949; Snyder, 1978; Laughhunn, Payne and Crum, 1980; Payne, Laughhunn and Crum, 1981) and organizations (Mayhew, 1979; Bowman, 1982). It forms the basis for several modern treatments of context-dependent risk-taking (Maynard Smith, 1978; Kahneman and Tversky, 1979; Lopes, 1986; March, 1988).

There are unresolved problems, however. The idea of risk-taking in the face of adversity certainly finds support, but the idea that major innovations and change are produced by misery is not well supported by history. For example, Hamilton (1978) analyzed the structural sources of adventurism using demographic data from the days of the gold rush in California. He found that gold rush 'entrepreneurs' were primarily professionals, upper class and young. They were not from marginal social groups. More inclusive studies of innovation (Mansfield, 1968) and revolution (Brinton, 1938) similarly suggest that risk-taking is not connected to adversity in a simple way.

Dealing with Risk

In conventional decision theory formulations, choice involves a trade-off between risk and expected return. Risk-averse decision-makers prefer relatively low risks and are willing to sacrifice some expected return in order to reduce the variation in possible outcomes. Risk-seeking decision-makers prefer relatively high risks and are willing to sacrifice some expected return in order to increase the variation. The theory assumes that decision-makers deal with risks by first calculating and then choosing among the alternative risk-return combinations that are available.

It is not clear that actual decision-makers treat risk in such a way. For example, Israeli defense decision-makers seem to have dealt with the subject of shelter construction in a way that ignored a decision theory definition of risk (Lanir and Shapira, 1984). There are indications that decision-makers sometimes deny risk, saying that there is no risk or that it is so small that it can be ignored. A common form of denial involves acceptance of the actuarial reality of the risk combined with a refusal to associate that reality with one's self (Weinstein, 1980). The word 'denial' suggests a psychological pathology; it may, of course, be a more philosophical rejection of the relevance of probabilistic reasoning for a single case, or a belief in the causal basis of events. The tendency for individuals to perceive chance events to be causal and under control has been documented in various experiments (Langer, 1975), as has the tendency to develop causal theories of events even when the relations between events are known to be only incidental (Tversky and Kahneman, 1982).

Managerial Perspectives

Two recent studies of managerial perceptions of risk (MacCrimmon and Wehrung, 1986; Shapira, 1986) can be used to consider managerial perspectives on these issues.[1] The study by MacCrimmon and Wehrung is based on questionnaire responses from 509 high-level executives in Canadian and American firms and interviews with 128 of those executives (all from Canadian firms). The study by Shapira is based on interviews with 50 American and Israeli executives. The MacCrimmon and Wehrung

1 A more complete description of the Shapira study, its methodology, and its results is available on request from the TIMS office in Providence, Rhode Island.

studies were conducted in 1973–1974. The Shapira study was conducted in 1984–1985. Taken together, these studies provide some rather consistent observations on how managers define risk, their attitudes toward risk, and how they deal with risk.

The Definition of Risk

The managers see risk in ways that are both less precise and different from risk as it appears in decision theory. In particular, there is little inclination to equate the risk of an alternative with the variance of the probability distribution of possible outcomes that might follow the choice of the alternative. Three differences from decision theory are obvious: First, most managers do not treat uncertainty about positive incomes as an important aspect of risk. Possibilities for gain are of primary significance in assessing the attractiveness of alternatives (MacCrimmon and Wehrung, 1986), but 'risk' is seen as associated with the negative outcomes. Shapira (1986) asked respondents: 'Do you think of risk in terms of distribution of all possible outcomes? Just the negative ones? Or just the positive ones?' Eighty per cent of the executives said they considered the negative ones only. There is, therefore, a persistent tension between 'risk' as a measure (e.g., the variance) on the distribution of possible outcomes from a choice and 'risk' as a danger or hazard. From the former perspective, a risky choice is one with a wide range of possible outcomes. From the latter perspective, a risky choice is one that contains a threat of a very poor outcome.

Secondly, for these managers, risk is not primarily a probability concept. About half (54 per cent) of the managers interviewed by Shapira (1986) saw uncertainty as a factor in risk, but the magnitudes of possible bad outcomes seemed more salient to them. A majority felt that risk could better be defined in terms of amount to lose (or expected to be lost) than in terms of moments of the outcome distribution. This led the vice-president of a venture capital firm to say, 'I take large risks regarding the probability but not the amounts.' And a vice-president for finance reported, 'I don't look at the probability of success or failure but at the volume of risk.' In describing the difference between risk-taking and gambling one manager said, 'A gamble of one million dollars in terms of success in a project is risk; however, a gamble of half a dollar is not a risk.' This tendency to ignore or downplay the probability of loss compared to the amount is probably better defined as loss-aversion (Kahneman and Tversky, 1982) or as regret-aversion (Bell, 1983) than as risk-aversion in conventional terms. It is also reflected in the tendency found by MacCrimmon and Wehrung (1986) for less risk-taking when greater stakes were involved. In evaluating uncertain prospects, 80 per cent of Shapira's executives asked for estimates of the 'worst outcome' or the 'maximum loss'. From such responses, it is difficult to assess the extent to which there are considerations of 'plausibility' introduced in determining the possible exposure involved in the alternative. Nevertheless, it is clear that these managers are much more likely to use a few key values to describe their exposure than they are to compute or use standard summary statistics grounded in ideas of probability.

Thirdly, although quantities are used in discussing risk, and managers seek precision in estimating risk, most show little desire to reduce risk to a single quantifiable construct. When MacCrimmon and Wehrung (1986) asked executives to rank nine investment alternatives, the ranks matched an ordering based on expected value in only 11 per cent of the respondents. Even fewer executives ranked the alternatives strictly in terms of maximizing major gain, breaking even, minimizing major loss, or minimizing variation. A vice-president for finance reported (Shapira, 1986) that 'No one is interested in getting quantified measures'; and a senior vice-president observed, 'You don't quantify the risk, but you have to be able to feel it'. Recognizing that there are financial, technical, marketing, production and other aspects of risk, a majority of the interviewees in the Shapira study felt that risk could not be captured by a single number or a distribution, that quantification of risks was not an easy task; and 42 per cent argued that there was no way to translate a multi-dimensional phenomenon into one number. On the other hand, 24 per cent of the same managers felt it could be done and with additional probing said that actually it should be. As one project manager said, 'Everything should be expressed in terms of the profit (or loss) at the end of the project, shouldn't it?' Several felt that one should average the different dimensions and get an overall weighted index of risk, but even among those who thought such a number should be produced, most reported that they didn't do it that way.

Attitudes towards Risk

Managerial risk-taking propensities vary across individuals and across contexts. Among the managers interviewed by Shapira (1986), the variation across individuals is seen as resulting from incentives and experience. In keeping with much of the literature, they think some people are more risk-averse than others, that there are intrinsic motivational factors associated with risk and encoded as a part of an individual personality (McClelland, 1961; Atkinson, 1964; Deci, 1975). They see these differences, however, as less significant than differences produced by incentives and normative definitions of proper managerial behavior. They feel that a manager who fails to take risks should not be in the business of managing. When asked if they could identify risk-prone and risk-averse managers, middle level managers were inclined to say that risk-prone individuals disappear as you move up the hierarchy. Higher level managers, on the other hand, feel there is a definite need to educate new managers into the importance of risk-taking. In the Shapira study, the inclination to encourage others to take risks increased as one moved up the hierarchy, and MacCrimmon and Wehrung (1986) found that higher level executives scored higher on their risk-taking measures than did lower level executives.

Managers recognize both the necessity and the excitement of risk-taking in management, but they report that risk-taking in organizations is sustained more by personal than by organizational incentives. Shapira (1986) found that managers at all levels generally picture organizational life as inhibiting risk-taking on the part of managers. As a result, and in contrast to their normative enthusiasm for risk-taking, these respondents were mostly conservative when asked what practical advice they would give to a new manager. They did not encourage risk-taking. Rather, they said things like: 'Let other managers participate in your decisions.' 'Don't gamble.' 'Arrange for a blanket.' This negative attitude toward individual risk-taking is particularly characteristic of managers who see risk as unconnected to uncertainty, that is as being defined in terms of the magnitude of a projected loss or gain rather than that magnitude weighted by its likelihood.

Despite this pessimism about organizational incentives for risk-taking, or perhaps because of it, most of the managers interviewed by Shapira (1986) portrayed themselves as judicious risk-takers and as less risk-averse than their colleagues. Similarly, MacCrimmon and Wehrung (1986) found that managers tended to believe they were greater risk-takers than they were. The executives studied by Shapira explained their willingness to take calculated risks in terms of three powerful motivations. First, they said that risk-taking is essential to success in decision-making. Eighty-seven per cent of the executives felt that risk and return were related, though they added 'ifs', 'buts' and 'it depends' to qualify this relation. In general, the managers studied by Shapira (1986) expect the choice of an alternative to be justified if large potential losses are balanced by similarly large potential gains, but they do not seem to think that they would require the expected value of a riskier alternative to be greater than that of the less risky in order to justify choice.

Secondly, these managers associate risk-taking more with the expectations of their jobs than with a personal predilection. They believe that risk-taking is an essential component of the managerial role. In the words of a senior vice-president of one firm, 'If you are not willing to assume risks, go deal with another business.' This link between risk-taking and management is less a statement of the measurable usefulness of risk-taking to a manager than an affirmation of a role. As the president of an electronic firm said, 'risk-taking is synonymous with decision-making under uncertainty.' In keeping with contemporary managerial ideology, he might have added that management is synonymous with decision-making. Consistent with such a spirit, both MacCrimmon and Wehrung (1986) and Shapira (1986) found that managers are inclined to show greater propensity toward risk-taking when questions are framed as business decisions than when they are framed as personal decisions.

Thirdly, these managers recognize the emotional pleasures and pains of risk-taking, the affective delights and thrills of danger. Risk-taking involves emotions of anxiety, fear, stimulation and joy. Many of the Shapira (1986) respondents seemed to believe that the pleasures of success were augmented by the threat of failure. One president said, 'Satisfaction from success is directly related to the degree of risk taken.' As we shall note below, this excitement with danger is confounded by a concomitant anticipation of mastery, the expectation that danger will be overcome.

These three motivational factors are background for a greater variation in risk-taking attributable to contextual factors. The managers interviewed by Shapira (1986) saw themselves and other managers as exhibiting different risk-preferences under different conditions, and the MacCrimmon and Wehrung (1986) measures of managerial risk-propensity were poorly correlated across decision situations. Some of this variation appears to be idiosyncratic to the details of particular situations, but there is one consistent theme. Both the managers interviewed by Shapira and those interviewed by MacCrimmon and Wehrung believe that fewer risks should, and would, be taken when things are going well. They expect riskier choices to be made when an organization is 'failing'. In short, risk-taking is affected by the relation between current position and some critical reference points (Kahneman and Tversky, 1979).

Two comparisons organize managerial thinking about how things are going. The first of these is a comparison between some performance or position (e.g., profit, liquidity, sales) and an aspiration level or 'target' for it. Most managers seem to feel that risk-taking is more warranted when faced with failure to meet targets than when targets were secure. In 'bad' situations risks would be taken. Some also feel that attention to the survival of an individual as a manager is involved, that executives will take riskier actions when their own positions or jobs are threatened than when they are safe. A second comparison is between the current position of an organization and its demise. There is strong sentiment that survival should not be risked. Over 90 per cent of the executives interviewed by Shapira said they would not take risks where a failure could jeopardize the survival of the firm, although one executive commented that 'in situations where a competitor threatens the market position of the firm, you have to take one of two risks: not surviving on the one hand and risking new strategies on the other.'

There is some obvious ambiguity in the ideas. Generally, the argument is that a strong position leads to conservative behavior with respect to risk, that the danger of falling below a target is minimized. At the same time, however, the greater the asset position relative to the target, the less the danger from any particular amount of risk (Arrow, 1965). As one vice-president said (Shapira, 1986), 'Logically and personally I'm willing to take more risks the more assets I have.' Conversely, performance below a target is argued to lead to greater willingness to take risks, in order to increase the chance of reaching the target; but the poorer the position, the greater the danger reflected in the downside risk. This would suggest that the value attached to alternatives differing in risk may depend not only on whether they are 'framed' as gains or losses but also on which of two targets (the 'success' target or the 'survival' target) is evoked (Lopes, 1986).

Dealing with Risk

Early studies of managers (Cyert and March, 1963) concluded that business managers avoid risk rather than accept it. They avoid risk by using short-run reaction to short-run feedback rather than anticipation of future events. They avoid the risk of an uncertain environment by negotiating uncertainty-absorbing contracts. In a similar way, MacCrimmon and Wehrung (1986) found managers avoiding risks in a simulated in-basket task. They delay decisions and delegate them to others.

Other studies suggest that managers avoid accepting risk by seeing it as subject to control. They do not accept the idea that the risks they face are inherent in their situation (Strickland, Lewicki, and Katz, 1966). Rather, they believe that risks can be reduced by using skills to control the dangers. Keyes (1985) pictured entrepreneurs and other risk-takers as seeking mastery over the odds of fate, rather than simply accepting long shots. Adler (1980) distinguished managers who were risk-avoiders, risk-takers and risk-makers. The latter are those who not only take risks but try to manage and modify them. The managers interviewed by MacCrimmon and Wehrung (1986) and by Shapira (1986) are similar. They believe that risk is manageable. Seventy-five per cent of the Shapira respondents saw risk as controllable. As a result, they make a sharp distinction between gambling (where the odds are exogenously determined and uncontrollable) and risk-taking (where skill or information can reduce the uncertainty). The situations they face seem to them to involve risk-taking, but not gambling. They report seeking to modify risks, rather than simply accepting them; and they assume that normally such a modification will be possible. As the president of a successful high technology company told Shapira, 'In starting my company I didn't gamble; I was confident we were going to succeed.'

In cases in which a given alternative promises a good enough return but presents an unacceptable danger, managers focus on ways to reduce the danger while retaining the gain. One simple action is to reject the estimates. Thus, only two of the 50 executives interviewed by Shapira (1986) said they accept estimates of risk as given to them. In most cases, rejection is supplemented by efforts to revise estimates. Seventy-four per cent of the managers said they tried to modify the descriptions of risk, partly by securing new information, partly by attacking the problem with different perspectives. More importantly, however, they try to change the odds. Managers see themselves as taking risks, but only after modifying and working on the dangers so that they can be confident of success. Prior to a decision, they look for risk-controlling strategies. Most managers believe that they can do better than is expected, even after the estimates have been revised. This tactic, called 'adjustment' by MacCrimmon and Wehrung (1986), is reported as a standard executive reponse to risk. In the Shapira interviews, managers spoke of 'eliminating the unknowns' and 'controlling the risk'. Managerial confidence in the possibilities for post-decision reduction in risk comes from an interpretation of managerial experience. Most executives feel that they have been able to better the odds in their previous decisions. Thus, managers accept risks, in part, because they do not expect that they will have to bear them.

Implications for Understanding Risk-Taking by Managers

These empirical observations call attention to three pervasive features of managerial treatment of risk that deviate from simple conceptions of risk and are important for understanding managerial decision-making.

Insensitivity of Risk-Taking to Probability Estimates

There are strong indications in these studies, as well as in others (Slovic, 1967; Kunreuther, 1976; Fischhoff, Lichtenstein, Slovic, Derby and Keeney, 1981), that individuals do not trust, do not understand, or simply do not much use precise probability estimates. Crude characterizations of likelihoods are used to exclude certain possibilities from entering the decision calculus. Possible outcomes with very low probabilities seem to be ignored, regardless of their potential significance. Where low prior probability is combined with high consequence, as in the case of unexpected major disasters or unanticipated major discoveries, the practice of excluding very low probability events from consideration makes a difference. In a world containing a very large number of very low probability, very high consequence possible events, it is hard to see how an organization can reasonably consider all of them. But if, as seems likely, *some* particular very low probability, high consequence events are certain to occur, the organization is placed in the position of preparing for a world that is certain not to be realized (i.e., a world in which *no* low probability, high consequence events occur). It is, of course, not necessarily given that there is an attractive solution to this dilemma, regardless of the treatment of probability estimates; but the practice of ignoring very low probability events has the effect of leaving organizations persistently surprised by, and unprepared for, realized events that had, *a priori*, very low probabilities.

The insenstivity to probability estimates extend beyond the case of very low probability events, however. Within a wide range of plausibility, it appears to be the magnitude of the value of the outcome that defines risk for managers, rather than some weighting of that magnitude by its likelihood. This is reflected in the use of terms such as 'maximum exposure', 'opportunity', or 'worst or best (plausible) case'. The behavior has consequences. It leads to a propensity to accept greater risk (in the sense of variance) when the probability distribution of possible outcomes is relatively rectangular than where there are relatively long tails.

Although it is arguable that this behavior is less intelligent than taking a fuller account of variations in likelihood, it may be useful to observe that the 'confusions' of managers about risk are echoes of ambiguity in the choice engineering literature. In decision theory terms, risk refers to the probabilistic uncertainty of outcomes stemming from a choice. In recent treatises on risk-assessment and risk-management, on the other hand, risk has become increasingly a term referring not to the *unpredictability* of outcomes but to their *costs*, particularly their costs in terms of mortality and morbidity (Fischhoff, Watson and Hope, 1984). Within the latter terminology, the main focus of concern has been not on variability but on defining trade-offs between a specific 'risk' and other costs, for example, between the frequency and severity of injury and the monetary costs of safety measures. The typical style is to deal with the expected value of the probability distribution over adverse outcomes, rather than any higher moments. Thus, 'risk' becomes 'hazard', the expected value of an outcome rather than its variability; and the central insight of theories of decision-making under risk, the importance of considering the whole distribution of possible outcomes, tends to become obscured in considerations of 'risk'.

Managerial insensitivity to probability estimates may, in part, reflect such terminological elasticity among writers on risk- and decision-engineers. It may also be attributable to some realities of decision-making that are not habitually noted by students of rational choice. Typically, the guesses of choice are not easy ones. Estimating the probabilities of outcomes is difficult, as is estimating the returns to be realized and the subjective value that might be associated with such returns when they are realized is unclear. Information is compromised by conflict of interest between the source of the information and the recipient. Since these difficulties are particularly acute in the estimation of probabilities, it is entirely sensible for a manager to conclude that the credibility of probability estimates is systematically less than is the credibility of estimates of the value of an outcome; and it is certainly arguable that the relative credibility of estimates should affect the relative attention paid to them.

The Importance of Attention Factors for Risk-Taking

Empirical studies of risk-taking, including the ones discussed here, indicate that risk-preference varies with context. Specifically, the acceptability of a risky alternative depends on the relation between the dangers and opportunities reflected in the risk and some critical aspiration levels for the decision-maker. From a behavioral point of view, this contextual variation in risk-taking seems to stem less from the revision of a coherent preference for risk (March, 1988) than from a change in focus among a set of inconsistent and ambiguous preferences (March, 1978). As a result of changing fortunes or aspirations, focus is shifted away from the dangers involved in a particular alternative and toward its opportunities (Lopes, 1986).

The tendency for managerial evaluations of alternatives to focus on a few key aspects of a problem at a time is a recurrent theme in the study of human problem solving. Consider, for example, the discussion of 'elimination by aspects' by individual decision-makers (Tversky, 1972), analyses of attention in human problem solving (Nisbett and Ross, 1980), the 'sequential attention to goals' by organizational decision-makers (Cyert and March, 1963), or 'garbage-can models of choice' (March and Olsen, 1976). These observations suggest that choice behavior normally interpreted as being driven primarily by preferences and changes in them is susceptible to an alternative interpretation in terms of attention. Theories that emphasize the sequential consideration of a relatively small number of alternatives (Simon, 1955; March and Simon, 1958), that treat slack and search as stimulated or reduced by a comparison of performance with aspirations (Cyert and March, 1963; Levinthal and March, 1981; Singh, 1986), or that highlight the significance of order of presentation and agenda effects (Cohen, March and Olsen, 1972; Kingdon, 1984) are all reminders that understanding action in the face of incomplete information may depend more on ideas about attention than on ideas about decision.

In several of these theories, there is a single critical focal value for attention, for example, the aspiration level that divides subjective success from subjective failure. The present observations with respect to the shifting focus of attention in risk seem to confirm the importance of two focal values rather than a single one (Lopes, 1986; March, 1988). The most frequently mentioned values are a target level for performance (e.g., breakeven) and a survival level. These two reference points partition possible states into three: success, failure and extinction. The addition of a focus value associated with extinction changes somewhat the predictions about attention (or risk-preference) as a function of success.

In general, if one is above a performance target, the primary focus is on avoiding actions that might place one below it. The dangers of falling below the target dominate attention; the opportunities for gain are less salient. This leads to relative risk-aversion on the part of successful managers, particularly those who are barely above the target. As long as the distribution of outcomes is symmetrical, the dangers and the opportunities covary; but since it is the dangers that are noticed, the opportunities are less important to the choice. For successful managers, attention to opportunities and thus risk-taking is stimulated only when performance exceeds the target by a substantial amount.

For decision-makers who are, or expect to be, below the performance target, the desire to reach the target focuses attention in a way that leads generally to risk-taking. In this case, the opportunities for gain receive attention, rather than the dangers, except when nearness to the survival point evokes attention to that level. If performance is well above the survival point, the focus of attention results in a predilection for relatively high variance alternatives, thus risk-prone behavior. If performance is close to the survival point, the emphasis on high variance alternatives is moderated by a heightened awareness of their dangers.

Risk-Taking, Gambling and Managerial Conceit

Managers have a strong normative reaction to risk and risk-taking. They care about their reputations for risk-taking and are eager to expound on their sentiments about the deficiencies of others and on the inadequacy of organizational incentives for making risky decisions intelligently. The rhetoric of these values is, however, decidedly two-pronged. On the one hand, risk-taking is valued, treated as essential to innovation and success. At the same time, however, risk-taking is differentiated from 'playing the odds'. A good manager is seen as 'taking risks' but not as 'gambling'. To a student of statistical decision theory, the distinction may be obscure since the idea of decision-making under risk in that tradition is paradigmatically captured by a vision of betting, either against nature or against other strategic actors. From that perspective, the choice of a particular business strategy depends on the same general considerations as the choice of a betting strategy in a game of poker. The significance of this parallel has been recognized by decision-engineers who have tried, with only modest success, to champion a criterion for evaluating managers that rewards 'good decisions' rather than 'good outcomes', arguing that the determination of a proper choice should not be confounded with the chance realizations of a risky situation.

We believe that managers distinguish risk-taking from gambling primarily because the society that evaluates them does, and because their experience teaches them that they can control fate. Society values risk-taking but not gambling, and what is meant by gambling is risk-taking that turns out badly. From the point of view of managers and a society dedicated to good management, the problem is to develop and maintain managerial reputations for taking 'good' (i.e., ultimately successful) risks and avoiding 'bad' (i.e., ultimately unsuccessful) risks, in the face of (possibly inherent) uncertainties about which are which. The situation was described rather precisely to Shapira (1986) by one senior vice-president. He said, 'You have to be a risk-taker, but you have to win more than you lose.'

Managers can engage in relatively conscious strategies designed to inflate the perceived riskiness of successful actions, but deliberate efforts on the part of managers to portray themselves as risk-takers are only a minor part of the story. Managerial reputations for risk-taking rather than gambling are sustained by the ordinary social processes for interpreting life and getting ahead. In historical perspective, we have no difficulty distinguishing those who have been brilliant risk-takers from those who have been foolish gamblers, however obscure the difference may have been at the time they were making their decisions. *Post hoc* reconstruction permits history to be told in such a way that 'chance', either in the sense of genuinely probabilistic phenomena or in the sense of unexplained variation, is minimized as an explanation (Fischhoff, 1975; Fischhoff and Beyth, 1975). Thus, risky choices that turn out badly are seen, after the fact, to have been mistakes. The warning signs that were ignored seem clearer than they were; the courses that were followed seem unambiguously misguided.

History not only sorts decision-makers into winners and losers but also interprets those differences as reflecting differences in judgment and ability. The experience of successful managers teaches them that the probabilities of life do not apply to them. Neither a society nor a manager has any particular reason to doubt the validity of the assessment that successful managers have the skill to choose good risks and reject bad risks, thus that they can solve the apparent inconsistency of social norms that demand both risk-taking and assured success. Managers believe, and their experience appears to have told them, that they can change the odds, that what appears to be a probabilistic process can usually be controlled. The result is to make managers somewhat more prone to accept risks than they might otherwise be.

Such risk-taking also fits into social definitions of managerial roles. Managers are expected to make things happen, to take (good) risks. Managerial ideology pictures managers as making changes, thus leading to a tendency for managers to be biased in the direction of making organizational changes and for others to be biased in expecting them to do so (March, 1981b). In a similar fashion, managerial ideology also portrays a good manager as being a risk-taker. Managerial conceits include beliefs that it is possible at the time of a decision to tell the difference between risks with good outcomes and risks with bad outcomes, and that it is possible to manage risks so as to improve on the apparent odds. And such conceits make risk-taking seem entirely consistent with the normative expectation that decisions will also reliably turn out well (Keyes, 1985).

Conclusion

In the tradition of behavioral studies of organizational decision-making (March and Simon, 1958; March and Shapira, 1982), behavioral decision research (Edwards, 1954; 1961; Nisbett and Ross, 1980; Kahneman, Slovic and Tversky, 1982), and the behavioral assessment of risk-perception (Slovic, Fischhoff, and Lichtenstein, 1985; Englander, Farago, Slovic, and Fischhoff, 1985), we have examined how executives actually define and react to risk, rather than how they ought to do so. We conclude not only that managers fail to follow the canons of decision theory, but also that the ways they think about risk are not easily fitted into classical theoretical conceptions of risk.

Standard conceptions of risk, with their emphasis on trait differences among individual decision-makers, are problematic as bases for talking about managerial risk-taking behavior. To a substantial extent, probability estimates are treated as unreliable and subject to post-decision control, and considerations of trade-offs are framed by attention factors that considerably affect action. Managers look for alternatives that can be managed to meet targets, rather than assess or accept risks. Although they undoubtedly vary in their individual propensities to take risks, those variations are obscured by processes of selection that reduce the heterogeneity among managers and encourage them to believe in their ability to control the odds, by systems of organizational controls and incentives that dictate risk-taking behavior in significant ways, and by variations in the demand for risk-taking produced by the context within which choice takes place. These factors are embedded in a managerial belief system that emphasizes the importance of risk and risk-taking for being a manager.

These features of managerial approaches to risk have implications not only for understanding decision-making in organizations, but also for the engineering of risk-taking and risk-management. It is conventional in modern discussions of management to deplore the pattern of risk-taking observed in management. Individual managers are often criticized for taking too many (or too few) risks, as is management as a whole. Proposals for changing the incentives for risk-taking are common. The present observations suggest that some of the policies proposed to change risk-taking may not match the situation as it is seen by managers. In the short run, if we wish to encourage, or inhibit, risk-taking on the part of managers, we probably need to shape our interventions to meet the ways in which managers think. For example, it may be more efficacious to try to modify managerial attention patterns and conceits than to try to change beliefs about the likelihood of events or to try to induce preferences for high variance alternatives.

In the longer run, there are possible implications for the education of managers. The managers who participated in these studies do not follow decision theory very closely. They do not reject the theory in an informed, reasoned way, but rather act according to some rules and procedures that are implicitly at variance with the theory, even while acknowledging it as decision dogma. This suggests that there might be solid prospects for changing managerial perspectives through direct training in decision-theoretic approaches to risk and risk-management. As we have recorded above, however, the perspectives that managers have are not simply matters of individual taste but are embedded in social norms and expectations. History and common sense both suggest that changes may be relatively slow, responding more to broad shifts in beliefs and formulations than to simple changes in the selection or training of managers.

Before we leap too enthusiastically into a program of comprehensive managerial education and social reform, moreover, we may wish to recognize the elements of intelligence in these managerial perspectives. Although there is ample evidence that the risk-taking behavior of managers is often far from optimal, we may want to examine the extent to which the managerial beliefs and behaviors we observe are accommodations of human organizations and their managers to the subtle practical problems of sustaining appropriate risk-taking in an imperfectly comprehended world. It is not hard to show that contextually varying risk-preferences, insensitivity to probabilities, and managerial illusions are intelligent under plausible conditions (Ibsen, 1884; Einhorn, 1986; March, 1988). Perhaps the most troubling feature of decision theory in this context is the invitation it provides to managerial passivity. By emphasizing the calculation of expectations as a response to risk, the theory poses the problem of choice in terms appropriate to decision-making in an uncontrollable world, rather than in a world that is subject to control. It is not intrinsic to that frame that decision-makers become passive with respect to modifying the probabilities they face, but that danger is real. We may prefer to have managers imagine (sometimes falsely) that they can control their fates, rather than suffer the consequences of their imagining (sometimes falsely) that they cannot. What are harder to specify are the details of the ways in which such impulses for discovering methods to improve the odds can be meshed with standard 'rational' calculations to induce more sensible managerial behavior.

References

Adler, Stanley (1980) Risk-making management, *Business Horizons*, 23(2): 11–14.

Alderfer, Clayton, P., and Harold Bierman, Jr. (1970) Choices with risk: beyond the mean and variance, *Journal of Business*, 43: 341–53.

Allais, Maurice (1953) Le comportement de l'homme rationnel devant le risque: critique des postulats et axiomes de l'école americaine, *Econometrica*, 21: 503–46.

Allison, Graham T. (1971) *Essence of Decision*. Boston, MA: Little, Brown.

Arrow, Kenneth J. (1965) *Aspects of the Theory of Risk Bearing*. Helsinki: Yrjö Jahnssonis Säätio.

Atkinson, John W. (1964) *An Introduction to Motivation*. New York, NY: Van Nostrand.

Bell, David E. (1983) Risk premiums for decision regret, *Management Science*, 29: 1156–66.

Boussard, Jean-Marc, and Michel Petit (1967) Representation of farmers behavior under uncertainty with a focus-loss constraint, *Journal of Farm Economics*, 49: 869–80.

Bowman, Edward H. (1980) A risk-return paradox for strategic management, *Sloan Management Review*, 21: 17–31.

Bowman, Edward H. (1982) Risk seeking by troubled firms, *Sloan Management Review*, 23: 33–42.

Brenner, Menachem and Zur Shapira (1983) Environmental uncertainty as determining merger activity, in Walter Goldberg (ed.), *Mergers: Motives, Modes, Methods*. New York, NY: Nichols, pp. 51–65.

Brinton, Crane (1938) *Anatomy of Revolution*. New York, NY: Norton.

Brockhaus, Robert H., Sr. (1980) Risk-taking propensity of entrepreneurs, *Academy of Management Journal*, 23: 509–20.

Budescu, David V., and Thomas S. Wallsten, (1985) Consistency in interpretation of probabilistic phrases, *Organizational Behavior and Human Decision Processes*, 36: 391–405.

Cohen, Michael D., James G. March, and Johan P. Olsen, (1972) A garbage can model of organizational choice, *Administrative Science Quarterly*, 17: 1–25.

Coombs, Clyde H. (1983) *Psychology and Mathematics*. Ann Arbor, MI: University of Michigan Press.

Crouch, Edmund A. C., and Richard Wilson (1982) *Risk/Benefit Analysis*. Cambridge, MA: Ballinger.

Cyert, Richard M., and James G. March (1963) *A Behavioral Theory of the Firm*. Englewood Cliffs, NJ: Prentice Hall.

Deci, Edward L. (1975) *Intrinsic Motivation*, New York: Plenum.

Douglas, Mary and Aaron Wildavsky (1982) *Risk and Culture*. Berkeley: University of California Press.

Edwards, Ward (1954) The theory of decision-making, *Psychological Bulletin*, 51: 380–417.

Edwards, Ward (1961) Behavioral decision theory, *Annual Review of Psychology*, 12: 473–98.

Einhorn, Hillel (1986) Accepting errors to make less error, *Journal of Personality Assessment*, 50: 387–95.

Englander, Tibor, Klara Farago, Paul Slovic, and Baruch Fischhoff (1985) A comparative analysis of risk perception in Hungary and the United States, unpublished ms.

Fischhoff, Baruch (1975) Hindsight ≠ foresight: The effect of outcome knowledge on judgement under uncertainty, *Journal of Experimental Psychology: Human Perception and Performance*, 1: 288–99.

Fischhoff, Baruch, and Ruth L. Beyth (1975) I knew it would happen – remembered probabilities of once-future things, *Organizational Behavior and Human performance*, 3: 552–64.

Fischhoff, Baruch, Sarah Lichtenstein, Paul Slovic, Stephen L. Derby, and Ralph Keeney (1981) *Acceptable Risk*. New York, NY: Cambridge University Press.

Fischhoff, Baruch, Stephen R. Watson, and Chris Hope (1984) Defining risk, *Policy Sciences*, 17: 123–39.

Fishburn, Peter C. (1977) Mean-risk analysis with risk associated with below-target returns, *American Economic Review*, 67: 116–26.

Gibbons, Michael R. (1982) Multivariate tests of financial models: A new approach, *Journal of Financial Economics*, 10: 3–27.

Griffith, R. M. (1949) Odds adjustments by American horse race bettors, *American Journal of Psychology*, 62: 290–94.

Hamilton, Gary G. (1978) The structural sources of adventurism: the case of the California gold rush, *American Journal of Sociology*, 83: 1466–90.

Hastorf, Albert, and Alice M. Isen, (eds) (1982) *Cognitive Social Psychology*. New York, NY: Elsevier.

Ibsen, Henrik (1884) *The Wild Duck*. Norton Critical Edition (1968), Dounia B. Christiani (trans.). New York, NY: W. W. Norton.

Johnson, Eric J., and Amos Tversky, (1983) Affect, generalization and the perception of risk, *Journal of Personality and Social Psychology*, 45: 20–31.

Kahneman, Daniel, Paul Slovik, and Amos Tversky (1982) *Judgment under Uncertainty: Heuristics and Biases.*Cambridge: Cambridge University Press.

Kahneman, Daniel, and Amos Tversky (1979) Prospect theory: an analysis of decision under risk, *Econometrica*, 47: 263–91.

Kahneman, Daniel, and Amos Tversky (1982) Variants of uncertainty, *Cognition*, 11: 143–57.

Kamil, Alan C., and Herbert L. Roitblat (1985) The ecology of foraging behavior: implications for animal learning and memory, *Annual Review of Psychology*, 36: 141–69.

Keyes, Ralph (1985) *Chancing it*. Boston, MA: Little, Brown.

Kingdon, John (1984) *Agendas, Alternatives, and Public Policies*. Boston, MA: Little, Brown.

Kogan, Nathan, and Michael A. Wallach (1964) *Risk-taking*. New York, NY: Holt, Rhinehart and Winston.

Kunreuther, Howard (1976) Limited knowledge and insurance protection, *Public Policy*, 24: 227–61.

Langer, Ellen J. (1975) The illusion of control, *Journal of Personality and Social Psychology*, 32: 311–28.

Lanir, Zvi, and Zur Shapira (1984) Analysis of decisions concerning the defense of rear areas in Israel: a case study in defense decision-making, in Zvi Lanir (ed.), *Israel's Security Planning in the 1980s*. New York, NY: Praeger.

Laughhunn, Dan J., John W. Payne, and Roy L. Crum (1980) Managerial risk-preferences for below target returns, *Management Science*, 26: 1238–49.

Levinthal, Daniel, and James G. March (1981) A model of adaptive organizational search, *Journal of Economic Behavior and Organization*, 2: 307–333.

Levy, Haim, and Harry M. Markowitz (1979) Approximating expected utility by a function of mean and variance, *American Economic Review*, 69: 308–17.

Levy, Haim and Marshall Sarnat (1984) *Portfolio and Investment Selection*. Englewood Cliffs, NJ: Prentice Hall.

Lindley, D. V. (1973) *Making Decisions*. London: John Wiley.

Lopes, Lola L. (1987) Between hope and fear: the psychology of risk, *Advances in Experimental Social Psychology*, 20: 255–95.

MacCrimmon, Kenneth R., and Donald A. Wehrung (1986) *Taking Risks: The Management of Uncertainty*. New York, NY: Free Press.

Mansfield, Edwin (1968) *The Economics of Technological Change*. New York, NY: Norton.

March, James G. (1978) Bounded rationality, ambiguity, and the engineering of choice, *Bell Journal of Economics*, 9: 587–608.

March, James G. (1981a) Decisions in organizations and theories of choice, in Andrew Van de Van, and William Joyce (eds), *Assessing Organizational Design and Performance*. New York: Wiley Interscience, pp. 205–244.

March, James G. (1981b) Footnotes to organizational change, *Administrative Science Quarterly*, 26: 563–77.

March, James G. (1988) Variable risk preferences and adaptive aspirations, *Journal of Economic Behavior and Organizations*, in press.

March, James G., and Johan P. Olsen (1976) *Ambiguity and Choice in Organizations*. Bergen, Norway: Universitetsforlaget.

March, James G., and Zur Shapira (1982) Behavioral decision theory and organizational decision theory, in Gerardo R. Ungson and Daniel N. Braunstein (eds), *Decision Making: An Interdisciplinary Inquiry*. Boston, MA: Kent, pp. 92–115.

March, James G., and Herbert A. Simon (1958) *Organizations*. New York, NY: Wiley.

Markowitz, Harry M. (1952) The utility of wealth, *Journal of Political Economy*, 60: 151–58.

Mayhew, Lewis B. (1979) *Surviving the Eighties*. San Francisco, CA: Jossey-Bass.

Maynard Smith, J. (1978) Optimization theory in evolution, *Annual Review of Ecology and Systematics*, 9: 31–56.

McClelland, David (1961) *The Achieving Society*. New York, NY: Van Nostrand.

Mueller, Dennis C. (1969) A theory of conglomerate mergers, *Quarterly Journal of Economics*, 83: 643–59.

Nisbett, Richard, and Lee Ross (1980) *Human Inference: Strategies and Shortcomings of Social Judgment*. Englewood Cliffs, NJ: Prentice-Hall.

Olsen, Johan P. (1983) *Organized Democracy*. Oslo: Universitetsforlaget.

Payne, John W., Dan J. Laughhunn, and Roy L. Crum (1981) Further tests of aspiration level effects in risky choice behavior, *Management Science*, 27: 953–8.

Peters, Tom, and Robert Waterman (1982) *In Search of Excellence*. New York, NY: Harper and Row.

Pratt, John W. (1964) Risk-aversion in the small and in the large, *Econometrica*, 32: 122–36.

Ross, Stephen A. (1981) Some stronger measures of risk-aversion in the small and in the large with applications, *Econometrica*, 49: 621–38.

Schoemaker, Paul J. H. (1980) *Experiments on Decisions under Risk: The Expected Utility Hypothesis*. Boston, MA: Nijhoff.

Schoemaker, Paul J. H. (1982) The expected utility model: its variants, purposes, evidence and limitations, *Journal of Economic Literature*, 20: 529–63.

Shapira, Zur (1986) Risk in managerial decision-making. Unpublished ms.

Sharpe, William F. (1964) Capital asset prices: a theory of market equilibrium under conditions of risk, *Journal of Finance*, 19: 425–42.

Sharpe, William F. (1977) The capital asset pricing model: a multi-beta interpretation, in Haim Levy and Marshall Sarnat (eds), *Financial Decision Making under Uncertainty*. New York, NY: Academic Press, pp. 127–136.

Simon, Herbert A. (1955) A behavioral model of rational choice, *Quarterly Journal of Economics*, 69: 99–118.

Singh, Jitendra V. (1986) Performance, slack, and risk-taking in strategic decisions, *Academy of Management Journal*, 29: 562–85.

Slovic, Paul (1967) The relative influence of probabilities and payoffs upon perceived risk of a gamble, *Psychonomic Science*, 9: 223–4.

Slovic, Paul, Baruch Fischhoff, and Sarah Lichtenstein (1977) Behavioral decision theory, *Annual Review of Psychology*, 28: 1–39.

Slovic, Paul, Baruch Fischhoff, and Sarah Lichtenstein (1982) Facts versus fears: understanding perceived risk, in Daniel Kahneman, Paul Slovic and Amos Tversky (eds), *Judgement under Uncertainty: Heuristics and Biases*. Cambridge: Cambridge University Press, pp. 463–492.

Slovic, Paul, Baruch Fischhoff, and Sarah Lichtenstein (1985) Characterizing perceived risk, in Robert W. Kates and Christoph Hohenemser (eds), *Perilous Progress: Managing the Hazards of Technology*. Boulder, CO: Westview Press, pp. 91–125.

Snyder, Wayne W. (1978) Horse racing: Testing the efficient markets model, *Journal of Finance*, 33: 1109–18.

Strickland, Lloyd, Roy J. Lewici, and Arnold M. Katz (1966) Temporal orientation and perceived control as determinants of risk taking, *Journal of Experimental Social Psychology*, 2: 143–51.

Tversky, Amos (1972) Elimination by aspects: a theory of choice, *Psychological Review*, 79: 281–99.

Tversky, Amos, and Daniel Kahneman (1974) The framing of decisions and the psychology of choice, *Science*, 185: 1124–31.

Tversky, Amos, and Daniel Kahneman (1982) Causal schemas in judgment under uncertainty, in Daniel Kahneman, Paul Slovic and Amos Tversky (eds), *Judgment under Uncertainty: Heuristics and Biases*. New York, NY: Cambridge University Press, pp. 117–28.

Ungson, Gerardo, R., and Daniel N. Braunstein (1982) *Decision Making: an Interdisciplinary Inquiry*. Boston, MA: Kent.

Vlek, Charles, and Pieter-Jan Stallen (1980) Rational and personal aspects of risk, *Acta Psychologica*, 44: 273–300.

Weinstein, N. D. (1980) Unrealistic optimism about future life events, *Journal of Personality and Social Psychology*, 39: 806–20.

Part II
Conflict in Organizations

5

The Business Firm as a Political Coalition

James G. March

The modern business firm is an organization for making and implementing decisions within a market economy. In most major industries of well-developed economies, most firms are large, complex organizations. These organizations render a set of key decisions for the economy. They establish prices, determine outputs, make investments, and allocate resources. These decisions and the consequences ensuing from them are the focus for the economic study of the firm. The economic theory of the firm attempts (1) to specify the decisions that business firms will make (as a basis for more aggregate predictions of the economy); and (2) to prescribe appropriate decision-rules for a rational firm operating in a market economy.

Except as it enters as a participant in the general political arena, the business firm has not been a focus of study for political scientists. Political scientists have generally defined their field in a relatively modest way, limiting their attention to phenomena that occur in, or in close conjunction with, explicitly governmental institutions. Except for a few attempts to define the field in terms of the study of power (or its variants), the major criterion for delimiting the field has been descriptive rather than analytic. By any reasonable descriptive definition of political science, the business firm is outside the domain. Similarly, economists have largely ignored political systems except as they impinge on the market. Although it is conventional for economists to identify their field in terms of an analytic

This paper was first published in *Journal of Politics* 24 (1962) 662–678. It is based on a paper presented at the annual meetings of the American Political Science Association in St Louis, 7 September, 1961. The research underlying it was conducted jointly with R. M. Cyert under a grant from the Ford Foundation for the study of organizational behavior. I wish to acknowledge the major contribution of Professor Cyert to the ideas expressed here.

definition (e.g., the study of the allocation of scarce resources), the vast bulk of economic research is linked to a descriptive definition of the field. For practical purposes, economics is the study of markets. The main attention to politics comes as a side issue in the area of economic policy.

At the risk of offending both economists and political scientists, I will assert that this division of labor is dysfunctional. It contributes to our inability as students to understand and predict the firm; it contributes to our inability as public-policy-makers to control and direct the firm. More specifically, I will argue that the business organization is properly viewed as a political system and that viewing the firm as such a system both clarifies conventional economic theories of the firm and (in conjunction with recent developments in theoretical languages) suggests some ways of dealing with classical problems in the theory of political systems generally. The argument depends on a general statement of the theoretical problem involved in decision models of complex systems, an evaluation of two major alternative approaches to that problem, and an examination of the implications of some recent attempts to develop a revised theory of the firm on the basis of a few key political concepts.

Conflict Systems

Consider a general class of purposive systems characterized by two attributes:

1 *There are consistent basic units.* Each elementary unit in the system can be described as having a consistent preference ordering defined over the possible states of the system. By a consistent preference ordering is meant an ordering such that for any realizable subset of possible states of the system there exists at least one state as good as any other state in the subset. Thus we require that the elementary units be able to make a choice among alternative states of the system (allowing for a chance decision-rule for the special case in which there is more than one state at least as good as all other states).

2 *There is conflict.* The preference orderings of the elementary units are mutually inconsistent relative to the resources of the system. Conflict, in this sense, arises when the most preferred states of all elementary units cannot be simultaneously realized. In order for conflict (in this sense) to exist it must be true that there is no allocative decision such that no one of the elementary units would prefer an alternative state of the system.

These two simple postulated attributes underlie a wide variety of theories about conflict resolution, choice, or the allocation of scarce resources.

Whether we are talking about the behavior of individuals in a simple learning experiment, the internal dynamics of a small group solving a problem, the interaction of parties and pressure groups in a legislative setting, or the pricing of commodities in a market system, we frequently make these two postulates. For convenience, let us call them the postulates of conflict. Any system satisfying the postulates we can call a conflict system.

One feature of studies of conflict systems that is puzzling from the point of view of the postulates of conflict is the extent to which the elementary units in one study are the conflict systems of another. The individual is treated as the system in some cases (e.g., in learning) and as the elementary unit in other (e.g., studies of small groups). Similarly, small groups are treated both as systems and as elementary units (e.g., in studies of organizations). Since the first postulate of conflict is essentially that the basic units themselves not be conflict systems, it seems awkward to be able to view a single system as either an elementary unit or a conflict system depending on the level of aggregation involved. In fact, most systems studied in the social sciences are apparently conflict systems of conflict systems.

The assumption of consistent basic units is justified by asserting either of two other characteristics of the macro-system involved. We may assert that the preference ordering of the subsystem (which we wish to identify as the elementary unit) is causally antecedent, and independent of, the decisions of the larger system. In such a case, we treat the preference ordering of the subsystem as given without considering the way in which that ordering is derived. Alternatively, we may assert that variation in system behavior due to conflict within the subsystem is trivial because of scale differences between the conflict within the subsystem on the one hand and conflict among subsystems on the other. In such a case, we take the preference ordering of the subsystem as subject to some minor error without attempting to eliminate the error entirely.

Such assertions are not simple technicalities. Consider, for example, either labor–management bargaining or bargaining among nations. Most of the literature and models of these phenomena accept the postulates of conflict. Since it is clear that (at the least) labor unions and nation states are themselves conflict systems, the theories are required to make some assertions that will allow the postulates of conflict to be made. A casual reading of this literature would suggest that either the assumption of causal antecedence or the assumption of scale difference is typically made. A casual reading of the literature also suggests, however, that the assumptions are suspect. In fact, one of the major recent developments in the study of these particular conflict systems has been a consideration of the complexities of interaction between the resolution of conflict within the subsystems and the resolution of conflict within the larger systems.

Despite such observations on the difficulties of satisfying the first postulate of conflict, most theories of conflict resolution essentially accept it as a reasonable approximation. If we restrict our attention to more or less well-defined theories susceptible to technical manipulation, virtually all theories use the postulate.

Political theory deals primarily with conflict systems as thus defined; and a rather large proportion of studies of the political process are concerned with discovering how conflict is resolved within a system revolving around some explicitly political institutions. Similarly, economic theory and economic studies focus to a large extent on conflict systems identified with explicitly economic institutions. In recent years a modest resurgence of political economy as a field of study has led to some important applications of economic concepts to the analysis of political conflict systems. This is particularly conspicuous in the work of Downs,[2] Davis and Whinston,[3] and Buchanan and Tullock.[4] In these attempts, allocation problems in politics have been studied from the point of view of concepts developed for economic systems. In some cases (e.g., Downs), this has meant the translation of a standard form of economic analysis into political terms. In other cases (e.g., Davis and Whinston), the general approach is clearly economic but the detailed form of analysis is relatively new for economics as well as politics. At the same time, some recent work in organization theory seems to indicate the utility of applying political concepts to the study of economic systems, particularly to the study of economic organizations. In many respects, March and Simon,[5] Thompson,[6] and Cyert and March[7] view the business organization as a socio-political conflict system subject to economic constraints.

Theories of Conflict Resolution

Given that we wish to describe a system as satisfying the postulates of conflict, and given that we wish to describe this system as 'acting', 'behaving', 'choosing', or 'deciding', we are required to introduce some mode of conflict resolution. By saying that the system does in fact 'act',

2 A. Downs, *An Economic Theory of Democracy* (New York, 1957).

3 O. A. Davis and A. B. Whinston, The Economics of Urban Renewal, *Law and Contemporary Problems*, 26, 1961, 105–17.

4 J. M. Buchanan and G. Tullock, *The Calculus of Consent* (Ann Arbor, 1962).

5 J. G. March and H. A. Simon, *Organizations* (New York, 1958).

6 V. A. Thompson, *Modern Organization* (New York, 1961).

7 R. M. Cyert and J. G. March, *A Behavioral Theory of the Firm* (New York, forthcoming).

we accept the proposition that the system in *some sense* prefers some state of the world to other possible states of the world. By describing the system as a conflict system, we assert that the system does not have a preference ordering in the usual sense of that term. The devices used to move from conflict to conflict resolution comprise the core of a theory of a conflict system. In general, extant theories take one of two directions for resolving conflict. Either they impute a superordinate goal in terms of which the conflict can be mediated, or they describe a process by which decisions are reached without explicit comparison of utilities. The latter approach is typical of theories of political coalitions; the former is typical of theories of business firms.

The Imputation of a Superordinate Goal

Any conflict system that can be observed and that can be described as 'behaving' is susceptible to description in terms of a superordinate goal. Given a sequence of behaviors, we impute a superordinate goal by accepting two simple assumptions: First, we assume there exists a joint preference ordering for the system at any particular point in time. Second, we assume the system always chooses the alternative behavior that is most preferred. Consider, for example, the familiar example of a conspicuous conflict system – a tree.[8] Is it reasonable to say that a tree seeks to maximize its total exposure to the sun subject to certain behavior limitations on the species, nutrients available, and environmental conditions? If, in fact, the behavior of the tree is such as to resolve conflict over a scarce resource (sunlight) so as to maximize total exposure, there is no reason why we cannot impute such a goal to a tree. Moreover, there may be many reasons why we would want to do so.

The usual objection to the imputation of a superordinate goal to conflict systems other than the human organism (or perhaps animals generally) is a curious one. Any such effort bears the onus of anthropomorphism. Yet in so far as a goal is simply an inferred rule for allocating resources, it is no more unique to anthropoids that is change of state. In the tree example, in fact, it can be argued that the concept of a goal is (under the assumed conditions) a more powerful tool for studying trees than it is for studying human beings. It permits us to make predictions about a variety of important phenomena (e.g., the location and movement of leaves and branches).

The tree example suggests two necessary conditions for effective use of an imputed superordinate goal in the construction of a theory. First,

8 M. Friedman, *Essays in Positive Economics* (Chicago, 1953), pp. 3–43; E. Rotwein, On the 'Methodology of Positive Economics', *Quarterly Journal of Economics,* 73, 1959, 554–78.

the goal must be stable (or at least change in a predictable way). Second, the goal must be meaningful. If the goal is not meaningful, it cannot be used for predictive purposes and simply becomes a restatement of the axiom that the system always chooses the most preferred alternative. A goal of maximizing subjective utility can, for example, be imputed to any system; but the imputation is largely useless unless operational meaning that is independent of the choices studied can be given to subjective utility. If the goal is not stable, the axioms underlying the importance of a superordinate goal are largely futile since the theory can only be applied *a posteriori*.

The Description of a Conflict Resolution Process

Just as any system that 'behaves' can be described as having a superordinate goal, it can also be described as having a conflict resolving process. If we adopt the process approach to a conflict system, we do not attempt to identify a joint preference ordering with respect to the ultimate decision. We replace the axioms of superordinate goals with two different assumptions. First, we assume that the ultimate decision results from a series of elementary decisions. Second, we assume that some sort of joint preference ordering exists for the elementary decisions.

If we consider the case of the tree again, it is clear that we can describe the tree in terms of a conflict resolution process. In fact, this is apparently the more common theoretical tool. We might, for example, stipulate a series of elementary decisions by individual leaves that, taken together, allocate sunshine to the various parts of the tree. Furthermore, we might be able to demonstrate the consistency of the process and a particular superordinate goal. This would be true, for example, if we could demonstrate that the elementary leaf decisions necessarily resulted in an ultimate allocation that maximized total exposure for the tree. The botanical invisible hand as it were.

The usual objection to a process description of a conflict system is its tendency to become analytically grotesque. A large elm tree has more than a million leaves on it. Even if we had a theory of leaf decision-making and could (conceptually) link leaf decisions to an aggregate exposure allocation, it is not easy to see how we analyze such a system.

Thus, two necessary conditions for effective use of a process description in the development of a theory for conflict systems are: (1) that the elementary decision processes be susceptible to treatment as consistent basic units; and (2) that analytic procedures be available with which to explore the properties of the model. The first is required to make the theory well-defined; the second is required to permit the theory to make meaningful predictions.

Studies of the Firm as an Economic Conflict System

Economic treatment of the firm as a conflict system is heavily influenced by the fact that the firm in economic theory is more commonly treated as the basic unit of a larger conflict system (industry, market, economic system) than as a conflict system itself. As a result, the economic theory of the firm is almost invariably constructed by explicitly imputing a superordinate goal to the conflict system represented by a business firm. In its classic form the theory asserts that the objective of the firm is to maximize long-run expected profits. The objective is accomplished by determining an output to be produced given a production function, a cost function, and a price. Given a set of factor prices, the firm determines the minimum cost-factor mix and the optimum output. Theories of imperfect competition are primarily modifications of this basic structure and do not change the basic approach. In the main, they modify the market structure faced by the firm or introduce new decision variables (e.g., price).

Thus, the economic theory of the firm assumes a joint preference ordering for the firm. In the standard form, that joint preference ordering is defined by profit-maximization. Such a characterization of business firm objectives has been subject to more or less continuous minority attack. Part of that attack we can ignore for present purposes. It stems from some misgivings about the social welfare implications of profit-maximization as a goal. The other source of the attack is more critical, however. It suggests that a theory assuming a profit-maximization goal is a poor predictive theory. Consequently, in some attempts at revision, profit-maximization is replaced by a more general utility function[9] or by an alternative goal (e.g., revenue-maximization).[10] In some revisions the preference ordering is a partial rather than complete ordering.[11] For the most part, the theory suppresses as outside its domain the process by which an organization composed of a rather complex mixture of people with considerable heterogeneity of individual goals generates a single preference ordering. It is assumed that conflict is resolved by the employment contract, or – more generally – by the factor prices and that the result is a joint preference ordering of some sort or other.

This implicit assumption that the firm represents a conflict system susceptible to useful description in terms of a superordinate goal (whether profit maximization or some other) is shared by most economists. It is apparently convenient for the construction of theories of macroeconomic

9 A. Papandreau, Some Basic Problems in the Theory of the Firm, in B. F. Haley (ed.) *A Survey of Contemporary Economics*, vol. 2 (Homewood, Illinois, 1952).

10 W. J. Baumol, *Business Behavior, Value and Growth* (New York, 1959).

11 H. A. Simon, *The New Science of Management Decision* (New York, 1961).

systems. Most economic theories build upon it (although not all necessarily depend upon it). It is relatively amenable to theoretical manipulation. It lends itself to the geometry and calculus familiar to economic thought.

Nevertheless, the assumption is almost certainly wrong as a micro-description of a business firm. It is extremely difficult to define a superordinate goal for a business firm that meets the two technical requirements of stability and meaningfulness as well as the empirical requirement of validity. Generally speaking, profit-maximization can be made perfectly meaningful (with some qualifications); but when made meaningful, it usually turns out to be invalid as a description of firm behavior. To achieve validity, we can substitute utility maximization; but this turns out to be either not stable or not meaningful. Thus, Machlup, who set out to save the profit-maximization assumption by generalizing it to utility-maximization, ended by reducing it largely to a definition[12] in so far as a micro-theory is concerned. With few exceptions, modern observers of actual firm behavior report persistent and significant contradictions between firm behavior and the classical assumptions.[13]

Despite their inadequacies, the assumptions have persisted. They have persisted for a simple but compelling reason. The alternative mode of theory – the process description of a conflict system – also has generally failed to satisfy its technical requirements. Until quite recently, case descriptions of the decision process in a business firm had approximately the same impact on a theorist of economic behavior as experiments on ESP had on a theorist of human perception. They were horror stories. They tended to demonstrate that there existed some unexplained variance in received theories. They did not provide us devices for reducing the variance. No matter how much we might think we knew about the decision process without the firm, we had no analytical apparatus for dealing with a process model. Such a disability means that few of the implications of the process could be determined except by direct observation and that a revised theory of the firm could not satisfactorily be grafted to existing economic theory. For most economists, such difficulties have seemed of decisive importance.

Studies of Political Conflict Systems

Whatever the reason may be, analytical disabilities appear to have had less impact on the development of political science than on economics.

12 F. Machlup, Marginal Analysis and Empirical Research, *American Economic Review*, 36, 1946, 519–54; F. Machlup, Rejoinder to an Anti-marginalist, *American Economic Review*, 37, 1947, 148–54.

13 For example, R. L. Hall and C. J. Hitch, Price Theory and Business Behavior, in T. Wilson (ed.) *Oxford Studies in Price Mechanisms* (Oxford, 1951); B. Fog, *Industrial Pricing Policies* (Amsterdam, 1960); Cyert and March, *A Behavioral Theory of the Firm*.

There is no political theory in the sense in which there is economic theory; and with only a few exceptions, little effort has been made to develop analytically tractable theories of political conflict systems. Generally speaking, there has been little pressure for simplification comparable to the pressure for simplification in the theory of the firm imposed by the needs of aggregation. The major exception (and only a partial one) is the study of international relations. In some treatments of bargaining among nation states, attempts have been made to characterize the behavior of the individual states in terms of simple models analogous in a loose way to the marginalist assumptions of economic theory.[14]

Most conspicuous by its absence in most of the modern literature on political conflict resolution is the imputation of a superordinate goal to political organizations. Except for some students of international relations, most modern observers have viewed concepts of the 'general will', 'national interest', or the 'common interest' as unsatisfactory concepts in the development of a theory of how political systems behave. 'Public interest' as a theoretical tool suffers from the standard problems of superordinate goals. It is almost impossible to make it simultaneously meaningful, stable, and valid. Because of such difficulties and because the existence of unresolved conflict is conspicuous in political systems, students of such systems have moved heavily toward process descriptive case studies of specific political organizations or decisions. By and large, these case studies have not yielded a set of theoretical propositions on which there is general agreement. The richness of specific case detail has tended to emphasize the uniqueness of the cases rather than contribute to theoretical model building.

Nevertheless, the basic outline of a process-oriented political theory of conflict resolution can be detected.[15] The theory assumes that there exist various interest groups in the system and that these groups make various demands. It further assumes that decisions within the system on the allocation of resources (i.e., in response to demands) are made by coalitions of interest groups and that each potential coalition has made a certain potential control over the system. The process postulated is one in which a broker – the politician – attempts to organize a coalition of interests that is viable (that is, one in which the demands are less than or equal to the resources available on the coalition). The theory ordinarily highlights phenomena such as bargaining, compromise, negotiation, inconsistency, and more or less continual conflict. In the descriptions of political systems

14 A. Rapport, Lewis Richard's Mathematical Theory of War, *Journal of Conflict Resolution*, 1, 1957, 249–99.

15 For example, see D. B. Truman, *The Governmental Process* (New York, 1951); R. A. Dahl and C. E. Lindblom, *Politics, Economics, and Welfare* (New York, 1953).

there is an emphasis of power, internal struggle, and expediency; a de-emphasis of order, cooperation, and problem-solving.

In so far as the interest group theory of political decision-making is a theory, it is a theory with modest analytic pretensions but rather impressive generality as a framework for observation. Most recent students of political organizations accept it in one form or another despite the obvious fact that the theory neither is particularly well-defined nor has a particularly powerful language. Thus, where the economic theory of the firm has moved to the imputation of a superordinate goal in order to gain analytic simplicity, the political theory of decision-making has moved to process description in order to gain empirical validity.

The Firm as a Political Coalition

The choice between an analytically elegant but empirically sterile theory on the one hand and an empirically fecund but analytically crude theory on the other is hardly a happy choice. Nor, I think, any longer a necessary one. To illustrate, let me outline a revised theory of the business firm and particularly a revised theory of the goals of a business firm. It is a theory that in some respects is more pristinely classic than many currently conventional economic conceptions of the firm, but it also bears a rather close relationship to current conceptions of political conflict systems. It is a theory that R. M. Cyert and I have used in developing some behavioral models of business firm decision-making.[16]

Basically, we assume that a business firm is a political coalition and that the executive in the firm is a political broker. The composition of the firm is not given; it is negotiated. The goals of the firm are not given; they are bargained.

We assume that there is a set of potential participants in the firm. At least initially, we think of such classes of potential participants as investors (stockholders), suppliers, customers, governmental agents and various types of employees. More realistically, we might supplement such a list with such actual or potential participants as investment analysts, trade associations, political parties and labor unions. Each potential participant makes demands on the system. These demands are essentially the price required for participation in the coalition. The demands are partly in the form of payments commonly assumed in economic theories (e.g., money) but they also are partly in the form of demands for policy commitments, personal treatment, etc. Thus, each set of demands can be characterized as having some degree of consistency with each combination of other demands. Some pairs of demands may be strictly inconsistent (under no

16 Cyert and March, *A Behavioral Theory of the Firm*.

circumstances can they both be satisfied). Some pairs of demands may be more or less consistent depending on external conditions (e.g., so long as the resources available to the coalition are substantial they may be consistent). Some pairs of demands may be completely complementary (e.g., if one demand is satisfied so also is the other one necessarily and without additional resource expenditure). As a result of this complementarity, we can describe the marginal 'cost' of any participant to any given coalition.

At the same time, we assume that the demands of the potential participants are subject to two important dynamic properties. First, the level of demand shifts in response to experience (both actual and vicarious). Second, attention to demands – the extent to which they are seen as relevant to action – shifts in response to the perception of problems.

We also assume that each possible coalition of participants has a certain 'value' with respect to the environment involved. It can gain a certain return from that environment. Thus, an over-simple model of a governmental coalition in a parliamentary democracy might assume that any coalition including more than 50 per cent of the voters would be able to do anything permissible within the system (thus would have maximum power) and that any coalition including less than 50 per cent of the voters would be able to do nothing (thus would have minimum power). In a similar way, alternative business coalitions can gain different returns from the economic system in which they operate; and we can (at least approximately) specify the marginal value of a particular given participant to a particular given coalition.

One way (not the only one) of describing the theory is from the point of view of the executive. Assume that the executive wishes to use the organization to maximize his own utility. His problem then is (in so far as he is able) to select a coalition so as to maximize the difference between the demands of his coalition members and the potential return from the environment of the coalition. The executive-political broker problem is twofold. On the one hand, he must select a coalition that has relatively low 'costs' of maintenance and relatively high returns from the environment. On the other hand, he must so structure the payments made to coalition members as to make the shifts in demands conducive to increasing the difference between total demands and total resources. The theory to this point becomes well-defined when we can specify the dimensions of participant demands, some measure of their complementarity, the functions by which they change over time, and the short-run internal constraints on the bargaining process by which goals are formed.

The terms 'marginal cost' and 'marginal value' suggest the sense in which this theory of business coalitions is close to classic economic views. Why do we describe the coalition involved as a political coalition? There are four critical ways in which the theory deviates from conventional economic views in the direction of a more 'political' treatment.

First, the focus of attention shifts from the owners (and their objectives) to the actual, operating organizers of the coalition – whoever they may be. In general, we view stockholders much as a theory of political systems might view citizens. Their demands form loose constraints on the more active members of the coalition. Their initiative in policy formation and in determining the nature of the coalitions is small.

Second, the theory emphasizes the non-uniqueness of short-run solutions to the coalition problem. At any point in time, there are a number of possible coalitions that are viable (that is, their total value exceeds their total cost of maintenance). As in the case of most political theories, some of the more interesting features of the theory depend on short-run deviations from a long-run position of equilibrium.

Third, the theory does not solve the problem of conflict by simple payments to participants and agreement on a superordinate goal. Rather it emphasizes the importance of policy demands and payments and of sequential rather than simultaneous mediation of demands.

Fourth, the theory emphasizes the importance of institutional constraints on the solution of the coalition problem. Most conspicuously there are constraints imposed: (1) by the institutionalization of commitments through the organizational structure, precedents, and budgetary agreements; (2) by the reification of attachments through identification and indoctrination; and (3) by the limitations in coordination and control imposed on an executive.

A theory of the business firm as a political coalition has both face validity and a certain amount of empirical support. In particular, such a theory seems more consistent than other available theories with the following widely observed attributes of business decision-making:

1 Organization goals seem to be a series of more or less independent constraints.
2 Business firms seem to tolerate a rather large amount of apparent inconsistency in goals and decisions, both over time and from one part of the organization to another.
3 Goals and decisions tend to be paired and decentralized with loose cross connections.
4 The extent to which decisions within the firm involve extensive conflict and 'marginal' decisions varies with the munificence of the environment.
5 The goals and commitments of business firms shift slowly over time in response to shifts in the coalition represented in the firm.

The fact (if it is one) that a description of a business firm as a political coalition is a more valid description than the classic economic description of the firm as an entrepreneur does not, however, solve the theoretical dilemma posed by the classic problems of analysis. For many years, economists as well as others have belabored the point that firms are organizations rather than entrepreneurs; only in the last few years have such strictures had any impact on the theory of the firm. Those students who were prepared to accept the evidence had no choice but to abandon not only the theory but also the field, since few of them were sympathetic intellectually with the journalist role implicit in the proliferation of case studies.

In recent years, the introduction of the computer and the computer program model to the repertoire of the theorist has changed dramatically the theoretical potential of process description models of conflict systems. Complex process description models of organizational behavior permit the development of a microeconomic theory of the firm. To illustrate, let me mention briefly three specific models:

First, a model of discretionary pricing and ordering decisions in a large departmental store. Cyert, March, and Moore have been able to simulate quite well three kinds of pricing decisions: regular pricing, scheduled sale pricing, and markdown pricing. In addition, they have been able to predict the amount and timing of orders (both original orders and reorders) with (as nearly as can be determined) reasonable accuracy.[17]

Second, a model of output determination in a duopoly, the American Can industry. On the basis of a few theoretical assumptions about differences between American and Continental Can Companies, Cyert, Feigenbaum, and March have been able to develop a model of decision-making within the industry. This model predicts quite well both the profit ratio of the two firms and their share of market over the 1913–56 period.[18]

Third, a general model of price and output determination. As a framework for other specific models and as a basis for investigation of the macroeconomic implications of a behavioral theory of the firm (including the assumption that the firm is a political coalition), Cohen, Cyert, March, and Soelberg have developed a general model of price and output determination in a modern oligopoly. The model has not been fully analyzed, but preliminary results seem to indicate a general correspondence between the output of the model and empirical data.[19]

Each of these models is written in the language of a computer program. All of them are process description models. Other comparable models of organizational behavior built on assumptions that differ in detail but are

17 Ibid.
18 Ibid.
19 Ibid.

generally process descriptive, are in various stages of development. Balderston and Hoggatt have developed a model of the wholesale lumber market.[20] Howard has developed a model of another wholesale market.[21] Clarkson has developed a model of the investment decisions of a trust bank.[22] Haines has developed a model of decision-making by an experimental group playing a complex business game.[23]

Not all of these models assume that the best characterization of a business firm is as a political coalition; however, they all illustrate the point that we are now in a position to explore the implications of viewing the firm as such a coalition. Process-descriptive, computer models are a natural form of theory in this area. As a result, theoretically-oriented students of the firm can afford to take seriously the detailed case studies of conflict systems both economic and political. For example, the recent work on a behavioral theory of the firm described briefly above has drawn rather heavily on political concepts. Within these models, it has been possible to introduce such 'political' features as unmediated conflict, multidimensional goals, and sequential attention to subunit pressures.

Implications for the Study of Political Conflict Systems

With a few exceptions, studies of political conflict systems have been largely atheoretical or quasi-theoretical in the past. Lacking an adequate theoretical language, we have had to work within the confines of simple verbal formulations. Nevertheless, some of these formulations seem to contribute to an understanding of the operation of the business firm, particularly when they are introduced into computer models of organizational decision-making. In the context of such models, I think it is quite likely that we will be able to expose both the theory of the firm as a coalition and the theory of political coalitions in general to new analytic attention.

Thus, we can identify three major implications for political science of recent research on the business firm as a decision-making coalition:

1 Recent experience indicates that the business firm can plausibly be conceived as a political conflict system; indeed the firm provides a useful test of the extent to which political phenomena are modified by a non-governmental setting.

---

20 F. E. Balderston and A. C. Hoggatt, *The Simulation of Market Processes* (Berkeley, 1960).

21 J. A. Howard, *Marketing: Executive and Buyer Behavior* (New York, forthcoming), chapter 2.

22 G. P. E. Clarkson, *Portfolio Selection: A Simulation of Trust Investment* (New York, 1962).

23 G. H. Haines, Jr, The Rote Marketer *Behavioral Science*, 6, 1961, 357–65.

2 Successes with computer program models in the analysis of political systems within business firms support the view that computer programs provide a powerful language for treatment of political conflict systems generally.
3 The apparent theoretical similarity between the political coalition in business and the political coalition in governmental organizations suggests that the substantive features of recent behavioral models of the firm may be useful as a basis for comparable models of governmental decision-making.

Finally, we should identify the major theoretical job that remains to be done. Although they are adaptive in many respects, the models of firm decision-making discussed above have not gone beyond the static implications of the fact that firms are political coalitions. Essentially they assert that certain phenomena occur in the firm because of its character as a coalition. They do not attempt to reflect shifts in coalitions *per se*. The latter task – leading to a more general theory of coalition development – has hardly been touched except conceptually. The significance of such a theory to a theory of the business firm and its growth is obvious. Even more obvious, however, is the significance of such a theory to the development of a theory of politics.

6

The Power of Power

James G. March

Introduction

Power is a major explanatory concept in the study of social choice. It is used in studies of relations among nations, of community decision-making, of business behavior, and of small-group discussion. Partly because it conveys simultaneously overtones of the cynicism of *Realpolitik*, the glories of classical mechanics, the realism of elite sociology, and the comforts of anthropocentric theology, *power* provides a prime focus for disputation and exhortation in several social sciences.

Within this galaxy of nuances, I propose to consider a narrowly technical question: To what extent is one specific concept of power useful in the empirical analysis of mechanisms for social choice? The narrowness of the question is threefold. First, only theories that focus on mechanisms of choice are considered. Second, only considerations of utility for the development or testing of empirically verifiable theories are allowed. Third, only one concept of power – or one class of concepts – is treated. The question is technical in the sense that it has primary relevance for the drudgery of constructing a predictive theory; the immediate implications for general theories of society, for the layman confronted with his own

---

This paper first appeared in David Easton (ed.) *Varieties of Political Theory* (New York, Prentice-Hall, 1966). It received the American Political Science Association Pi Sigma Alpha Award for the best paper presented at the Association's annual meetings in 1963.

The author has profited considerably from the comments of John C. Harsanyi, Herbert Kaufman, Norton E. Long, Duncan MacRae, Jr, Dale T. Mortensen, and Raymond E. Wolfinger, and by a pre-publication reading of Robert A. Dahl's forthcoming article: 'The Power Analysis Approach to the Study of Politics', in the *International Encyclopedia of the Social Sciences*.

complex environment, or for the casual student, are probably meager. They certainly are not developed here.

By a mechanism for social choice, I mean nothing more mysterious than a committee, jury, legislature, commission, bureaucracy, court, market, firm, family, gang, mob, and various combinations of these into economic, political, and social systems. Despite their great variety, each of these institutions can be interpreted as a mechanism for amalgamating the behavior (preferences, actions, decisions) of subunits into the behavior of the larger institution; thus, each acts as a mechanism for social choice. The considerations involved in evaluating the usefulness of power as a concept are the same for all of the mechanisms cited above, although it is patently not necessarily true that the conclusions need be the same.

By an empirically verifiable theory, I mean a theory covered by the standard dicta about prediction and confirmation. We will ask under what circumstances the use of *power* contributes to the predictive power of the theory.

The specific concept of power I have in mind is the concept used in theories having the following general assumptions:

1 The choice mechanism involves certain basic components (individuals, groups, roles, behaviors, labels, etc.).
2 Some amount of power is associated with each of these components.
3 The responsiveness (as measured by some direct empirical observation) of the mechanism to each individual component is monotone increasing with the power associated with the individual component.

There are a number of variations on this general theme, each with idiosyncratic problems; but within a well-defined (and relatively large) class of uses of the concept of power, power plays the same basic role. It is a major intervening variable between an initial condition, defined largely in terms of the individual components of the system, and a terminal state, defined largely in terms of the system as a whole.

In order to explore the power of power in empirical theories of social choice, I propose to do two things: First, I wish to identify three different variations in this basic approach to power as an intervening variable to suggest the kinds of uses of *power* with which we will be concerned. Second, I wish to examine six different classes of models of social choice that are generally consistent with what at least one substantial group of students means by *social power*. In this examination, I will ask what empirical and technical problems there are in the use of the concept of power and in the use of alternative concepts, and under what circumstances the concept of power does, or can, contribute to the effective prediction of social choice.

Three Approaches to the Study of Power

The Experimental Study

The great variety of types of studies of power in the experimental literature is clear from a perusal of recent compendia and review articles.[1] Since many of these studies are only marginally relevant to the concerns of this paper, I will assume general awareness of the experimental literature rather than attempt to review it. This brief introduction is intended simply to provide a relatively coherent characterization of a class of approaches to the study of power. Although these approaches are predominantly used in experimental studies, the experimental setting is neither a necessary nor a sufficient condition for the approaches; the label 'experimental studies' is simply shorthand for the general approach.

Conceptual basis. The experimental studies of power are generally Newtonian. Many of them are directly indebted to Lewin, who defined the power of *b* over *a* 'as the quotient of the maximum force which *b* can induce on *a*, and the maximum resistance which *a* can offer'.[2] In general, the experimental studies assume that the greater the power of the individual, the greater the changes induced (with given resistance) and the more successful the resistance to changes (with given pressure to change).

The experimental studies tend to be reductionist. Although they are ultimately (and sometimes immediately) interested in the power of one individual over another, they usually seek to reduce that relationship to more basic components. Thus, we distinguish between the power of behavior and the power of roles, and characterize specific individuals as a combination of behavior and roles.[3] Or, we distinguish factors affecting the agent of influence, the methods of influence, and the agent subjected to influence.[4]

The experimental studies of interest here are generally synthetic. They attempt to predict the result of the interaction of known (experimentally manipulated) forces rather than to determine the forces by analysis of

1 See Dorwin Cartwright, (ed.) *Studies in Social Power* (Ann Arbor: University of Michigan Press, 1959): Dorwin Cartwright and A. F. Zander, (eds), *Group Dynamics* (New York: Harper & row, Publishers, 1959); and Dorwin Cartwright, Influence, Leadership, Control, in *Handbook of Organizations*, ed. J. G. March (Chicago: Rand McNally & Co., 1965).

2 Kurt Lewin, *Field Theory in Social Science* (New York: Harper & Row, Publishers, 1951), p. 336.

3 See J. G. March, Measurement Concepts in the Theory of Influence, *Journal of Politics*, XIX, 1957, 202–26.

4 See Cartwright, Influence, Leadership, Control.

known (or hypothetical) results. The problem is generally not to determine the power distribution, but to test the consequences of various power distributions.

Procedures. The procedures used in this class of experimental studies are the classic ones. We determine power by some *a priori* measure or experimental manipulation, use a relatively simple force model to generate hypotheses concerning differences in outcomes from different treatments, and compare the observed outcomes with the predicted outcomes.

One of the better known variations on the basic Lewinian model is the one by French as further developed by Harary.[5] In this model, we predict shifts in opinion as a result of communication among subjects characterized by initial positions. Power exerted in a given direction is a function of the distribution of underlying power and the distances between the initial positions. In the two-person version of the model, change in opinion is inversely proportional to power. If we view an *n*-person group as being connected by a communication structure defining who can (or does) talk to whom, the model predicts the time series of opinion changes and the equilibrium opinions for various power distributions and communication structures. Theorems for the equal-power case are presented by French and Harary. Few theorems have been adduced for the unequal-power case in general, but the model can easily be used to generate specific predictions in specific cases.

Although few other models approach the specificity of the graph-theory version, the inverse relation between opinion- or behavior-change and power is normally used to derive hypotheses about differences among treatments.

Results. There are several studies of social power that are substantially irrelevant for the present discussion. Studies of the consequences of apparent power for non-task or non-opinion behavior are potentially relevant, but they have rarely been interpreted in a way that fits this framework. For example, the responses to power are classified nominally, rather than along a continuum. Similarly, many of the studies of factors in differential influence (e.g., content of the communication) are only marginally relevant here.

For present purposes, two general results are particularly germane:

1 It is possible to vary power of a specific subject systematically and (within limits) arbitrarily in an experimental setting. This can be done

---

5 See J. R. P. French, Jr, A Formal Theory of Social Power, *Psychological Review,* LXIII, 1956, 181–94; and Cartwright, *Studies in Social Power.*

by manipulating some elements of his reputation[6] or by manipulating some elements of his power experience.[7] This apparently innocuous – and certainly minimal – result is in fact not so unimportant. It permits us to reject certain kinds of social-choice models for certain kinds of situations.

2 The effectiveness of *a priori* power (i.e., manipulated, or *a priori* measured power) in producing behavior change is highly variable. Although there are indications that some kinds of leadership behavior are exhibited by some people in several different groups,[8] most studies indicate that the effectiveness of specific individuals, specific social positions, and specific behaviors in producing behavior change varies with respect to the content and relevancy of subject matter,[9] group identifications,[10] and power base.[11] In fact, much of the literature is devoted to identifying these factors.

The Community Study

A second major approach to the study of power can be called *the community power approach*; it is typical of, but not limited to, community studies.[12] This paper is limited to the base problems of power and consequently does not do justice to the variety of substantive concerns represented in the research. As in the case of the experimental literature, it also exaggerates the conceptual homogeneity of the studies; I think, though, that there is general homogeneity with respect to the questions of interest here.

Conceptual basis. The conceptual definition of power implicit (and often explicit) in the community studies is clearly Newtonian. The first two 'laws' of social choice form a simple definition:

6 See C. I. Hovland, I. L. Janis, and H. H. Kelley, *Communication and Persuasion* (New Haven: Yale University Press, 1953).

7 See B. Mausner, The Effect of Prior Reinforcement on the Interaction of Observer Pairs *Journal of Abnormal and Social Psychology,* XLIX, 1954, 65–8, and The Effect of One Partner's Success or Failure in a Relevant Task on the Interaction of Observer Pairs *Journal of Abnormal and Social Psychology*, XLIX, 1954, 577–60.

8 See E. F. Borgatta, A. S. Couch, and R. F. Bales, Some Findings Relevant to the Great Man Theory of Leadership, *American Sociological Review*, XIX, 1954, 755–59.

9 J. G. March, Influence Measurement in Experimental and Semi-Experimental Groups *Sociometry*, XIX, 1956, 260–71

10 Cartwright, *Studies in Social Power*.

11 Cartwright, *Studies in Social Power*.

12 For reviews of the literature, see P. H. Rossi, Community Decision Making, *Administrative Science Quarterly*, I, 1957, 415–43; and L. J. R. Herson, In the Footsteps of Community Power, *American Political Science Review*, LV, 1961, 817–30.

1 Social choice will be a predictable extension of past choices unless power is exerted on the choice.
2 When power is exerted, the modification of the choice will be proportional to the power.

The laws may lack some of the operational precision of Newton; in fact, it is not clear that they are any more Newton than Aristotle. But the community power studies generally assume that the decisions made by the community are a function of the power exerted on the community by various power holders. They assume some kind of 'power field' in which individual powers are summed to produce the final outcome.

The community studies are analytic in the sense that they attempt to infer the power of individuals within the community by observing (either directly or indirectly) their net effects on community choice. That is, they assume that a decision is some function of individual powers and the individual preferences. Hence, they observe the decision outcome and the preferences, and estimate the powers.

The community studies are personal in the sense that power is associated with specific individuals. The estimation procedures are designed to determine the power of an individual. This power, in turn, is viewed as some function of the resources (economic, social, etc.), position (office, role, etc.), and skill (choice of behavior, choice of allies, etc.); but the study and the analysis assume that it is meaningful to aggregate resource power, position power, and skill power into a single variable associated with the individual.

Procedures. The controversy over the procedures used in community studies is well known.[13] Since that controversy forms part of the background to the more general discussion below, I will simply lay the descriptive groundwork here. The procedure most generally used involves some variation of asking individuals within the community to assess the relative power of other individuals in the community. Essentially the panel is given the following task: On the basis of past experience (both your

13 See W. V. D'Antonio and H. J. Ehrlich, *Power and Democracy in America* (South Bend, Ind.: Notre Dame University Press, 1961); W. V. D'Antonio and E. C. Erickson, The Reputational Technique as a Measure of Community Power: An Evaluation Based on Comparative and Longitudinal Studies *American Sociological Review*, XXVII, 1962, 362–76; N. W. Polsby, Three Problems in the Analysis of Community Power *American Sociological Review*, XXIV, 1959, 796–803; N. W. Polsby, Community Power: Some Reflections on the Recent Literature *American Sociological Review*, XXVII, 1962, 838–41; and R. E. Wolfinger, Reputations and Reality in the Study of Community Power *American Sociological Review*, XXV, 1960, 636–44.

own and that of other people with whom you have communicated), estimate the power of the following individuals.[14] In some cases the domain of power is specified only broadly (e.g., political decisions); in some cases it is specified relatively narrowly (e.g., urban renewal decisions).

A second procedure involves the direct observation of decision outcomes and prior preferences over a series of decisions.[15] Essentially, we define a model relating power to decisions, draw a sample of observations, and estimate the power of individuals on the basis of that model and those observations.

It seems rather clear that neither the direct nor the indirect method of estimation is necessarily better. As we will note below, there are many 'reasonable' models of power; and the estimation problems are somewhat different for the different models.

Results. At a general level, the results of the community studies can be described in terms of three broad types of interests. First, we ask how power is distributed in the community. Second, we ask what relation exists between power and the possession of certain other socio-economic attributes. Third, we ask how power is exerted.

With respect to the distribution of power, most studies indicate that most people in most communities are essentially powerless. They neither participate in the making of decisions directly nor accumulate reputations for power. Whatever latent control they may have, it is rarely exercised. As a result, such control cannot be demonstrated by the power-measurement procedures of the community studies. Beyond the simple statement that only a minority of the population appears to exercise power, the studies are not really designed to elaborate the description of the power distribution. Some general statements of comparative variances can be made, but nothing approximating a systematic measure of power variance has been reported.

With respect to the relation between power and other individual characteristics, rather sharp differences among communities have been observed. Two results are conspicuous. First, in every study reported, the business and economic elite is overrepresented (in terms of chance expectations) among the high power-holders. By any of these measures, the economic notable is more powerful in the community than the average man. Second, the main influences on the extent to which non-economic characteristics are found to be important seem to be the procedures used

14 See F. Hunter, *Community Power Structures* (Chapel Hill: University of North Carolina Press, 1953).

15 See R. A. Dahl, *Who Governs?* (New Haven: Yale University Press, 1961).

in the investigation and the academic license of the investigator.[16] On the whole, studies using the general reputational technique seem to show business–economic characteristics[17] as more important than do studies using the direct-observation technique or a more narrowly defined reputation.[18] And studies by sociologists usually show business–economic characteristics as more important than do studies by political scientists. The two factors are hopelessly cross-contaminated, of course; and there are exceptions. If we assume that the correlation between results and technique (or discipline) is spurious, it may be possible to argue that the results are consistent with the hypothesis that power in somewhat older communities (e.g., English City, New Haven) is less linked to economic factors than is power in somewhat newer communities (e.g., Regional City, Pacific City).

With respect to the exercise of power, the studies have focused on specialization, activation, and unity of power-holders. Most studies have identified significant specialization in power: Different individuals are powerful with respect to different things. But most studies also have shown 'general leaders': Some individuals have significant power in several areas. Some studies have reported a significant problem associated with power activation: the more powerful members of the community are not necessarily activated to use their power, while less powerful members may be hyperactivated. The activation factor may be long-run[19] or short-run.[20] Although few systematic observations have been used to explore unity among the powerful, there has been some controversy on the extent to which the group of more powerful individuals represents a cohesive group with respect to community decisions. Some studies indicate a network of associations, consultations and agreements among the more powerful; other studies indicate rather extensive disagreement among the more powerful.[21]

The Institutional Study

The third alternative approach to the study of power is in one sense the most common of all. It is the analysis of the structure of institutions to

16 See N. W. Polsby, The Sociology of Community Power: A Reassessment *Social Forces,* XXXVII, 1959, 232–36; and P. Bachrach and M. S. Baratz, Two Faces of Power, *American Political Science Review,* LVI, 1962, 947–52.

17 See, for example, Hunter, *Community Power Structures.*

18 See, for example, Dahl, *Who Governs?*

19 See Dahl, *Who Governs?*

20 See R. C. Hanson, Predicting a Community Decision: A Test of the Miller-Form Theory *American Sociological Review*, XXIV, 1959, 662–71.

21 See W. H. Form and W. V. D'Antonio, Integration and Cleavage among Community Influentials in Two Border Cities *American Sociological Review,* XXIV, 1959, 804–14; and H. Scoble, Leadership Hierarchies and Political Issues in a New England Town in *Community Political Systems,* Morris Janowitz (ed.) New York: Free Press of Glencoe, Inc., 1961).

determine the power structure within them. Such studies are the basis of much of descriptive political science. Systematic attempts to derive quantitative indices of power from an analysis of institutional structure are limited, however. The approach will be characterized here in terms of the game-theory version, but other alternative *a priori* institutional interpretations of power would fall in the same class.[22]

The possibility of using the Shapley value for an *n*-person game as the basis for a power index has intrigued a number of students of bargaining and social-decision systems.[23] The present discussion will assume a general knowledge of game theory, the Shapley value,[24] and the original Shapley and Shubik article.[25]

Conceptual basis. The Shapley value is Neumannian. We assume the General von Neumann concept of a game: There are *n* players, each with a well-defined set of alternative strategies. Given the choice of strategies by the player (including the mutual choice of coalitions), there is a well-defined set of rules for determining the outcome of the game. The outcomes are evaluated by the individual players in terms of the individual orderings of preference. The Shapley value for the game to an individual player (or coalition of players) has several alternative intuitive explanations. It can be viewed as how much a rational person would be willing to pay in order to occupy a particular position in the game rather than some other position. It can be viewed as the expected marginal contribution of a particular position to a coalition if all coalitions are considered equally likely and the order in which positions are added to the coalition is random. It can be viewed as how much a rational player would expect to receive from a second rational player in return for his always selecting the strategy dictated by the second player. Or, it can be viewed simply as a computational scheme with certain desirable properties of uniqueness.

The Shapley value is impersonal. It is associated not with a specific player but rather with a specific position in the game. It is not conceived to measure the power of President Kennedy or President Eisenhower; it is conceived to measure the power of the presidency.

22 See, for example, Karl Marx, *Capital* (New York, 1906).

23 Dahl, *Who Governs?* and H. A. Simon, *Models of Man* (New York: John Wiley & Sons, Inc., 1957), both of whom are conceptually much closer to the other approaches outlined here, seem to have been supportive. W. H. Riker, A Test of the Adequacy of the Power Index *Behavioral Science*, IV, 1959, 276–90, applies the value in an empirical study: and J. C. Harsanyi, Measurement of Social Power, Opportunity Costs, and the Theory of Two-Person Bargaining Games, *Behavioral Science*, VII, 1962, 67–80, extends the value.

24 L. S. Shapley, A Value for *n*-Person Games, in *Contributions to the Theory of Games,* H. W. Huhn and A. W. Tucker (eds), (Princeton: Princeton University Press, 1953), II.

25 L. S. Shapley and M. Shubik, A Method for Evaluating the Distribution of Power in a Committee System *American Political Science Review*, XLVIII, 1954, 787–92.

The value is analytic in the sense that it is derived from the rules of the game (e.g., the legislative scheme) rather than vice versa. The value is *a priori* in the sense that it does not depend on empirical observations and has no necessary empirical implications.

How do we move from such a conception of value to a conception of power? One way is to restrict ourselves to a parsimonious definition: 'When we use the word *power* in the rest of this paper, it shall mean only the numerical representation of rewards accruing to coalitions as evaluated by the members of these coalitions.'[26] Although such a procedure is defensible, it will not help us significantly in the present discussion. We need to relate the Shapley–Shubik measure to the Newtonian approaches previously described. In the standard Newtonian versions of power, power is that which induces a modification of choice by the system. Quite commonly, we measure the power by the extent to which the individual is able to induce the system to provide resources of value to him. We are aware that power, in this sense, is a function of many variables; we suspect that informal alliances and allegiances influence behavior; and we commonly allege that power is dependent on information and intelligence as well as formal position.

Suppose that we want to assess the contribution to power of formal position alone. One way to do so would be an empirical study in which we would consider simultaneously all of the various contributing factors, apply some variant of a multiple regression technique, and determine the appropriate coefficients for the position variables. A second way would be an experimental study in which non-position factors are systematically randomized. A third way would be the one taken by Shapley and Shubik. We can imagine a game involving position variables only (e.g., the formal legislative scheme), and we can assume rationality on the part of the participants and ask for the value of each position under that assumption. Since this value is a direct measure of the resources the individual can obtain from the system by virtue of his position in the game alone, it is a reasonable measure of the power of that position. Alternatively, we can view the resources themselves as power.[27]

Procedures. There are two main ways in which we can use the Shapley–Shubik index in an empirical study: (1) We can construct some sort of empirical index of power, make some assumptions about the relation between the empirical and *a priori* measures, and test the consistency of the empirical results with the *a priori* measures. Thus, we might assume that

26 R. D. Luce and A. A. Rogow, A Game Theoretic Analysis of Congressional Power Distributions for a Stable Two-Party System, *Behavioral Science,* I, 1956, 85.

27 See R. D. Luce, 'Further Comments on Power Distributions for a Stable Two-Party Congress', Paper read at American Political Science Association meetings (1956): and Riker, 'A Test of the Adequacy of the Power Index'.

the empirical measure consists of the *a priori* measure plus an error term representing various other (non-position) factors. If we can make some assumptions about the nature of the 'error', we can test the consistency. Or, (2), we can deduce some additional propositions from the model underlying the index and test those propositions.

The first of these alternatives was suggested by Shapley and Shubik and considered by Riker. But neither they nor others have seen a way around the major obstacles in the way. The second alternative was the basis for a series of papers by Luce, Rogow, and Riker.[28]

Results. The main results in the application of the Shapley value have had only casual testing. Luce and Rogow have used the basic Shapley–Shubik approach in conjunction with Luce's conception of Ø-stability to generate some power distributions consistent with a stable two-party system. In this approach, one first assumes a two-party legislature and a President belonging to one of the two parties. Within each party, there is a subset that always votes with the party, a subset that is willing to defect to the other party, and a subset that is willing to form a coalition with a defecting subset from the other party. The President may be constrained always to vote with his party or to defect only to the coalition of defectors. Alternatively, he may be completely free to defect. This legislature operates under some voting rules which define (along with the size of parties, the permissible defections, and the size of defecting subsets) a set of coalitions that are able to pass a bill. The analysis produces a series of observations on the stability and other properties of power distributions found under various combinations of restrictions on the President and the size of the party subsets. These detailed results lead then to more general statements of the form: 'The richer the defection possibilities . . . the greater the localization of power'.[29] Although some of the results obtained seem intuitively sensible, only a footnoted bit of data has been adduced in support of them. In fact, most of the propositions are stated in a form that would require an empirical measure of power – and that would drive us back to the difficulty previously observed.

Riker has applied the basic Shapley–Shubik measure to the French Assembly to derive changes in power indices for the various parties in the French Assembly during the period 1953–4, as 34 migrations from one party to another produced 61 individual changes in affiliation.[30] On the assumption that party power is equally distributed among individual members, Riker tested the proposition that shifts in party affiliation tended

28 Luce and Rogow, 'A Game Theoretic Analysis'; Luce, 'Further Comments on Power Distributions'; and Riker, 'A Test of the Adequacy of the Power Index'.

29 Luce, 'Further Comments on Power Distributions', p. 10.

30 Riker, 'A Test of the Adequacy of the Power Index'.

to result in increases in individual power. The data did not support the hypothesis. In subsequent work, Riker has almost entirely abandoned the Shapley–Shubik approach.[31]

Six Models of Social Choice and the Concept of Power

The three general approaches described above illustrate the range of possible uses of the concept of power, and include most of the recent efforts to use the concept in empirical research or in empirically-oriented theory. I wish to use these three examples as a basis for exploring the utility of the concept of power in the analysis of systems for social choice. The utility depends first, on the true characteristics of the system under investigation. The concept of power must be embedded in a model and the validity of the model is a prerequisite to the utility of the concept. Second, the utility depends on the technical problems of observation, estimation, and validation in using the concept in an empirically reasonable model.

I shall now consider six types of models of social choice, evaluate their consistency with available data, and consider the problems of the concept of power associated with them. By a *model* I mean a set of statements about the way in which individual choices (or behavior) are transformed into social choices, and a procedure for using those statements to derive some empirically meaningful predictions. The six types of models are:

1 Chance models, in which we assume that choice is a chance event, quite independent of power.
2 Basic force models, in which we assume that the components of the system exert all their power on the system with choice being a direct resultant of those powers.
3 Force-activation models, in which we assume that not all the power of every component is exerted at all times.
4 Force-conditioning models, in which we assume that the power of the components is modified as a result of the outcome of past choices.
5 Force-depletion models, in which we assume that the power of the components is modified as a result of the exertion of power on past choices.
6 Process models, in which we assume that choice is substantially independent of power but not a chance event.

---

31 W. H. Riker, *The Theory of Political Coalitions* (New Haven: Yale University Press, 1962).

The list is reasonably complete in so far as we are interested in empirically oriented models of social choice. The approaches to the study of social power previously discussed and a fair number of other theories of social choice can be fitted into the framework.

Chance Models

Let us assume that there are no attributes of human beings affecting the output of a social-choice mechanism. Further, let us assume that the only factors influencing the output are chance factors, constrained perhaps by some initial conditions. There are a rather large number of such models, but it will be enough here to describe three in skeleton form.

The unconstrained model. We assume a set of choice alternatives given to the system. These might be all possible bargaining agreements in bilateral bargaining, all possible appropriations in a legislative scheme, or all experimentally defined alternatives in an experimental setting. Together with this set of alternatives, we have a probability function. Perhaps the simplest form of the function would be one that made the alternatives discrete, finite, and equally probable; but we can allow any form of function so long as the probabilities do not depend on the behavior, attitudes, or initial position of the individual components in the system.

The equal-power model. We assume a set of initial positions for the components of the system and some well-defined procedures for defining a social choice consistent with the assumption of equal power. For example, the initial positions might be arranged on some simple continuum. We might observe the initial positions with respect to wage rates in collective bargaining, with respect to legislative appropriations for space exploration, or with respect to the number of peas in a jar in an experimental group. A simple arithmetic mean of such positions is a social choice consistent with the assumption of equal power. In this chance model, we assume that the social choice is the equal-power choice plus some error term. In the simplest case, we assume that the error around the equal-power choice is random and normally distributed with mean zero and a variance that is some function of the variance of initial positions.

The encounter model. We assume only two possible choice outcomes: We can win or lose; the bill can pass or fail; we will take the left or right branch in the maze. At each encounter (social choice) there are two opposing teams. The probability of choosing a given alternative if the teams have an equal number of members is 0.5. If the teams are unequal in size, we have three broad alternatives:

1 We can make the probability of choosing the first alternative a continuous monotone increasing function of the disparity between the sizes of the two teams.
2 We can assume that the larger teams always win.
3 We can assume that the probability is 0.5 regardless of the relative size of the teams, thus making the model a special case of the unconstrained model.

What are the implications of such models? Consider the encounter model. Suppose we imagine that each power encounter occurs between just two people chosen at random from the total population of the choice system. Further, assume that at each encounter we will decide who prevails by flipping a coin.[32] If the total number of encounters per person is relatively small and the total number of persons relatively large, such a process will yield a few people who are successful in their encounters virtually all the time, others who are successful most of the time, and so on. In a community of 4,000 adults and about a dozen encounters per adult, we would expect about 12 or 13 adults to have been unsuccessful no more than once. Similarly, if we assume that all encounters are between teams and that assignment to teams is random, the other encounter models above will yield identical results. A model of this general class has been used by Deutsch and Madow to generate a distribution of managerial performance and reputations.[33]

Similar kinds of results can be obtained from the unconstrained-chance model. If we assume that social choice is equi-probable among the alternatives and that individual initial positions are equi-probable among the alternatives, the only difference is that the number of alternatives is no longer necessarily two. In general, there will be more than two alternatives; as a result the probability of success will be less than 0.5 on every trial and the probability of a long-run record of spectacular success correspondingly less. For example, if we assume a dozen trials with ten alternatives, the probability of failing no more than once drops to about 10^{-10} (as compared with about 0.0032 in the two alternative cases).

Finally, generally similar results are obtained from the equal-power model. If we assume that the initial position is normally distributed with mean, M, and variance, V, and that the error is normally distributed around M with a variance that is some function of V, we obtain what amounts to variations in the continuous version of the discrete models.

32 See H. White, Uses of Mathematics in Sociology *Mathematics and the Social Sciences*, J. C. Charlesworth (ed.) (Philadelphia: American Academy of Political and Social Science, 1963).

33 K. W. Deutsch and W. G. Madow, A Note on the Appearance of Wisdom in Large Organizations *Behavioral Science*, VI, 1961, 72–8.

If we set the error variance equal to V, the relationship is obvious. Our measures of success now become not the number (or proportion) of successes but rather the mean deviation of social choices from individual positions; and we generate from the model a distribution of such distances for a given number of trials.[24]

All of the chance models generate power distributions. They are spurious distributions in the sense that power, as we usually mean it, had nothing to do with what happened. But we can still apply our measures of power to the systems involved. After observing such a system, one can make statements about the distribution of power in the system and describe how power was exercised. Despite these facts, I think that most students of power would agree that if a specific social-choice system is in fact a chance mechanism, the concept of power is not a valuable concept for that system.

To what extent is it possible to reject the chance models in studies of social choice? Although there are some serious problems in answering that question, I think we would probably reject a pure-chance model as a reasonable model. I say this with some trepidation because studies of power have generally not considered such alternative models, and many features of many studies are certainly consistent with a chance interpretation. The answer depends on an evaluation of four properties of the chance models that are potentially inconsistent with data either from field studies or from the laboratory.

First, we ask whether power is stable over time. With most of the chance models, knowing who won in the past or who had a reputation for winning in the past would not help us to predict who would win in the future. Hence, if we can predict the outcome of future social choices by weighting current positions with weights derived from past observations or from *a priori* considerations, we will have some justification for rejecting the chance model. Some efforts have been made in this direction, but with mixed results.[35] Even conceding the clarity of the tests and the purity of the procedures and assuming that the results were all in the predicted direction, the argument for the various power models against a chance model would be meager. The 'powerful' would win about half the time even under the chance hypothesis.

Second, we ask whether power is stable over subject matter. Under the chance models, persons who win in one subject-matter area would be no more likely to win in another area than would people who lost in the first area. Thus, if we find a greater-than-chance overlap from one area to another, we would be inclined to reject the chance model. The evidence on

34 See D. MacRae, Jr, and H. D. Price, Scale Positions and 'Power' in the Senate *Behavioral Science*, IV, 1959, 212–18.

35 See, for example, Hanson, 'Predicting a Community Decision'.

this point is conflicting. As was noted earlier, some studies suggest considerable specialization of power, while others do not. On balance, I find it difficult to reject the chance model on the basis of these results; although it is clear that there are a number of alternative explanations for the lack of stability, non-chance explanations are generally preferred by persons who have observed subject-matter instability.[36]

Third, we ask whether power is correlated with other personal attributes. Under the chance model, power is independent of other attributes. Although it might occasionally be correlated with a specific set of attributes by chance, a consistent correlation would cast doubt on the chance hypothesis. It would have to be saved by some assumption about the inadequacy (that is, irrelevance) of the power measure or by assuming that the covariation results from an effect of power on the correlated attribute. Without any exception of which I am aware, the studies do show a greater-than-chance relation between power and such personal attributes as economic status, political office, and ethnic group. We cannot account under the simple chance model for the consistent underrepresentation of the poor, the unelected, and the Negro.

And fourth, we ask whether power is *susceptible to experimental manipulation.* If the chance model were correct, we could not systematically produce variations in who wins by manipulating power. Here the experimental evidence is fairly clear. It is possible to manipulate the results of choice mechanisms by manipulating personal attributes or personal reputations. Although we may still want to argue that the motivational or institutional setting of real-world choice systems is conspicuously different from the standard experimental situation, we cannot sustain a strictly chance interpretation of the experimental results.

Chance models are extremely naïve; they are the weakest test we can imagine. Yet we have had some difficulty in rejecting them, and in some situations it is not clear that we can reject them. Possibly much of what happens in the world is by chance. If so, it will be a simple world to deal with. Possibly, however, our difficulty is not with the amount of order in the world, but with the concept of power. Before we can render any kind of judgment on that issue, we need to consider some models that might be considered more reasonable by people working in the field.

Basic Force Models

Suppose we assume that power is real and controlling, and start with a set of models that are closely linked with classical mechanics although

36 See, for example, N. W. Polsby, How to Study Community Power: The Pluralist Alternative *Journal of Politics,* XXII, 1960, 474–84.

the detailed form is somewhat different from mechanics. In purest form, the simple force models can be represented in terms of functions that make the resultant social choice a weighted average of the individual initial positions – the weights being the power attached to the various individuals. Let us identify three variations on this theme:

The continuous case. Let C_j be the outcome (social choice) on the jth issue and A_{ij} *be the initial position on the* jth issue of the ith individual power source. C_j and the A_{ij} may be vectors, but they have the same dimensions. Let m_{ij}^* be the total power resources available to the ith component at the jth issue, and let m_{ij} be the normalized form of this. Thus:

$$m_{ij} = m_{ij}^* / \sum_{i=1}^{n} m_{ij}^*,$$

where n is the number of components.

The basic force model, in which we assume that m_{ij}^* is a constant over all j, is elegant in its simplicity:

$$C_j = \sum_{i=1}^{n} m_i A_{ij}.$$

Given a set of power indices and initial positions, we can predict the outcomes. Given a set of outcomes and the associated initial positions, we can determine the power indices.

The probabilistic binary case. Suppose C_j and A_{ij} can assume only two values (yes-no, pro-con, pass-fail, up-down, etc.). Associate the nominal values 1 and -1 with the two alternatives. Let P_j be the probability that $C_j = 1$. Then the basic force model assumes the form

$$P_j = \frac{1 + \sum_{i=1}^{n} m_i A_{ij}}{2}.$$

Alternative, we can define any function that maps $(-1, 1)$ onto $(0, 1)$, is monotone increasing, and is symmetric around the point $(0, 0.5)$. Most data suggest, in fact, that the function is not linear.[37]

Given the function, a set of power indices, and the initial positions, we can predict the outcomes subject to some chance error. Given the function, a set of outcomes, and the associated initial positions, we can determine the power indices subject to some errors in estimation.

37 F. M. Tonge, Models of Majority Influence in Unanimous Group Decision. Unpublished (1963).

The nearly determinate binary case. In this special form of the binary case, we assume that the more powerful team carries the day unequivocally. Thus

$$P_j = \begin{Bmatrix} 1 \\ .5 \\ 0 \end{Bmatrix} \text{ if } \sum_{i=1}^{n} m_i A_{ij} \begin{Bmatrix} > \\ = \\ < \end{Bmatrix} 0.$$

As before, we can use the model to predict outcomes given the power and initial positions, or to estimate power given outcomes and initial positions. In the latter case, we would normally have a family of solutions rather than a single solution.

The only serious problem with the use of these models lies in potential difficulties in estimation. But it is clear that the estimation problems are relatively minor unless the required observations are difficult to obtain. Consider the continuous case. Since we know that

$$m_k = \frac{C_j - \sum_{i \neq k} m_i A_{ij}}{A_{kj}} \qquad i = 1, \ldots, n$$

we need only $n-1$ distinct observations to determine the power (m_k) weights in a system having n distinct power sources. If the system involves only two individuals, we require only one observation to determine the weights. We get similar results in the case of the nearly determinate binary case, although if we deal in inequalities. If we ignore the possibility of a tie between the two sides, we know that

$$m_k < C_j \sum_{i \neq k} m_i A_{ij} \quad i = 1, \ldots, \text{n}.$$

Thus, given a set of observations we can define a family of values for the m_i that are consistent with the observations.

In the probabilistic case, the observations are the basis for estimating a set of weights that control the results (outcomes) only up to a probability value. If we have s observations, we know that

$$m_k = \frac{1 - 2\sum_{i=1}^{s} P_j - \sum_{i \neq k} \sum_{j=1}^{s} m_i A_{ij}}{\sum_{j=1}^{s} A_{kj}} \qquad i = 1, \ldots, \text{n}.$$

However, we do not know $\sum_{j=1}^{s} P_j$, but have to estimate it from $\sum_{j=1}^{s} C_j$. As a result, our estimate of m_k is subject to sampling variation.

None of these estimation problems are severe. In fact, the first two models are determinate and trivial; the third involves the binomial distribution but is not overly complicated.

The force models, therefore, are reasonably well-defined and pose no great technical problems, and the estimation procedures are straightforward. The observations required are no more than the observations required by any model that assumes some sort of power. What are the implications of the models? First, unless combined with a set of constraints (such as the power-structure constraints of the French and Harary formulation), the models say nothing about the distribution of power in a choice system. Thus, there is no way to test their apparent plausibility by comparing actual power distributions with derived distributions.

Second, in all of the models, the distance between the initial position of the individual and the social choice (or expected social choice) is inversely proportional to the power when we deal with just two individuals. As we noted earlier, this is also a property of French's model. With more than two individuals, the relation between distance and power becomes more complex, depending on the direction and magnitude of the various forces applied to the system. Since the models are directly based on the ideas of center of mass, these results are not surprising. Given these results, we can evaluate the models if we have an independent measure of power, such as the Shapley–Shubik measure. Otherwise, they become, as they frequently have, simply a definition of power.

Third, we can evaluate the reasonableness of this class of models by a few general implications. Consider the basic characteristics of the simple force models:

1 There are a fixed number of known power sources.
2 At any point in time, each of these sources can be characterized as affecting the social choice by exerting force in terms of two dimensions, magnitude (power) and direction (initial position or behavior).
3 Any given source has a single, exogenously determined power. That is, power is constant (over a reasonable time period and subject-matter domain of observation) and always fully exercised.
4 The result (social choice) is some sum of the individual magnitudes and directions.

In so far as the determinate models are concerned, both experimental and field observations make it clear that the models are not accurate portrayals of social choice. In order for the models to be accepted, the m_i (as defined in the models) must be stable. As far as I know, no one has ever reported data suggesting that the m_i are stable in a determinate model. The closest thing to such stability occurs in some experimental groups where the choices consistently come close to the mean, and in some highly formal voting schemes. In such cases, the power indices are occasionally close to stable at a position of equal power. Nevertheless, few students of power have claimed stability of the power indices.

When we move to the probabilistic case – or if we add an error term to the determinate models – the situation becomes more ambiguous. Since it has already been observed that rejection of a purely chance model is not too easy with the available data, the argument can be extended to models that assume significant error terms, or to models in which the number of observations is small enough to introduce significant sampling variation in the estimate of underlying probabilities. However, most observers of power in field situations are inclined to reject even such variations on the theme, although no very complete test has been made.

The basis for rejecting the simple force models (aside from the necessity of making them untidy with error terms) is twofold:

1 There seems to be general consensus that either potential power is different from actually exerted power or that actually exerted power is variable. If, while potential power is stable, there are some unknown factors that affect the actual exercise of power, the simple force models will not fit; they assume power is stable, but they also assume that power exerted is equal to power. If actually exerted power is unstable, the simple force models will fit only if we can make some plausible assertions about the nature of the instability. For example, we can assume that there are known factors affecting the utilization of power and measure those factors. Or, we can assume that the variations are equivalent to observational errors with known distributions.

2 There appears to be ample evidence that power is not strictly exogenous to the exercise of power and the results of that exercise. Most observers would agree that present reputations for power are at least in part a function of the results of past encounters. Although the evidence for the proposition is largely experimental, most observers would probably also agree that power reputation, in turn, affects the results of encounters. If these assertions are true, the simple force model will fit in the case of power systems that are in equilibrium, but it will not fit in other systems.

These objections to the simple force model are general; we now need to turn to models that attempt to deal with endogenous shifts in power and with the problem of power activation or exercise. As we shall see, such models have been little tested and pose some serious problems for evaluation on the basis of existing data. We will consider three classes of models, all of which are elaborations of the simple force models. The first class can be viewed as *activation models*. They assume that power is a potential and that the exercise of power involves some mechanism of activation. The second class can be described as *conditioning models*. They assume that power is partly endogenous – specifically that apparent power leads to actual power. The third class can be classified as *depletion models*. They assume that power is a stock, and that exercise of power leads to a depletion of the stock.

Force-Activation Models

All of the models considered thus far accept the basic postulate that all power is exerted all of the time. In fact, few observers of social-choice systems believe this to be true, either for experimental groups or for natural social systems. With respect to the latter, Schulze argues that 'the Cibola study appears to document the absence of any neat, constant, and direct relationship between *power as a potential for determinative action, and power as determinative action itself*'.[38] Wolfinger criticizes the reputational method for attributing power on the grounds that it 'assumes an equation of potential for power with the realization of the potential'.[39] And Hanson suggests that predictions based on the Miller–Form theory will be less accurate 'when the issue does not arouse a high level of community interest and activity'.[40]

As before, let m_{ij}^* represent the total power resources of the *i*th component at the *j*th choice, and let x_{ij} be the share $(0 \leq x_{ij} \leq 1)$ of the total power resources that are exercised by the *i*th component at the *j*th choice. We associate the force activation models to the basic force models by means of the simple accounting expression

$$m_{ij} = \frac{x_{ij} m_{ij}^*}{\sum_{i=1}^{n} x_{ij} m_{ij}^*}.$$

We can consider two general variations on this theme:

The partition model. Suppose we let x_{ij} assume only two values, 1 and 0. That is, we assume that components in the system are either active or inactive on any particular choice. It is frequently suggested that power must be made relative to a specific set of actions or domain of joint decisions.[41]

38 R. O. Schulze, The Role of Economic Dominants in Community Power Structure *American Sociological Review*, XXXII, 1958, 9.

39 Wolfinger, 'Reputation and Reality'.

40 Hanson, 'Predicting a Community Decision'.

41 See H. A. Simon, Notes on the Observation and Measurement of Political Power *Journal of Politics*, XV, 1953, 500–16; J. G. March, An Introduction to the Theory and Measurement of Influence *American Political Science Review*, LIX, 1955, 431–51; March, Measurement Concepts; and R. A. Dahl, The Concept of Power *Behavioral Science*, II, 1957, 201–15.

The specialization hypothesis is one form of such a model. We assume that once we have made the basic partition, we can treat the activated group as the total system and apply the basic force model to it.

The continuous model. Suppose we let x_{ij} assume any value between 0 and 1. That is, we assume that the participants in the system can vary their exercised power from zero to the total of their power resource. Thus, a relatively weak person can sometimes exert more power than a relatively strong one simply by devoting more attention to the choice problems involved.

Consider the problem of relating the activation models to observations of reality. Let us assume initially that potential power (m_{ij}^*) is constant over all choices. We assume that there is something called *potential power* that is associated with a component of the choice system and that this power resource does not depend on the choice. In effect, this assumes that m_{ij}^* is also constant over time, for we will require a time series of observations in order to make our estimates. We will relax this assumption in subsequent classes of models, but the constancy assumption is characteristic of most activation models.

Given the assumption of fixed potential power, we have two major alternatives. First, we can attempt to determine the value of x_{ij} for each component and each choice and use that information to estimate the potential power for each component. If we can determine by direct observation either the level of power utilization or the distribution of power utilization (or if we can identify a procedure for fixing the extent of utilization), we can estimate the potential power by a simple modification of our basic force models.

Suppose, for example, that we have some measures of the activation of individual members of a modern community. One such measure might be the proportion of total time devoted by the individual to a specific issue of social choice. We could use such a measure, observations of initial positions and social choices, and one of the basic force models to assign power indices (potential power) to the various individuals in the community. Similarly, if we took a comparable measure in an experimental group (e.g., some function of the frequency of participation in group discussions), we could determine some power indices. Because direct observational measures of the degree of power utilization are not ordinarily the easiest of measurements to take, the partition version of the model has an important comparative advantage from the point of view of estimation problems. Since we assume that the x_{ij} must be either 1 or 0, we need only observe whether the individual involved did or did not participate in a choice, rather than the degree of his participation.

If we are unable or do not choose to observe the extent of utilization directly, we can, at least in principle, estimate it from other factors in the situation. For example, if we can determine the opportunity costs[42] to the individual of the exercise of power, we might be able to assume that the individual will exercise power only up to the point at which the marginal cost equals the marginal gain. If we can further assume something about the relation between the exercise of power and the return from that exercise, we can use the opportunity costs to estimate the power of utilization. The general idea of opportunity costs, or subjective importance,[43] as a dimension of power has considerable intuitive appeal. If procedures can be developed to make the concepts empirically meaningful, they will be of obvious utility in an activation model of the present type. This route, however, has not yet attracted most persons doing empirical studies.

The second major alternative, given the assumption of constant potential power, is also to assume a constant utilization of power over all choices. Under such circumstances, the product $x_{ij}m_{ij}^*$ is a constant over all j. If both utilization and potential power are constant, we are back to the simple force model and can estimate the product $x_i m_i$ in the same way we previously established the m_i. Under such circumstances, the introduction of the concepts of power utilization and power potential is unnecessary and we can deal directly with power exercised as the core variable.[44]

The force activation model has been compared with empirical data to a limited extent. Hanson and Miller undertook to determine independently the potential power and power utilization of community members and to predict from those measures the outcome of social choices.[45] Potential power was determined by *a priori* theory; utilization was determined by inviews and observation. The results, as previously noted, were consistent not only with the force activation model but also with a number of other models. The French and Harary graph theory models are essentially activation force models (with activation associated with a communication structure) and they have been compared generally with experimental data for the equal potential power case. The comparison suggests a general consistency of the data with several alternate models. Dahl used a force activation model as a definition of power in his study of New Haven.[46]

42 See Harsanyi, 'Measurement of Social Power, Opportunity Costs. . . .'

43 See R. Dubin, Power and Union-Management *Administrative Science Quarterly*, II (1957), 60–81; and A. S. Tannenbaum, An Event Structure Approach to Social Power and to the Problem of Power Comparability, *Behavioral Science*, VII, 1962, 315–31.

44 See Dahl, *Who Governs?* and Wolfinger, 'Reputation and Reality'.

45 Hanson, 'Predicting a Community Decision', D. C. Miller, The Prediction of Issue Outcome in Community Decision-Making, *Research Studies of the State College of Washington*, XXV, 1957, 137–47.

46 Dahl, *Who Governs?*

That is, he assumed the constancy of the x_{ij} and the m^*_{ij} within subject-matter partitions in order to estimate power. On the basis of other observations, Dahl, Polsby, and Wolfinger[47] seem to have concluded that it is meaningful to separate the two elements for certain special purposes (thus the classification as a force activation model rather than a simple force model). A New Haven test of the model, however, requires a subsequent observation of the stability of the indices.

It is clear from a consideration both of the formal properties of activation models and of the problems observers have had with such models that they suffer from their excessive *a posteriori* explanatory power. If we observe that power exists and is stable and if we observe that sometimes weak people seem to triumph over strong people, we are tempted to rely on an activation hypothesis to explain the discrepancy. But if we then try to use the activation hypothesis to predict the results of social-choice procedures, we discover that the data requirements of 'plausible' activation models are quite substantial. As a result, we retreat to what are essentially degenerate forms of the activation model – retaining some of the form but little of the substance. This puts us back where we started, looking for some device to explain our failures in prediction. Unfortunately, the next two types of models simply complicate life further rather than relieve it.

Force-conditioning Models

The conditioning models take as given either the basic force model or the activation model. The only modification is to replace a constant power resource with a variable power resource. The basic mechanisms are simple: (1) People have power because they are believed to have power. (2) People are believed to have power because they have been observed to have power. It is possible, of course, to have models in which one or the other of these mechanisms is not present. If we assume the first but not the second, we have a standard experimental paradigm. If we assume the second but not the first, we have an assortment of prestige learning models.[48]

Furthermore, it is clear that if power is accurately specified by observations and if social choices are precisely and uniquely specified by the power distribution, then the conditioning models are relatively uninteresting. They become interesting because of non-uniqueness in the results of the exercise of power or because of non-uniqueness in the attributions of power.

Let us assume that the C_js are ordered according to the time of their occurrence. C_1 occurs immediately before C_2, and so on. Then we can

47 Dahl, *Who Governs?* Polsby, How to Study Community Power; Wolfinger, Reputation and Reality.

48 White, Uses of Mathematics in Sociology.

view the general form of conditioning models as one of the basic force models as well as a procedure for modifying the m^*_{ij} as a consequence of the C_j. Consider, for example, the following model. We assume that the system re-evaluates the power of the individual components after each choice. At that time, it has information on the choice (C_j) and the previous power reputations, $R_{j-1} = (r_{1,j-1}, r_{2,j-1}, \ldots, r_{n,j-1})$. It must assign a new set of power attributions, R_j. In assigning the new attributions, we might reasonably assume that the system affects the classic compromise of adaptive systems between (1) making the new solutions as consistent as possible with the immediate past experience, and (2) making the new solutions as consistent as possible with the old solutions. In order to identify a dimension along which to affect this compromise, we define a minimum distance, $\overline{D}_j$, between the old attribution and the new choice: $\overline{D}_j\overline{Q}_j - \overline{R}_{j-1}$, where $\overline{Q}_j$ is chosen so as to minimize

$$\sum_{i=1}^{n} (r_{i,j=1} - q_{ij})^2,$$

subject to

$$\sum_{i=1}^{n} q_{ij}A_{ij} = C_j.$$

We can define an equivalent form for the other basic force models.

Now we can assume $\overline{R}_j = \overline{R}_{j-1} + a\overline{D}_j$, *where* $0 \leq a \leq 1$. If a is 0, we have a degenerate case of a system that does not adapt. If a is 1, we have a system that always adapts the power reputations to be completely consistent with the past observations. If actual power does not depend on the perceived power and is constant, this system simply solves the set of equations (that is, learns the correct answer) or (in the case of the error elements) improves the estimates of power. Under these latter circumstances, it seems reasonable to assume that reputational techniques for assessing power will be preferable to direct observational techniques.

Our interest here, however, is in combining this mechanism with a second one, making actual power a function of perceived power. Within one of our basic force models (or an activation force model) we can define a reputation error, $e_{ij} = r_{ij} - m_{ij}$, and a simple form of adaptation, $m_{ij} = m_{i,j-1} + be_{i,j-1}$ where $0 \leq b \geq 1$. If b is 0, we have our constant power model. If b is 1, we have a model that adjusts power immediately to reputation.

Models of this general class have not been explored in the power literature. Experimental studies have demonstrated the realism of each of the two mechanisms – success improves reputation, reputation improves success. As a result, conditioning models cannot be rejected out of hand. Moreover, they lead directly to some interesting and relevant predictions.

In most of the literature on the measurement of power, there are two nagging problems – the problem of the chameleon who frequently jumps in and agrees with an already decided issue and the satellite who, though he himself has little power, is highly correlated with a high-power person. Since these problems must be at least as compelling for the individual citizen as they are for the professional observer, they have served as a basis for a number of strong attacks on the reputational approach to the attribution of power. But the problem changes somewhat if we assume that reputations affect outcomes. Now the chameleon and the satellite are not measurement problems but important phenomena. The models will predict that an association with power will lead to power. Whether the association is by chance or by deliberate imitation, the results are substantially the same.

To the best of my knowledge, no formal efforts have been made to test either the satellite prediction in a real-world situation, or to test some of its corollaries, which include:

1 Informal power is unstable. Let the kingmaker beware of the king.
2 Unexercised power disappears. Peace is the enemy of victory.
3 Undifferentiated power diffuses. Beware of your allies lest they become your equals.

Moreover, it is really not possible to re-evaluate existing data to examine the plausibility of conditioning models. Virtually all of the studies are cross-sectional rather than longitudinal. The data requirements of the conditioning models are longitudinal. They are also substantially more severe than for the basic force models. Consider the minimally complex adaptive model outlined above. We have added two new parameters (a and b) and a changing m_{ij} to our earlier estimation problems. In order to have much chance of using the model (or variants on it), we will probably need to have data on variables in addition to simply social choice and individual attitudes or behavior. For example, we will probably need reputational data. We will need data that is subscripted with respect to time. We will probably have to make some additional simplifying assumptions, particularly if we want to allow for probabilistic elements in the model or introduce error terms. I do not think these are necessarily insuperable problems, but I think we should recognize that even simple conditioning models of this type will require more and different data than we have been accustomed to gather.

Force-Depletion Models

Within the conditioning models, success breeds success. But there is another class of plausible models in which success breeds failure. As in the conditioning models, we assume that power varies over time. As in the force-activation models, we assume that not all power is exercised at every point in time. Thus,

$$m_{ij} = x_{ij} m^*_{ij} / \sum_{i=1}^{n} x_{ij} m^*_{ij}.$$

The basic idea of the model is plausible. We consider power to be a resource. The exercise of power depletes that resource. Subject to additions to the power supply, the more power a particular component in the system exercises, the less power there is available for that component to use. In the simplest form we can assume

$$m^*_{ij} = m^*_{i,j-1} - x_{i,j-1} m^*_{i,j-1} = m^*_{i,j-1}(1 - x_{i,j-1}).$$

And, if we assume that there are no additions to the power resources,

$$m^*_{ij} = m^*_{i,0}(1 - x_{i,0}) \ldots (1 - x_{i,j-1}).$$

If the withdrawal rate is constant,

$$m^*_{ij} = m^*_{i,0}(1 - x_i)^j.$$

We can modify this to make the depletion proportional to utilization of power (rather than equal to it) without changing the basic structure of the model.

Under this scheme, it is quite possible for power to shift as a result of variations in the rates of power utilization. So long as additions to the power supply are independent of the exercise of power, the use of power today means that we will have less to use tomorrow. We can show various conditions for convergence and divergence of power resources or exercised power. We can also generate a set of aphorisms parallel to – but somewhat at variance with – the conditioning model aphorisms:

1 Formal power is unstable. Let the king beware of the kingmaker.
2 Exercised power is lost. Wars are won by neutrals.
3 Differentiation wastes power. Maintain the alliance as long as possible.

As far as I know, no one has attempted to apply such a model to power situations, although there are some suggestions of its reasonableness (at least as a partial model). Hollander has suggested a model of this class for a closely related phenomenon, the relation between the exercise of independence by a member of a group and the tolerance of independent behavior by the group; but his primary focus was on a system that involved, at the same time, systematic (but independent) effects on the resource (tolerance).[49] Some of the studies of interpersonal relations in organizations indicate that the exercise of power is often dysfunctional with regard to the effective exercise of power in the future. In those cases, the mechanism ordinarily postulated involves the impact of power on sentiments[50] rather than our simple resource notion. Nonetheless the grosser attributes of observed behavior in such studies are consistent with the gross predictions of models that view power as a stock.

Even if power resources are exogenous, the problems of testing a simple depletion model are more severe than the problems of testing the basic activation model. As in the case of the conditioning model, we require longitudinal data. Thus, if we can assume that power resources or increments to power resources are a function of social or economic status, skill in performing some task, or physical attributes (e.g., strength), the model probably can be made manageable if the simplifying assumptions made for force activation models are sensible. On the other hand, if we combine the depletion model with a conditioning model – I think we probably ought to – we will have complicated the basic force model to such a point that it will be difficult indeed to be sanguine about testing.

One way of moderating the test requirements is to use experimental manipulation to control some variables, and experimental observation to measure others. If we can control the resources available and directly measure the extent to which power is exercised, we can develop depletion and depletion-conditioning models to use in experimental situations.

If, however, we want to apply any of the more elaborate force models to a natural system, or if we want to develop natural-system predictions from our experimental studies, we will need far more data than recent research provides. Perhaps a model that includes considerations of activation, conditioning, and power depletion can be made empirically manageable, but such a model (and associated observations) would be a major technical achievement. We are not within shouting distance of it now.

Once we do get such a model, we may well find that it simply does not fit and that a new elaboration is necessary. From a simple concept of power in a simple force model, we have moved to a concept of power that is further and further removed from the basic intuitive notions captured by the simple model, and to models in which simple observations of power are less and less useful. It is only a short step from this point to a set of models that are conceptually remote from the original conception of a social-choice system.

49 E. P. Hollander, Conformity, Status, and Idiosyncrasy Credit *Psychological Review*, LXV, 1958, 117–27.

50 See W. G. Bennis, Effecting Organizational Change: A New Role for the Behavioral Sciences *Administrative Science Quarterly*, VIII, 1963.

Process Models

Suppose that the choice system we are studying is not random. Suppose further that power really is a significant phenomenon in the sense that it can be manipulated systematically in the laboratory and can be used to explain choice in certain social-choice systems. I think that both those suppositions are reasonable. But let us further suppose that there is a class of social-choice systems in which power is insignificant. Unless we treat *power* as true by definition, I think that suppression is reasonable. If we treat *power* as a definition, I think it is reasonable to suppose there is a class of social-choice systems in which power measurement will be unstable and useless.

Consider the following process models of social choice as representative of this class:

An exchange model. We assume that the individual components in the system prefer certain of the alternative social choices, and that the system has a formal criterion for making the final choices (e.g., majority vote, unanimity, clearing the market). We also assume that there is some medium or exchange by which individual components seek to arrange agreements (e.g., exchanges of money or votes) that are of advantage to themselves. These agreements, plus the formal criterion for choice, determine the social decision. This general type of market system is familiar enough for economic systems and political systems.[51] It is also one way of viewing some modern theories of interpersonal influence[52] in which sentiments on one dimension ('I like you') are exchanged for sentiments on another ('You like my pots') in order to reach a social choice ('We like us and we like my pots').

A problem-solving model. We assume that each of the individual components in the system has certain information and skills relevant to a problem of social choice, and that the system has a criterion for solution. We postulate some kind of process by which the system calls forth and organizes the information and skills so as systematically to reduce the difference between its present position and a solution. This

51 See, for example, Anthony Downs, *An Economic Theory of Democracy* (New York: Harper & Row, Publishers, 1957); J. M. Buchanan and Gordon Tullock, *The Calculus of Consent* (Ann Arbor: University of Michigan Press, 1962); and Riker, *The Theory of Political Coalitions*.

52 Dale Carnegie, *How to Win Friends and Influence People* (New York: Simon and Schuster, Inc., 1936); Leon Festinger, *A Theory of Cognitive Dissonance* (New York, Harper & Row, 1957).

general type of system is familiar to students of individual and group problem solving.[53]

A communication-diffusion model. We assume that the components in the system are connected by some formal or informal communication system by which information is diffused through the system. We postulate some process by which the information is sent and behavior modified, one component at a time, until a social position is reached. This general type of system is familiar to many students of individual behavior in a social context.[54]

A decision-making model. We assume that the components in the system have preferences with respect to social choices, and that the system has a procedure for rendering choices. The system and the components operate under two limitations:

1 Overload: they have more demands on their attention than they can meet in the time available.
2 Undercomprehension: the world they face is much more complicated than they can handle.

Thus, although we assume that each of the components modifies its behavior and its preferences over time in order to achieve a subjectively satisfactory combination of social choices, it is clear that different parts of the system contribute to different decisions in different ways at different times. This general type of system is a familiar model of complex organizations.[55]

In each of these process models, it is possible to attribute power to the individual components. We might want to say that a man owning a section of land in Iowa has more power in the economic system than a man owning a section of land in Alaska. We might want to say that, in a pot-selling competition, a man with great concern over his personal status has less power than a man with less concern. We might want to say that a man who knows Russian has more power than a man who does not in a group deciding

53 See, for example, A. Newell, J. C. Shaw, and H. A. Simon, Elements of a Theory of Human Problem Solving *Psychological Review*, LXV, 1958, 151–66; and D. W. Taylor, Decision Making and Problem Solving, in March (ed.) *Handbook of Organizations*.

54 See, for example, Elihu Katz and P. F. Lazarsfeld *Personal Influence* (New York: Free Press of Glencoe, Inc., 1955); and Angus Campbell, Philip Converse, W. E. Miller, and Donald Stokes, *The American Voter* (New York: John Wiley & Sons, Inc., 1960).

55 See C. E. Lindblom, The Science of Muddling Through *Public Administration Review*, XIX, 1959, 79–88; and R. M. Cyert and J. G. March, *A Behavioral Theory of the Firm* (Englewood Cliffs, NJ.: Prentice-Hall, Inc., 1963).

the relative frequency of adjectival phrases in Tolstoy and Dostoyevsky. Or, we might want to say that, within an organization, a subunit that has problems has more power than a subunit that does not have problems. But I think we would probably not want to say any of these things. The concept of power does not contribute much to our understanding of systems that can be represented in any of these ways.

I am impressed by the extent to which models of this class seem to be generally consistent with the reports of recent (and some not so recent)[56] students of political systems and other relatively large (in terms of number of people involved) systems of social choice. 'Observation of certain local communities makes it appear that inclusive over-all organization for many general purposes is weak or non-existent', Long writes. 'Much of what occurs seems to just happen with accidental trends becoming commulative over time and producing results intended by nobody. A great deal of the communities' activities consist of undirected cooperation of particular social structures, each seeking particular goals and, in doing so, meshing with the others'.[57]

Such descriptions of social choice have two general implications. On the one hand, if a system has the properties suggested by such students as Coleman, Long, Riesman, Lindblom, and Dahl, power will be a substantially useless concept. In such systems, the measurement of power is feasible, but it is not valuable in calculating predictions. The measurement of power is useful primarily in systems that conform to some variant of the force models. In some complex process systems we may be able to identify subsystems that conform to the force model, and thus be able to interpret the larger system in terms of a force-activation model for some purposes. But I think the flavor of the observations I have cited is that even such interpretations may be less common-sensible than we previously believed.[58]

On the other hand, the process models – and particularly the decision-making process models – look technically more difficult with regard to estimation and testing than the more complex modifications of the force model. We want to include many more discrete and nominal variables, many more discontinuous functions, and many more rare combinations of events. Although some progress has been made in dealing with the problems, and some predictive power has been obtained without involving the force model, the pitfalls of process models are still substantially uncharted.

56 For example, David Riesman, *The Lonely Crowd* (New Haven: Yale University Press, 1951).

57 N. E. Long, The Local Community as an Ecology of Games *American Journal of Sociology*, XLIV, 1958, 252.

58 See Bachrach and Baratz, Two Faces of Power.

The Power of Power

If I interpret recent research correctly, the class of social-choice situations in which power is a significantly useful concept is much smaller than I previously believed. As a result, I think it is quite misleading to assert that, 'Once decision-making is accepted as one of the focal points for empirical research in social science, the necessity for exploring the operational meaning and theoretical dimensions of influence is manifest.'[59] Although *power* and *influence* are useful concepts for many kinds of situations, they have not greatly helped us to understand many of the natural social-choice mechanisms to which they have traditionally been applied.

The extent to which we have used the concept of power fruitlessly is symptomatic of three unfortunate temptations associated with power:

Temptation No. 1: the obviousness of power. To almost anyone living in contemporary society, power is patently real. We can scarcely talk about our daily life or major political and social phenomena without talking about power. Our discussions of political machinations consist largely of stories of negotiations among the influentials. Our analyses of social events are punctuated with calculations of power. Our interpretations of organizational life are built on evaluations of who does and who does not have power. Our debates of the grand issues of social, political, and economic systems are funneled into a consideration of whether *i* has too little power and *j* has too much.

Because of this ubiquity of power, we are inclined to assume that it is real and meaningful. There must be some fire behind the smoke. 'I take it for granted that in every human organization some individuals have more influence over key decisions than do others.'[60] Most of my biases in this regard are conservative, and I am inclined to give some credence to the utility of social conceptual validation. I think, however, that we run the risk of treating the social validation of power as more compelling than it is simply because the social conditioning to a simple force model is so pervasive.

Temptation No. 2: the importance of measurement. The first corollary of the obviousness of power is the importance of the measurement problem. Given the obviousness of power, we rarely re-examine the basic model by which social choice is viewed as some combination of individual

59 March, 'An Introduction', p. 431.

60 R. A. Dahl, A Critique of the Ruling Elite Model *American Political Science Review*, LII, 1958.

choices, the combination being dependent on the power of the various individuals. Since we have a persistent problem discovering a measurement procedure that consistently yields results which are consistent with the model, we assert a measurement problem and a problem of the concept of power. We clarify and re-clarify the concept, and we define and redefine the measures.

The parallel between the role played by power in the theories under consideration here and the role played by subjective utility in theories of individual choice is striking. Just as recent work in power analysis has been strongly oriented toward conceptual and measurement problems, so recent work on utility theory has been strongly oriented toward conceptual and measurement problems.

Although I have some sympathy with these efforts, I think our perseveration may be extreme. At the least, we should consider whether subsuming all our problems under the rubric of conceptual and measurement problems may be too tempting. I think we too often ask *how* to measure power when we should ask *whether* to measure power. The measurement problem and the model problem have to be solved simultaneously.

Temptation No. 3: the residual variance. The second corollary of the obviousness of power is the use of *power* as a residual category for explanation. We always have some unexplained variance in our data – results that simply cannot be explained within the theory. It is always tempting to give that residual variance some name. Some of us are inclined to talk about God's will; others talk about errors of observation; still others talk about some named variable (e.g., power, personality, extrasensory perception). Such naming can be harmless; we might just as well have some label for our failures. But where the unexplained variance is rather large, as it often is when we consider social-choice systems, we can easily fool ourselves into believing that we know something simply because we have a name for our errors. In general, I think we can roughly determine the index of the temptation to label errors by computing the ratio of uses of the variable for prediction to the uses for a posteriori explanation. On that calculation, I think power exhibits a rather low ratio, even lower than such other problem areas as personality and culture.

Having been trapped in each of these cul-de-sacs at one time or another, I am both embarrassed by the inelegance of the temptations involved and impressed by their strength. We persist in using the simple force model in a variety of situations in which it is quite inconsistent with observations. As a result, we bury the examination of alternative models of social choice under a barrage of measurement questions.

I have tried to suggest that the power depends on the extent to which a predictive model requires and can make effective use of such a concept.

Thus, it depends on the kind of system we are confronting, the amount and kinds of data we are willing or able to collect, and the kinds of estimation and validation procedures we have available to us. Given our present empirical and test technology, power is probably a useful concept for many short-run situations involving the direct confrontations of committed and activated participants. Such situations can be found in natural settings, but they are more frequent in the laboratory. Power is probably not a useful concept for many long-run situations involving the problems of component-overload and undercomprehension. Such situations can be found in the laboratory but are more common in natural settings. Power may become more useful as a concept if we can develop analytic and empirical procedures for coping with the more complicated forms of force models, involving activation, conditioning, and depletion of power.

Thus, the answer to the original question is tentative and mixed. Provided some rather restrictive assumptions are met, the concept of power and a simple force model represent a reasonable approach to the study of social choice. Provided some rather substantial estimation and analysis problems can be solved, the concept of power and more elaborate force models represent a reasonable approach. On the whole, however, power is a disappointing concept. It gives us surprisingly little purchase in reasonable models of complex systems of social choice.

7

Implementation and Ambiguity

Vicki Eaton Baier, James G. March and Harald Sætren

Abstract

Studies of implementation have established two conspicuous things: First, policies can make a difference. Bureaucracies often respond to policy changes by changing administrative actions. Second, policy as implemented often seems different from policy as adopted. Organizational actions are not completely predictable from policy-directives. Efforts to tighten the connection between policy and administration have, for the most part, emphasized ways of augmenting the competence and reliability of bureacracies, of making them more faithful executors of policy directives. Alternatively, they look for ways of making policy makers more sophisticated about bureaucratic limitations. Such recommendations, however, assume that policies either are clear or can be made so arbitrarily. By describing discrepancies between adopted policies and implemented policies as problems of implementation, students of policy-making obscure the extent to which ambiguity is important to policy-making and encourage misunderstanding of the processes of policy-formation and administration.

The 'Implementation Problem'

One of the oldest topics in the study of organizations is the relation between policy and practice, the way general directives and programs adopted by legislatures, boards of directors, or top managements are executed,

---

This paper was first published in the *Scandinavian Journal of Management Studies*, May 1986. The authors are grateful for the assistance of Julia Ball; for the comments of David Brereton, Anne Miner, Johan Olsen, and David Weckler, and for grants from the Spencer Foundation, the Hoover Institution, and the Stanford Graduate School of Business.

modified, and elaborated by administrative organizations. Contemporary forms of this interest are found in studies of program evaluation and policy implementation. Although there is no question that central policies affect organizational behavior (Attewell and Gerstein, 1979; Randall, 1979), students of implementation frequently report complications in moving from adoption of a policy to its execution (Marshall, 1974). They often describe a scenario in which the wishes of central offices and policy making bodies are frustrated by the realities of a decentralized administrative organization (Levine, 1972; Pressman and Wildavsky, 1973; Edwards and Sharkansky, 1978; Hanf and Scharpf, 1978).

Two interpretations of implementation problems are common. The first interpretation attributes difficulties in implementation to bureaucratic incompetence. Sometimes bureaucracies are unable to accomplish the tasks they are assigned. The technical difficulties of organizing for major programs are often substantial; the technical skills needed for a specific job may be unavailable (Allison and Halperin, 1971; Pressman and Wildavsky, 1973; Bardach, 1977). The second interpretation attributes difficulties in implementation to conflict of interest between policy makers and bureaucratic agents, and thus to deficiencies in organizational control. A bureaucracy responds to objectives and pressures from many persons within and outside the organization; bureaucrats are self-interested actors; they evade control (Tullock, 1965; Niskanen, 1971; Davis, 1972; Halperin, 1974).

The two interpretations are not mutually exclusive, and they are sensible. In the present article, however, we wish to suggest some limitations to such analyses and the importance of including an appreciation of the policy-making process in a discussion of implementation. At the limit, it has been observed that the details of a policy's execution can be systematically less important to policy makers than its proclamation (Christensen, 1976; Kreiner, 1976; Rein and White, 1977). Analyses of the United States Congress, for example, suggest that the act of voting for legislation with appropriate symbolic meaning can be more important to legislators than either its enactment or its implementation (Mayhew, 1974). This is not because legislators are unusually hypocritical. It comes from practical concerns with maintaining electoral support and the substantial symbolic significance of political actions. Voters seek symbolic affirmations as well as mundane personal or group advantage. An interest in the support of constituents, whether voters or stockholders or clients, leads policy makers to be vigorous in enacting policies and lax in enforcing them.

A desire to maintain the values, ideals, and commitments of an organization or society can easily lead to a similar course (March and Olsen, 1976). Political actors, citizens as well as legislators, workers as well as managers, symbolize their virtues and proclaim their values by seeking and securing policy changes. Policies are not simply guidelines for action. Often they are more significantly expressions of faith, acknowledgements of virtue, and instruments of education (Olsen, 1970; Christensen, 1976; Feldman and March, 1981; March and Sevon, 1984). Individuals and groups support (often with extraordinary vigor and at considerable cost) the adoption of policies that symbolize important affirmations, even where they are relatively unconcerned with the ultimate implementation of the policies. As Arnold (1935, p. 34) observed: 'It is part of the function of Law to give recognition to ideals representing the exact opposite of established conduct. Most of the complications arise from the necessity of pretending to do one thing, while actually doing another.'

Cases of such clear intentionality are, however, only a minor part of the story. They dramatize the limitations of talking about 'implementation problems', but they do not define those limitations. We will argue the more general point that an understanding of implementation cannot be divorced from an understanding of the processes that generate policies, and that some conspicuous features of policy-making contribute directly to the phenomena we have come to label as problems of implementation.

Bureaucracies as Instruments of Policy

Despite the pervasiveness and effectiveness of bureaucratic organization, there are ample grounds for doubting that a modern administrative agency will fulfill any policy directive that it might be assigned. For example, bureaucratic inability to cope with the size or scope of new responsibilities has been used to explain the difficulties of some business organizations implementing policies that lead them into foreign markets and of military organizations implementing policies that ask them to fight limited wars. One typical situation in the public sector involves the implementation of new national programs through local departments or bureaus seemingly ill-equipped to administer them.

Consider, for example, Sutherland's (1975, pp. 74–6) portrayal of problems in implementing the Elementary and Secondary Education Act of 1965 in the United States:

> Although some state agencies in 1965 were considered to be well managed, most were thought to lack sufficient personnel to supervise existing state programs or the capability to assume new responsibilities needed to meet future educational needs. Although all state departments of education had professionals capable of providing consultative and technical service to local educational agencies, the number of staff members available on a full-time basis was limited. Only one-fifth of the states had two or more supervisors of

> teacher education and 15 did not have a part-time employee for this activity. One-third of the states provided no services or supervision of school libraries. Twenty-nine did not provide for the supervision of industrial arts programs and the remaining states had only a supervisor of vocational education. Four state agencies had no full-time staff members to consult with local school systems for special education and only 13 had one or more full-time consultants for the development of programs for the gifted. . . . Persons in possession of skills and the training to conduct research, evaluate findings and test and implement new instructional programs were also needed by state educational agencies. Although more than two-thirds of the state agencies had departments that included the word 'research' as a part of the title, only 108 persons were employed for research purposes, and nine state departments of education listed no research personnel.

Sutherland's description is specific to a particular mismatch between an educational policy and an educational bureaucracy, but it echoes a common concern in the implementation literature (Bardach, 1977). The idea that implementation is made difficult by the possibly unavoidable, and certainly ubiquitous, problems of bureaucratic and individual incompetence is found in many analyses of modern administrative agencies. Logistic complications are not solved in time. Coordination among agencies is not accomplished, even when there is no significant conflict among them (Pressman and Wildavsky, 1973). Materials, plans, and people are not available when needed (Bardach, 1977); personnel are not trained properly or are given inadequate instructions or supervision (Allison and Halperin, 1971).

Agencies are sometimes sloppy, disorganized, inadequately trained, poorly staffed and badly managed; but gross incompetence is not required to produce significant bureaucratic inadequacy. Some tasks are not feasible; some policies are ill-suited to administrative agencies. Moreover, it is possible to recognize the considerable individual and organizational skills represented in a bureaucracy and still observe a mismatch between a particular organization and a particular task. For example, the United States Forest Service has had difficulty playing the role of a narcotics police force in national forests.

These difficulties are frequently further complicated by a need to coordinate several different organizations in order to implement a single general policy (Elmore, 1975; Hanf and Scharf, 1978). Central policy may require coordination among organizations with sharply contrasting objectives, styles, or normal activities. Managing several relatively autonomous groups often demands capacities beyond those of elaborate bureaucratic structures, not to mention the largely ad hoc structures that are sometimes used. Policy-makers often ignore, or underestimate considerably, the administrative requirements of a policy, and thus make policies that assure administrative incapacity.

The problems of incompetence are paired with problems of control. Administrative organizations are neither reliably neutral nor easily controlled. They seem persistently to modify policies in the course of implementing them. Descriptions of such local adaptations tend to overestimate the extent to which official policy, as interpreted by interested observers, can be equated either with the public interest or with the intentions of legislatures (Lynn, 1977). They are likely to picture national officials, top management, or major policy makers as defending general interests against the predations of local officials, subordinates, and special interest (Moynihan, 1969; Lowi, 1972; Murphy, 1974). The core idea, however, does not depend on that particular representation of a morality play. Whenever an agent is used to execute the policy of a principal, control problems arise. The problems are endemic to organization and have been extensively discussed in the literature on organizations (March and Simon, 1958; Crozier, 1964), as well as in treatises on optimal contracts, incentive schemes, and theories of agency (Hirschleifer and Riley, 1979).

Bureaucracies appear often to be thoroughly political, responding to claims made in the name of subunits, clients, and individual organizational actors. Political processes continue as policies filter through a bureaucracy to first-level administrative officials. Agencies adopt projects and implement programs in response to political pressure or financial incentives; they exercise discretion in order to improve their local position or address specific problems of interest to them (Berman and McLaughlin, 1976; Mayntz, 1976); they interpret policy directives in ways that transform their prior desires into the wishes of policy makers. For example, the Fort Lincoln project, seen by political leaders as a way to help poor people escape city slums, was converted into a program to build model communities and to try out the newest ideas in community planning (Derthick, 1972).

In dealing with organizational actors, policy makers find it hard to assure that incentives for following official policy are adequate to overcome incentives to deviate from it (Christie, 1964). Organizations, their clients, and their subunits pursue political tactics seeking renegotiation of policies and practices (Mayntz, 1977). Since from the point of view of most other groups and institutions, any new policy announced by policy makers is primarily an opportunity to pursue their own agenda (Bardach, 1977), those responsible for implementing policy have constituents who seek deviations from policy (Derthick, 1972; Pressman and Wildavsky, 1973; Nelson and Yates, 1978; Weiss, 1979). Some parts of any administrative organization will have incentives for pursuing objectives that deviate from any policy that might be adopted (Downs, 1967; Murphy, 1974).

The difficulties in coordinating the agendas of multiple actors are compounded by the way political and organizational actors move in and out of the arena in response to various claims on their attention (March and Olsen, 1976; Sproull, Weiner and Wolf, 1978). An organization is pressed to meet the inconsistent demands of a continually changing group of actors. Pressman and Wildavsky (1973) suggest some reasons for the inconstancy of attention: actors may find their commitments to a policy incompatible with other important commitments; they may have preferences for other programs; they may be dependent on others who lack the same sense of urgency; they may have differences of opinion on leadership or proper organizational roles; they may be constrained by legal or procedural questions or demands. In general, a shifting pattern of demands for attention made on the individuals involved in and around an organization tends to make the climate of implementation unstable in many small ways that cumulatively affect the course of events (Kaufman, 1981).

Programs for Reform of the Policy Process

Because it is part of classical administrative dogma, and because bureaucratic organizations do, in fact, have a rather impressive record for successfully coordinating large numbers of people in service of policies imposed from outside, it is persistently tempting to picture administrative agents as natural implements of prior policy. They are made innocent by an act of will or good management. In this spirit, problems of implementation lead to proposals to increase competence and control by hiring new personnel, developing new training or procedures, improving accountability, and providing new incentives. For example, foreign service organizations may respond to diagnoses of incompetence by increasing the length of service at a particular station for individual officers; they may respond to diagnoses of lack of control by requiring more frequent rotation of officers through stations. Implementation failures may lead to new organizational forms, for example, divisional management; to new investments, for example, in management information systems; to new routines, for example, evaluation studies; or to new personnel, for example, new top executives.

Such changes are intended to make an organization into a competent, reliable agent, executing a wide range of possible policies (Maass, 1951; Kaufman, 1960). They picture the problems of implementation as problems of securing neutral administrative compliance with prior, exogenous policies. This view of administration has, however, long been in disrepute among students of organizations (Herring, 1936; Leiserson, 1942; Truman, 1951). It suggests more clarity in the distinction between policy-making and administration than can usually be sustained; and it leads to a mechanistic perspective on the management of organizations that seems likely to be misleading. Trying to keep administrators innocent may, of course, simply reflect an instinct to use unachievable aspirations as a means of achieving less heroic, but admirable outcomes (March, 1978; 1979); but it tends to delusion. Consequently, many sophisticated observers of organizations take a more strategic posture with respect to designing administrative organizations.

Suppose we accept the proposition that bureaucracies are limited instrumentalities, that there are constraints on our abilities to make them more competent or to avoid the demands of self-interest. Then implementation problems are attributed not to characteristics of organizations – which are taken as essentially intractable – but to the *naïveté* of policy makers. In this view, policy makers do not specify objectives clearly enough (Løchen and Martinsen, 1962; Jacobsen, 1966; Lowi, 1969; Sabatier and Mazmanian, 1980), provide inadequate resources (Allison and Halperin, 1971; Bardach, 1977), fail to build a proper administrative organization (Williams, 1971; Derthick, 1972), fail to consult with affected groups (Bunkers, 1972; Derthick, 1972), or have too high expectations (Elmore, 1975; Bardach, 1977; Timpane, 1978). Such a strategic vision leads to recommendations to improve the policies, make them clearer and more consistent with the attitudes of the groups involved, and strengthen the incentives and capabilities for bureaucratic conformity to policy directives.

An example of such advice is found in Bardach's (1977, p. 253) discussion of policy design.

> . . . a management game is played against the entropic forces of social nature, and there is no permanent solution. Once this fact is recognized, the implication for policy designers is clear, design simple, straight-forward programs that require as little management as possible. To put it another way, if the management game is a losing proposition, the best strategy is to avoid playing. Programs predicated on continuing high levels of competence, on expeditious interorganizational coordination, or on sophisticated methods for accommodating diversity and heterogeneity are very vulnerable. They are not necessarily doomed to failure, but they are asking for trouble. . . . Other things equal, policy designers would prefer to operate through manipulating prices and markets rather than writing and enforcing regulations, through delivering cash rather than services, through communicating by means of smaller rather than larger units of social organizations, and through seeking clearances from fewer rather than more levels of consultation and review.

The advice seems well-taken. Many problems in implementation might be avoided if policy makers made less ambiguous policies and designed simple procedures that protected their intentions from the inadequacies and self-interest of administrative agencies. Rather than expecting to change the character of administrative organizations, we might design strategic policies, quasi-price systems, and incentive contracts that are likely to lead to desired ends even when executed by administrative organizations that are neither perfect nor neutral.

These efforts to increase the sophistication of policy makers in dealing with administrative agencies, like earlier attempts to improve the competence and reliability of the agencies, are vital to good administration. Without a struggle to link policy and action, any social system suffers. However, we want to argue that the problems of implementation are obscured by the terminology of implementation, even in its more sophisticated forms, that discussions of implementations assume a coherence in policy objectives that rarely exists. Understanding administrative implementation cannot be separated from understanding the ways in which policies are made and the implications of the policy-making process for administrative action.

Policy-Making and Policy Ambiguity

Proposals for implementations reform treat policy – or policy objectives – as given. They assume that policy goals and directives are (or can be) clear, that policy makers know what they want, and that what they want is consistent, stable, and unambiguous. The assumptions are similar to assumptions about preferences made in standard decision theory, and they have some of the same advantages (Raiffa, 1968). They made administration, like decision-making, a difficult technical job of optimization, subject to prior exogenous policies established by legitimate authority. They also have many of the same disadvantages (March, 1978; Elster, 1979; Cronbach et al., 1980).

In particular, the assumptions are often not true. They are frequently false in a way that makes the concept of implementation not only inaccurate as a portrayal of organizational reality, but often an inappropriate base for organizational reform. For example, the frequent advice that policies should be clear seems to assume that policy makers can arbitrarily choose the level of clarity of a policy, that policies are ambiguous because of some form of inadequacy in policy-making. Such a view ignores what we know about the making of policies. In fact, policies are negotiated in a way that makes the level of clarity no more accessible to arbitrary choice than other vital parts of the policy.

Forming a coalition in order to support a policy, whether in a legislature or a boardroom, involves standard techniques of horse-trading, persuasion, bribes, threats, and management of information. These are the conventional procedures of discussion, politics, and policy-formation. They are well-conceived to help participants form coalitions, explore support for alternative policies, and develop a viable policy. Much of the genius of modern organizational leadership lies in skills for producing policy from the conflicting and inchoate ideas, demands, preconceptions, and prejudices of the groups to which organizational leadership must attend. At the heart of several of these techniques for achieving policies, however, are features that make implementation problematic.

Adopted policies will, on average, be oversold. Even unbiased expectations about possible policies will lead to bias in the expectations with respect to those that are adopted. Since proposed programs for which expectations are erroneously pessimistic are rarely adopted, the sample of adopted programs is more likely to exhibit errors of over-optimism than of over-pessimism (Harrison and March, 1984). Inflated expectations about programs that are successful in gaining support from policy makers make subsequent disappointment likely. Thus, great hopes lead to action, but great hopes are invitations to disappointment. This, in turn, leads both to an erosion of support and to an awareness of 'failures of implementation'.

Such a structural consequence of intelligent decision-making under conditions of uncertainty is accentuated in situations of collective choice. Competition for policy support pushes advocates to imagine favorable outcomes and to inflate estimates of the desirability of those outcomes. Developing and communicating such expectations are a major part of policy discussions. Expectations become part of the official record, part of collective history, and part of individual beliefs. Others will, of course, try to deflate the estimates of advocates; but the advocates usually write the stories for their preferred policies and often come either to believe them or to be committed publicly to them. Tactical supporters of policies (i.e., those who support policies for reasons extraneous to their content) do not resist being misled. Extravagant claims justify their support and provide a basis, if one is ever needed, for claims that they are duped.

In addition, the centripetal processes of policy-making exaggerate the real level of support for policies that are adopted. Although commitment to a policy or program in its own right may be important for some coalition members, few major policies could be adopted without some supporters for whom the policy is relatively unimportant except as a political bargain. They may be persuaded to join a coalition by a belief the policy is sensible, by claims of loyalty or friendship, or by a logroll in which their support is offered in trade for needed support on other things in which they have a direct concern. There is no assurance that such groups and individuals will be equally supportive of its implementation. Except in so far as their continued active support is a part of the coalition agreement, and such extended coalition agreements are difficult to arrange and enforce, supporters will turn to other matters. Consequently, a winning coalition can easily be an illusion (Sætren, 1983).

Finally, one common method for securing policy support is to increase the ambiguity of a proposed policy (Page, 1976). It is a commonplace observation of the legislative process that difficult issues are often 'settled' by leaving them unresolved or specifying them in a form requiring subsequent interpretation. A similar observation can be made about policies in armies, hospitals, universities, and business firms. Particularly where an issue is closely contested, success in securing support for a program or policy is likely to be associated with increasing, rather than decreasing ambiguity. Policy ambiguity allows different groups and individuals to support the same policy for different reasons and with different expectations, including different expectations about the administrative consequences of the policy.

Thus, official policy is likely to be vague, contradictory, or adopted without generally shared expectations about its meaning or implementation. Aubert, in his study of the enactment of a Housemaid Law in Norway (Aubert, 1969, p. 125), discusses the apparent anomaly of legislation that paired a policy proclaiming the protection of household workers with a set of procedures for redress that were effectively inaccessible to victims:

> What is pretended in the penal clause of the Housemaid Law is that effective enforcement of the law is envisaged. And what the legislature is actually doing is to see to it that the privacy of the home and the interest of housewives are not ignored. . . . The ambivalence and the conflicting views of the legislators, as they can be gleaned from the penal clause, appear more clearly in the legislative debate. A curious dualism runs through the debates. It was claimed, on the one hand, that the law is essentially a codification of custom and established practice, rendering effective enforcement inessential. On the other hand, there was a tendency to claim that the Housemaid Law is an important new piece of labour legislation with a clearly reformatory purpose, attempting to change an unacceptable status quo. . . . The crucial point here is the remarkable ease with which such apparently contradictory claims were suffused in one and the same legislative action, which in the end received unanimous support from all political groups.

In this way, the ambiguity of a policy increases the chance of its adoption, but at the cost of creating administrative complications. For example, Øyen (1964) observed that the ambiguous text of a Norwegian welfare statute was simultaneously a necessary condition for the unanimity of its political support and a basis for considerable administrative discretion. As a policy unfolds into action, the different understandings of an ambiguous political agreement combine with the usual transformation of preferences over time to become bases for abandoning support, deploring administrative sabotage of the program, or embracing a special fantasy of what the policy means. As a result, many coalition members can easily feel betrayed; and observers can easily become confused.

In the long run, of course, political institutions learn from their experience. Administrative agencies seem likely to adapt to a history of ambiguous, contradictory, and grandiose policies by an administrative posture that tends to emphasize creative autonomy. They learn to establish independent political constituencies, to treat normal policies as problematic (or at least subject to interpretation), and to expect policy makers to be uncertain, or in conflict, about the expected consequences of a policy, or its importance. They come to realize that they cannot escape criticism by arguing that they were following policy but must develop an independent political basis for their actions.

Similarly, policy makers learn from their experiences with administrative agencies. As administrative practices become flexible, it becomes easier to use policy ambiguity as a basis for forming coalitions. It becomes plausible to attribute failures in programs to failures in implementation and thus to avoid possible criticism for mistakes. Policy ambiguity encourages administrative autonomy, which in turn encourages more policy ambiguity. Thus, it is not hard to see why we might observe organizations functioning with only a loose coupling between policies and actions, between plans and behavior, and between policy makers and administrators (March and Olsen, 1976; Weick, 1976).

The Concept of Implementation

The terminology of implementation conjures up a picture of clear, consistent, and stable policy directives waiting to be executed. It encourages us to think that a reasonable and responsible person can easily measure the discrepancy between policy and bureaucratic action, that the discrepancy can be attributed to some properties of the organization (e.g., its competence and reliability) or to some properties of the policy (e.g., its clarity and consistency), and that the properties of the organization and the properties of the policy can be chosen arbitrarily and independently in order to reduce the discrepancy.

As we have noted, studies of policy-making cast doubt on such a characterization. The implementation of policies is frequently problematic; but the difficulties cannot be treated as independent of the confusions in the policy. Those confusions, in turn, cannot be treated as independent of the ways in which winning policy coalitions are built. Policies are frequently ambiguous; but their ambiguities are less a result of deficiencies in policy makers than a natural consequence of gaining necessary support for the policies, and of changing preferences over time. Conflict of interest is not just a property of the relations between policy makers on the one hand and administrators on the other; it is a general feature of policy negotiation and bureaucratic life. As a result, policies reflect contradictory intentions and expectations and considerable uncertainty.

It may be tempting to deplore a policy process that sometimes seems to restrict us to a choice between inaction and ambiguity, and to wish for some alternative system in which policy agreements would be clear and their execution unproblematic. But that concern should be paired with an awareness of the complications. The problems involved in establishing and maintaining an effective policy-making and an administrative system that provides responsiveness, coherence, and symbolic affirmation of social values have occupied philosophers and managers for long enough to suggest that they are not trivial. Certainly, contemporary theories of policy-making and administration have not solved them. Nor have we. As a preface to such an effort, however, we have argued that the terms of discourse for discussing policy-making and implementation are misleading. Any simple concept of implementation, with its implicit assumption of clear and stable policy intent, is likely to lead to a fundamental misunderstanding of the policy process and to disappointment with efforts to reform it.

References

Allison, Graham T., and Morton H. Halperin (1971) Bureaucratic politics: A paradigm and some policy implications. *World Politics*, 24: 40–79.

Arnold, Thurman (1935) *The Symbols of Government* New Haven, CT: Yale University Press.

Attewell, Paul, and Dean R. Gerstein (1979) Government policy and local practice. *American Sociological Review*, 44: 311–27.

Aubert, Wilhelm (1969) Some social functions of legislation. In Vilhelm Aubert (ed.), *Sociology of Law*, London: Penguin.

Bardach, Eugene (1977) *The Implementation Game*, Cambridge, MA: MIT Press.

Berman, Paul, and Milbrey McLaughlin (1976) *Implementation Problems: Patterns and Parameters – Implications for Macro Policy*. Santa Monica, CA: Rand Corporation.

Bunker, Douglas R. (1972) Policy sciences perspectives on implementation processes. *Policy Sciences*, 3: 71–80.

Christensen, Søren (1976) Decision-making and socialization. In James G. March and Johan P. Olsen, *Ambiguity and Choice in Organizations*, pp. 351–85. Bergen: Universitetsforlaget.

Christie, Nils (1964) Edruelighetsnemnder: Analyse av en velferdslov. (Temperance committees: Analysis of a welfare statute), *Nordisk Tidskrift for Kriminalvitenskap*, 52: 89–118.

Cronbach, Lee J., et al. (1980) *Toward Reform of Program Evaluation*. San Francisco: Jossey-Bass.

Crozier, Michel (1964) *The Bureaucratic Phenomenon*. Chicago: University of Chicago Press.

Davis, David H. (1972) *How the Bureaucracy Makes Foreign Policy*. Lexington, MA: Lexington Books.

Derthick, Martha (1972) *New Towns – In Town*. Washington, DC: Urban Institute.

Downs, Anthony (1967) *Inside Bureaucracy*. Boston: Little, Brown.

Edwards, George C., and Ira Sharkansky (1978) *The Policy Predicament*, San Francisco: W. H. Freeman.

Elmore, Richard F. (1975) Lessons from follow through. *Policy Analysis*, 1: 459–67.

Elster, Jon (1979) *Ulysses and the Sirens*. Cambridge: Cambridge University Press.

Feldman, Martha S., and James G. March (1981) Information in organizations as signal and symbol. *Administrative Science Quarterly*, 26: 171–86.

Halperin, Morton H. (1974) *Bureaucratic Politics and Foreign Policy*. Washington DC: Brookings.

Hanf, Kenneth, and Fritz W. Scharpf (1978) *Interorganizational Policy Making: Limits to Coordination and Central Control*. London: Sage.

Harrison, J. Richard, and James G. March (1984) Decision-making and post-decision surprises. *Administrative Science Quarterly* 29: 26–42.

Herring, E. Pendleton (1936) *Public Administration and the Public Interest*. New York: McGraw-Hill.

Hirschleifer, J., and John C. Riley (1979) The analytics of uncertainty and information – An expository survey. *Journal of Economic Literature*, 17: 1375–421.

Jacobsen, Knut D, (1966) Public administration under pressure: the role of the expert in the modernization of traditional agriculture. *Scandinavian Political Studies*, 1: 69–93.

Kaufman, Herbert (1960) *The Front Ranger*, Baltimore: Johns Hopkins University Press.

Kaufman, Herbert (1981) *The Administrative Behavior of Federal Bureau Chiefs*. Washington, DC: Brookings Institution.

Kreiner, Kristian (1976) Ideology and management in a garbage can situation. In James G. March and John P. Olsen, *Ambiguity and Choice in Organizations*, pp. 156–73. Bergen: Universitetsforlaget.

Leiserson, Avery (1942) *Administrative Regulation: A Study in Representation of Interests*. Chicago: University of Chicago Press.

Levine, Robert A. (1972) *Public Planning: Failure and Redirection*. New York: Basic Books.

Løchen, Yngvar, and Arne Martinsen (1962) Samarbeidsproblemer ved gjennomføringen av lovene om attføringshjelp og unføretrygd. (Cooperation problems in the implementation of laws dealing with aid to the handicapped and disability insurance), *Tidsskrift for Samfunnsforskning*, 3: 133–68.

Lowi, Theodore J. (1969) *The End of Liberalism*. New York: W. W. Norton.

Lowi, Theodore J. (1972) Four systems of policy, politics and choice. *Public Administration Review*, 32: 298–310.

Lynn, Laurence E. (1977) Implementation: Will the hedgehogs be outfoxed? *Policy Analysis*, 3: 277–80.

Maass, Arthur A. (1951) *Muddy Waters: The Army Engineers and the Nation's Rivers*. Cambridge, MA: Harvard University Press.

March, James G. (1978) Bounded rationality, ambiguity, and the engineering of choice. *Bell Journal of Economics*, 9: 587–608.

March, James G. (1979) *Science, Politics, and Mrs. Gruenberg* Washington, DC: National Academy of Sciences.

March, James G., and Johan P. Olsen (1976) *Ambiguity and Choice in Organizations*: Bergen: Universitetsforlaget.

March, James G., and Guje Sevón (1984) Gossip, information and decision making. In Lee S. Sproull and Patrick D. Larkey (eds), *Advances in Information Processing in Organizations*, pp. 95–107. Greenwich, CT: JAI Press.

March, James G., and Herbert A. Simon (1958) *Organizations*. New York: Wiley.

Marshall, Dale Rogers (1974) Implementation of federal poverty and welfare policy: A review essay. *Policy Studies Journal*, 2: 152–7.

Mayhew, David R. (1974) *Congress: The Electoral Connection*. New Haven, CT: Yale University Press.

Mayntz, Renate (1976) Environmental policy conflicts: The case of the German Federal Republic. *Policy Analysis,* 2: 577–88.

Mayntz, Renate (1977) Die Implementation Politischer Programme: Theoretische Uberlegungen zu einem neuen Forschungsgebiet. (Implementation of political programs: Theoretical considerations for a new research area), *Die Verwaltung*, 10: 51–66.

Moynihan, Daniel P. (1969) *Maximum Feasible Misunderstanding*. New York: Free Press.

Murphy, Jerome T. (1974) *State Education Agencies and Discretionary Funds.* Lexington, MA: Lexington Books.

Nelson, Richard, and Douglas Yates (1978) *Innovation and Implementation in Public Organizations*. Lexington, MA: Lexington Books.

Niskanen, William A. (1971) *Bureaucracy and Representative Government*. Chicago: Aldine.

Olsen, Johan P. (1970) Local budgeting - Decision-making or ritual act. *Scandinavian Political Studies*, 5: 85–118.

Øyen, Else (1964) *Sosialomsorgen og dens Forvaltere* (Social care and its managers), Bergen: Universitetsforlaget.

Page, Benjamin I. (1976) The theory of political ambiguity. *American Political Science Review*, 70: 742–52.

Pressman, Jeffrey L., and Aaron B. Wildavsky (1973) *Implementation*. Berkeley, CA: University of California Press.

Raiffa, Howard (1968) *Decision Analysis*. Reading, MA: Addison Wesley.

Randall, Ronald (1979) Presidential power versus bureaucratic intransigence: The influence of the Nixon administration on welfare policy. *American Political Science Review*, 73: 795–810.

Rein, Martin, and Sheldon H. White (1977) Policy research: Belief and doubt. *Policy Analysis*, 3: 239–71.

Sabatier, Paul, and Daniel Mazmanian (1980) The implementation of public policy: A framework of analysis. *Policy Studies Journal,* 8: 538–60.

Sætren, Harald (1983) *Iverksetting av offentlig politikk*. (Implementation of public policy). Bergen: Universitetsforlaget.

Sproull, Lee S. Stephen Weiner, and David Wolf (1978) *Organizing an Anarchy*. Chicago: University of Chicago Press.

Sutherland, B. H. (1975) *Federal Grants to State Departments of Education for the Administration of the Elementary and Secondary Education Act of 1965*. Ann Arbor, MI: University of Michigan Press.

Timpane, Michael P. (1978) *The Federal Interest in Financing Schooling*. Cambridge, MA: Ballinger.

Truman, David (1951) *The Governmental Process*. New York: Knopf.

Tullock, Gordon (1965) *The Politics of Bureaucracy*. Washington, DC.: Public Affairs Press.

Weick, Karl (1976) Educational organizations as loosely coupled systems. *Administrative Science Quarterly,* 21: 1–19.

Weiss, Carol (1979) Many meanings of research utilization *Public Administration Review*, 39: 426–31.

William, Walter (1971) *Social Policy Research and Analysis*. New York: Elsevier.

Part III
Adaptive Rules

8

Footnotes to Organizational Change

James G. March

Abstract

Five footnotes to change in organizations are suggested. They emphasize the relation between change and adaptive behavior more generally, the prosaic nature of change, the way in which ordinary processes combine with a confusing world to produce some surprises, and the implicit altruism of organizational foolishness.

Introduction

Organizations change. Although they often appear resistant to change, they are frequently transformed into forms remarkably different from the original. This paper explores five footnotes to research on organizational change, possible comments on what we know. The intention is not to review the research results but to identify a few speculations stimulated by previous work.

Footnote 1. Organizations are continually changing, routinely, easily, and responsively, but change within them cannot ordinarily be arbitrarily controlled. Organizations rarely do exactly what they are told to do.

This paper was first published in *Administrative Science Quarterly*, 26, in 1981: 563–77. The author would like to acknowledge the assistance of Julia Ball; the comments and collaboration of David Anderson, Vicki Eaton, Martha Feldman, Daniel Levinthal, Anne Miner, J. Rounds, Philip Salin and Jo Zettler; and support by the Spencer Foundation, the National Institute of Education, the Hoover Institution, and the National Center for Higher Education Management Systems.

Footnote 2. Changes in organizations depend on a few stable processes. Theories of change emphasize either the stability of the processes or the changes they produce, but a serious understanding of organizations requires attention to both.

Footnote 3. Theories of change in organizations are primarily different ways of describing theories of action in organizations, not different theories. Most changes in organizations reflect simple responses to demographic, economic, social, and political forces.

Footnote 4. Although organizational response to environmental events is broadly adaptive and mostly routine, the response takes place in a confusing world. As a result, prosaic processes sometimes have surprising outcomes.

Footnote 5. Adaptation to a changing environment involves an interplay of rationality and foolishness. Organizational foolishness is not maintained as a conscious strategy, but is embedded in such familiar organizational anomalies as slack, managerial incentives, symbolic action, ambiguity, and loose coupling.

Stable Processes of Change

A common theme in recent literature, particularly in studies of the implementation of public policy, is that of attempts at change frustrated by organizational resistance. There are well-documented occasions on which organizations have failed to respond to change initiatives or have changed in ways that were, in the view of some, inappropriate (Gross, Giaquinta, and Bernstein, 1971; Nelson and Yates, 1978).

What most reports on implementation indicate, however, is not that organizations are rigid and inflexible, but that they are impressively imaginative (Pressman and Wildavsky, 1973; Bardach, 1977). Organizations change in response to their environments, but they rarely change in a way that fulfills the intentions of a particular group of actors (Attewell and Gerstein, 1979; Crozier, 1979). Sometimes organizations ignore clear instructions; sometimes they pursue them more forcefully than was intended; sometimes they protect policy makers from folly; sometimes they do not. The ability to frustrate arbitrary intention, however, should not be confused with rigidity; nor should flexibility be confused with organizational effectiveness. Most organizational failures occur early in life when organizations are small and flexible, not later (Aldrich, 1979). There is considerable stability in organizations, but the changes we observe are substantial enough to suggest that organizations are remarkably adaptive, enduring institutions, responding to volatile environments routinely and easily, though not always optimally.

Because of the magnitude of some changes in organizations, we are inclined to look for comparably dramatic explanations for change, but the search for drama may often be a mistake. Most change in organizations results neither from extraordinary organizational processes or forces, nor from uncommon imagination, persistence or skill, but from relatively stable, routine processes that relate organizations to their environments. Change takes place because most of the time most people in an organization do about what they are supposed to do; that is, they are intelligently attentive to their environments and their jobs. Bureaucratic organizations can be exceptionally ineffective, but most of the organizations we study are characterized by ordinary competence and minor initiative (Hedberg, Nystrom, and Starbuck, 1976). Many of the most stable procedures in an organization are procedures for responding to economic, social, and political contexts. What we call organizational change is an ecology of concurrent responses in various parts of an organization to various interconnected parts of the environment. If the environment changes rapidly, so will the responses of stable organizations; change driven by such shifts will be dramatic if shifts in the environment are large.

The routine processes of organizational adaptation are subject to some complications, and a theory of change must take into account how those processes can produce unusual patterns of action. Yet, in its fundamental structure a theory of organizational change should not be remarkably different from a theory of ordinary action. Recent research on organizations as routine adaptive systems emphasizes six basic perspectives for interpreting organizational action:

1 *Rule following*. Action can be seen as the application of standard operating procedures or other rules to appropriate situations. The underlying process is one of matching a set of rules to a situation by criteria of appropriateness. Duties, obligations, roles, rules, and criteria evolve through competition and survival, and those followed by organizations that survive, grow, and multiply come to dominate the pool of procedures. The model is essentially a model of selection (Nelson and Winter, 1974).

2 *Problem solving*. Action can be seen as problem solving. The underlying process involves choosing among alternatives by using some decision-rule that compares alternatives in terms of their expected consequences for antecedent goals. The model is one of intendedly rational choice under conditions of risk and is familiar in statistical decision theory, as well as microeconomic and behavioral theories of choice (Lindblom, 1958; Cyert and March, 1963).

3 *Learning*. Action can be seen as stemming from past learning. The underlying process is one in which an organization is conditioned through

trial and error to repeat behavior that has been successful in the past and to avoid behavior that has been unsuccessful. The model is one of experiential learning (Day and Groves, 1975).

4 *Conflict*. Action can be seen as resulting from conflict among individuals or groups representing diverse interests. The underlying process is one of confrontation, bargaining, and coalition, in which outcomes depend on the initial preferences of actors weighted by their power. Changes result from shifts in the mobilization of participants or in the resources they control. The model is one of politics (March, 1962; Gamson, 1968; Pfeffer, 1981).

5 *Contagion*. Action can be seen as spreading from one organization to another. The underlying process is one in which variations in contact among organizations and in the attractiveness of the behaviors or beliefs being imitated affect the rate and pattern of spread. The model is one of contagion and borrows from studies of epidemiology (Rogers, 1962; Walker, 1969; Rogers and Shoemaker, 1971).

6 *Regeneration*. Action can be seen as resulting from the intentions and competencies of organizational actors. Turnover in organizations introduces new members with different attitudes, abilities, and goals. The underlying process is one in which conditions in the organization (e.g., growth, decline, changing requirements for skills) or deliberate strategies (e.g., cooptation, raiding of competitors) affect organizational action by changing the mix of participants. The model is one of regeneration (Stinchcombe, McDill, and Walker, 1968; White, 1970; McNeil and Thompson, 1971).

These six perceptives are neither esoteric, complicated, nor mutually exclusive. Although we may sometimes try to assess the extent to which one perspective or another fits a particular situation, it is quite possible for all six to be pertinent or for any particular history to involve them all. An organization uses rules, problem-solving, learning, conflict, contagion, and regeneration to cope with its environment, actively adapt to it, avoid it, seek to understand, change, and contain it. The processes are conservative. That is, they tend to maintain stable relations, sustain existing rules, and reduce differences among organizations. The fundamental logic, however, is not one of stability in behavior; it is one of responsiveness. The processes are stable; the resulting actions are not.

Some Complexities of Change

Organizations change in mundane ways, but elementary processes sometimes produce surprises in a complex world. As illustrations of such complexities, consider five examples: the unanticipated consequences of ordinary action, solution-driven problems, the tendency for innovations and organizations to be transformed during the process of innovation, the endogenous nature of created environments, and the interactions among the system requirements of individuals, organizations, and environments.

Unanticipated Consequences of Ordinary Action

Each of the six perspectives on action described above portrays organizations as changing sensibly; that is, solving problems, learning from experience, imitating others, and regenerating their capabilities through turnover of personnel. These processes, however, may be applied under conditions which, though difficult to distinguish from usual conditions, are sufficiently different to lead to unanticipated outcomes. In particular we can identify three such conditions.

First, the rate of adaptation may be inconsistent with the rate of change of the environment to which the organization is adapting. Unless an environment is perfectly stable, of course, there will always be some error arising from a history-dependent process (e.g., learning, selection); but where an environment changes quickly relative to the rate at which an organization adapts, a process can easily lose its claim to being sensible. It is also possible for an anticipatory process (e.g., problem-solving) to result in changes that outrun the environment and thereby become unintelligent. Second, the causal structure may be different from that implicit in the process. If causal links are ignored, either because they are new, or because their effects in the past have been benign, or because the world is inherently too complex, then changes that seem locally adaptive may produce unanticipated or confusing consequences. Such outcomes are particularly likely in situations in which belief in a false or incomplete model of causality can be reinforced by confounded experience. Third, concurrent, parallel processes of *prima facie* sensibility may combine to produce joint outcomes that are not intended by anyone and are directly counter to the interests motivating the individual actions (Schelling, 1978).

Most of the time, these unanticipated outcomes are avoided, but they are common. Consider the following illustrations:

Learning from the response of clients. Clients and customers send signals to organizations, the most conspicuous one being the withdrawal of their patronage. We expect organizations to respond to such signals. For example, although customer withdrawal is a major device used by market organizations to maintain product quality, it is not always effective. As Hirschman (1970) observed, it is likely that the first customers to abandon a product of declining quality will be those customers with the highest quality standards. If it is assumed that new customers are a random sample from the market, a firm is left with customers whose standards are, on the average, lower and who complain less about the reduced quality. This leads to further decay of quality, and the cycle continues until the quality consciousness of new customers equals that of lost customers; i.e., until the firm's most quality-conscious customers are no more concerned about quality than the average customers in the market. This cycle of regeneration can lead to a fairly rapid degradation in product or service.

Rewarding friends and coopting enemies. Employees of governmental regulatory agencies sometimes subsequently become employees of the organizations they regulate. The flow of people presumably affects the relations between the organizations. In particular, the usual presumption is that expectations of future employment will lead current governmental officials to treat the organizations involved more favorably than they would otherwise. However, if the regulated organizations provide possible employment as an incentive for favorable treatment, they risk producing a pattern of turnover in the regulatory agency in which friends leave the agency, and only those unfriendly to the organization remain. Alternatively, some organizations attempt to coopt difficult people (e.g., rebels), on the assumption that cooptation leads to controlled change, since opponents are socialized and provided with modest success. However, in so far as the basic strategy of cooptation is to strip leadership from opposition groups by inducing opposition leaders to accept more legitimate roles, a conspicuous complication is the extent to which cooptation provides an incentive for being difficult, and thereby increases, rather than reduces opposition.

Competency multipliers. Organizations frequently have procedures to involve potentially relevant people in decision-making, planning, budgeting, or the like. The individuals vary in status, knowledge about a problem, and interest in it. Initial participation rates reflect these variations; however, individuals who participate slightly more than others become slightly more competent at discussing the problems of the group than others. This induces them to participate even more, which makes them even more competent. Before long, the *de facto* composition of the group can change dramatically (Weiner, 1976). More generally organizations learn from experience, repeating actions that are successful. As a result, they gain greater experience in areas of success than in areas of failure. This increases their capabilities in successful areas, thus increasing their chances of being successful there. The sensibleness of such specialization depends on the relation between the learning rates and the rate of change in the environment.

The process can easily lead to misplaced specialization if there are infrequent, major shifts in the environment.

Satisficing. It has been suggested that organizations satisfice, that is, that they seek alternatives that will satisfy a target goal rather than look for the alternative with the highest possible expected value (March and Simon, 1958; Cyert and March, 1963). Satisficing organizations can be viewed as organizations that maximize the probability of achieving their targets, but it is not necessary to assume quite such a precise formulation to suggest that organizations that satisfice will follow decision-rules that are risk-avoiding in good times, when the best alternatives have expected values greater than the target, and risk-seeking in bad times, when the best alternatives have expected values less than the target (Tversky and Kahneman, 1974). As is noted below, the association of risk-seeking behavior with adversity requires some qualification; but in so far as such a pattern is common, it has at least two important consequences. First, organizations that are facing bad times will follow riskier and riskier strategies, thus simultaneously increasing their chances of survival through the present crisis and reducing their life expectancy. Choices that seek to reverse a decline, for example, may not maximize expected value. As a result, for those organizations that do not survive, efforts to survive will have speeded the process of failure (Hermann, 1963; Mayhew, 1979). Second, if organizational goals vary with organizational performance and the performance of other comparable organizations, most organizations will face situations that are reasonably good most of the time. Consequently, the pool of organizations existing at any time will generally include a disproportionate number that are risk-avoiding.

Performance criteria. Organizations measure the performance of participants. For example, business firms reward managers on the basis of calculations of profits earned by different parts of the organization. The importance of making such links precise and visible is a familiar theme of discussions of organizational control, as is the problem of providing similar performance measures in non-business organizations. However, in an organization with a typical mobility pattern among managers, these practices probably lead to a relative lack of concern about long-term consequences of present action. Performance measurement also leads to exaggerated concern with accounts, relative to product and technology. Measured performance can be improved either by changing performance or by changing the accounts of performance. Since it is often more efficient, in the short run, to devote effort to the accounts rather than to performance (March, 1978a), a bottom-line ideology may over-stimulate the cleverness of organizational participants in manipulating accounts.

Superstitious learning. Organizations learn from their experience, repeating actions that have been associated with good outcomes, avoiding actions that have been associated with bad ones. If the world makes simple sense, and is stable, then repeating actions associated with good outcomes is intelligent. Yet relative to the rate of our experience in it, the world is sometimes neither stable enough nor simple enough to make experience a good teacher (March and Olsen, 1976). The use of associational, experiential learning in complex worlds can result in superstitious learning (Lave and March, 1975). Consider, for example, the report by Tversky and Kahneman (1974) of the lessons learned by pilot trainers who experimented with rewarding pilots who make good landings and punishing pilots who make bad ones. They observe that pilots who are punished generally improve on subsequent landings, while pilots who are praised generally do worse. Thus, they learn that negative reinforcement works; positive reinforcement does not. The learning is natural, but the experience, like all experience, is confounded, in this case by ordinary regression to the mean.

These six examples of unanticipated consequences are illustrative of the variation in behavior that can be generated by elementary adaptive processes functioning under special conditions. They suggest some ways in which undramatic features of organizational life can lead to surprising organizational change.

Solution-Driven Problems

There seems to be ample evidence that when performance fails to meet aspirations, organizations search for new solutions (Cyert and March, 1963), that is, for new people, new ways of doing things, new alliances. However, changes often seem to be driven less by problems than by solutions. Daft and Becker (1978) have argued the case for educational organizations and Kay (1979) for industrial organizations; but the idea is an established one, typical of diffusion theories of change.

We can identify at least three different explanations for solution (or opportunity) driven change. In the first, organizations face a large number of problems of about equal importance, but only a few solutions. Thus, the chance of finding a solution to a particular problem is small; if one begins with a solution, however, there is a good chance that the solution will match some problem facing the organization. Consequently, an organization scans for solutions rather than problems, and matches any solution found with some relevant problem. A second explanation is that the linkage between individual solutions and individual problems is often difficult to make unambiguously. Then, almost any solution can be linked to almost any problem, provided they arise at approximately the same time (Cohen, March, and Olsen, 1972; March and Olsen, 1975). When causality and technology are ambiguous, the motivation to have particular solutions adopted is likely to be as powerful as the motivation to have particular problems solved, and many of the changes we observe will be better predicted by a knowledge of solutions than by a knowledge of problems. A third interpretation is that change is stimulated not by adversity but by success, less by a sense of problems than by a sense of competence and a belief that change is possible, natural, and appropriate (Daft and Becker, 1978). Professionals change their procedures and introduce new technologies because that is what professionals do and know how to do. An organization that is modern adopts new things because that is what being modern means. When a major stimulus for change comes from a sense of competence, problems are created in order to solve them, and solutions and opportunities stimulate awareness of previously unsalient or unnoticed problems or preferences.

Transformation of Innovations and Organizations

Students of innovation in organizations have persistently observed that both innovations and organizations tend to be transformed during the process of innovation (Browning, 1968; Brewer, 1973; Hyman, 1973). This is sometimes treated as a measurement problem. In that guise, the problem is to decide whether a change in one organization is equivalent to a change in another, or to determine when a change has been implemented sufficiently to be considered a change, or to disentangle the labeling of a change from the change itself. To treat such problems as measurement problems, however, is probably misleading. Seeing innovations as spreading unchanged through organizations helps link studies of innovation to models drawn from epidemiology; but where a fundamental feature of a change is the way it is transformed as it moves from invention to adoption to implementation to contagion, such a linkage is not helpful.

Organizational change develops meaning through the process by which it occurs. Some parts of that process tend to standardize the multiple meanings of a change, but standardization can be very slow, in some cases so slow as to be almost undetectable. When a business firm adopts a new policy (Cyert, Dill, and March, 1958), or a university a new program (March and Romelaer, 1976), specifying what the change means can be difficult, not because of poor information or inadequate analysis, but because of the fundamental ways in which changes are transformed by the processes of change. The developing character of change makes it difficult to use standard ideas of decision, problem-solving, diffusion, and the like, because it is difficult to describe a decision, problem solution, or innovation with precision, to say when it was adopted, and to treat the process as having an ending.

Organizations are also transformed in the process. Organizations develop and redefine goals while making decisions and adapting to environmental pressures; minor changes can lead to larger ones, and initial intent can be entirely lost. For example, an organization of evangelists becomes a gym with services attached (Zald and Denton, 1963); a social movement becomes a commercial establishment (Messinger, 1955; Sills, 1957); a radical rock radio station becomes an almost respectable part of a large corporation (Krieger, 1979); and a new governmental agency becomes an old one (Selznick, 1949; Sproull, Weiner and Wolf, 1978).

These transformations seem often to reflect occasions on which actions taken by an organization (for whatever reasons) become the source of a new definition of objectives. The possibility that preferences and goals may change in response to behavior is a serious complication for rational theories of choice (March, 1972, 1978a). Organizations' goals, as well as the goals of individuals in them, change in the course of introducing deliberate innovations, or in the course of normal organizational drift. As a result, actions affect the preferences in the name of which they are taken; and the discovery of new intentions is a common consequence of intentional behavior.

Created Environments

In simple models of organizational change, it is usually assumed that action is taken in response to the environment but that the environment is not affected by organizational action. The assumptions are convenient, but organizations create their environments in part, and the resulting complications are significant. For example, organizations are frequently combined into an ecology of competition, in which the actions of one competitor become the environment of another. Each competitor, therefore, partly determines its own environment as the competitors react to each other, a situation familiar to studies of prey-predator relations and markets (Mayr, 1963; Kamien and Schwartz, 1975). Also, if we think of adaptation as learning about a fixed environment, the model is somewhat different from one in which the environment is simultaneously adapting to the organization. The situation is a common one. Parents adapt to children at the same time that children adapt to parents, and customers and suppliers adapt to each other. The outcomes are different from those observed in the case of adaptation to a stable environment, with equilibria that depend on whether the process is one of hunting or mating and on the relative rates of adaptation of the organization and the environment (Lave and March, 1975). Finally, organizations create their own environments by the way they interpret and act in a confusing world. It is not just that the world is incompletely or inaccurately perceived (Slovic, Fischhoff, and Lichtenstein, 1977; Nisbet and Ross, 1980), but also that actions taken as a result of beliefs about the environment do, in fact, construct the environment, as, for example, in self-fulfilling prophecies and the construction of limits through avoidance of them (Meyer and Rowan, 1977; Weick, 1977, 1979).

It is possible, of course, for organizations to act strategically in an environment they help create, but created environments are not ordinarily experienced in a way different from other environments. For example, the experience of learning in a situation in which the environment is simultaneously adapting to the organization is not remarkably different from the experience of learning in simpler situations. The outcomes are, however, distinctive. When environments are created, the actions taken by an organization in adapting to an environment are partly responses to previous actions by the same organization; reflected through the environment. A common result is that small signals are amplified into large ones, and the general implication is that routine adaptive processes have consequences that cannot be understood without linking them to an environment that is simultaneously, and endogenously, changing.

Individuals, Organizations, and Environments

Although it is an heroic simplification out of which theoretical mischief can come, it is possible to see an organization as the intermeshing of three systems: the individual, the organization, and the collection of organizations that can be called the environment. Many of the complications in the study of organizational change are related to the way those three systems intermesh, as is reflected in the large number of studies that discuss managing change in terms of the relations between organizations and the individuals who inhabit them (Coch and French, 1948; Burns and Stalker, 1961; Argyris, 1965), between organizations and their environment (Starbuck, 1976; Aldrich, 1979), and among organizations (Evan, 1966; Benson, 1975).

Much of classical organization theory addresses the problems of making the demands of organizations and individuals consistent (Barnard, 1938; Simon, 1947; March and Simon, 1958); the same theme is frequent in modern treatments of information (Hirschleifer and Riley, 1979) and incentives (Downs, 1967). Although it is an old problem, it continues to be interesting for the analysis of organizational change. In particular, it seems very likely that both the individuals involved in organizations and systems of organizations have different requirements for organizational change than the organization itself. For example, individual participants in an organization view their positions in the organizations, e.g., their jobs, as an important part of their milieu. They try to arrange patterns of stability and variety within the organization to meet their own desires. However, there is no particular *a priori* reason for assuming that individual desires for change and stability will be mutually consistent or will match requirements for organizational survival. Moreover, the survival of an organization is a more compelling requirement for the organization than it is for a system of organizations. Survival of the system of organizations may require organizational changes that are inappropriate for the individual organization; it may require greater organizational flexibility or rigidity than makes sense for the individual organization. The organizational failure rates that are optimal for systems of organizations are somewhat different from those that are optimal for individual organizations. Complications such as these are common in any combination of autonomous systems. They form a focus for some standard issues in contemporary population genetics (Wright, 1978), as well as extensions of those ideas into social science in general (Wilson, 1975; Hannan and Freeman, 1977). That observed systems of individuals, organizations, and environments have evolved to an equilibrium is questionable, but it is possible that some of the features of organizations that seem particularly perverse make greater sense when considered from the point of view of the larger system of organizations.

Other illustrations of complications could easily be added, including problems introduced by the ways in which humans make inferences (Nisbet and Ross, 1980), and by the ways in which organizational demography affects regeneration (Reed, 1978). Each of the complications represents either a limitation in one of the standard models or a way in which a model of adaptation can be used to illuminate organizational change under complicated or confounding conditions. Familiar activities, rules, or procedures sometimes lead to unanticipated consequences.

Foolishness, Change and Altruism

Organizations need to maintain a balance (or dialectic) between explicitly sensible processes of change (problem-solving, learning, planning) and certain elements of foolishness that are difficult to justify locally but are important to the broader system (March, 1972, 1978a; Weick, 1979). Consider, for example, a classic complication of long-range planning. As we try to anticipate the future, we will often observe that there are many possible, but extremely unlikely, future events which would dramatically change the consequences of present actions and thus the appropriate choice to be made now. Because there are so many very unlikely future events that can be imagined, and each is so improbable, we ordinarily exclude them from our more careful forecasts, though we know that some very unlikely events will certainly occur. As a result, our plans are based on a future that we know, with certainty, will not be realized. More generally, if the most favorable outcomes of a particular choice alternative depend on the occurrence of very unlikely events, the expected value of that alternative will be low, and it would not be sensible to choose it. Thus, the best alternative after the fact is unlikely to be chosen before the fact by a rational process. For similar reasons, the prior expected value of any specific innovation is likely to be negative, and organizations are likely to resist proposals for such change. Indeed, we would expect that an institution eager to adopt innovative proposals will survive less luxuriantly and for shorter periods than others. Though some unknown change is almost certainly sensible, being the first to experiment with a new idea is not likely to be worth the risk.

The problem becomes one of introducing new ideas into organizations at a rate sufficient to sustain the larger system of organizations, when such action is not intelligent for any one organization. The conventional solution for such problems involves some kind of collaboration that pools the risk (Hirschleifer and Riley, 1979). Explicit risk-sharing agreements exist, but for the most part, organizational systems have evolved a culture of implicit altruism which introduces decentralized non-rational elements into rational choice procedures rather than relying on explicit contractual arrangements. These cultural elements of manifest foolishness have latent implications for innovation and change in organizations. New ideas are sustained in an organization by mechanisms that shield them, altruistically, from the operation of normal rationality, for example, by organizational slack, managerial incentives, symbolic action, ambiguity, and loose coupling.

Slack protects individuals and groups, who pursue change for personal or professional reasons, from normal organizational controls. As a result, it has been argued that one of the ways in which organizations search when successful is through slack (Cyert and March, 1963; Wilson, 1966). Several studies of change seem to lend support to this idea (Mansfield, 1968; Staw and Szwajkowski, 1975; Manns and March, 1978); but Kay (1979) concludes that it is hard to see consistent evidence for slack search in the data on research and development expenditures. Daft and Becker (1978) suggest that slack is associated not with excess resources but with high salaries and a consequent high level of professionalism.

Since managers and other leaders are selected by a process that is generally conservative (Cohen and March, 1974), it is probably unreasonable to see them as sources of intentional foolishness. Managerial incentives seem unlikely to stimulate managerial playfulness; incentive schemes try to tie individual rewards to organizational outcomes, so that managers help themselves by helping the organization. The ideology of good management, however, associates managers with the introduction of new ideas, new organizational forms, new technologies, new products, new slogans, or new moods. Consequently, some fraction of organizational resources is dedicated to running unlikely experiments in changes as unwitting altruistic contributions to the larger world.

Choice and decision-making touch some of the more important values of modern developed cultures, and thereby become major symbolic domains in contemporary organizations. Symbolic values, including those associated with change, are important enough and pervasive enough to dominate other factors in a decision situation (Christensen, 1976; Kreiner, 1976; Feldman and March, 1981). Symbolism shades into personal motivations easily for professionals (e.g., engineers, doctors) or managers, since they express their competence and authority by the introduction of changes or symbols of changes (Daft and Becker, 1978) in a more general way, the symbolic elaboration of processes of choice becomes more important than the outcomes, and the outcomes thus reflect more foolishness than would otherwise be expected.

Organizations do not always have a well-defined set of objectives; their preferences are frequently ambiguous, imprecise, inconsistent, unstable, and affected by their choices (March, 1978a; Elster, 1979). As a result, problem-solving and decision-making assume some of the features of a garbage can process (Cohen, March, and Olsen, 1972), learning becomes confounded by the ambiguity of experience (Cohen and March, 1974; March and Olsen, 1976), and actions become particularly sensitive to the participation and attention patterns of organizational actors (Olsen, 1976). Moreover, the uncertainties associated with trying to guess future preferences increase considerably the variance in any estimates that might be made of the expected utility of present action and thus decrease the reliability of the process.

Finally, organizations are complex combinations of activities, purposes, and meanings; they accomplish coordinated tasks that would be inconceivable without them, and without which it is difficult to imagine a modern developed society. This impressive integration of formal organizations should not, however, obscure the many ways in which organizations are loosely coupled. Behavior is loosely coupled to intentions; actions in one part of the organization are loosely coupled to actions in another part; decisions today are loosely coupled to decisions tomorrow (Cohen and March, 1974; March and Olsen, 1976; Weick, 1976, 1979). Such loose coupling does not appear to be avoidable. Rather, limits on coordination, attention, and control are inherent restrictions on the implementation of rationality in organizational action.

These organizational phenomena ensure that some level of foolishness will occur within an organization, no matter how dedicated to rational coordination and control it may be. Although it is easy to argue that foolishness is a form of altruism by which systematic needs for change are met, it is much harder to assess whether the mixture of rationality and foolishness that we observe in organizations is optimal. The ideology underlying the development of decision-engineering probably underestimates the importance of foolishness, and the ideology underlying enthusiasm for some versions of undisciplined creativity probably underestimates the importance of systematic analysis. What is much more difficult is to determine whether a particular real system errs on the side of excessive reason or excessive foolishness. We can solve the problem of appropriate foolishness within a specific model by assuming some characteristics of the environment over the future; solving the problem in a real situation, however, is not ordinarily within our ability.

Nor is it easy to devise realistic insurance, information, or contractual schemes that will reliably ensure reaching an optimum. Not only are the difficulties in analysis substantial, but, quite aside from those problems, there is also a difficulty posed by the cultural character of the existing solution. The mix of organizational foolishness and rationality is deeply embedded in the rules, incentives, and beliefs of the society and organization. It is possible to imagine changing the mix of rules, thereby changing the level of foolishness; but it is hard to imagine being able to modify broad cultural and organizational attributes with much precision or control.

Discussion

The five footnotes to organizational change suggested at the outset are comments on change, not a theory of change. Nevertheless, they may have some implications for organizational leadership and for research on adaptation in organizations. The general perspective depends on the proposition that the basic processes by which organizations act, respond to their environments, and learn are quite stable, and possibly comprehensible. These stable processes of change, however, produce a great variety of action and their outcomes are sometimes surprisingly sensitive to the details of the context in which they occur.

A view of change as resulting from stable processes realized in a highly contextual and sometimes confusing world emphasizes the idea that things happen in organizations because most of the time organizational participants respond in elementary ways to the environment, including that part of the environment that might be called management or leadership. Managers and leaders propose changes, including foolish ones; they try to cope with the environment and to control it; they respond to other members of the organization; they issue orders and manipulate incentives. Since they play conventional roles, organizational leaders are not likely to behave in strikingly unusual ways. And if a leader tries to march toward strange destinations, an organization is likely to deflect the effort. Simply to describe leadership as conventional and constrained by organizational realities, however, is to risk misunderstanding its importance. Neither success nor change requires dramatic action. The conventional, routine activities that produce most organizational change require ordinary people to do ordinary things in a competent way (March, 1978b). Moreover, within some broad constraints, the adaptiveness of organizations can be managed. Typically, it is not possible to lead an organization in any arbitrary direction that might be desired, but it is possible to influence the course of events by managing the process of change, and particularly by stimulating or inhibiting predictable complications and anomalous dynamics.

Such a view of managing organizations assumes that the effectiveness of leadership often depends on being able to time small interventions so that the force of natural organizational processes amplifies the interventions. It is possible to identify a few minor rules for such actions (Cohen and March, 1974), but a comprehensive development of managerial strategies (as well as of effective strategies for frustrating managers) requires a more thorough understanding of change in organizations, not a theory of how to introduce any arbitrary change, but a theory of how to direct somewhat the conventional ways in which an organization responds to its environment, experiences, and anticipations. The footnotes to change elaborated in this paper are much too fragmentary for such a task, but they indicate a possible way of understanding change. They argue for considering the fundamental adaptive processes by which change occurs, in terms of broader theoretical ideas about organizational action. They direct attention particularly to how substantial changes occur, as the routine consequence of standard procedures or as the unintended consequence of ordinary adaptation. And they suggest that understanding organizational change requires discovering the connections between the apparently prosaic and the apparently poetic in organizational life.

References

Aldrich, Howard E. (1979) *Organizations and Environments*. Englewood Cliffs, NJ: Prentice-Hall.

Argyris, Chris (1965) *Organization and Innovation*. Homewood, IL: Irwin-Dorsey.

Attewell, Paul, and Dean R. Gerstein (1979) Government policy and local practice. *American Sociological Review*, 44: 311–27.

Bardach, Eugene (1977) *The Implementation Game*. Cambridge, MA: MIT Press.

Barnard, Chester I. (1938) *Functions of the Executive*. Cambridge, MA: Harvard University Press.

Benson, J. Kenneth (1975) The interorganizational network as political economy. *Administrative Science Quarterly* 20: 229–49.

Brewer, Garry D. (1973) *Politicians, Bureaucrats and the Consultant: A Critique of Urban Problem Solving*. New York: Basic Books.

Browning, Rufus P. (1968) Innovation and non-innovation decision processes in governmental budgeting. In Robert T. Golembiewski (ed.), *Public Budgeting and Finance*, pp. 128–45. Itasca, IL: F. E. Peacock.

Burns, Tom, and G. M. Stalker (1961) *The Management of Innovation*. London: Tavistock.

Christensen, Søren (1976) Decision making and socialization. In James G. March and Johan P. Olsen (eds), *Ambiguity and Choice in Organizations*, pp. 351–85. Bergen, Norway: Universitetsforlaget.

Coch, Lester, and John R. P. French, Jr (1948) Overcoming resistance to change. *Human Relations*, 1: 512–32.

Cohen, Michael D., and James G. March (1974) *Leadership and Ambiguity: The American College President*. New York: McGraw-Hill.

Cohen, Michael D., James G. March, and Johan P. Olsen (1972) A garbage can model of organizational choice. *Administrative Science Quarterly*, 17: 1–25.

Crozier, Michel (1979) *On ne Change pas la Société par Décret*. Paris: Grasset.

Cyert, Richard M., William Dill, and James G. March (1958) The role of expectations in business decision making. *Administrative Science Quarterly*, 3: 307–40.

Cyert, Richard M., and James G. March (1963) *A Behavioral Theory of the Firm*. Englewood Cliffs, NJ: Prentice-Hall.

Daft, Richard L., and Selwyn W. Becker, (1978) *The Innovative Organization*. New York: Elsevier.

Day, R. H., and T. Groves (eds) (1975) *Adaptive Economic Models*. New York: Academic Press.

Downs, Anthony (1967) *Inside Bureaucracy*, Boston: Little, Brown.

Elster, Jon (1979) *Ulysses and the Sirens*. Cambridge: Cambridge University Press.

Evan, William M. (1966) The organization set: Toward a theory of interorganizational relations. In James D. Thompson (ed.), *Approaches to Organizational Design*, pp. 173–91. Pittsburgh: University of Pittsburgh Press.

Feldman, Martha S., and James G. March (1981) Information in organizations as signal and symbol. *Administrative Science Quarterly*, 26: 171–86.

Gamson, William A. (1968) *Power and Discontent*. Homewood, IL: Dorsey.

Gross, Neal, Joseph B. Giaquinta, and Marilyn Bernstein (1971) *Implementing Organizational Innovations: A Sociological Analysis of Planned Educational Change*. New York: Basic Books.

Hannan, Michael T., and John Freeman (1977) The population ecology of organizations. *American Journal of Sociology*, 82: 929–66.

Hedberg, Bo L. T., Paul C. Nystrom, and William H. Starbuck (1976) Camping on seesaws: Prescriptions for a self-designing organization. *Administrative Science Quarterly*, 21: 41–65.

Hermann, Charles F. (1963) Some consequences of crisis which limit the viability of organizations. *Administrative Science Quarterly* 8: 61–82.

Hirschleifer, J., and John G. Riley (1979) The analytics of uncertainty and information – An expository survey. *Journal of Economic Literature*. 17: 1375–421.

Hirschman, Albert O. (1979) *Exit, Voice, and Loyalty*. Cambridge, MA: Harvard University Press.

Hyman, Herbert H. (ed.) (1973) *The Politics of Health Care: Nine Case Studies of Innovative Planning in New York City*. New York: Praeger.

Kamien, Morton I., and Nancy L. Schwartz (1975) Market structure and innovation: A survey. *Journal of Economic Literature*. 13: 1–37.

Kay, Neil M. (1979) *The Innovating Firm: A Behavioral Theory of Corporate R & D*. New York: St Martin's.

Kreiner, Kristian (1976) Ideology and management in a garbage can situation. In James G. March and Johan P. Olsen (eds), *Ambiguity and Choice in Organizations:* 156–73. Bergen, Norway: Universitetsforlaget.

Krieger, Susan (1979) *Hip Capitalism*. Beverly Hills, CA: Sage.

Lave, Charles A., and James G. March (1975) *An Introduction to Models in the Social Sciences*. New York: Harper and Row.

Lindblom, Charles E. (1958) The science of muddling through. *Public Administration Review*, 19: 79–88.

Manns, Curtis L., and James G. March (1978) Financial adversity, internal competition, and curriculum change in a university. *Administrative Science Quarterly*, 23: 541–52.

Mansfield, Edwin (1968) *The Economics of Technological Change*. New York: Norton.

March, James G. (1962) The business firm as a political coalition. *Journal of Politics*, 24: 662–78.

March, James G. (1972) Model bias in social action. *Review of Educational Research*. 42: 413–29.

March, James G. (1978a) Bounded rationality, ambiguity, and the engineering of choice. *Bell Journal of Economics*, 9: 587–608.

March, James G. (1978b) American public school administration: A short analysis. *School Review*, 86: 217–50.

March, James G., and Johan P. Olsen (1975) The uncertainty of the past: Organizational learning under ambiguity. *European Journal of Political Research*. 3: 147–71.

March, James G., and Johan P. Olsen (1976) *Ambiguity and Choice in Organizations*. Bergen, Norway: Universitetsforlaget.

March, James G., and Pierre J. Romelaer (1976) Position and presence in the drift of decisions. In James G. March and Johan P. Olsen (eds), *Ambiguity and Choice in Organizations*, pp. 251–76. Bergen, Norway: Universitetsforlaget.

March, James G., and Herbert A. Simon (1958) *Organizations*. New York: Wiley.

Mayhew, Lewis B. (1979) *Surviving the Eighties*. San Francisco: Jossey-Bass.

Mayr, Ernst (1963) *Population, Species, and Evolution*. Cambridge, MA: Harvard University Press.

McNeil, Kenneth, and James D. Thompson (1971) The regeneration of social organizations. *American Sociological Review*, 36: 624–37.

Messinger, Sheldon L. (1955) Organizational transformation: A case study of a declining social movement. *American Sociological Review*, 20: 3–10.

Meyer, John W., and Brian Rowan (1977) Institutionalized organizations: Formal structure as myth and ceremony. *American Journal of Sociology*, 83: 340–60.

Nelson, Richard R., and Sidney G. Winter (1974) Neoclassical vs. evolutionary theories of economic growth: Critique and prospectus. *Economic Journal*, 84: 886–905.

Nelson, Richard R., and Douglas Yates, (eds) (1978) *Innovation and Implementation in Public Organizations*. Lexington, MA: D. C. Heath.

Nisbet, Richard, and Lee Ross (1980) *Human Inference: Strategies and Shortcomings of Social Judgment*. Englewood Cliffs, NJ: Prentice-Hall.

Olsen, Johan P. (1976) Reorganization as a garbage can. In James G. March and Johan P. Olsen (eds), *Ambiguity and Choice in Organizations*, pp. 314–37. Bergen, Norway: Universitetsforlaget.

Pfeffer, Jeffrey (1981) *Power in Organizations*. Marshfield, MA: Pitman.

Pressman, Jeffrey, and Aaron Wildavsky (1973) *Implementation*. Berkeley, CA: University of California Press.

Reed, Theodore L. (1978) Organizational change in the American foreign service, 1925–1965: The utility of cohort analysis. *American Sociological Review*, 43: 404–21.

Rogers, Everett M. (1962) *Diffusion of Innovations*. New York: Free Press.

Rogers, Everett M., and F. Floyd Shoemaker (1971) *Communication of Innovations*. New York: Free Press.

Schelling, Thomas C. (1978) *Micromotives and Macrobehavior*. New York: Norton.

Selznick, Philip (1949) *TVA and the Grass Roots*. Berkeley, CA: University of California Press.

Sills, David L. (1957) *The Volunteers*. New York: Free Press.

Simon, Herbert A. (1947) *Administrative Behavior*. New York: Macmillan.

Slovic, Paul, Bernard Fischhoff, and Sarah Lichtenstein (1977) Behavioral decision theory. *Annual Review of Psychology*, 28: 1–39.

Sproull, Lee S., Stephen S. Weiner, and David Wolf (1978) *Organizing an Anarchy*. Chicago: University of Chicago Press.

Starbuck, William H. (1976) Organizations and their environments. In Marvin D. Dunnette (ed.), *Handbook of Industrial and Organizational Psychology*: 1069–124. Chicago: Rand McNally.

Staw, Barry M., and Eugene Szwajkowski (1975) The scarcity–munificence component of organizational environments and the commission of illegal acts. *Administrative Science Quarterly*, 20: 345–54.

Stinchcombe, Arthur L., Mary Sexton McDill, and Dollie R. Walker (1968) Demography of organizations. *American Journal of Sociology*, 74: 221–29.

Tversky, Amos, and Daniel Kahneman (1974) Judgment under uncertainty: Heuristics and biases. *Science*. 185: 1124–131.

Walker, Jack L. (1969) The diffusion of innovations among the American states. *American Political Science Review*, 63: 880–99.

Weick, Karl E. (1976) Educational organizations as loosely-coupled systems. *Administrative Science Quarterly*, 21: 1–19.

Weick, Karl E. (1977) Enactment processes in organizations. In Barry M. Staw and Gerald R. Salancik (eds), *New Directions in Organizational Behavior*. 267–300. Chicago: St Clair.

Weick, Karl E. (1979) *The Social psychology of Organizing*, 2nd edn, Reading, MA: Addison-Wesley.

Weiner, Stephen S. (1976) Participation, deadlines and choice. In James G. March and Johan P. Olsen (eds). *Ambiguity and Choice in Organizations*; pp. 225–50. Bergen, Norway: Universitetsforlaget.

White, Harison C. (1970) *Chains of Opportunity: System Models of Mobility in Organizations*. Cambridge, MA: Harvard University Press.

Wilson, Edward O. (1975) *Sociobiology: The New Synthesis*. Cambridge, MA: Harvard University Press.

Wilson, James Q. (1966) Innovation in organizations: Notes toward a theory. In James D. Thompson (ed.) *Approaches to Organizational Design*; 193–218. Pittsburgh: University of Pittsburgh Press.

Wright, Sewall (1978) *Evolution and Genetics of Populations*, vol. 4. Chicago: University of Chicago Press.

Zald, Mayer N., and Patricia Denton (1963) From evangelism to general service: The transformation of the YMCA. *Administrative Science Quarterly*, 8: 214–234.

9

A Model of Adaptive Organizational Search

Daniel Levinthal and James G. March

Abstract

A model of organizational change through adaptive search for new technologies is developed and explored. The model is in the tradition of behavioral models of organizational choice and learning associated with work by Winter, Nelson, and Radner. It permits the exploration of simultaneous organizational adaptation in search strategies, competences, and aspirations under conditions of environmental instability and ambiguity. The model exhibits the extent to which variation in organizational behavior and performance reflect the distributional consequences of simple adaptation in ambiguous environments, as well as some adverse consequences of rapid learning.

Adaptive Search and Technological Change

In this paper, we present a model of adaptive search and technological change. By technology we mean any semi-stable specification of the way in which an organization deals with its environment, functions and prospers. Thus, it may be a production function, as in theories of the firm; it may be a normative structure, as in some theories of professional service organizations; it may be a constituency structure, as in some theories of political organizations. Our analysis is in the tradition of previous work

---

This paper was first published in the Journal of Economic Behavior and Organization 2 (1981), pp. 307–33. The research has been supported by grants from the Spencer Foundation, the National Institute of Education, the Hoover Institution, and the Stanford Graduate School of Business. The authors are grateful for comments by Julia Ball, Michael D. Cohen, Scott Herriott, John F. Padgett, Allyn Romanow, Harrison White, and Sidney Winter.

by Winter (1971), Radner (1975), and Nelson and Winter (1978). It is intended as an elaboration of their ideas, with some variations on the theme.

The model focuses on the search for new technologies through refinement and innovation, on the uncertain outcomes of that search, and on organizational learning as a result of experience in developing and implementing new technologies. It does not consider the effects of competition, imitation, or other interaction among organizations. It explores some ways simple adaptation might lead to organizational change, and how that process might be complicated by the confusions of a changing and autonomous environment and by the interrelation of different adaptive processes. The basic speculation (quite possibly wrong) is that significant elements of variation in organizational histories reflect the distributional characteristics of simple adaptation in ambiguous environments, rather than the results of fundamentally different processes or even significantly different environmental conditions. The model considers effects due primarily to interactions among five features of organizational life that have been observed in behavioral studies of decision-making.

1 The inclination of organizations to distinguish between success and failure, thus between slack times and harsh times, in allocating resources to innovation and refinement.
2 The tendency for organizations to modify search strategies on the basis of apparent experience with them.
3 The increase of organizational competence through experience, thus the effect of experience on the relative efficiency of alternative search strategies.
4 The adaptation of aspirations to performance and the consequent change in definitions of subjective success and failure.
5 The tendency for experience to be confounded by random fluctuations, systematic exogenous effects, and uncontrolled environmental change.

We assume the success of an organization depends partly on its technology. The connection may be partly obscured by many other factors, and causal inferences about the relation between technological change and improvement in performance may be difficult to make with assurance; but technology affects success. We treat research and development or other forms of search as equivalent to drawing from a distribution of search outcomes (in the form of possible technological opportunities). The number of draws is a function of the size of the expenditure on search and its efficiency; the expected result of a draw is a function of the distribution of technological opportunities associated with a particular mode of search and a particular technology. In the absence of learning, the optimization problem is straightforward as long as information is available on costs, the distribution of opportunities, and the way in which opportunities are sampled through search. The interest here, however, is not in solving the optimization problem. Though we examine the efficacy of learning in finding optimal solutions in simple situations, our primary intention is to model the behavior of organizations as they make decisions and learn about their search expenditures. We describe decision-making as a result of experiential learning, that is, as a consequence of an organization's successes and failures in meeting performance targets, of search expenditures made and their outcomes, and of the (sometimes mistaken) inferences made from experience.

Organizational experience leads to three distinct kinds of learning in such a situation. The first is adaptation of search *strategies*. Organizations attempt to modify their propensities to search for new technologies, as well as propensities to direct that search toward refinement or innovation, on the basis of experience. Second, organizations improve their search *competences*. The greater the experience in looking for refinement (or innovation) in a technology, the greater the efficiency in discovering them. Finally, organizations adapt their *aspirations*. They learn what to hope for. Discussions of organizational learning with respect to strategies (March and Olsen, 1976), competences (Alchian, 1959; Preston and Keachie, 1964), and aspirations (Cyert and March, 1963) are familiar. The present model extends those efforts to a consideration of some consequences of their interrelations.

In the spirit of behavioral studies of decision-making, we assume organizations both react to their environments in terms of existing rules and, at the same time, modify the rules. The first-order responses to experience are what Cyert and March (1963) called 'problemistic search' and what Steinbruner (1974) characterized as 'cybernetic'. The ideas are usually associated with Simon (1957) and others (March and Simon, 1958; Lindblom, 1959; Cyert and March, 1963; Allison, 1971; Kay, 1979). The organization is assumed to have a performance target (goal) against which it compares actual achievement. If the target exceeds performance, an organization searches for solutions to the problem. That search emphasizes relatively immediate refinements in the existing technology, greater efficiency, and discoveries in the near neighborhood of the present activities. Depending on the pool of opportunities for small changes in present behavior, search for technological refinements generates new actions that reduce, or eliminate, the discrepancy between target and performance.

If, on the other hand, performance exceeds the target, organizational slack accumulates. Slack is the difference between the potential performance of an organization and the performance actually achieved.

It represents various ways in which resources and energy that might have been devoted to pursuing organizational goals have been channeled into other things. It includes such manifest inefficiencies as over-designed equipment, over-qualified personnel, undiscovered improvements in current technology, and relaxed managerial control procedures. Although it is not ordinarily justified in such terms, organizational slack contributes to organizational adaptation in two similar ways. First, it conserves the pool of unexploited refinements in a technology. By failing to discover a refinement today, an organization maintains an inventory of possible refinements as a buffer against future uncontrolled exogenous adversity. Second, it allows 'irresponsible' search (slack search). By relaxing organizational controls, slack encourages search activities that cannot be justified in terms of their expected return for the organization. They are initiated because of their attractiveness to some individuals or subunits, and tolerated because of the organization's current success in achieving targets.

Some fraction of these slack search activities results (essentially fortuitously) in discoveries of value to parts of the organization other than the original subunit involved. The prototypes are the pet projects of playful engineers, but the phenomenon extends to a wide variety of substantially foolish investments and activities with negative expected values from the point of view of the organization. Organizational slack may, therefore, be sensible under some circumstances (Knight, 1967; Keen, 1977). It is certainly possible that organizational procedures leading to slack have evolved in a mix of environments that encourages their endurance (Winter, 1975; Hannan and Freeman, 1977). For our purposes, however, slack exists simply as a characteristic of organizational behavior that has been widely observed.

First-order responses are rapid and match standard operating procedures to environmental signals. Second-order responses are slower. They involve changes in performance targets, technological opportunities, search behavior, and knowledge about opportunities. These changes occur in response to organizational actions taken and (possibly misleading) information received on their consequences. Aspirations adapt to actual performance. Organizations learn what is reasonable to expect by observing what they achieve. Typically, however, such adaptation takes time (and, of course, performance also changes simultaneously). Opportunities adapt to search and discoveries. A technological pool can become depleted by ordinary refinements; alternatively, it can be enriched by new innovations. Search behavior adapts through trial and error. Behavior that is associated with success tends to be repeated; behavior that is associated with failure tends not to be repeated. At the same time, the values of alternatives are clarified by implementing them and experiencing their consequences.

These elementary forms of learning occur in a world in which it is possible for experience to be misleading. If a stable environment associates particular performance outcomes with particular organizational actions, experiential learning can be an efficient mechanism for discovering intelligent rules for behavior. However, organizations often appear to be trying to learn in somewhat more confusing environments (March and Olsen, 1976). We wish to examine the consequences of adaptive search behavior in situations in which outcomes are affected by both random fluctuations and systematic exogenous effects, and where the rate of change in environmental conditions exceeds the adaptation rate. It is easy to show that basically sensible learning can lead to superstitious belief under such conditions (Cohen and March, 1974; Lave and March, 1975). Thus, we consider the impacts of systematic exogenous changes and environmental uncertainty on organizational learning when search strategies, search competences, and aspirations for performance outcomes are all simultaneously adapting to experience.

A Model

We assume that an organization sets a performance target, G_t, for each time period and modifies that target on the basis of performance experience. If P_t is an organization's performance in period t:

$$G_t = \mathrm{b}_1 P_{t-1} + (1 - b_1) G_{t-1}. \tag{1}$$

As a result, the target is an exponentially weighted moving average of past performance.

Organizational learning is driven by the relationship between G_t and P_t, and thus by variations in both. We assume that the organization's performance in period t depends on the state of its technology at time t, $T_{*,t}$, the costs of search that it has undertaken, and an exogenous and randomly varying environmental variable, a_t. Specifically,

$$P_t = (1 + a_t) T_{*,t} - R_t - I_t, \tag{2}$$

where R_t and I_t are the levels of expenditure on the two types of search processes considered, refinement search and innovation search. By refinement we mean the fine-tuning and economizing designed to improve the efficiency of an existing technology. The second kind of search is technological innovation, finding a new improved technology. The distinctions are taken from Radner (1975) and are similar to those made by Knight (1967) and Nelson and Winter (1978).

The technology in period t, $T_{*,t}$, depends on the technology of the previous period and the realized outcomes of search. If we ignore the complications in forecasting the consequences of technologies before they are implemented, $T_{*,t}$ is the maximum of the technological outcomes from two search processes (the search for refinement and the search for innovation), and the (possibly changed) technology of the previous period. That is, it is assumed that existing technology changes by a constant factor, b_2. It is possible for technology to decay (i.e., $b_2 < 1$), remain constant (i.e., $b_2 = 1$), or improve (i.e., $b_2 > 1$) in the absence of search. Thus,

$$T_{*,t} = \max\ (T_{r,t}, T_{i,t}, b_2 T_{*,t-1}), \tag{3}$$

where $T_{r,t}$ is the value of the best technology discovered through refinement search during period t, and $T_{i,t}$ is the value of the best technology discovered through innovation search during period t. If the consequences of technological changes are subject to error, $T_{*,t}$ is the true value of the technology that appeared best, according to estimates at the time of decision.

Organizations are assumed to search by sampling some number of opportunities and to implement the best of those, provided it is believed to be better than the existing technology. The outcomes from search are a joint consequence of the sample size, the current technology, and the distributions of possible technologies. Assuming errors of estimation are unbiased, the technology expected as a result of search is better than the expected value of the pool of opportunities; and an increase in the variance of the distribution in the pool increases the expected improvement in technology to be realized from search (Kohn and Shavell, 1974).

The distributions of technological opportunities are assumed to be different for the two kinds of search. In the case of refinement, it is assumed that the distribution of opportunities is a normal distribution of changes from $b_2 T_{*,t-1}$ with a mean $= 0$, and a standard deviation, $V_{r,t}$, which declines with search until a new technology is invented and adopted (at time y). The initial standard deviation for a newly innovated technology is proportional to the value of the technology when adopted. Thus,

$$V_{r,y} = c_1 T_{*,y}, \text{ and} \tag{4}$$

$$V_{r,t+1} = c_2 V_{r,t} \text{ (if a refinement draw was made in period } t\text{).} \tag{5}$$

In the case of search for innovation, it is assumed that opportunities are distributed as a log normal distribution of changes from $b_2 T_{*,t-1}$ with a mean $= 0$, and a fixed standard deviation V_t, proportional to the value of the current (unrefined) technology. Thus,

$$V_t = c_3 T_{*,y}, \tag{6}$$

The value of a refinement or innovation discovered by search is assumed to be known with certainty once it is implemented. However, the values of unimplemented technological modifications may be known only up to some error. As a result, it is possible for search to result in technological decline rather than improvement even though choices of the best apparent technology are made; and it is possible for an organization to learn not to search because of estimation errors and thereby reduce the experience in search that would make search more useful. We assume that estimation errors are distributed normally with mean zero and a standard deviation that is initially greater in the case of innovation ($V_{e,i,t}$) than in the case of refinement ($V_{e,r,t}$). The standard deviation for errors for each kind of search declines with experience in implementing new technological change. Note that even though errors of estimation are assumed to be unbiased, the errors observed with respect to implemented technologies will more commonly be overestimates than underestimates, and that increasing the variance of (unbiased) errors decreases the expected real improvements to be realized from search.

We assume an organization affects its performance by changing search expenditures. Returns to search are assumed to depend on the size of current expenditures, current efficiencies in search, and current technological opportunities. We imagine that search consists of sampling opportunities from the pool of technological possibilities associated with either refinement or innovation. Each draw results in the 'discovery' of some opportunity. Many of these will be less attractive than the present technology; some may be more attractive. Thus the likelihood of discovering technological improvements depends on the sample size. We assume the sample size for each of the two kinds of search is proportional to the product of the current expenditure on search and current search efficiency. Thus, if we let $E_{r,t}$ be the efficiency in refinement search at time t and $E_{i,t}$ be the efficiency in innovation search, the sample sizes for refinement, $K_{r,t}$, and innovation, $K_{i,t}$, are given by the integer values of

$$K_{r,t} = k_r R_t E_{r,t}, \tag{7}$$

and

$$K_{i,t} = k_i I_t E_{i,t}, \tag{8}$$

We assume that efficiency in search increases with increasing search within a given technology, but at a decreasing rate. The carry-over of efficiency from the previous technology is proportional to the difference between the two technologies. Let

$$F_{d,t} = F_{d,y-1}(T_{*,y-1}/T_{*,y}) + \sum_{j=y}^{t-1} K_{d,j} \text{ if } T_{*,y-1} \leqq T_{*,y}, \tag{9}$$

and

$$F_{d,t} = F_{d,y-1}(T_{*,y}/T_{*,y-1}) + \sum_{j=y}^{t-1} K_{d,j} \text{ if } T_{*,y-1} > T_{*,y},$$

where y is the time period of the last adopted innovation, and d represents the particular mode of search (refinement or innovation). Then

$$E_{d,t} = (F_{d,t})^{1/wd}. \tag{10}$$

Note that the efficiency of search is not affected by b_2, the exogenous change in technology, and that the cost of a sample declines with experience in the standard learning curve way (log linear in total sampling to date), except that each innovation of a new technology discounts prior experience.

We assume that the pools of resources available to the two kinds of search are different. The organization is assumed to have a (changing) propensity to search, $S_{s,t}$. This propensity establishes the fraction of apparent organizational resources that are available for search activities at times $t, U_{s,t}$. Thus,

$$\begin{aligned} U_{s,t} &= S_{s,t}(P_{t-1} + R_{t-1} + I_{t-1}) \\ &= S_{s,t}[(1 + a_{t-1})\, T_{*,t-1}]. \end{aligned} \tag{11}$$

The pool of resources available to innovation search and refinement search depends on, but does not equal, $U_{s,t}$. This partial decoupling of the investment budget and the allocation of resources to specific projects has been noted by several authors (Allen, 1970; Reeves, 1958). We assume that the primary source of resources for innovation, $U_{i,t}$, is organizational slack. That is, the model reflects a tendency for organizations to support search for innovation from 'excess' resources and to contract such search when resources are apparently short, and for successful firms to make more radical product and process innovations than unsuccessful firms (Mansfield, 1963). If the organization has been successful in meeting its performance goal in the previous time period, a relatively large pool of organizational resources is potentially available. If the goal has not been reached, the pool of resources potentially available is curtailed. Conversely, resources available for refinement, $U_{r,t}$, are greater after a failure to reach the performance goal than they are after success. Thus, if the performance goal was achieved:

$$U_{i,t} = U_{s,t}, \text{ and} \tag{12}$$

$$U_{r,t} = (U_{s,t})^{1/h_r}, \text{ where } h_r \geqq 1. \tag{13}$$

If the performance goal was not achieved:

$$U_{r,t} = U_{s,t}, \text{ and} \tag{14}$$

$$U_{i,t} = (U_{s,t})^{1/h_i}, \text{ where } h_i \geqq 1. \tag{15}$$

These resources are available for allocation in each time period. We assume that organizations adapt their actual search expenditures to their (possibly confusing) experiences in the following way. First, they observe the apparent relation between changes in search expenditures and changes in performance. Then they adjust their search propensity, an index of intention to allocate resources to search, in a direction that appears to be suggested by a simple consideration of the results. Thus, if search increased and targets subsequently were achieved, then search propensity increases; if search increased and targets subsequently were not achieved, then search propensity decreases; if search decreased and targets subsequently were achieved, then search propensity decreases; if search decreased and targets subsequently were not achieved, then search propensity increases.

The general propensity to devote resources to search of either type, $S_{s,t}$, the search propensity for refinement, $S_{r,t}$, and the search propensity for innovation, $S_{i,t}$, are numbers between 0 and 1. They are determined in the following way:

$$S_{r,t} = Q_{r,t}b_3 + S_{r,t-1}(1 - b_3), \tag{16}$$

$$S_{i,t} = Q_{i,t}b_4 + S_{i,t-1}(1 - b_4), \tag{17}$$

$$S_{s,t} = Q_{s,t}b_5 + S_{s,t-1}(1 - b_5). \tag{18}$$

Each Q is assigned a value of one or zero that reflects previous changes in search and subsequent experience (see above). For example, if refinement search increased in the previous period and the performance target was subsequently achieved, or if refinement search decreased and the target was not achieved, then $Q_{r,t}$ is assigned a value of one. The learning rates, b_3, b_4, b_5, are here treated as constants.

By applying the propensities to the resources available, we can specify the amount of search expenditure in period t. The effect of the general propensity to search $S_{s,t}$, has already been specified in defining $U_{s,t}$ above. Thus,

$$R_t = S_{r,t} U_{r,t}, \tag{19}$$

$$I_t = S_{i,t} U_{i,t}. \tag{20}$$

These expenditures determine, stochastically, the outcomes and subsequent adaptation of the organization to its experience.

Some Results

The model generates a time series of decisions, results, and goals, the details of which depend on a number of initial conditions and parameters, as well as on stochastic variation. Table 9.1 displays one particular time series based on one specific set of parameters.[1] Repeated replication with any particular set of parameters produces a distribution of organizational histories. Although significant variation across replications with identical parameters is a distinctive feature of the model, the history in table 9.1 is typical in the sense that it is not conspicuously distinguishable from many others. In the remainder of this section we identify four general characteristics of the model derived from inspecting such histories.

Sensibility

We speculate that some interesting features of organizational learning result from an interaction between a sensible learning process and a confusing world. The present model exhibits both some properties of sensibility and some limitations imposed on sensibility by ambiguity and uncertainty. An elementary indication of sensibility in the model is the tendency for organizations to improve their performance over time. We observe a pattern of modest improvement with small oscillations for most organizations, and spectacular improvement for some. Figure 9.1 displays a 20-period record of the average performance of the model.

Since it is possible that improvement in performance is due more to properties of the search environment than to the learning process, we explore the sensibility of the process further by comparing learned propensities to invest, refine, and innovate with apparent optima for those propensities. By apparent optima we mean values for the three propensities that would result in maximum return if they were held fixed. The definition of maximum return is, however, ambiguous. In general, if we wish to

1 The initial conditions and parameter values are given in the program listing in the Appendix (lines 1140–570). Unless otherwise noted, these values are used in all results reported here.

Table 9.1 A 20-period sample of output from the model

	Propensities			Expenditures					
Period	*r*	*i*	*s*	*ref*	*inn*	*Outcome*	*Technology*	*Performance*	*Success*
1	0.45	0.45	0.45	7	10	innovate	51	33	failure
2	0.40	0.40	0.50	10	7	innovate	59	41	success
3	0.46	0.36	0.55	11	11	refine	60	39	success
4	0.51	0.42	0.59	13	16	refine	60	33	failure
5	0.46	0.38	0.53	15	9	refine	61	34	failure
6	0.41	0.44	0.58	14	11	refine	63	37	failure
7	0.47	0.40	0.52	15	9	refine	63	35	failure
8	0.42	0.46	0.57	15	11	refine	64	40	success
9	0.38	0.51	0.61	11	21	refine	65	34	failure
10	0.44	0.46	0.55	16	12	refine	65	35	failure
11	0.40	0.51	0.59	15	14	refine	65	37	failure
12	0.46	0.46	0.53	16	12	refine	66	36	failure
13	0.41	0.51	0.58	15	14	refine	67	38	success
14	0.37	0.56	0.62	11	24	refine	67	28	failure
15	0.43	0.51	0.56	15	13	refine	67	39	success
16	0.49	0.45	0.50	12	16	refine	68	37	success
17	0.44	0.51	0.45	9	15	refine	69	41	success
18	0.39	0.46	0.41	8	12	refine	69	50	success
19	0.35	0.41	0.37	7	11	refine	69	49	success
20	0.32	0.37	0.33	5	8	refine	69	55	success

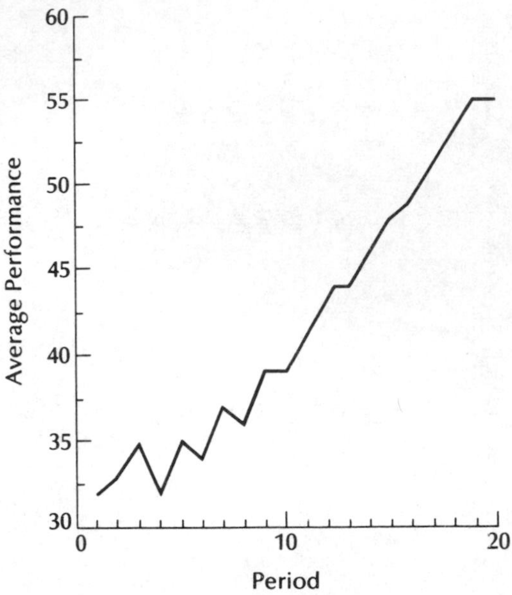

Figure 9.1. Average performance over time, 100 organizations

maximize expected value over the next n periods, the optimal value for the search propensities is either 0 or 1, depending on the value of n. For relatively short time horizons, it is best not to spend any resources on search; for relatively long time horizons it is best to spend as much as possible. Figure 9.2 shows average nth-period performance for various fixed propensities to invest and various time horizons for a particular set of parameters. Other parameters would change the specific results but not the general picture.

The model does not, in general, result in the extreme values for search propensities indicated by the previous analysis. Search propensitites near 1 are quite unusual. Propensities near zero are adopted frequently by organizations with very rapid propensity learning rates, but not by others. There is a tendency for most organizations to learn to set search propensities at a fairly low level, in the range of 0.1 to 0.4. This might be interpreted as an implicit setting of a short planning horizon, but the behavior stems from the learning process rather than any explicit calculation and suggests that the learning environment may not guarantee the development of optimal search propensities when the optimum propensity is 1. At the same time, it should be noted that large search propensities are associated with large variation in performance across runs of the model. The results for the propensity to search are shown in figure 9.3. Thus, if the criterion for maximum performance were to involve considerations of risk, the optimal propensity for large values of n might differ from 1.

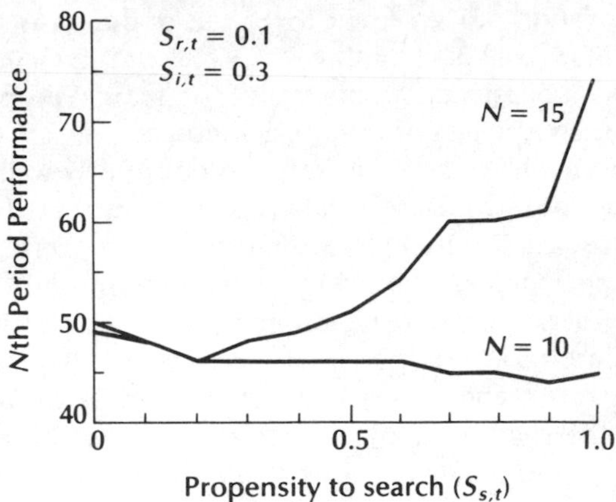

Figure 9.2. *N*th-period average performance as a function of propensity to search, 100 organizations

In order to examine the outcome of the model in a situation having a relatively clear optimum other than 0 or 1, the reward for refinement and innovation search can be set at some fixed number with no variance. Even under these circumstances, determination of the optimum propensities is a non-trivial problem. The mean of the reward from refinement search decays with refinement draws, thereby mitigating the desirability of refinement search; but the efficiency of search declines with each new innovation, so complete reliance on innovation search is not optimal. However, by searching the propensity space in increments of 0.1, we can approximate an optimum. If the mean reward for refinement and the mean

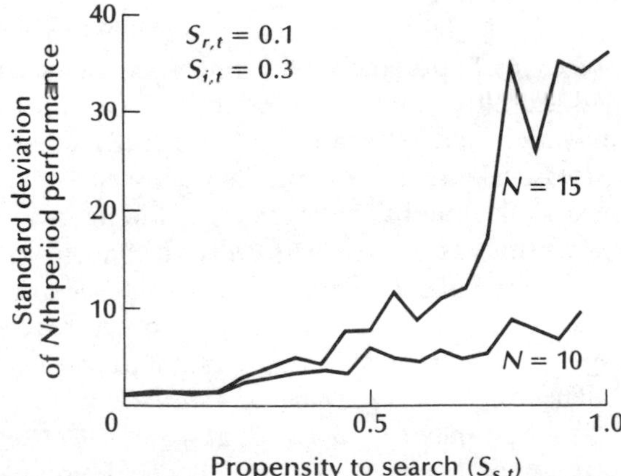

Figure 9.3. Standard deviation of *n*th-period performance as a function of propensity to search, 100 organizations

reward for innovation are set equal to 10, an optimum is found in the neighborhood of $S_{r,t}=0.2$, $S_{i,t}=0.3$, $S_{s,t}=0.3$ and $S_{r,t}=0.3$, $S_{i,t}=0.4$, $S_{s,t}=0.2$. Under modest adaptation rates for search propensities, the model reaches such a neighborhood, on average.

In general, the model learns in a way that does fairly well with strong signals. In situations in which search is clearly unwarranted, it generally learns to reduce search, though ordinarily not to zero. Where the technological opportunities make discovery of an improved technology likely, learning generally leads to higher propensities. Numerous exceptions to such results are observed, however. The process is sensitive to the learning rates involved, and the sensibility of the process is often obscured, particularly in the short run, by the uncertainties of evaluating technologies, by the limited number of draws, and by the fact that expenditure is affected by slack as well as propensities.

Success

The model leads to subjectively successful organizations. Despite the way goals adjust to performance as it improves, thus discounting past levels of performance in assessing current success, most organizations in stable environments are successful in their own terms most of the time. Table 9.2 shows the percentage of the time periods that the model achieves subjective success as a function of environmental uncertainty and exogenous changes in the technology. In cases where there is no uncertainty, and no exogenous change in the technology, goals are achieved about 93 per cent of the time. The precise fraction for any particular run depends, of course, on stochastic variation within the model and as we note below, on learning rates.

The tendency of the model to produce successful organizations under conditions of steady or improving environments has consequences for expenditures and learning. Period to period variations in resources allocated to innovation and refinement are generally due more to the amount of resources available and whether they are seen as slack resources (i.e, whether the organization has been successful in its own terms) than to the search propensities associated with the two. Short-run changes in resource allocation are, that is, less responsive to learning than to organizational success and failure. Thus, they both obscure the significance of adaptive propensities and provide the perturbations of decisions on which learning depends. The magnitude of the slack effect depends on the values of h_r and h_i. When $h_r=h_i=1$, there is no effect of success or failure on allocations. As h_r and h_t increase above 1, subjective feelings of success and failure have an increasing effect on the allocation of expenditures. Total expenditures on search are also affected by the slack

Table 9.2 Per cent successes, 100 organizations, periods 11-20, varying environmental uncertainty (*a*) and exogenous changes in technology (b_2)

Environmental uncertainty	*Exogenous changes in technology*				
	$b_2=0.975$	$b_2=0.990$	$b_2=1.000$	$b_2=1.010$	$b_2=1.025$
$a=0$	23	77	93	99	99
$a=0.05$	35	86	94	97	97
$a=0.10$	35	71	78	83	84
$a=0.15$	36	64	69	70	79
$a=0.20$	38	58	64	67	75
$a=0.25$	40	56	63	65	71
$a=0.50$	47	53	54	57	60

components. Increase in h_r and h_i will, other things being equal, decrease the allocation of resources to search.

The general pattern of success in steady or improving environments means that the model shows, under those conditions, a tendency for organizations to spend relatively more on innovation than refinement, and to become relatively more efficient at it. Conversely, any tendency to failure produces relatively more spending on refinement than innovation, and leads to an organization becoming relatively more efficient at it. Thus, the extent to which the propensity to refine and the propensity to innovate diverge depends in large measure on the relative frequency of successes and failures. An inspection of table 9.2 suggests that organizational differentiation in the propensity to engage in refinement and innovation search will depend, therefore, on the level of environmental uncertainty and the exogenous changes in technology as much as on differences in the efficacy of the two types of search. An exogenously declining technology will, by increasing the frequency of failure, increase relative efficiency in refinement search and result in relatively high propensities to engage in such search. On the other hand, an improving technology will, by increasing the frequency of success, produce refinement propensities that are relatively low. Environmental uncertainty tends to vitiate such effects. That is, high uncertainty reduces the frequency of subjective success when the technology is improving or declining slightly; it reduces the frequency of failure when the technology is declining significantly (i.e., when b_2 is less than 0.98).

Path Dependence

Two common properties of stochastic processes are conspicuous in the model. First, draws from the technological distributions occasionally yield extreme values. For the most part, low extreme values are irrelevant; but high extreme values (major innovations) affect the position of the organization significantly and, in most cases, permanently. Second, the consequence of one (random) step is often to change the probabilities associated with the next step. This is most obvious in the way in which the good fortune of discovering a major innovation not only makes substantial changes in technology, but also in the allocation of resources to search, in aspirations, and in efficiencies at search. These adaptations, in turn, lead to different sequences of events than would have been experienced in the absence of such discoveries. Organizational histories are produced through a combination of chance events and adaptations to those events that, in some cases, considerably amplify the effects of chance.

Path dependence is particularly notable in the case of extreme draws from the distribution of possible technologies, but it is also exhibited by the more prosaic tendency for a subjective success to lead to a subsequent success and a subjective failure to lead to a subsequent failure. The model produces fewer period-to-period changes from success to failure or failure to success than would be expected merely from their relative frequencies. This serial correlation is sensitive to the rate at which an organization adapts its goal to performance, the degree of environmental uncertainty, and the size of exogenous changes in the technology. The basic results are shown in table 9.3, where we record the number of organizations (out of ten) for which period-to-period changes from success to failure, or failure to success, exceeded the number that would have been expected simply from chance and the overall proportions of the two outcomes for that organization. Cases in which the number of changes precisely equaled the expected number are treated as being one-half above and one-half below expectations. If there were no serial correlation in results, the numbers in the table should vary around 5. Over most of the situations examined, the numbers are less than that (positive serial correlation), but high levels of environmental uncertainty in combination with rapid goal adaptation lead to more frequent changes than would be expected (negative serial correlation).

A positive serial correlation of successes and failures accentuates the effects of success and failure on the development of efficiencies in search and the propensities to search. Organizational slack tends to remain high, or low, for several periods, and the organization builds efficiency in one or the other of the types of search. At the same time, a series of successes has the effect (on average) of increasing expenditures on innovations and thus of increasing the propensity to invest in a search for innovations. When there is a shift from failure to success, the level of expenditure on innovation rises, due primarily to the slack condition. Subsequently, the propensity to search for innovation rises as a result of success (which is

Table 9.3 Number of organizations (out of 10) showing more than expected changes from success to failure or failure to success, 20 periods, varying environmental uncertainty (a), exogenous changes (b_2), and goal learning rate (b_1)

	Environmental uncertainty		
	$a=0$	$a=0.05$	$a=0.10$
Exogenous decline ($b_2=0.99$)			
$b_1=0.1$	0	0	2
$=0.3$	0	0	2
$=0.5$	0	0	5
$=0.7$	0	3	8
$=0.9$	0	7	9
No exogenous change ($b_2=1$)			
$b_1=0.1$	0	0	1
$=0.3$	0	0	3
$=0.5$	0	0	6
$=0.7$	0	2	9
$=0.9$	0	5	7.5
Exogenous increase ($b_2=1.005$)			
$b_1=0.1$	0	0	1
$=0.3$	0	0	4
$=0.5$	0	2	4
$=0.7$	0	1	8
$=0.9$	0	5	10

likely because of the serial correlation of successes). The two effects combine to produce a further increase in expenditure, followed by further success, and so on. This result occurs even under conditions in which no actual innovation takes place, and does not depend on the relative desirability of innovation and refinement.

Sensitivity to Learning Rates

As is clear from the earlier discussion of the model's sensibility, one basic decision problem in the model is the following: given an indefinitely long planning horizon, the best search strategy is to set search propensities as high as possible and keep them there. Such a strategy will maximize the long-run potential of the technology and thus maximize performance in the long run. However, the return on that investment is highly chancy, and a discovery may take many time periods. Until a discovery is made, high search expenditures reduce the performance of the organization. As a result, the net advantage (or disadvantage) of high search propensities relative to low search propensities depends on the performance horizon (see figure 9.2).

A possible inference from such observations would be that, given indefinitely long experience, all organizations should learn to have relatively high search propensities, that average search propensity should increase over time and its variance decline, and that the main effect of learning rates would be on the time it took an organization to adopt high search propensities. The speculation is not quite correct. In an indefinitely long period all organizations will, in fact, ultimately make discoveries that put them into new technologies and dramatically improved performance. This result, however, does not depend on learning to have a large propensity to search, but comes simply from the stochastic features of the search assumptions. Each organization has, at each time period, a non-zero probability (however small) of discovering a spectacular technology and embarking on a long string of successes.

The expected length of time that it takes different organizations to make new discoveries depends, however, on variations that are produced in their search propensities by their learning experiences and the adaptation rates for propensities, efficiencies, and goals. Thus, an organization's performance expectations are a function of its learning rates. It is not, in general, true that fast learning is best. Fast learners adapt quickly to correct signals; they also adapt quickly to false signals. If the false signals lead them to take actions that reduce the experience on which they might correct the error, rapid adaptation can lead to persistent mistakes. In particular, fast learners may fairly easily learn to reduce expenditures on search to a low level and thus reduce the probability of technological improvement. Conversely, slow learners are not confused as much by false signals, but neither do they respond as quickly to correct signals. If their slow response leads them to continue erroneous policies, slow adaptation can also lead to persistent mistakes.

Within the present model, long-run performance is, on average, improved by relatively slow, relatively imprecise learning. Search propensities tend to be less than 0.5, and average propensities for different sets of parameters normally vary between about 0.1 and 0.4. In the long run, performance will be highest if an organization can learn to set relatively high search propensities in the face of short-run experience that indicates, most of the time, that expenditures on search are unwarranted, and in a situation in which the average quality of outcomes increases with experience. Quick, precise learning of propensities will do well in the short run, but not in the long run unless there is a lucky early discovery of a new technology or very rapid goal adaptation. Learning is slowed by having a relatively low rate of propensity adaptation. It is made imprecise by having a relatively high rate of goal adaptation (and relatively high environmental uncertainty).

Figure 9.4 shows, for horizons varying from one period to 100 periods, the average cumulative performance as a function of the propensity learning rate, where $b_3 = b_4 = b_5$. Differences in the outcomes produced by values from 0.2 to 0.9 are modest, but if the rate of learning is reduced to 0.1, the effect on performance is substantial. There appear to be two major reasons for such a result. First, organizations that adapt propensities rapidly to experience rather quickly reduce the propensities to relatively low levels. This, in turn, reduces expenditures and reduces the chances of making a major discovery. Second, low expenditures on search reduce the accumulation of efficiency at search, and thus make discoveries even more difficult. A comparable analysis with respect to the rate of goal adaptation shows a quite different picture. As figure 9.5 shows, the goal learning rate has no appreciable effect for planning horizons up to about 30 periods, but after that fast goal learners do systematically better than slow learners. Rapidly adjusting goals make the success experience of the organization problematic, make learning linked to success and failure difficult, and tend to keep an organization from learning the false lesson that search expenditures are undesirable.

The relation between learning rates and performance is complicated not only by the length of time considered but also by interactions among the learning rates. For example, figure 9.6 shows the cumulative average performance for various planning horizons and four different values for the propensity learning rates for the extreme case in which the goal learning rate is 1.0. This is the case in which the organization, in effect, compares performance at period t with performance at period $t-1$ in deciding

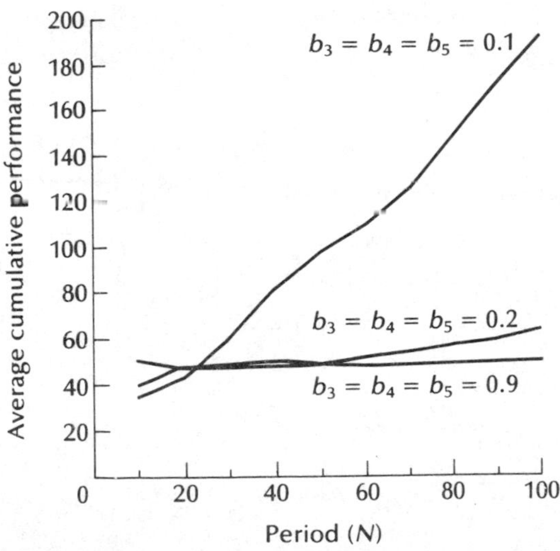

Figure 9.4. Average cumulative performance up to period n, as a function of propensity adaptation rate, 100 organizations

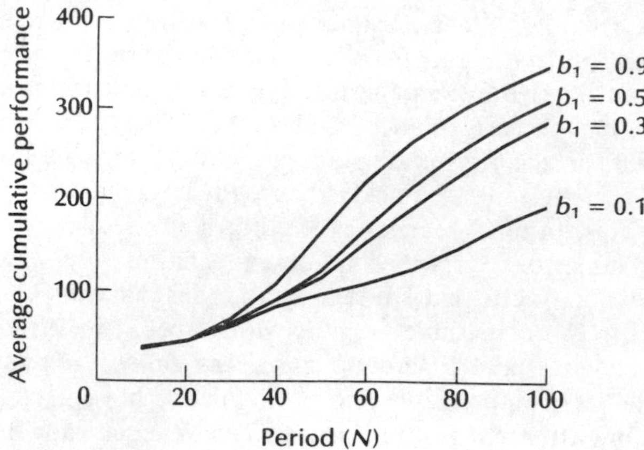

Figure 9.5. Average cumulative performance up to period *n*, as a function of goal adaptation rate, 100 organizations

whether to consider the new performance a success or failure. In this specific situation, the best propensity learning rate is 0.2 with a planning horizon less than 20 periods; it is 0.1 with a planning horizon between 20 and 80 periods; but it is 1.0 with a planning horizon between 80 and 100 periods. The details of these results, as well as the specific numbers involved, are, of course, a function of the other parameters and initial conditions in the model; but they illustrate the possibilities for significant interactions.

Learning rates also affect the likelihood of subjective success. As is clear from the discussion above, subjective success and performance are loosely coupled within the model. Most organizations are successful but

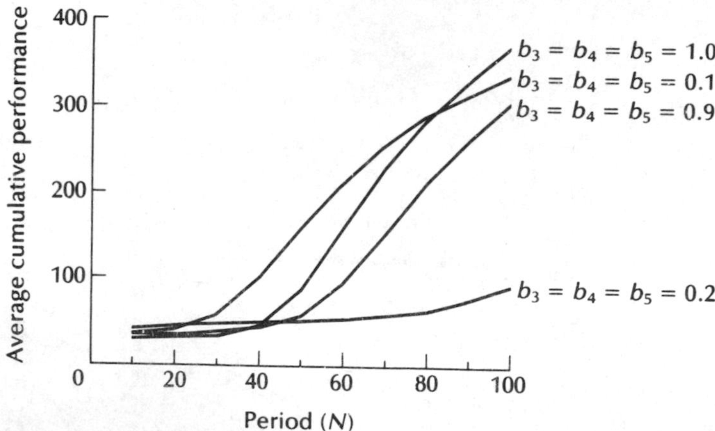

Figure 9.6. Average cumulative performance up to period *n*, as a function of propensity learning rate, with goal learning rate = 1,100 organizations

organizations with the lowest proportion of successes (about 50 per cent) can show some of the highest performances. Indeed, low success rates and rapid alternation in success and failure are ways that false learning is avoided. Figure 9.7 shows the percentage of successes achieved over the first 50 periods for different rates of propensity and goal adaptation. Since the model is one in which organizations normally improve performance under conditions of no exogenous changes in technology, slowly adapting goals make it fairly easy to keep performance above the goal; thus, regardless of the propensity learning rate, success is associated with slowly adjusting goals. On the other hand, the propensity learning rate that is best for subjective success depends on the goal learning rate. For slowly adapting goals, rapid propensity learning leads to maximizing the proportion of periods in which subjective success is achieved; for rapidly adjusting goals, slow propensity learning maximizes the proportion of successes.

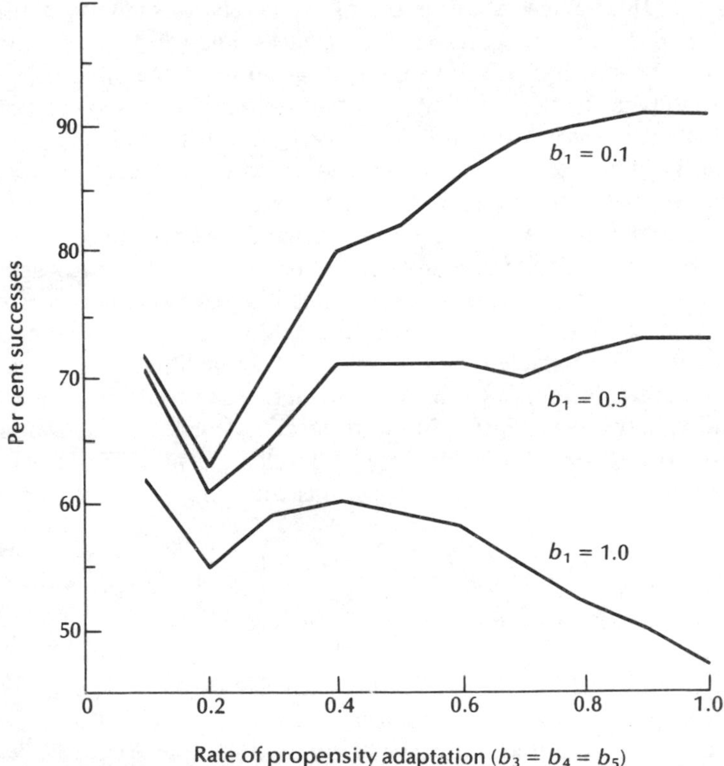

Figure 9.7. Per cent of success over 50 periods as a function of propensity and goal learning rates, 100 organizations.

Summary

The model is obviously incomplete. It does not consider the effects of competition and imitation among competitors; it ignores the problems produced by conflict of interest within a learning organization; it does not introduce any significant elements of cognition into a basically behavioral learning process; it assumes a very simple goal structure and a very simple conception of search. Despite this, or perhaps because of it, the model may tell us something about learning in organizations as a form of behavior and intelligence. The major assumptions we have used are drawn from the organizational literature. The four clusters of results are neither surprising nor inconsistent with what we think we know about organizations. The main claim for the model is that it may provide some link between speculations about organizational learning and observed patterns of organizational adaptation to experience.

By elaborating somewhat our potrayal of the relations among learning search strategies, developing search competences, and forming aspirations for search, the model provides an interpretation for some difficulties we have had in identifying consistent factors associated with organizational change (March, 1981). In particular, it suggests how experiences with exogenously or stochastically driven success or failure can lead to relatively large and relatively permanent changes in organizational behaviors, as well as to substantial differentiation among identical organizations learning in probabilistically identical environments. It shows some of the learning consequences of satisficing, of sharp organizational distinctions between subjective success and failure. It describes a behavioral process that makes successes serially correlated. And it identifies some situations in which sensible learning processes will lead to less than sensible learning, specifically, how the intelligence of rapid learning depends on the planning horizon involved and the ways in which false learning about search strategies or aspirations can lead to actions that tend to compound the error.

Appendix: A Listing of a Basic Program for the Model

```
00100 REM: DIRECTORY OF VARIABLES
00110 REM: A— maximum variation of a random factor that affects
00120 REM:    performance achieved from a technology (0< =a< =1).
00130 REM: B1—the weight given performance in changing goals.
00140 REM: B2—the period-to-period constant change in technology.
00150 REM: B3—controls rate of change of refinement search
```

```
00160 REM:   propensity.
00170 REM: B4—controls rate of change in innovation search
00180 REM:   propensity.
00190 REM: B5—controls rate of change of investment propensity.
00200 REM:
00210 REM:
00220 REM: C1—relates variance in refinement to new technology
00230 REM: C2—reduces variance in refinement draws with experience
00240 REM: C3—relates variance in innovation to new technology
00250 REM: C4—changes mean of refinement with experience
00260 REM: C5—reduces variance in innovation errors with innovation
00270 REM: C6—reduces variance in refinement errors with refinement
00280 REM: C7—changes mean of innovation with experience
00290 REM:
00300 REM:
00310 REM: E(r,t)—efficiency of refinement
00320 REM: E(i,t)—efficiency of innovation
00330 REM:
00340 REM: G(t)—the goal in the current time period.
00350 REM: G(t-1)—the goal in the previous period.
00360 REM:
00370 REM: h(r)—refinement slack investment exponent
00380 REM: h(i)—innovation non-slack investment exponent
00390 REM:
00400 REM: I(t)—innovation investment in the current period.
00410 REM: I(t-1)—innovation investment in the previous period.
00420 REM: I(t-2)—innovation investment in period (t-2).
00430 REM:
00440 REM: K(r,t)—number of refinement draws this period.
00450 REM: K(i,t)—number of innovation draws this period.
00460 REM:
00470 REM: Kr—constant for converting to refinement draws
00480 REM: Ki—constant for converting to innovation draws
00490 REM:
00500 REM: M—the total resources of the firm.
00510 REM:
00520 REM: N—the total number of time periods.
00530 REM: N1—the number of the current time period.
00540 REM:
00550 REM: P(t)—performance in the current time period.
00560 REM: P(t-1)—performance in the previous time period.
00570 REM:
00580 REM: Q. . Q9 the Q-variables are all used to make internal
```

```
00590 REM:    calculations.
00600 REM:
00610 REM: R(t)—refinement investment in the current period.
00620 REM: R(t-1)—refinement investment in the previous period.
00630 REM: R(t-2)—refinement investment in period (t-2)
00640 REM:
00650 REM: S(r,t)—refinement search propensity this period.
00660 REM: S(r,t-1)—refinement search propensity last period.
00670 REM: S(i,t)—innovation search propensity this period.
00680 REM: S(i,t-1)—innovation search propensity last period.
00690 REM: S(s,t)—propensity to invest this period
00700 REM: S(s,t-1)—propensity to invest last period
00710 REM:
00720 REM:
00730 REM: S9  used for calculating only (standard deviation)
00740 REM:
00750 REM: T1  T(*,t)—technology at start of period
00760 REM: T2  b1T(*,t-1)—the current technology
00770 REM: T3  the initial value of the current technology
00780 REM: T4  b1T3(t-1)—unrefined changed value of current
               technology.
00790 REM:
00800 REM: U(t)  U(s,t)—the resources available for investment
00810 REM: U(t-1)  U(s,t-1)—resources available for investment last
               period
00820 REM: U(t-2)  U(s,t-2)—the resources available for investment
               at (t-2)
00830 REM:
00840 REM: V(r,t)—the standard deviation of the distribution
00850 REM:             of refinement opportunities (this period)
00860 REM: V(i,t)—the standard deviation of the distribution
00870 REM:             of innovation opportunities (this period)
00880 REM: Ve(r,t)—standard deviation of refinement estimation error
00890 REM: Ve(i,t)—standard deviation of innovation estimation error
00900 REM:
00910 REM:
00920 REM: w(r)—refinement efficiency exponent
00930 REM: w(i)—innovation efficiency exponent
00940 REM:
00950 REM: X5  current mean of distribution of refinement opportunities
00960 REM: X6  current mean of distribution of innovation opportunities
00970 REM: X7  mean of refinement estimation errors
00980 REM: X8  mean of innovation estimation errors
```

```
00990 REM: X9  used for calculating only (mean)
01000 REM:
01010 REM: Z    used for calculating only (random normal generator)
01020 REM:
01030 !
01040 !
01050 !
01060 REM: ESTABLISHING RANDOM NORMAL NUMBER
           FUNCTION
01070 RANDOMIZE
01080 DEF FNN(X9,S9)=X9+SGR(-2*LOG(RND))*COS
           (RND*6.28)*S9
01090 !
01100 !
01110 GOTO 3470 !MAIN PROGRAM LOOP
01120 !
01130 !
01140 REM: SETTING INITIAL VALUES
01150 r=0\i=1\s=2\t=3 !setting values for indexes
01160 A=05
01170 B1=.1
01180 B2=1
01190 B3=1
01200 B4=1
01210 B5=1
01220 C1=.01
01230 C2=.98
01240 C3=.0135
01250 C4=.9
01260 C5=.98
01270 C6=.98
01280 C7=.9
01290 E(r,t)=0
01300 E(i,t)=0
01310 Q(t)=40
01320 h(r)=1.1
01330 h(i)=1.1
01340 I(t)=5
01350 I(t-1)=5
01360 K(r,t)=3
01370 K(i,t)=3
01380 kr=.2
01390 ki=.2
```

```
01400 N=20
01410 P(t)=40
01420 R(t)=5
01430 R(t-1)=5
01440 S(r,t)=.5
01450 S(i,t)=.5
01460 S(s,t)=.5
01470 T1=50
01480 Ve(r,t)=.5
01490 Ve(i,t)=.75
01500 w(r)=3.5
01510 w(i)=3.5
01520 X5=0
01530 X6=0
01540 X7=0
01550 X8=0
01560 U(t)=50
01570 U(t-1)=50
01580 REM: INITIAL VALUES (NEW TECHNOLOGY)
01590 T3=T1
01600 V(r,t)=c1*T3
01610 V(i,t)=c3*T3
01620 RETURN
01630 !
01640 !
01650 REM: UPDATING VALUES
01660 G(t-1)=G(t)
01670 I(t-2)=I(t-1)
01680 I(t-1)=I(t)
01690 P(t-1)=P(t)
01700 R(t-2)=R(t-1)
01710 R(t-1)=R(t)
01720 S(r,t-1)=S(r,t)
01730 S(i,t-1)=S(i,t)
01740 S(s,t-1)=S(s,t)
01750 T2=T1*B2
01760 T4=T3*B2
01770 U(t-1)=U(t)
01780 U(t-1)=U(t)
01790 !
01800 !
01810 !
01820 REM: DETERMINING SEARCH PROPENSITIES
```

```
01830 G=0
01840 IF G(t-1)>P(t-1) THEN G=1
01850   G3=0
01860   IF R(t-1)>R(t-2) THEN G3=1
01870     G4=0
01880     IF I(t-1)>I(t-2) THEN G4=1
01890 G1=1
01900 IF G=G3 THEN G1=0
01910   G2=1
01920   IF G=G4 THEN G2=0
01930 G5=0
01940 IF U(t-1)>U(t-2) THEN G5=1
01950   G6=1
01960   G=G5 THEN G6=0
01970 S(r,t)=(G1*B3)+(S(r,t-1)*(1-B3))
01980 S(i,t)=(G2*B4)+(S(i,t-1)*(1-B4))
01990 S(s,t)=(G6*B5)+((1-B5)*S(s,t-1))
02000 !
02010 !
02020 REM: DETERMINING SEARCH INVESTMENTS
02030 M=P(t-1)+I(t-1)+R(t-1)
02040 U(t)=S(s,t)*M
02050 IF G=1 THEN GOTO 2090
02060 R(t)=S(r,t)*(U(t)∧(1/h(r)))
02070 I(t)=S(i,t)*U(t)
02080 GOTO 2130
02090 R(t)=S(r,t)*U(t)
02100 I(t)=S(i,t)*(U∧(1/h(i)))
02110 !
02120 !
02130 REM: COMPUTING SEARCH EFFICIENCIES
02140 E(r,t)=E(r,t)+K(r,t)
02150 E(i,t)=E(i,t)+K(i,t)
02160   IF E(r,t)=0 THEN G1=0
02170   G1=E(r,t)∧(1/w(r))
02180   IF E(i,t)=0 THEN G2=0
02190   G2=E(i,t)∧(1/w(i))
02200 !
02210 !
02220 REM: FIXING SAMPLE SIZES
02230 K(r,t)=INT(Kr*R(t)*G1)
02240 K(i,t)=INT(Ki*I(t)*G2)
02250 !
```

```
02260 !
02270 REM: SEARCHING FOR THE BEST REFINEMENT
02280 G1=T2
02290 G2=T2
02300 IF K(r,t)<1 THEN 2580
02310 G=0
02320 G5=-100000000000
02330 V(r,t)=c2*V(r,t)
02340 X5=c4*X5
02350 REM: FIRST, DRAW A REFINEMENT
02360 X9=X5
02370 S9=V(r,t)
02380 G7=FNN(X9,S9)
02390 REM: SECOND, ADD THE ESTIMATION ERROR
02400 X9=X7
02410 S9=Ve(r,t)
02420 G8=FNN(X9,S9)
02430 REM: THIRD, COMPARE WITH OTHERS IN THIS SAMPLE
02440 G9=T2+G7+G8
02450 IF G9< =G5 THEN GOTO 2480
02460 G5=G9
02470 G2=T2+G7
02480 G=G+1
02490 IF G=K(r,t) THEN GOTO 2520
02500 GOTO 2360
02510 REM: FOURTH, RECORD THE BEST REFINEMENT FOUND
02520 IF G5>T2 THEN GOTO 2540
02530 GOTO 2570
02540 G1=G5
02550 !
02560 !
02570 REM: SEARCHING FOR THE BEST INNOVATION
02580 G3=T2
02590 G4=T2
02600 IF K(i,t)<1 THEN GOTO 2880
02610 G=0
02620 G6=10000000000
02630 X6=c7*X6
02640 REM: FIRST, DRAW AN INNOVATION
02650 X9=X6
02660 S9=V(i,t)
02670 G7=EXP(FNN(X9,S9))-EXP(X9+·5*(S9∧2))
02680 REM: SECOND, ADD THE ESTIMATION ERROR
```

```
02690 X9=X8
02700 S9=Ve(i,t)
02710 G8=FNN(X9,S9)
02720 REM: THIRD, COMPARE WITH OTHERS IN THIS SAMPLE
02730 G9=T4+G7+G8
02740 IF G9<=G6 THEN GOTO 2770
02750 G6=G9
02760 G4=T4+G7
02770 G=G+1
02780 IF G=K(i,t) THEN GOTO 2810
02790 GOTO 2650
02800 REM: FOURTH, RECORD THE BEST INNOVATION
            FOUND
02810 IF G6>T2 THEN GOTO 2830
02820 GOTO 2860
02830 G3=G6
02840 !
02850 !
02860 REM: ESTABLISHING THE NEW TECHNOLOGY
02870 CH$="NONE"
02880 IF G3>G1 THEN GOTO 2960
02890  IF G1>T2 THEN GOTO 2920
02900      T1=T2
02910    GOTO 3130
02920     T1=G2
02930     Ve(r,t)=c6*Ve(r,t)
02940     CH$="REFINEMENT"
02950  GOTO 3130
02960 IF G3>T2 THEN GOTO 2990
02970 T1=T2
02980 GOTO 3130
02990  T1=G4
03000  T3=T1
03010 IF G4<T2 THEN GOTO 3050
03020 E(r,t)=E(r,t)*(T2/G4)
03030 E(i,t)=E(i,t)*(T2/G4)
03040 GOTO 3070
03050  E(r,t)=E(r,t)*(G4/T2)
03060  E(i,t)=E(i,t)*(G4/T2)
03070 V(r,t)=c1*T3
03080 V(i,t)=c3*T3
03090 Ve(i,t)=c5*Ve(i,t)
03100 CH$="INNOVATION"
```

```
03110 !
03120 !
03130 REM: CALCULATING PERFORMANCE AND CHANGING
          GOALS
03140 G=RND
03150 G1=RND
03160 IF G1<.5 THEN G=G*(-1)
03170 G=G*A
03180 REM: FIRST, THE PERFORMANCE
03190 P(t)=((1+G)*T1)-R(t)-1(t)
03200 REM: SECOND, THE GOALS
03210 G(t)=((1-B1)*G(t-1))+(B1*P(t-1))
03220 SF$="SUCCESS"
03230 IF G(t)>P(t) THEN SF$="FAILURE"
03240 RETURN
03250 !
03260 !
03270 REM: PRINTING THE RESULTS
03280 !
03290 IF N1> THEN GOTO 3320
03300 PRINT
03310 PRINT "TIME", " ", "REFINE", "INNOVATE", "INVEST",
          "TECH", "PERFORMANCE"
03320 PRINT
03330 PRINT N1.
03340 IF CH$="NONE" THEN GOTO 3370
03350 PRINT CH$, INT(T1)
03360 GOTO 3380
03370 PRINT " "
03380 PRINT " ", "PROPENSITY", INT(S(r,t)*100)/100, INT(S(i,t)*
          100)/100,
03390 PRINT INT(S(s,t)*100)(100,INT(T1),INT(P(t))
03400 PRINT " ", "INVESTMENT", INT(R(t)),INT(I(t))," "," ",SF$
03410 PRINT " ", "DRAWS", K(r,t),K(i,t)
03420 PRINT
03430 RETURN
03440 !
93459 !
03460 !
03470 REM: MAIN PROGRAM LOOP
03480 GOSUB 1140 !INITIAL VALUES
03490 FOR N1=1 TO N
03500 GOSUB 1650 !MAIN PROGRAM
```

```
03510 GOSUB 3270 !PRINT RESULTS
03520 NEXT N1
03530 !
03540 !
03550 !
03560 !
03570 END
```

References

Alchian, Armen (1959) Cost and output. In Moses Abramovitz et al. (eds), *The Allocation of Economic Resources: Essays in Honor of B. F. Haley*. CA: Stanford University Press, Stanford.

Allen, J. M. (1970) A survey into the R&D evaluation and control procedures currently used in industry. *Journal of Industrial Economics*, 18, 16–81.

Allison, Graham T. (1971) Essence of Decision. MA: Little Brown, Boston.

Cohen, Michael, and James G. March (1974) *Leadership and Ambiguity: The American College President*. New York: McGraw-Hill.

Cyert, Richard M., and James G. March (1963). *A Behavioral Theory of the Firm*. Englewood Cliffs, NJ: Prentice Hall.

Hannan, Michael, and John Freeman (1977) The population ecology of organizations. *American Journal of Sociology*, 82, 929–61.

Kay, Neil M. (1979) *The Innovating Firm: A Behavioral Theory of Corporate R&D*. New York: St Martin's.

Keen, Peter G. W. (1977) The evolving concept of optimality. *TIMS Studies in the Management Sciences*, 6, 31–57.

Knight, Kenneth E. (1967) A descriptive model of the intra-firm innovative process. *The Journal of Business*, 40, 478–96.

Kohn, Meir G., and Steven Shavell (1974) Optimal adaptive search. *Journal of Economic Theory*, 9(2), 93–124.

Lave, Charles A., and James G. March (1975) *An Introduction to Models in the Social Sciences*. New York: Harper and Row.

Lindblom, Charles E. (1959) The science of muddling through. *Public Administration Review*, 19, 79–88.

Mansfield, Edwin (1963) Size of firm, market structure, and innovation. *Journal of Political Economy*, 71, 556–76.

March, James G. (1981) Footnotes to organizational change. *Administrative Science Quarterly*, 26, 563–77.

March, James G., and Johan P. Olsen (1976) *Ambiguity and Choice in Organizations*. Bergen: University Press of Norway.

March, James G., and Herbert A. Simon (1958) *Organizations*. New York: Wiley.

Nelson, Richard R., and Sidney G. Winter (1978) Forces generating and limiting concentration under Schumpeterian competition. *Bell Journal of Economics*, 9, 524–48.

Preston, L. D., and E. C. Keachie (1964) Cost functions and progress functions: an integration. *American Economic Review*, 54, 100–08.

Radner, Roy (1975) A behavioral model of cost reduction. *Bell Journal of Economics*, 6, 196–215.

Reeves, E. D. (1958) Development of the research budget. *Research Management*, 1, 133–42.

Simon Herbert A. (1957) *Models of Man*. New York: Wiley.

Steinbruner, John D. (1974) *The Cybernetic Theory of Decision: New Dimensions of Political Analysis*. Princeton, NJ: Princeton University Press.

Winter, Sidney G. (1971) Satisficing, selection and the innovating remnant. *Quarterly Journal of Economics*, 85, 237–61.

Winter, Sidney G. (1975) Optimization and evolution in the theory of the firm. In Richard H. Day and Theodore Groves (eds), *Adaptive Economic Models*. New York: Academic Press.

10

Learning from Experience in Organizations

Scott R. Herriott, Daniel Levinthal, and James G. March

Abstract

This paper sketches a class of difference equation models for examining incremental experiential learning by economic actors, particularly organizations. The models reflect features of adaptive behavior drawn from observations of decision-making in organizations. They picture choice as stemming from decision-rules that adjust cumulatively on the basis of trial-by-trial monitoring of the success or failure associated with past adjustments. Such models are in a broad tradition that includes previous work not only in organizational learning and adaptive economics, but also hill-climbing optimization techniques, control theory, and modeling of elementary learning by humans and other animals. Some modest complexities associated with learning are introduced, particularly ways in which learning occurs along several interacting dimensions and within an ecology of learning.

Models of Experiential Learning

We assume a simple choice situation in which a fixed budget is allocated among several alternative, independent activities. Each of the activities provides a return that is proportional to the allocation and the competence (efficiency) of the system at that activity. In the absence of competition, total performance is the potential (or capacity) of each activity weighted by the allocation to that activity and the competence at it, summed over

---

This paper first appeared in the *American Economic Review*, 75 (1985) pp. 298–302. The research has been supported by grants from the Spencer Foundation, the Mellon Foundation, the Stanford Graduate School of Business, and the Hoover Institution.

the activities. If $A_{i,t}$ is the fraction of the budget allocated to activity i at time t, $k_{i,t}(0<k_{i,t}<1)$ is the competence at activity i at time t, and $C_{i,t}$ is the potential return from activity i at time t, then, P_t, the performance at time t, is

$$P_t = \sum_i k_{i,t} A_{i,t} C_{i,t}. \tag{1}$$

Within this choice situation, simple trial-by-trial learning will commonly lead an actor to increase the allocation to activities for which $k_{i,t}C_{i,t}$ is relatively large, decrease it for those for which it is relatively small.

There are two sets of complications in discovering sensible allocations in this way. The first is that learning occurs along several simultaneous dimensions. Competences and goals adapt at the same time as allocations, and each affects the other. The second complication is that any one learner exists in an ecology of other learners whose actions, goals, and competences affect each other.

Dimensions of Learning

Adaptive allocations. We assume that decision-making consists in choosing an allocation $(A_{1,t}, A_{2,t}, \ldots, A_{n,t})$ to available alternatives that exhausts the budget. That choice is made by adjusting the previous allocation. The adjustment is made in two steps. At the first step, a proposed allocation to each activity, $A^*_{i,t}$, is determined:

$$A^*_{i,t} = A_{i,t-1} + b_1(L_{i,t} - A_{i,t-1}). \tag{2}$$

The learning limit $L_{i,t}$, for a proposed allocation to activity i at time t, assumes values of 0 or 1 (alternatively 0 and the total budget) with probability $1 - U_{i,t}$ and $U_{i,t}$. Thus, $U_{i,t}$ is the probability of proposing an increase in the fraction of the budget allocated to alternative i. The value of $U_{i,t}$ changes in response to experience, depending on the adjustment in allocation made on the previous trial and the outcome on that trial (P_{t-1}) relative to some goal (G_{t-1}). Specifically,

$$U_{i,t} = U_{i,t-1} + b_2(1 - U_{i,t-1}) \tag{3}$$

if $\quad A_{i,t-1} > A_{i,t-2};\ P_{t-1} > G_{t-1}$

or if $\quad A_{i,t-1} < A_{i,t-2};\ P_{t-1} < G_{t-1};$

$$= U_{i,t-1} - b_2 U_{i,t-1}$$

if $\quad A_{i,t-1} > A_{i,t-2};\ P_{t-1} < G_{t-1}$

or if $\quad A_{i,t-1} < A_{i,t-2};\ P_{t-1} > G_{t-1}.$

Equation (3) defines a variation on a standard stochastic learning model. Where $b_2 = 1$, the direction of the adaptations is determined without stochastic variation. The two learning parameters, b_1 and b_2, affect the rate at which adjustments in allocations are made. The adjustment of $A^*_{i,t-1}$ and $U_{i,t-1}$ from one trial to the next are proportional to the difference between the current values and the upper or lower limits of those variables. They can also be made proportional to the absolute difference between P_{t-1} and G_{t-1}, more specifically to $[|G_{t-1} - P_{t-1}|]/[G_{t-1} + P_{t-1}]$. In such a case, the adaptations are more finely tuned to the magnitude of success or failure. Another form of fine-tuning would disaggregate performance and goal, associating each with a specific activity rather than to their sum. Moving from $A^*_{i,t}$ to $A_{i,t}$ involves satisfying the constraint that the sum of allocation increases in individual activities must equal the sum of allocation decreases while maintaining the relative sizes of individual changes projected by $A^*_{i,t}$.

Adaptive competence. Models of adaptive learning (for example, binary choice learning, two-armed bandits) commonly assume that the outcome from a current choice is independent of the history of choices. In many situations of economic allocation, however, it seems more reasonable to assume that competence at an activity decreases with the passage of time and increases with allocation to the activity. Thus,

$$k_{i,t} = (1 - b_3)k_{i,t-1} + A_{i,t-1}b_4[1 - (1 - b_3)k_{i,t-1}]. \quad (4)$$

The coefficients of competence decay (b_3) and learning (b_4) control the rate at which efficiency at an activity responds to disuse and experience. Equation (4) is a variant of a standard learning-by-doing model.

Adaptive goals. We assume that performance aspirations adapt to past performance so that the goal in any time period is a mix between the previous goal and the previous performance.

$$G_t = (1 - b_5)G_{t-1} + b_5 P_{t-1}. \quad (5)$$

The result is to make the goal an exponentially weighted moving average of performance, with b_5 determining the relative weight attached to relatively recent performance results. If $b_5 = 1$, then $G_t = P_{t-1}$; and the adaptation responds simply to changes in performance. If $b_2 = 1 = b_5$, the model becomes a standard hill-climbing procedure.

The Ecology of Learning

Diffusion of Experience. In a social environment, learning from direct experience is supplemented by the diffusion of experience, that is, by copying others. From a rational perspective, copying can be seen as a way of increasing (on average) the amount of experience from which an individual draws while decreasing (on average) the linkage between that individual's situation and the experience base of action. From a behavioral perspective, it can be seen as a standard way by which adaptive systems deal with uncertainty and ambiguity.

If we let $A^*_{j,i,t}$ be the proposed allocation of individual j to activity i at time t, a natural extension of (2) yields

$$A^*_{j,i,t} = (1-d_1) \times [A_{j,i,t-1} + b_1(L_{i,t} - A_{j,i,t-1})] + d_1 \sum_{h\neq j} A_{h,i,t-1}/(n-1). \tag{6}$$

That is, allocations adapt to the mean allocation made by other actors, as well as to direct experience.

If we let $k_{j,i,t}$ be the competence of individual j at activity i at time t, a natural extension of (4) yields

$$k_{j,i,t} = (1-d_2)\{(1-b_3)k_{j,i,t-1} + A_{j,i,t-1}b_4[1-(1-b_3)k_{j,i,t-1}]\} + d_2 \max_h k_{h,i,t-1}. \tag{7}$$

That is, competences adapt to the highest level of competence exhibited within the population of actors.

If $G_{j,t}$ is the goal of individual j at time t, then a natural extension of (5) yields

$$G_{j,t} = (1-b_4)G_{j,t-1} + \mathrm{b}_4\left\{\left[d_3 \sum_{h\neq j} P_{h,i-1}/(n-1)\right] + [(1-d_3)P_{j,t-1}]\right\}. \tag{8}$$

That is, an actor's goals adapt to the mean performance of other actors, as well as to her own performance. The adaptation coefficients (d_1,d_2,d_3)

determine the rate at which allocations, competences, and goals spread from one learner to another.

Interdependence of experience. Where experience is interdependent, the performance realized by any one actor depends not only on that actor's allocations and competences, but also on the actions of others. The interdependencies may involve 'mating', in which actor's rewards for a particular activity are augmented by having other actors engaged in the same activity. They may involve competition, in which each actor's rewards for a particular activity are decreased by having other actors engaged in the same activity. They may involve 'hunting', in which the rewards of some actors are increased by the presence of other actors engaged in the same activity who, themselves, have their rewards decreased by the joint presence. In the present paper, we consider only the competitive case. If more than one actor allocates effort to a particular activity, the allocation and competence of each reduces the return for the others. Specifically, in any time period where $\Sigma_j k_{j,i,t} A_{j,i,t} > 1$, the return from activity i for actor j is

$$P_{j,i,t} = \frac{(k_{j,i,t} A_{j,i,t})^w}{\sum_{h \neq j} (k_{h,i,t} A_{h,i,t})^w} C_{i,t}. \tag{9}$$

The power w determines the way in which an overexploited activity is shared among competitors.

Organizational subunits. Many economic actors are organizations – firms, armies, public bureaucracies, schools, unions. Organizations have subunits whose actions affect outcomes and whose rewards are linked to local results, as well as to overall performance. We have modeled organizations consisting in subunits, similarly allocating among activities, while adapting allocation competences, and goals over time. Since allocations within subunits affect not only the performance of subunits but also the performance of the organization as a whole, organizational learning is heavily interactive. The details are omitted here. They parallel the earlier characterizations of learning but include some additional features to link the learning and performance of subunits with the overall organization.

Some Results

We report here some fragmentary results based on analysis of the determinate ($b_2 = 1$) case involving only two alternative activities with unchanging (but different) potentials. We address ourselves to four general questions relevant to assessing trial-by-trial learning as a form of intelligence:

1 To what extent does incremental learning of this type produce, after a suitably long period of time, sensible adaptations to environmental possibilities?
2 To what extent are long-run outcomes independent of initial allocations, competences, and goals?
3 To what extent is the long-run performance of learners improved by increasing the learning parameters?
4 To what extent is the long-run performance of learners improved by tuning the adjustment of allocations more finely to the magnitude of success or failure?

The Isolated Learner

If adjustment of allocations over time is roughly tuned (i.e., if b_1 is fixed), the isolated learner specializes. That is, an equilibrium is reached at which all resources are devoted to one alternative or the other, and where $k_i = b_4 A_i / (b_3 + b_4 A_i - b_3 b_4 A_i)$. Specialization is also characteristic of the stochastic version of the model (i.e., $b_2 < 1$). Specialization may not involve the superior alternative, however. The equilibrium outcome depends not only on the learning parameters but also on the initial allocation, competence, and goal. In general, as the initial conditions become more favorable to the inferior alternative, the set of learning values that result in specialization at the inferior value expands.

Given initial conditions in which competence in and allocation to an inferior alternative are high, specialization in that activity is likely. It can be avoided by slow adjustment of allocations and rapid adjustment of goals, or by learners whose absolute level of performance declines over time (thus producing failures). With fixed capacities for the two alternatives, the latter result requires that the competence decay rate (b_3) be high relative to the competence learning rate (b_4), that is, slow learning and fast forgetting.

In the 'finely tuned' case, where the adjustment of allocations is made proportional to the absolute disparity between performance and goal, the model also reaches a stable mixture of allocations, competences, goal, and performance; but the allocation does not, in general, reach 1 or 0. Rather, it locates an equilibrium combination at some interior, suboptimal point. Thus, fine-tuning yields higher performance in situations in which rough-tuning leads to specialization in the inferior alternative, but not in those cases where rough tuning leads to specialization in the superior alternative.

Diffusion of Experience

The effects of diffusion of experience among parallel (but non-interacting) learners depends on characteristics of the population of learners. The discussion here is limited to the case of a population heterogeneous with respect to the values of b_1 and b_5, but homogeneous with respect to the other learning rates (i.e., $b_2 = 1, b_3 = 0.1, b_4 = 0.5$). Diffusion of allocations decreases both the mean and the variance of performance within the population (relative to isolated learners), normally driving all actors to a common set of allocations, competences, and goals. Diffusion of competence, goals, or both normally increases average performance. In addition, the diffusion of competence changes the region of the parameter space that leads to specialization in the superior alternative, giving an advantage in that respect to learners who adjust allocations relatively quickly and adjust goals relatively slowly.

Goal diffusion, by making goals more homogeneous among learners than is performance, tends to divide a population of non-competing learners into one group with a history of subjective successes, another with a history of subjective failures. Since persistent success produces specialization and persistent failure produces non-specialization, goal diffusion partitions the population into three groups of actors. The first group allocates all its resources to the inferior alternative; the second allocates all its resources to the superior alternative; the allocation by the third group oscillates around an equal division between the two. The proportion in each group depends on the initial conditions and learning parameters. It also depends on whether the allocation adjustments are finely or roughly tuned, with fine-tuning tending to produce a large number of learners who fail consistently and thus divide their allocations equally among the alternatives.

Interdependence of Experience

The effects of competition depend on the number of competitors and the parameter w that controls the way in which the resources in an overexploited activity are divided among competitors, as well as the characteristics of the population of competitors. With small numbers of competitors ($n = 2, n = 3$), specialization is common. In the case of two competitors, this means each competitor specializes in a different activity. Under many, but not all, conditions, the slower learner becomes the specialist in the superior alternative, thus has higher performance. In the case of three competitors, a quite typical result is that one or two of the three specialize, while the other does not. Faster learners tend to become specialists, but whether that results in their also having higher performance depends on the alternative in which they specialize and the pattern of allocations by the others.

With larger numbers, both the analysis and the story become more complicated. In general, if $w > 1$, rapid adjustment of allocations leads to better performance than slow adjustment; if $w < 1$, the converse is true. If the adjustment of allocations is made proportional to the magnitude of success or failure (the fine-tuning option), the system reaches an apparent equilibrium which depends on the initial allocations and competences as well as the learning rates. In the fine-tuning case, moderate rates of goal adaptation often seem advantageous, but not always. There are also numerous situations with relatively idiosyncratic outcomes. In otherwise apparently smooth response surfaces mapping variations of performance onto variations in learning rates, substantial spikes appear.

Competition with Diffusion

If diffusion and competition are both present, we obtain many of the same basic results observed in the case of either alone. Goal diffusion, however, confounds the general observation that rapid, rough-tuned adjustment of allocations gives an advantage where $w > 1$. When goals diffuse, competitors who are persistently successful tend to become specialists in one activity or the other. Fast learners tend to specialize, but the fastest learners often specialize in the inferior alternative, leaving the superior alternative to the their somewhat slower cousins. In addition, variation in performance within the population of competitors tends to be decreased by allocation diffusion, but increased by competence or goal diffusion.

Organizational Subunits

Over a fair range of situations, the consequence of introducing learning subunits is to make both the intelligence of learning through trial-by-trial adaptation and its analysis somewhat problematic. The interactions make it less likely that organizations will specialize in inferior activities, but also less likely that they will specialize in superior activities. In this respect, the existence of subunits produces effects not unlike the presence of random error in performance. Although it seems likely that there are regular cycles in the resulting patterns of adaptations, we have not as yet discovered them.

Discussion

To provide a base for considering experiential learning as a form of adaptive intelligence, we have modeled a collection of behavioral observations about the forms of learning common in organizations. Since there is ample experimental and observational evidence for believing that simple experiential learning can be a powerful procedure for improving human performance and since the informational, computational, and coordinative requirements of adaptive intelligence seems to be closer to the capabilities of individual and organizational decision-makers than are the demands of anticipatory intelligence, we explore the conditions for sensibility of this kind of incremental adaptation.

Although analysis of the models is very incomplete and much of the structure remains unexplored, we can begin to answer the four questions with which the present discussion began.

1 Learning of the sort we have described leads reliably to optimal choices in some situations, but does not do so in others.
2 Allocations at equilibrium are not determined uniquely by activity potentials, but are extensively dependent on the rates at which adaptations take place and on initial allocations and competences.
3 Although fast learners often do better than slow learners, there are many plausible situations in which slow learners do better than fast learners.
4 Although fine-tuned adjustment of allocations facilitates locating an equilibrium, the equilibria achieved are not reliably better than the long-term results of a rougher-tuned adjustment, in fact, are often worse.

11

Decision-Making and Postdecision Surprises

J. Richard Harrison and James G. March

Abstract

Most ideas of intelligent choice assume that decision-making involves estimating the probable future values of currently available alternatives and choosing the best of them. Sometimes chosen alternatives turn out to be better than anticipated; sometimes they turn out to be worse. The difference between the predecision estimated value of a chosen alternative and its postdecision value, determined after some of its consequences have been experienced, can be defined as postdecision surprise. This paper examines a systematic bias in the distribution of postdecision surprises attributable to the structure of intelligent choice itself. It is shown that unbiased, random errors in estimation result in a structural tendency toward postdecision disappointment, which will be most characteristic of decision situations in which variation among the true values of alternatives is relatively small, the ambiguity or uncertainty in evaluation is relatively high, and the number of alternatives considered is relatively large. The decision dilemma is clear. Choosing apparently better alternatives will, on average, produce higher returns; however, in the absence of behavioral adjustments, higher expected benefits will be associated with greater expected disappointments. The effects are illustrated with results computed for the special case of normally distributed values and errors. Some implications are suggested for understanding postdecision surprise and the development of social norms of intelligent choice in individuals and organizations.

This paper was first published in *Administrative Science Quarterly*, 29, 1984, 26–42. The authors' research has been supported by grants from the Spencer Foundation, the Stanford Graduate School of Business, and the Hoover Institution. They are grateful for comments by Gerhard Arminger, Terry Connolly, Daniel Levinthal, John Meyer, Stephen Peters, and Allyn Romanow.

Postdecision Surprises

It is a canon of rationality that intelligent choices are based on beliefs about their consequences for personal or collective values. Although it is clear that actual human behavior frequently follows other kinds of logics with their own claims to intelligence (March, 1978), decisions made by individuals, organizations, and societies often are guided by an explicit calculation of the benefits and costs anticipated from alternative actions. These calculations reflect two kinds of guesses about the future, conditional on current action. The first guess is an estimate of probable future states of the world; the second is an estimate of probable future values, or tastes. Conventional decision procedures have a decision-maker combine the two guesses into estimates of the expected values of available alternatives and select the alternative with the highest expected value.

After a decision is made and its consequences experienced, additional information is available. This information normally clarifies the outcomes and values of the alternative that was selected; and it is, at least in principle, possible to examine the relation between expectations and realizations. We can ask whether forecasts of the net benefits to be achieved from a chosen alternative are unbiased estimates of those benefits; or whether there are features of pre- and postdecision processes that lead to systematic bias in the distribution of postdecision surprises, that is, realizations minus expectations.

Empirical studies of predecision expectations and postdecision evaluations in individuals and organizations are well known in the literature; but there is another, possibly prior, kind of question that can be raised about the relationship between intelligent choice and the distribution of surprises. We may be interested in whether there are structural features of decision-making that affect postdecision surprise. By structural features of decision-making, we mean consequences of the process that are implicit in the decision model itself, rather than a result of behavioral applications of the model. These structural characteristics are particularly important for understanding the inherent properties of intelligence, as it is reflected in calculated choice, and can be viewed both as defining a base-line distribution of surprises against which to compare the behavioral results and as a factor in the long-run adaptation of decision-making norms. In this paper we examine one such structural feature of intelligent choice, the way in which unbiased errors in making estimates about available alternatives produce biased distributions of postdecision surprises.

Calculated Choice with Unbiased Estimates

Consider standard problems of choice such as the following:

1 *The adoption of a new technology*: we evaluate alternative technologies and install the one we estimate to have the best ratio of efficiency to cost.
2 *The selection of a new manager*: we evaluate candidates for a job and choose the one whom we estimate to have the greatest ability.
3 *The passage of new legislation*: we evaluate alternative legislative programs in terms of their political consequences and support the one that seems to offer the greatest improvement in prospects for our reelection. Innumerable similar choices (e.g., choices of marital partners, occupations, products, investments, and foreign policies) are made by individuals, groups, and societies.

Such decisions can be viewed in the following general way: There is a pool of possible alternatives. These alternatives differ with respect to their values. These values are not known with certainty, but can be estimated. In order to make a choice, decision-makers evaluate some alternatives drawn from the pool and choose the alternative that they think will be best.

The process is conventional and general. It presumes a general process of choice, not a specific decision-rule. Thus, it includes the case in which decision-makers select the best option among a predetermined number of alternatives drawn from the pool, or one in which alternatives are considered sequentially and the first one that satisfies some predetermined aspiration level is selected, or one in which alternatives are considered sequentially and choice follows Bayesian rules. It does not require that all alternatives be considered, or that knowledge about them be complete or accurate.

Suppose estimates are unbiased, but subject to random error. Random error, or noise, in estimation can be seen as arising either from stochastic properties of the world or from problems of observation, measurement, communication, or inference. On the one hand, the underlying attributes of interest may be subject to random fluctuation in their realizations. For example, suppose good managers, on average, perform better than poor managers, but any level of talent produces a distribution of results. Fluctuations could arise from inherent stochastic properties of managerial ability, from random variation in the situations in which they are observed, or from random changes in the evaluation criteria. Similarly, the realizations of technologies or legislative programs may show random fluctuation around their average values. The history of such fluctuations will affect current estimations of the values, and future fluctuations will affect future realizations. On the other hand, random fluctuation may be introduced by the estimation or evaluation process. There may be random error in observations or measurements, or in the recording or transmittal of this information, or in forming inferences about the future. In the remainder of this paper we consider how the distribution of postdecision surprises is affected by random errors in estimation, without regard to whether that error is a property of the attributes of interest or their estimation. We restrict our discussion to the case in which alternatives are evaluated on a single criterion; the general results also hold for each attribute dimension of a multi-attribute decision problem.

Let X be the value of some attribute of an alternative. X is not precisely known to the decision-maker: it is a random variable. Let Y be the random error in the estimate of the attribute value. We assume that X and Y are stochastically independent, that Y has a mean of zero ($m_y = 0$), and that the estimated value for the alternative is $Z = X + Y$. Thus, Z is random also. The assumption that the error and underlying value combine additively to produce the estimate is not necessary to the general argument of the paper, but it is required for the detailed computations. Different quantitative results, but not a different basic conclusion, would be obtained if the errors entered multiplicatively (e.g., $Z = e^{(X+Y)}$). The distributions of attribute values, X, and of the errors, Y, depend on the particular choice situation involved. If X is distributed with mean m_x and standard deviation s_x, and Y is distributed with mean zero and standard deviation s_y, then Z has mean $m_z = m_x$, and standard deviation $s_z = (s_x^2 + s_y^2)^{1/2}$. If we think of X as a signal and Y as noise, then we can define $w = s_x^2/s_y^2$ as the signal-to-noise ratio (Marschak and Radner, 1972). In discussions of communication channels, $s_x^2/(s_x^2 + s_y^2)$ is known as the reliability, k, of a channel. In the present situation, k might be defined as the reliability of an estimation process. It is easy to see, from equation (2) below, that $k = w/(w+1) = r_{xz}^2$; and that $w = k/(1-k)$. We assume that all alternatives have the same signal-to-noise ratio, which is a structural property of the estimation process. Consequently, the variances of X and Y, given Z, do not depend on the particular value of Z.

Let x_c, y_c, and z_c be the value, error, and estimate respectively for a *chosen* alternative. The chosen alternative is determined so that $z_c \geqq z_i$ for all $i \neq c$, where z_i is the estimated value of the ith of n alternatives considered. We wish to examine the distribution of y_c, given an estimate z_c, and to determine the probability that y_c will be positive. In the absence of postdecision behavioral adjustment, the distribution of y_c over a set of decisions is the distribution of postdecision surprises. A surprise-neutral decision process is one that implies a symmetric distribution around a mean of zero, thus one whose structure is equally likely to produce euphoria (positive surprise) or disappointment (negative surprise), and on average produces neither. We ask whether a standard rational decision process is surprise-neutral in such a sense. The answer is that it is not.

Regression to the Mean

A basic structural property of decision-making processes such as those we have described is that an alternative with a relatively high estimated value will have associated with it, on average, a relatively large positive error, so that choosing the alternative with the highest estimated value will tend to elicit postdecision disappointment. This property stems from the well-known (Pearson, 1897; Snedecor, 1946) fact that the covariance of Y and Z must be positive. In fact, the correlation between the two, r_{yz}, depends only on the value of w and the assumption that X and Y are independent random variables. Specifically:[1]

$$r_{yz} = 1/(w+1)^{1/2}. \tag{1}$$

On average, the greater the value of z_i, the greater the value of y_i. Thus, if we make a decision by estimating the value of several alternatives, the higher the estimated value of the chosen alternative, the more disappointed we are likely to be in it. As Capen, Clapp, and Campbell (1971) observed in studying oil-lease bidding, 'In competitive bidding, the winner tends to be the player who most overestimates true tract value'. The result has come to be called 'the winner's curse'.

These disappointments, i.e., $E(y_c) > 0$, generated by making decisions intelligently are a form of regression to the mean. The phenomenon occurs in situations in which the future value of a variable having some random components is estimated on the basis of previously observed values of that variable. As equation (1) suggests, relatively extreme observations will be associated with relatively extreme random components, and less extreme observations will be associated with less extreme random components. Thus, if an extreme value is observed, the next observation can be expected to be less extreme, i.e., closer to the mean. Regression to the mean has long been recognized and widely discussed by biologists, statisticians, and social scientists. It was discussed as early as 1877 by Galton (1879), who observed that large sweet peas produced offspring with slightly smaller seeds. Regression to the mean has been noted in IQ scores (Anastasi, 1958), as a characteristic of managerial evaluation (March and March, 1978),

1 The derivations for all equations are straightforward. Those that may not be immediately obvious are shown in the Appendix.

and as a problem in such empirical research as measuring attitude change (Hovland, Lumsdaine, and Sheffield, 1949), assessing the impact of communication (Campbell and Clayton, 1961), and studying consumer attitudes (Morrison, 1973). Most treatments have emphasized the specific complications associated with specific examples rather than the generality of the phenomenon in any estimation or choice situation. Perhaps as a result, many people, including those with knowledge of statistics, do not reliably take regression into consideration in making predictions or in making decisions or judgments in uncertain situations. They do not seem to expect regression in many situations in which it is bound to occur (in the absence of behavioral reevaluations); and they invent spurious causal explanations for regression when it is observed (Tversky and Kahneman, 1974; Ross, 1977; Kahneman and Tversky, 1979; Nisbett and Ross, 1980; Hogarth, 1980).

Although higher estimated values are associated with greater disappointment, they are also associated with greater underlying values. The correlation between X and Z is also positive:

$$r_{xz} = [\, w/(w+1)]^{1/2}. \tag{2}$$

Or:

$$r_{xz} = r_{yz}(w^{1/2}). \tag{3}$$

The decision dilemma is clear. Choosing apparently better alternatives will, on average, produce higher returns. Thus, it is sensible to choose alternatives that are estimated to be relatively good. However, such a procedure is not surprise neutral. In the absence of behavioral adjustments, higher expected benefits will be associated with greater expected disappointments.

The Signal-to-Noise Effect

Any choice based on noisy estimates can be expected to exhibit a structural tendency toward disappointment. As is obvious from the equations above, the magnitude of the expected disappointment is a function of the signal-to-noise ratio, w. Large values of w produce a high correlation between estimates (z_i) and realizations (x_i), and a low correlation between estimates (z_i) and errors (y_i). As a result, high signal-to-noise ratios result in smaller disappointments.

To illustrate the magnitude of the signal-to-noise effect for one general class of decision situations, we introduce the assumption that X and Y, and consequently Z, are normally distributed. We can then determine the expected values of x_i and y_i for any given z_i as a function of w. These expectations of x_i and y_i are valid for *any* noisy estimate z_i (assuming normality), including the z_i that is associated with the chosen alternative. The expectation of x_i, given an estimate z_i, is given by:

$$E(x_i|z_i)=m_x+r_{xz}(s_x/s_z)(z_i-m_z). \tag{4}$$

Using equation (2), we can rewrite equation (4) as:

$$E(x_i|z_i)=m_z+r_{xz}^2(z_i-m_z). \tag{5}$$

Or, as a function of w:

$$E(x_i|z_i)=m_z+[w/(w+1)](z_i-m_z). \tag{6}$$

Analogously, using equation (1), we can estimate the magnitude of the error, y_i, given the estimate, z_i, as:

$$E(y_i|z_i=\mathrm{r}_{yz}^2(z_i-m_z). \tag{7}$$

Or, as a function of w:

$$E(y_i|z_i)=(z_i-m_z)/(w+1). \tag{8}$$

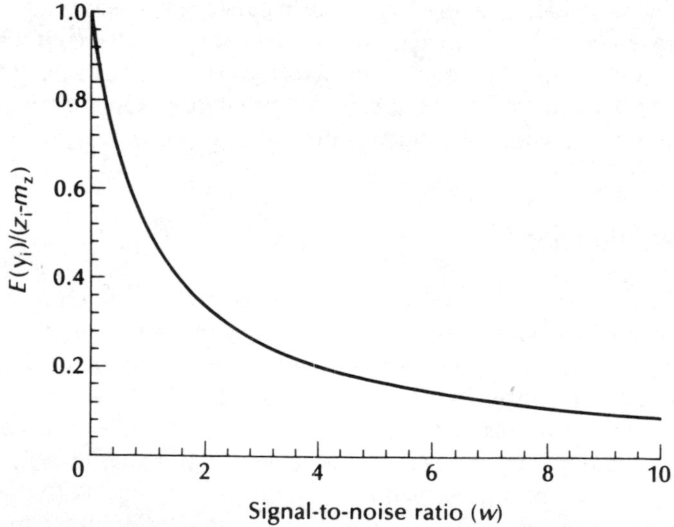

Figure 11.1. Expected fraction of deviation from the mean attributable to estimation error as a function of the signal-to-noise ratio (w)

In figure 11.1, we use these estimates to show, for any given deviation of z_i from $m_z = m_x$, the expected proportion of that deviation attributable to estimation error, as a function of w. The expected proportion attributable to the underlying value is one minus the value plotted in figure 11.1. As the figure confirms, the average contribution of estimation error to the apparent quality of an alternative is large when the signal-to-noise ratio is small.

Using equations (1) and (2) and the well-known (e.g., Mood and Graybill, 1963, p. 202) fact that if x_i and y_i are normally distributed, their conditional standard deviations are $s_{xi|zi} = s_x(1 - r_{xz}{}^2)^{1/2}$, and $s_{yi|zi} = s_y(1 - r_{yz}{}^2)^{1/2}$, it is possible to specify the likelihood that structural postdecision disappointment will occur. The standard deviation of x_i given z_i, equals the standard deviation of y_i, given z_i, and is a function of the signal-to-noise ratio, w:

$$s_{xi|zi} = s_{yi|zi} = s_z[\, w^{1/2}/(\, w + 1)]\,. \tag{9}$$

Note that $s_{xi|zi}$ and $s_{yi|zi}$ are equal, although in general s_x and s_y are not, because $x_i + y_i = z_i$.

With equation (9), it is possible to determine the probability, for a given estimate $z_i > m_z$, that the estimation error y_i is positive:

$$\Pr(\, y_i > 0|_{zi}) = 1 - \Pr\{V_N > [\,(\, z_i - m_z)/(\, w^{1/2} s_z)\,]\,\}. \tag{10}$$

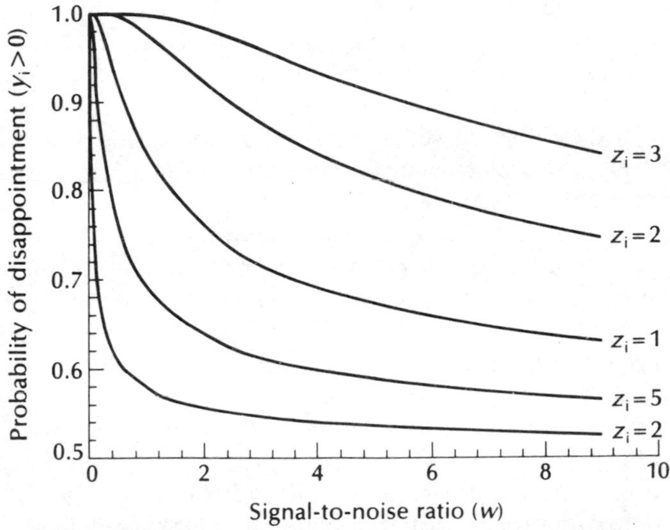

Figure 11.2. Probability of disappointment as a function of the signal-to-noise ratio (w) and the estimated value (z_i); $m_x = m_z = 0$; $s_z = 1$

where V_N is the standard normal variable. Figure 11.2 uses equation (10) to plot the probability that y_i is positive (i.e., the likelihood of disappointment) as a function of w, for various values of z_i, assuming $m_x = m_z = 0$ and $s_z = 1$. We have focused on y_i since it is the behavior of y_i that is associated with postdecision surprise. For a given z_i, a similar result could be obtained for the probability that $x_i > m_x$. Figure 11.2 quantifies the observation that the likelihood of postdecision disappointment decreases as the signal-to-noise ratio, w, increases. Specifically, the probability of positive expectation error approaches one as the signal-to-noise ratio approaches zero, and approaches 1/2 as the signal-to-noise ratio becomes large. Figure 11.2 also shows the effect of the magnitude of z_i on the probability of disappointment. The higher the estimated value, z_i, of an alternative, the greater the chance of disappointment. Since choices are made by selecting that alternative that has the highest estimated value among the alternatives considered, z_c is likely to be relatively high – and so is disappointment.

The Number of Alternatives Effect

The expected level of disappointment is also affected by the number of alternatives considered. As is clear from the previous analysis, both the expected amount of postdecision surprise and the probability that disappointment will occur depend on the signal-to-noise ratio, w, and the estimated value, z_c, of the chosen alternative. If a decision is made by choosing the best of several alternatives, then it is clear that z_c will, on average, increase with the number of alternatives considered. Suppose a decision-maker considers precisely n alternatives and estimates the value, z_i, of each. If these alternatives are arranged in decreasing order of their estimated values, we can designate the alternative with the largest estimated value as a_1, the second largest as a_2, and so forth to a_n. These ordered estimates are normally called order statistics. In general, their expected values and distributions depend on the number of alternatives considered, n, and the distribution, A, of estimated values for the population of possible alternatives.

The properties of order statistics can be computed for any ordered alternative, a_i; but the primary interest here is in the particular case of a_1, the highest estimated value among n different, randomly chosen alternatives. Although there are no simple formulae to calculate expected values and distributions for extreme order statistics (e.g., a_1, a_n), the expected values for order statistics of many commonly used distributions have been approximated to a high degree of accuracy using numerical methods (e.g., Hastings et al., 1947; Harter, 1969). If a decision-maker estimates $z_i = x_i + y_i$ for each of n alternatives drawn at random, the expected estimated value of the highest ranking alternative depends on n and the standard deviation of the estimates, $s_z = (s_x^2 + s_y^2)^{1/2} = s_x[(w+1)/w]^{1/2}$. For example, figure 11.3 plots the expected value of the largest of n items drawn from a standard normal distribution. If alternatives are not drawn at random from the pool of possibilities, the specific quantitative results would be different, but not the general implications. If a decision-maker excludes some (bad) alternatives on the basis of prior knowledge, then alternatives can be seen as drawn at random from the subset of alternatives that are left. Such a procedure has the consequence of reducing the s_x and thus also reducing w.

Given w,n, and assumptions about the distributions of X and Y, we can find the expected estimated value for the highest ranked alternative. Then we can use the estimates of the signal-to-noise effect from the previous section to find its expected value and expected error. To illustrate, suppose X and Y, and therefore Z, are normally distributed. If $A_1(n)$ is the expected estimated value for the highest ranking alternative out of n drawn from a normal distribution, A, of estimated values for alternatives, and N denotes the standard normal distribution, then:

$$E(z_c) = A_1(n) = m_z + s_z N_1(n). \qquad (11)$$

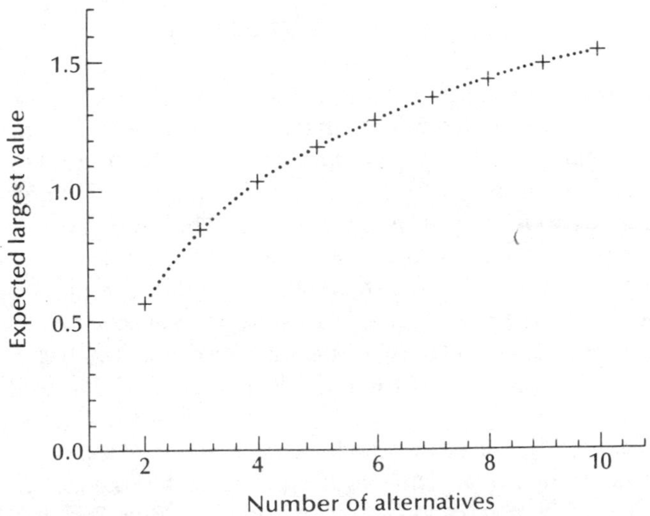

Figure 11.3. Expected value of largest alternative as a function of the number of alternatives (n), where alternatives are drawn from a standard normal distribution

Or:

$$E(z_c) = A_1(n) = m_x + s_x[(w+1)/w]^{1/2} N_1,(n), \tag{12}$$

where z_c is the estimated value of the chosen alternative.

We wish to determine the expectations of x_c and y_c, the true value and error for the chosen alternative. Since we have assumed normality, we can use equations (6) and (8) to specify the expectations for x_i and y_i:

$$E(x_i) = m_z + [w/(w+1)][E(z_i) - m_z]; \tag{13}$$

$$E(y_i) = [E(z_i) - m_z]/(w+1). \tag{14}$$

And from those and the expression for $E(z_c)$ in equation (11), we can derive the expectations for x_c and y_c:

$$E(x_c) = m_z + [w/(w+1)][s_z N_1(n)]; \tag{15}$$

$$E(y_c) = s_z N_1(n)/(w+1). \tag{16}$$

Or, in terms of the distribution of X:

$$E(x_c) = m_x + [w/w+1)]^{1/2}[s_x N_1(n)]: \tag{17}$$

$$E(y_c) = [s_x N_1(n)]/[w(w+1)]^{1/2}. \tag{18}$$

If we assume normality, equations (15), (16), (17), and (18) show the way in which the expected underlying value and expected surprise of the chosen alternative depend on the signal-to-noise ratio, w, and the number of alternatives considered, n. In particular, equations (16) and (18) give the amount by which the estimated value of a choice, on average, inflates the underlying value. Thus, they show the expected postdecision disappointment implicit in the structure of the decision-making process, as a function of w and n. Figure 11.4 shows the expected value of y_c as a function of w for a range of values of n, assuming X has a standard normal distribution. Using Monte Carlo procedures, figure 11.5 shows the probability that y_c is positive as a function of w for a range of values of n, assuming that X has a standard normal distribution.

The results show a significant level of expected postdecision disappointment as a structural feature of rational decision-making. Moreover, for any given signal-to-noise ratio, the level of structural disappointment increases with the number of alternatives considered. Since the expected value of the chosen alternative also increases with the number of alternatives, the pains

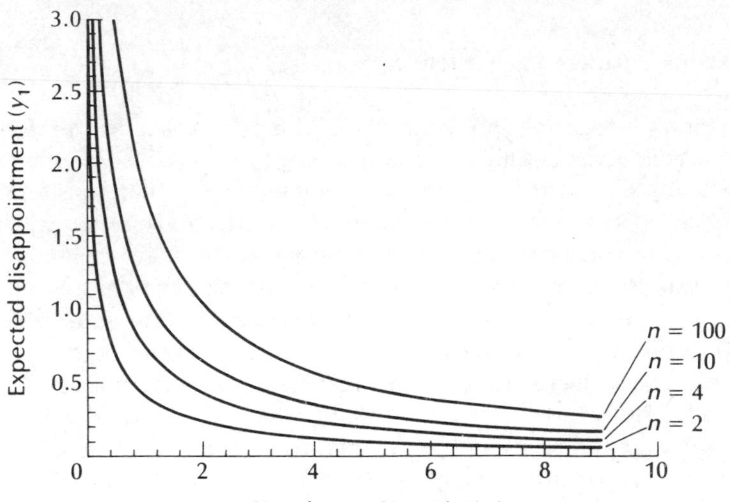

Figure 11.4. Expected disappointment as a function of the signal-to-noise ratio (w) and the number of alternatives (n), where x has a standard normal distribution

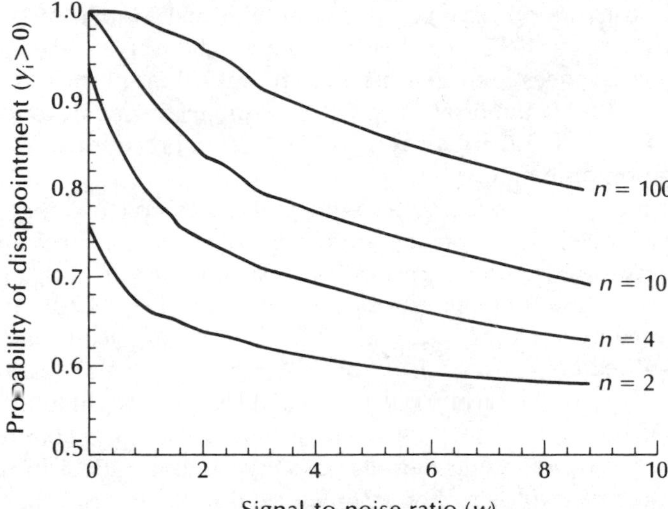

Figure 11.5. Probability of disappointment as a function of the signal-to-noise ratio (w) and the number of alternatives (n), where x has a standard normal distribution

of greater disappointment are presumably somewhat ameliorated by the pleasures of greater benefit. However, if neither prior corrections for the effect nor behavioral adjustments of expectations occur, each additional alternative evaluated before making a decision adds to the risk and expected magnitude of postdecision disappointment.

Managing Postdecision Structural Surprise

Structurally induced disappointment will be most characteristic of decision-making conditions in which variation among the true values of alternatives is relatively small, the ambiguity or uncertainty in evaluation is relatively high, and the number of alternatives considered is relatively large. Consider, for example, the choice of a top-level manager from a pool of senior executives. Eligible senior executives have already passed through a series of filters (promotions) that have, assuming the filters screen on similar criteria, substantially reduced the heterogeneity of the original cohort of beginning managers with respect to those criteria. That is, s_x^2 is small. The criteria for evaluation, on the other hand, are relatively ambiguous, and their use subject to significant error. That is, s_y^2 is large. Since the decision is important, a desire both to find the best person and to make the search process legitimate compel decision-makers to consider a relatively large number of candidates. That is, n is large. Consequently, the careful selection of top executives results in a structural tendency toward postselection disappointment (March and March, 1978). More generally, in any decision situation that is relatively novel, in which experience is modest, in which criteria are ambiguous or their estimation noisy, and that is important enough or prolonged enough to stimulate extended search for alternatives, sensible decision processes imply notable postdecision disappointment.

A recognition that postdecision disappointment is a structural characteristic of intelligent choice in many situations leads to attempts to avoid or manage postdecision surprises. An examination of such efforts is a natural extension of the previous analysis, but the discussion should be prefaced by at least one caveat. Our analysis has tried to distinguish *structural* features of a decision process from *behavioral* features and has focused on the former rather than the latter. Sensible advice on managing postdecision surprise should include attention to both features. Since the behavioral results indicate postdecision distributions of surprises that sometimes involve euphoria, sometimes disappointment, they cannot be understood as simple consequences of the properties of the decision process we have discussed. For example, although we have shown that the structural bias toward postdecision disappointment increases with the number of alternatives considered, there is some behavioral evidence that increasing the number of alternatives considered actually decreases the postdecision dissatisfaction of individuals (O'Reilly and Caldwell, 1981). Our analysis, by identifying a baseline of disappointment, makes such results even more striking than they might otherwise appear. At the same time, the behavioral results are cautions against basing managerial actions simply on structural features of the decision model (March, 1978)

The most obvious way to manage postdecision disappointment is to deflate expectations; assuming we wish to eliminate structural effects on postdecision surprise, deflating expectations seems sensible whenever it is feasible. If w is known and expectations can be arbitrarily adjusted, an appropriate correction will eliminate the structural bias. For the case of normally distributed errors, equation (8) defines the expected inflation of estimates as a function of w, and thus the necessary correction. Where w is not known with precision, it may be estimated. Alternatively, it is possible simply to introduce a less quantitative skepticism about expectations that varies with guesses about the signal-to-noise ratio and the number of alternatives. Murphy's Law for example. As Brown (1975) pointed out, such adjustments may be incorrectly interpreted by observers as 'risk aversion'.

In many situations, however, explicitly deflating expectations may not be feasible or desirable. When the decision process involves conflict, persuasion, discussion, and commitment, if one participant unilaterally deflates expectations, it simply makes that participant less persuasive, or makes that participant's commitment to a chosen alternative less than may be needed for its success. Consequently, we may want to consider an alternative form of surprise management. We can treat w and n as decision variables, chosen by allocating resources either to clarifying the values of known alternatives or to locating and evaluating new alternatives. If we ignore postdecision disappointment, any costless increase in either the signal-to-noise ratio, w, or the number of alternatives, n, is unambiguously advantageous in terms of increasing the expected returns from choice. The expected value of a chosen alternative will be increased if either w or n is increased. However, since increasing either w or n introduces costs of gathering and processing information, there is an optimization problem involved in allocating resources to them.

Given cost functions in terms of w and n, the expected net benefit of a choice conditional on w and n can be determined. By expected net benefit, we mean simply the expected value of the chosen alternative minus the expected information or search costs, $c(w,n)$, of achieving w and n. Relatively little is known about the cost of information (Marschak and Radner, 1972). Linear cost functions have been assumed for the cost of additional alternatives (Arrow, Blackwell, and Girschick, 1949; Wald, 1950; Savage, 1954), and it is possible to make similar linear assumptions about the cost of improving w. For example, it can be shown that increasing w by a strategy of multiple estimates of each alternative leads to a cost function linear in w if cost is linear in n. In figures 11.6 and 11.7 it is assumed that the cost of information is given by $c(n,w) = a + bnw$.

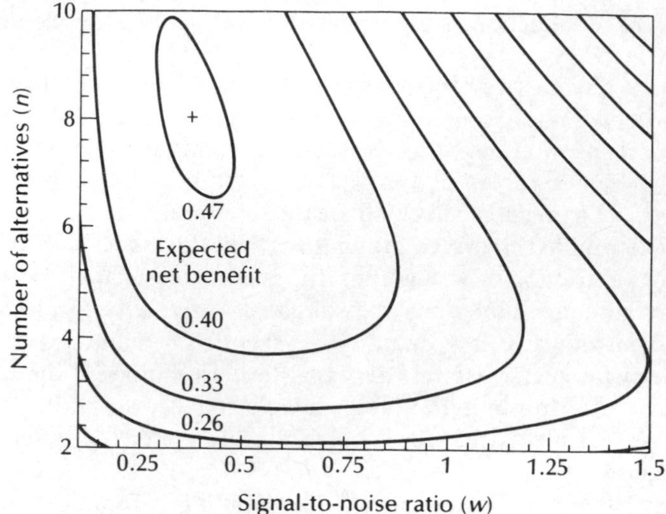

Figure 11.6. Expected net benefit as a function of the signal-to-noise ratio (w) and the number of alternatives (n)

It is also assumed that X has a standard normal distribution, and that Y is normally distributed with $m_y = 0$. Alternative cost and distribution assumptions would yield different quantitative results. Note also that figure 11.6 and 11.7 treat n as a continuous variable for illustrative purposes; only integer values of n are realizable.

Figure 11.6 shows a set of constant expected net benefit (indifference) curves conditional on w and n, and defines an optimum information policy for a decision-maker wanting to maximize expected net benefits. That is, it shows what level of w and n to choose, considering the costs of achieving those levels and the benefits accruing from them. Since increasing w or n offers improved expected performance, and each is costly, an optimal policy involves choosing between them. In the example displayed in figure 11.6, it would appear that major improvements in expected performance come less expensively from increases in n than from increases in w. Thus, at least in this particular case, there is some justification for devoting resources to expanding the number of alternatives rather than improving the precision of estimates about known alternatives.

Such an analysis, however, ignores the problems associated with post-decision disappointment. In general, if disappointment has negative utility, the above analysis will lead to overinvestment in n relative to w. Increasing the number of alternatives considered, n, increases expected realization, but it increases expected disappointment at the same time. Thus, each additional alternative considered increases the likelihood and expected magnitude of postdecision disappointment. On the other hand, increasing

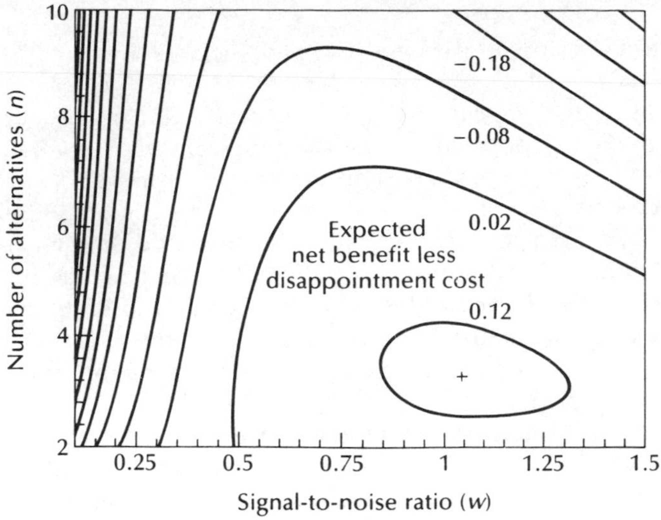

Figure 11.7. Expected net benefit minus disappointment cost ($d = 1/3$) as a function of the signal-to-noise ratio (w) and the number of alternatives (n)

the signal-to-noise ratio, w, both improves the expected value of the chosen alternative and reduces expected disappointment.

If we consider postdecision disappointment as one of the potential costs of making decisions, however, we can then examine possible trade-offs between the gains of net realized benefits and the losses of disappointments. As in the case of the information-cost analysis, an analysis involving disappointment involves assumptions about information costs, as well as assumptions about the exchange rate between outcomes and disappointments. That is, although realizations and disappointments are measured in the same units within the model, the utility of one unit of net benefit and the disutility of one unit of disappointment may be different. If we assume a simple exchange rate, d, we can plot the net gains minus the costs of disappointment as a function of w and n. Figure 11.7 shows net benefits minus disappointments for $d = 1/3$, for various values of w and n. When $d = 1/3$, a decision-maker is indifferent between increasing net benefits by one unit or decreasing disappointment by three units. In other words, the 'penalty' for a unit of disappointment is relatively low compared to the 'reward' for a unit of benefit. A comparison of figures 11.6 and 11.7 suggests that under some circumstances decision-makers might prefer – for reasons of disappointment costs – to invest in increasing w rather than in increasing n.

Structural Biases, Adaptive Behavior, and Social Norms

According to the present analysis, individuals and organizations are exposed to the risk of postdecision disappointment relatively frequently, not because they make poor decisions, nor because their world is unusually cruel, but simply because the way in which they (intelligently) make decisions leads them to expect too much. Intelligent decision-making with unbiased estimation of future costs and benefits implies a distribution of postdecision surprises that is biased in the direction of disappointment. Thus, a society that defines intelligent choice as normatively appropriate for individuals and organizations imposes a structural pressure toward postdecision unhappiness.

This does not mean that disappointment with decisions will be a necessary characteristic of individuals or organizations within such a society, however. The relation between structural biases and actual human behavior in a culture is not straightforward. In trying to identify biases inherent in the logic of the rules of decision-making, the present analysis is similar in spirit to game-theoretic efforts to describe power relations implicit in structural properties of a political system (Shapley and Shubik, 1954). Speculations about the impact of such structural properties on human behavior include two quite different kinds of propositions. The first, implicit in the analysis above, generates predictions about variations in reported postdecision surprise as a function of variations in signal-to-noise ratios and numbers of alternatives. The second considers the ways in which individuals, social norms, and social institutions have adapted to the bias over a history of experience with it, and the ways in which norms of choice fit with other important norms of social organization.

The second kind of speculation is more important. It is also more difficult. Differences in the magnitude of the structural bias are fundamental to understanding postdecision surprise; but they will not account directly for observed differences in surprise. Observed postdecision subjective experiences of euphoria and disappointment reflect behavioral adjustments to the structural biases of choice, as well as to other structural constraints on social life. The adjustments include both deliberate strategic actions and long-term adaptation. As was suggested in the previous section, it is possible to anticipate and manage the bias in postdecision surprise. Individuals and organizations can be taught to anticipate the bias, make corrections, and operate in terms of the corrected expectations. More importantly in the present context, adjustments to implicit bias in surprises may be found in less deliberate attributes of ordinary individual and organizational behavior, rules of thumb, motives, and sentiments.

For example, empirical studies of decision-making in political institutions and organizations indicate that surprises are often negative, that realizations from decisions tend to be disappointing (Pressman and Wildavsky, 1973; Bardach, 1977; Sproull, Weiner, and Wolf, 1978). Most empirical research on individual decision-making, on the other hand, reports positive post-decision surprises (Festinger, 1957, 1964; Staw, 1974, 1976; Salancik, 1977). It seems possible that psychological and normative mechanisms have evolved to offset the disappointment bias in individual decision-making; but the same mechanisms are either less powerful or less pervasive in collective choice.

A number of studies (Staw, 1974, 1976; Salancik, 1977) suggest that a key feature of individual postdecision satisfaction is the acceptance of personal responsibility for personal action, thereby for the consequences of that action, and thereby for discomfort with postdecision disappointment. That is, postdecision disappointment conflicts with individual norms of personal autonomy, control, and competence. The conventional response in cultures committed to such norms is to accept responsibility for the decisions (at least in the short run), deny disappointment, and behave as though the disconfirmations of expectations either did not occur or were unimportant (Aronson, 1968).

Similar acceptance of responsibility for past decisions is less conventional in the kind of collectivities that have been studied (but see Hägg, 1977). Rather, the norms are norms of conflict, competition, ambition, and turnover, and the expectation is that successors will be appropriately disappointed with the results of actions by predecessors. The conventional response in cultures committed to norms of competition and turnover is to accept disappointment, deny responsibility, and find justification for turnover in the failure to realize expectation. Disappointments are sustained by the way deliberative or political processes of decision undermine the commitment that is essential both to implementing decisions and to postdecision euphoria (Brunsson, 1982) and by the way advocates of alternative actions inflate their estimates of net return (Allison, 1969; Halperin, 1974; Williamson, 1975).

Thus, we suggest that organizational norms of turnover and competition for control and individual norms of personal responsibility can be understood as different adaptations to a bias introduced by intelligent choice. The suggestion may be overly brave, but it has the appeal of introducing a bit of sociology into a statistical analysis of a psychological problem. It may also lead us to ask whether the normative glorification of intelligent choice is to be considered simply a given of modern life or can be understood in terms of the fit between rules of intelligence and other social imperatives. Norms of intelligent choice are undoubtedly encouraged in both individuals and organizations by the way such choices improve average returns from decision-making. The norms may also be reinforced, particularly in organizations, by the way intelligent choice produces normatively appropriate disappointments. Where a central normative feature of social organization is competition for promotion and control, as it is in democratic political systems and many bureaucratic organizations, postdecision disappointment helps sustain important social norms.

Appendix: Derivations of Equations

The derivations of the equations in the text are substantially trivial. Those that are not immediately obvious are provided here.

Equation 1 (and, analogously, 2):

$$
\begin{aligned}
r_{yz} &= \mathrm{Cov}(Y,Z)/s_y s_z \\
&= E\,[(Y-m_y)(Z-m_z)]\,/s_y s_z \\
&= E[(Y-m_y)(X+Y-m_x-m_y)]\,/s_y s_z \\
&= E\,[(Y-m_y)(X-m_x)+(Y-m_y)^2]\,/s_y s_z \\
&= \{E[(Y-m_y)(X-m_z)] + E\,[(Y-m_y)^2]\}(s_y s_t \\
&= \{\mathrm{Cov}(Y,X)+s_y^2\}/s_y s_z \\
&= s_y^2/s_y s_z \quad \text{(since } X \text{ and } Y \text{ are independent)} \\
&= s_y/s_z \\
&= s_y/(s_x^2+s_y^2)^{1/2} \\
&= 1/[(s_x^2/s_y^2)+1]^{1/2} \\
&= 1/(w+1)^{1/2}
\end{aligned}
$$

Equation 4:

The result in equation (4) is well known (e.g., Mood and Graybill, 1963, p. 202; Marschak and Radner, 1972; Nisbett and Ross, 1980).

Equation 5 (and, analogously, 7):

$$
\begin{aligned}
E(x_i|z_i) &= m_x + r_{xz}(s_x/s_z)(z_i-m_z) \\
&= m_z + r_{xz}[s_x/(s_z^2+s_y^2)^{1/2}](z_i-m_z) \\
&= m_z + r_{xz}\{[s_x/s_y]/[(s_x^2/s_y^2)+1]^{1/2}\}(z_i-m_z) \\
&= m_z + r_{xz}[w/(w+1))]^{1/2}(z_i-m_z) \\
&= m_z + r_{xz}^2(z_i-m_z) \quad \text{(using equation 2).}
\end{aligned}
$$

Equation 9:

$$
\begin{aligned}
s_{x_i}|_{z_i} &= s_x(1-r_{xz}^2)^{1/2} \\
&= s_z(s_x^2/s_z^2)^{1/2}[1-(w/w+1)]^{1/2} \\
&= s_z\,[s_x^2/(s_x^2+s_y^2)]^{1/2}[1/(w+1)]^{1/2} \\
&= s_z[w/(w+1)]^{1/2}[1/(w+1)]^{1/2} \\
&= s_z[w^{1/2}/(w+1)].
\end{aligned}
$$

Similarly:

$$
\begin{aligned}
s_{y_i}|_{z_i} &= s_y(1-r_{yz}^2)^{1/2} \\
&= \ldots \\
&= s_z[w^{1/2}/(w+1)].
\end{aligned}
$$

Equation 10:

$$\Pr(y_i>0|z_i)=\Pr\{[\{y_i-E(y_i|z_i)\}/s_{y_i|z_i}]>[\{0-E(y_i|z_i)\}/s_{y_i}|z_i)\}$$
$$=\Pr\{V_N>[-(z_i-m_z)/(w+1)/[s_z w^{1/2}/(w+1)]]\}$$
$$=\Pr\{V_N>-[(z_i-m_z)/(w^{1/2}s_z)]\}$$
$$=1-\Pr\{V_N>[(z_i-m_z)/(w^{1/2}s_z)]\}$$

Equation 13 (and, analogously, 14):

$$E(x_i)E[E(x_i|z_i)]$$
$$=E\{m_z+[w/(w+1)](z_i-m_z)\}$$
$$=m_z+[w/(w+1)][E(z_i)-m_z].$$

References

Allison, Graham T. (1969) *Essense of Decision: Explaining the Cuban Missile Crisis*. Boston: Little Brown.

Anastasi, Anne (1958) *Differential Psychology*, 3rd edn New York: Macmillan.

Aronson, Elliot (1968) Disconfirmed expectancies and bad decisions – Discussion: Expectancy vs. other motives. In Robert P. Abelson, Elliot Aronson, William McGuire, Theodore Newcomb, Milton Rosenberg, and Percy H. Tannenbaum (eds), *Theories of Cognitive Consistency:* 491–3. Chicago: Rand McNally.

Arrow, Kenneth J., David Blackwell, and Meyer A. Girshick (1949) Bayes and minimax solutions of sequential decision problems. *Econometrica*, 17: 213–44.

Bardach, Eugene (1977) *The Implementation Game*. Cambridge, MA: MIT Press.

Brown, Keith C. (1975) A note on optimal fixed-price bidding with uncertain production cost. *Bell Journal of Economics*, 6: 695–97.

Brunsson, Nils (1982) The irrationality of action and action rationality: Decisions, ideologies and organizational actions. *Journal of Management Studies*, 19: 29–44.

Campbell, Donald T., and Keith T. Clayton (1961) Avoiding regression effects in panel studies of communication impact. *Studies in Public Communication*, 3: 99–118.

Capen, E. C., R. V. Clapp, and W. M. Campbell (1971) Competitive bidding in high-risk situations. *Journal of Petroleum Technology*, 23: 641–53.

Festinger, Leon (1957) *A Theory of Cognitive Dissonance*. Stanford, CA: Stanford University Press.

Festinger, Leon (ed.) (1964) *Conflict, Decision, and Dissonance*. Stanford, CA: Stanford University Press.

Galton, Francis (1879) Typical laws of heredity. *Proceedings of the Royal Institute of Great Britain (1875–8):* 282–301.

Hägg, Ingemund (1977) *Review of Capital Investments* Uppsala, Sweden: University of Uppsala, Department of Business Administration.

Halperin, Morton H. (1974) *Bureaucratic Politics and Foreign Policy*. Washington, DC: Brookings Institution.

Harter, Harmon L. (1969) *Order Statistics and Their Use in Testing and Estimation*, vol. 2. Wright-Patterson Air Force Base, OH: Aerospace Research Laboratories.

Hastings, Cecil, Jr., Frederick Mosteller, John W. Tukey, and Charles P. Winsor (1947) Low moments for small samples: A comparative study of order statistics. *Annals of Mathematical Statistics,* 18: 413–26.

Hogarth, Robin M. (1980) *Judgement and Choice. The Psychology of Decision.* New York: Wiley.

Hovland, Carl I., Arthur A. Lumsdaine, and Fred D. Sheffield (1949) *Experiments on Mass Communications.* Appendix D: 329–40. Princeton, NJ: Princeton University Press.

Kahneman, Daniel, and Amos Tversky (1979) Intuitive prediction: Biases and corrective procedures. *Management Science,* 12: 313–27.

March, James C., and James G. March (1978) Performance sampling in social matches. *Administrative Science Quarterly,* 23: 434–53.

March, James G. (1978) Bounded rationality, ambiguity, and the engineering of choice. *Bell Journal of Economics,* 9: 587–608.

Marschak, Jacob, and Roy Radner (1972) *Economic Theory of Teams.* New Haven, CT: Yale University Press.

Mood, Alexander M., and Franklin A. Graybill (1963) *Introduction to the Theory of Statistics.* New York: McGraw-Hill.

Morrison, Donald G. (1973) Reliability of tests: A technique using the 'regression to the mean' fallacy. *Journal of Marketing Research,* 10: 91–3.

Nisbett, Richard, and Lee Ross (1980) *Human Inference: Strategies and Shortcomings of Social Judgment.* Englewood Cliffs, NJ: Prentice-Hall.

O'Reilly, Charles A., and David F. Caldwell (1981) The commitment and job tenure of new employees: Some evidence of postdecisional justification. *Administrative Science Quarterly,* 26: 597–616.

Pearson, Karl (1897) Mathematical contributions to the theory of evolution. On: a form of spurious correlation which may arise when indices are used in the measurement of organs. *Proceedings of the Royal Society,* Series A, 60: 489–98.

Pressman, Jeffrey L., and Aaron B. Wildavsky (1973) *Implementation.* Berkeley, CA: University of California Press.

Ross, Lee (1977) The intuitive psychologist and his shortcomings: Distortion in the attribution process. In Leonard Berkowitz (ed.) *Advances in Experimental Psychology*: 173–220. New York: Academic Press.

Salancik, Gerald R. (1977) Commitment and the control of organizational behavior and belief. In Barry M. Staw and Gerald R. Salancik (eds), *New Directions in Organizational Behavior*; 1–54. Chicago: St. Clair.

Savage, Leonard J. (1954) *The Foundations of Statistics.* New York: Wiley.

Shapley, L. S., and Martin A. Shubik (1954) A method for evaluating the distribution of power in a committee system. *American Political Science Review,* 48: 787–92.

Snedecor, George W. (1946) *Statistical Methods,* 4th edn Ames, IO: Iowa State College Press.

Sproull, Lee S., Stephen Weiner, and David B. Wolf (1978) *Organizing an Anarchy.* Chicago: University of Chicago Press.

Staw, Barry M (1974) Attitudinal and behavioral consequences of changing a major organizational reward: A natural field experiment. *Journal of Personality and and Social Psychology,* 6: 742–51.

Staw, Barry M. (1976) Knee-deep in the Big Muddy: A study of escalating commitment to a chosen course of action. *Organizational Behavior and Human Performance*, 16: 27–44.

Tversky, Amos, and Daniel Kahneman (1974) Judgment under uncertainty: Heuristics and biases. *Science*, 185: 1124–31.

Wald, Abraham (1950) *Statistical Decision Functions*. New York: Wiley.

Williamson, Oliver E. (1975) *Markets and Hierarchies*. New York: Free Press.

Part IV

Decision-Making under Ambiguity

12

The Technology of Foolishness

James G. March

Choice and Rationality

The concept of choice as a focus for interpreting and guiding human behavior has rarely had an easy time in the realm of ideas. It is beset by theological disputations over free will, by the dilemmas of absurdism, by the doubts of psychological behaviorism, by the claims of historical, economic, social, and demographic determinism. Nevertheless, the idea that humans make choices has proven robust enough to become a major matter of faith in important segments of contemporary Western civilization. It is a faith that is professed by virtually all theories of social policy-making.

The major tenets of this faith run something like this:

> Human beings make choices. If done properly, choices are made by evaluating alternatives in terms of goals on the basis of information currently available. The alternative that is most attractive in terms of the goals is chosen. The process of making choices can be improved by using the technology of choice. Through the paraphernalia of modern techniques, we can improve the quality of the search for alternatives, the quality of information, and the quality of the analysis used to evaluate alternatives. Although actual choice may fall short of this ideal in various ways, it is an attractive model of how choices should be made by individuals, organizations, and social systems.

These articles of faith have been built upon, and have stimulated, some scripture. It is the scripture of theories of decision-making. The scripture is

---

This chapter is based on a paper first published in *Civiløkonomen* (Copenhagen) 18 (1971).

partly a codification of received doctrine and partly a source for that doctrine. As a result, our cultural ideas of intelligence and our theories of choice bear some substantial resemblance. In particular, they share three conspicuous interrelated ideas:

The first idea is the *pre-existence of purpose*. We find it natural to base an interpretation of human-choice behavior on a presumption of human purpose. We have, in fact, invented one of the most elaborate terminologies in the professional literature: 'values', 'needs', 'wants', 'goods', 'tastes', 'preferences', 'utility', 'objectives', 'goals', 'aspirations', 'drives'. All of these reflect a strong tendency to believe that a useful interpretation of human behavior involves defining a set of objectives that (a) are prior attributes of the system, and (b) make the observed behavior in some sense intelligent *vis-á-vis* those objectives.

Whether we are talking about individuals or about organizations, purpose is an obvious presumption of the discussion. An organization is often defined in terms of its purpose. It is seen by some as the largest collectivity directed by a purpose. Action within an organization is justified (or criticized) in terms of the purpose. Individuals explain their own behavior, as well as the behavior of others, in terms of a set of value premises that are presumed to be antecedent to the behavior. Normative theories of choice begin with an assumption of a pre-existent preference ordering defined over the possible outcomes of a choice.

The second idea is the *necessity of consistency*. We have come to recognize consistency both as an important property of human behavior and as a prerequisite for normative models of choice. Dissonance theory, balance theory, theories of congruency in attitudes, statuses, and performances have all served to remind us of the possibilities for interpreting human behavior in terms of the consistency requirements of a limited capacity information-processing system.

At the same time, consistency is a cultural and theoretical virtue. Action should be made consistent with belief. Actions taken by different parts of an organization should be consistent with each other. Individual and organizational activities are seen as connected with each other in terms of their consequences for some consistent set of purposes. In an organization, the structural manifestation of the dictum of consistency is the hierarchy with its obligations of coordination and control. In the individual, the structural manifestation is a set of values that generates a consistent preference ordering.

The third idea is the *primacy of rationality*. By rationality I mean a procedure for deciding what is correct behavior by relating consequences systematically to objectives. By placing primary emphasis on rational techniques, we implicitly have rejected – or seriously impaired – two other procedures for choice: (a) the processes of intuition, by means of which people may do things without fully understanding why; (b) the processes of tradition and faith, through which people do things because that is the way they are done.

Both within the theory and within the culture we insist on the ethic of rationality. We justify individual and organizational action in terms of an analysis of means and ends. Impulse, intuition, faith, and tradition are outside that system and viewed as antithetical to it. Faith may be seen as a possible source of values. Intuition may be seen as a possible source of ideas about alternatives. But the analysis and justification of action lie within the context of reason.

These ideas are obviously deeply imbedded in the culture. Their roots extend into ideas that have conditioned much of modern Western history and interpretations of that history. Their general acceptance is probably highly correlated with permeation of rationalism and individualism into the style of thinking within the culture. The ideas are even more obviously imbedded in modern theories of choice. It is fundamental to those theories that thinking should precede action; that action should serve a purpose; that purpose should be defined in terms of a consistent set of pre-existent goals; and that choice should be based on a consistent theory of the relation between action and its consequences.

Every tool of management decision that is currently a part of management science, operations research, or decision theory assumes the prior existence of a set of consistent goals. Almost the entire structure of microeconomic theory builds on the assumption that there exists a well-defined, stable, and consistent preference-ordering. Most theories of individual or organizational choice behavior accept the idea that goals exist and that (in some sense) an individual or organization acts on those goals, choosing from among some alternatives on the basis of available information. Discussions of educational policy, for example, with the emphasis on goal-setting, evaluation, and accountability, are directly in this tradition.

From the perspective of all of man's history, the ideas of purpose, consistency, and rationality are relatively new. Much of the technology currently available to implement them is extremely new. Over the past few centuries, and conspicuously over the past few decades, we have substantially improved man's capability for acting purposively, consistently, and rationally. We have substantially increased his propensity to think of himself as doing so. It is an impressive victory, won – where it has been won – by a happy combination of timing, performance, ideology, and persistence. It is a battle yet to be concluded, or even engaged, in many cultures of the world; but within most of the Western world, individuals and organizations see themselves as making choices.

The Problem of Goals

The tools of intelligence as they are fashioned in modern theories of choice are necessary to any reasonable behavior in contemporary society. It is difficult to see how we could, and inconceivable that we would, fail to continue their development, refinement, and extension. As might be expected, however, a theory and ideology of choice built on the ideas outlined above is deficient in some obvious, elementary ways, most conspicuously in the treatment of human goals.

Goals are thrust upon the intelligent man. We ask that he act in the name of goals. We ask that he keep his goals consistent. We ask that his actions be oriented to his goals. We ask that a social system amalgamate individual goals into a collective goal. But we do not concern ourselves with the origin of goals. Theories of individual organizational and social choice assume actors with pre-existent values.

Since it is obvious that goals change over time and that the character of those changes affects both the richness of personal and social development and the outcome of choice behavior, a theory of choice must somehow justify ignoring the phenomena. Although it is unreasonable to ask a theory of choice to solve all of the problems of man and his development, it is reasonable to ask how something as conspicuous as the fluidity and ambiguity of objectives can plausibly be ignored in a theory that is offered as a guide to human choice behavior.

There are three classic justifications. The first is that goal development and choice are independent processes, conceptually and behaviorally. The second is that the model of choice is never satisfied in fact that deviations from the model accommodate the problems of introducing change. The third is that the idea of changing goals is so intractable in a normative theory of choice that nothing can be said about it. Since I am unpersuaded of the first and second justifications, my optimism with respect to the third is somewhat greater than most of my fellows.

The argument that goal development and choice are independent behaviorally seems clearly false. It seems to me perfectly obvious that a description that assumes goals come first and action comes later is frequently radically wrong. Human choice behavior is at least as much a process for discovering goals as for acting on them. Although it is true enough that goals and decisions are 'conceptually' distinct, that is simply a statement of the theory. It is not defense of it. They are conceptually distinct if we choose to make them so.

The argument that the model is incomplete is more persuasive. There do appear to be some critical 'holes' in the system of intelligence as described by standard theories of choice. There is incomplete information, incomplete goal consistency, and a variety of external processes impinging on goal development – including tuition and tradition. What is somewhat disconcerting about the argument, however, is that it makes the efficacy of the concepts of intelligent choice dependent on their inadequacy. As we become more competent in the techniques of the model, and more committed to it, the 'holes' become smaller. As the model becomes more accepted, our obligation to modify it increases.

The final argument seems to me sensible as a general principle, but misleading here. Why are we more reluctant to ask how human beings might find 'good' goals than we are to ask how they might make 'good' decisions? The second question appears to be a relatively technical problem. The first seems more pretentious. It claims to say something about alternative virtues. The appearance of pretense, however, stems directly from the theory and the ideology associated with it.

In fact, the conscious introduction of goal discovery as a consideration in theories of human choice is not unknown to modern man. For example, we have two kinds of theories of choice behavior in human beings. One is a theory of children. The other is a theory of adults. In the theory of childhood, we emphasize choices as leading to experiences that develop the child's scope, his complexity, his awareness of the world. As parents, or psychologists, we try to lead the child to do things that are inconsistent with his present goals because we know (or believe) that he can only develop into an interesting person by coming to appreciate aspects of experience that he initially rejects.

In the theory of adulthood, we emphasize choices as a consequence of our intentions. As adults, or economists, we try to take actions that (within the limits of scarce resources) come as close as possible to achieving our goals. We try to find improved ways of making decisions consistent with our perceptions of what is valuable in the world.

The asymmetry in these models is conspicuous. Adults have constructed a model world in which adults know what is good for themselves, but children do not. It is hard to react positively to the conceit. The asymmetry has, in fact, stimulated a rather large number of ideologies and reforms designed to allow children the same moral prerogative granted to adults – the right to imagine that they know what they want. The efforts have cut deeply into traditional child-bearing, traditional educational policies, traditional politics, and traditional consumer economics.

In my judgment, the asymmetry between models of choice for adults and models of choice for children is awkward; but the solution we have adopted is precisely wrong-headed. Instead of trying to adapt the model of adults to children, we might better adapt the model of children to adults. For many purposes, our model of children is better. Of course, children know what they want. Everyone does. The critical question is whether they are encouraged to develop more interesting 'wants'. Values change. People become more interesting as those values and the interconnections made among them change.

One of the most obvious things in the world turns out to be hard for us to accommodate in our theory of choice: A child of two will almost always have a less interesting set of values (yes, indeed, a *worse* set of values) than a child of twelve. The same is true of adults. Values develop through experience. Although one of the main natural arenas for the modification of human values is the area of choice, our theories of adult and organizational decision-making ignore the phenomenon entirely.

Introducing ambiguity and fluidity to the interpretation of individual, organizational, and societal goals, obviously has implications for behavioral theories of decision-making. The main point here, however, is not to consider how we might describe the behavior of systems that are discovering goals as they act. Rather it is to examine how we might improve the quality of that behavior, how we might aid the development of interesting goals.

We know how to advise a society, an organization, or an individual if we are first given a consistent set of preferences. Under some conditions, we can suggest how to make decisions if the preferences are only consistent up to the point of specifying a series of independent constraints on the choice. But what about a normative theory of goal-finding behavior? What do we say when our client tells us that he is not sure his present set of values is the set of values in terms of which he wants to act?

It is a question familiar to many aspects of ordinary life. It is a question that friends, associates, students, college presidents, business managers, voters, and children ask at least as frequently as they ask how they should act within a set consistent and stable values.

Within the context of the normative theory of choice as it exists, the answer we give is: First determine the values, then act. The advice is frequently useful. Moreover, we have developed ways in which we can use conventional techniques for decision analysis to help discover value premises and to expose value inconsistencies. These techniques involve testing the decision implications of some successive approximations to a set of preferences. The object is to find a consistent set of preferences with implications that are acceptable to the person or organization making the decisions. Variations on such techniques are used routinely in operations research, as well as in personal counseling and analysis.

The utility of such techniques, however, apparently depends on the assumption that a primary problem is the amalgamation or excavation of pre-existent values. The metaphors – 'finding oneself', 'goal clarification', 'self-discovery', 'social welfare function', 'revealed pre-reference' – are metaphors of search. If our value premises are to be 'constructed' rather than 'discovered', our standard procedures may be useful; but we have no *a priori* reason for assuming they will.

Perhaps we should explore a somewhat different approach to the normative question of how we ought to behave when our value premises are not yet (and never will be) fully determined. Suppose we treat action as a way of creating interesting goals at the same time as we treat goals as a way of justifying action. It is an intuitively plausible and simple idea, but one that is not immediately within the domain of standard normative theories of intelligent choice.

Interesting people and interesting organizations construct complicated theories of themselves. In order to do this, they need to supplement the technology of reason with a technology of foolishness. Individuals and organizations need ways of doing things for which they have no good reason. Not always. Not usually. But sometimes. They need to act before they think.

Sensible Foolishness

In order to use the act of intelligent choice as a planned occasion for discovering new goals, we apparently require some idea of sensible foolishness. Which of the many foolish things that we might do now will lead to attractive value consequences? The question is almost inconceivable. Not only does it ask us to predict the value consequences of action, it asks us to evaluate them. In what terms can we talk about 'good' changes in goals?

In effect, we are asked either to specify a set of super-goals in terms of which alternative goals are evaluated, or to choose among alternatives *now* in terms of the unknown set of values we will have at some future time (or the distribution over time of that unknown set of future values). The former alternative moves us back to the original situation of a fixed set of values – now called 'super-goals' – and hardly seems an important step in the direction of inventing procedures for discovering new goals. The latter alternative seems fundamental enough, but it violates severely our sense of temporal order. To say that we make decisions now in terms of goals that will only be knowable later is nonsensical – as long as we accept the basic framework of the theory of choice and its presumptions of pre-existent goals.

I do not know in detail what is required, but I think it will be substantial. As we challenge the dogma of pre-existent goals, we will be forced to re-examine some of our most precious prejudices: the strictures against imitation, coercion, and rationalization. Each of those honorable prohibitions depends on the view of man and human choice imposed on us by conventional theories of choice.

Imitation is not necessarily a sign of moral weakness. It is a prediction. It is a prediction that if we duplicate the behavior or attitudes of someone else, the chances of our discovering attractive new goals for ourselves are relatively high. In order for imitation to be normatively attractive we need a better theory of who should be imitated. Such a theory seems to be eminently feasible. For example, what are the conditions for effectiveness of a rule that you should imitate another person whose values are in a close neighborhood of yours? How do the chances of discovering interesting goals through imitation change as the number of other people exhibiting the behavior to be imitated increases?

Coercion is not necessarily an assault on individual autonomy. It can be a device for stimulating individuality. We recognize this when we talk about parents and children (at least sometimes). What has always been difficult with coercion is the possibility for perversion that it involves, not its obvious capability for stimulating change. What we require is a theory of the circumstances under which entry into a coercive system produces behavior that leads to the discovery of interesting goals. We are all familiar with the tactic. We use it in imposing deadlines, entering contracts, making commitments. What are the conditions for its effective use? In particular, what are the conditions for coercion in social systems?

Rationalization is not necessarily a way of evading morality. It can be a test for the feasibility of a goal change. When deciding among alternative actions for which we have no good reason, it may be sensible to develop some definition of how 'near' to intelligence alternative 'unintelligent' actions lie. Effective rationalization permits this kind of incremental approach to changes in values. To use it effectively, however, we require a better idea of the kinds of metrics that might be possible in measuring value distances. At the same time, rationalization is the major procedure for integrating newly discovered goals into an existing structure of values. It provides the organization of complexity without which complexity itself becomes indistinguishable from randomness.

There are dangers in imitation, coercion, and rationalization. The risks are too familiar to elaborate. We should, indeed, be able to develop better techniques. Whatever those techniques may be, however, they will almost certainly undermine the superstructure of biases erected on purpose, consistency, and rationality. They will involve some way of thinking about action now as occurring in terms of a set of unknown future values.

Play and Reason

A second requirement for a technology of foolishness is some strategy for suspending rational imperatives toward consistency. Even if we know which of several foolish things we want to do, we still need a mechanism for allowing us to do it. How do we escape the logic of our reason?

Here, I think, we are closer to understanding what we need. It is playfulness. Playfulness is the deliberate, temporary relaxation of rules in order to explore the possibilities of alternative rules. When we are playful, we challenge the necessity of consistency. In effect, we announce – in advance – our rejection of the usual objections to behavior that does not fit the standard model of intelligence.

Playfulness allows experimentation. At the same time, it acknowledges reason. It accepts an obligation that at some point either the playful behavior will be stopped or it will be integrated into the structure of intelligence in some way that makes sense. The suspension of the rules is temporary.

The idea of play may suggest three things that are, in my mind, quite erroneous in the present context. First, play may be seen as a kind of Mardi Gras for reason, a release of emotional tensions of virtue. Although it is possible that play performs some such function, that is not the function with which I am concerned. Second, play may be seen as part of some mystical balance of spiritual principles: Fire and water, hot and cold, weak and strong. The intention here is much narrower than a general mystique of balance. Third, play may be seen as an antithesis of intelligence, so that the emphasis on the importance of play becomes a support for simple self-indulgence. My present intent is to propose play as an instrument of intelligence, not a substitute.

Playfulness is a natural outgrowth of our standard view of reason. A strict insistence on purpose, consistency, and rationality limits our ability to find new purposes. Play relaxes that insistence to allow us to act 'unintelligently' or 'irrationally', or 'foolishly' to explore alternative ideas of possible purposes and alternative concepts of behavioral consistency. And it does this while maintaining our basic commitment to the necessity of intelligence.

Although play and reason are in this way functional complements, they are often behavioral competitors. They are alternative styles and alternative orientations to the same situation. There is no guarantee that the styles will be equally well-developed. There is no guarantee that all individuals, all organizations, or all societies will be equally adept in both styles. There is no guarantee that all cultures will be equally encouraging to both.

Our design problem is either to specify the best mix of styles or, failing that, to assure that most people and most organizations most of the time use an alternation of strategies rather than perseverate in either one. It is a difficult problem. The optimization problem looks extremely difficult on the face of it, and the learning situations that will produce alternation in behavior appear to be somewhat less common than those that produce perseveration.

Consider, for example, the difficulty of sustaining playfulness as a style within contemporary American society. Individuals who are good at consistent rationality are rewarded early and heavily. We define it as intelligence, and the educational rewards of society are associated strongly with it. Social norms press in the same direction, particularly for men. Many of the demands of modern organizational life reinforce the same abilities and style preferences.

The result is that many of the most influential, best-educated, and best-placed citizens have experienced a powerful overlearning with respect to rationality. They are exceptionally good at maintaining consistent pictures of themselves, of relating action to purposes. They are exceptionally poor at a playful attitude toward their own beliefs, toward the logic of consistency, or toward the way they see things as being connected in the world. The dictates of manliness, forcefulness, independence, and intelligence are intolerant of playful urges if they arise. The playful urges that arise are weak ones.

The picture is probably overdrawn, but not, I believe, the implications. For societies, for organizations, and for individuals, reason and intelligence have had the unnecessary consequence of inhibiting the development of purpose into more complicated forms of consistency. In order to move away from that position, we need to find some ways of helping individuals and organizations to experiment with doing things for which they have no good reason, to be playful with their conception of themselves. It is a facility that requires more careful attention than I can give it, but I would suggest five things as a small beginning:

1 We can treat *goals as hypotheses*. Conventional decision theory allows us to entertain doubts about almost everything except the thing about which we frequently have the greatest doubt – our objectives. Suppose we define the decision process as a time for the sequential testing of hypotheses about goals. If we can experiment with alternative goals, we stand some chance of discovering complicated and interesting combinations of good values that none of us previously imagined.

2 We can treat *intuition as real*. I do not know what intuition is, or even if it is any one thing. Perhaps it is simply an excuse for doing something we cannot justify in terms of present values or for refusing to follow the logic of our own beliefs. Perhaps it is an inexplicable way of consulting that part of our intelligence that is not organized in a way anticipated by standard theories of choice. In either case, intuition permits us to see some possible actions that are outside our present scheme for justifying behavior.

3 We can treat *hypocrisy as a transition*. Hypocrisy is an inconsistency between expressed values and behavior. Negative attitudes

about hypocrisy stem from two major things. The first is a general onus against inconsistency. The second is a sentiment against combining the pleasures of vice with the appearance of virtue. Apparently, that is an unfair way of allowing evil to escape temporal punishment. Whatever the merits of such a position as ethics, it seems to me distinctly inhibiting toward change. A bad man with good intentions may be a man experimenting with the possibility of becoming good. Somehow it seems to me more sensible to encourage the experimentation than to insult it.

4 We can treat *memory as an enemy*. The rules of consistency and rationality require a technology of memory. For most purposes, good memories make good choices. But the ability to forget, or overlook, is also useful. If I do not know what I did yesterday or what other people in the organization are doing today, I can act within the system of reason and still do things that are foolish.

5 We can treat *experience as a theory*. Learning can be viewed as a series of conclusions based on concepts of action and consequences that we have invented. Experience can be changed retrospectively. By changing our interpretive concepts now, we modify what we learned earlier. Thus, we expose the possibility of experimenting with alternative histories. The usual strictures against 'self-deception' in experience need occasionally to be tempered with an awareness of the extent to which all experience is an interpretation subject to conscious revision. Personal histories, and national histories, need to be rewritten rather continuously as a base for the retrospective learning of new self-conceptions.

Each of these procedures represents a way in which we temporarily suspend the operation of the system of reasoned intelligence. They are playful. They make greatest sense in situations in which there has been an overlearning of virtues of conventional rationality. They are possibly dangerous applications of powerful devices more familiar to the study of behavioral pathology than to the investigation of human development. But they offer a few techniques for introducing change within current concepts of choice.

The argument extends easily to the problems of social organization. If we knew more about the normative theory of acting before you think, we could say more intelligent things about the functions of management and leadership when organizations or societies do not know what they are doing. Consider, for example, the following general implications.

First, we need to re-examine the functions of management decision. One of the primary ways in which the goals of an organization are developed is by interpreting the decisions it makes, and one feature of good managerial decisions is that they lead to the development of more interesting value-premises for the organization. As a result, decisions should not be seen as flowing directly or strictly from a pre-existent set of objectives. Managers who make decisions might well view that function somewhat less as a process of deduction or a process of political negotiation, and somewhat more as a process of gently upsetting preconceptions of what the organization is doing.

Second, we need a modified view of planning. Planning in organizations has many virtues, but a plan can often be more effective as an interpretation of past decisions than as a program for future ones. It can be used as a part of the efforts of the organization to develop a new consistent theory of itself that incorporates the mix of recent actions into a moderately comprehensive structure of goals. Procedures for interpreting the meaning of most past events are familiar to the memoirs of retired generals, prime ministers, business leaders, and movie stars. They suffer from the company they keep. In an organization that wants to continue to develop new objectives, a manager needs to be relatively tolerant of the idea that he will discover the meaning of yesterday's action in the experiences and interpretations of today.

Third, we need to reconsider evaluation. As nearly as I can determine, there is nothing in a formal theory of evaluation that requires that the criterion function for evaluation be specified in advance. In particular, the evaluation of social experiments need not be in terms of the degree to which they have fulfilled our *a priori* expectations. Rather we can examine what they did in terms of what we now believe to be important. The prior specification of criteria and the prior specification of evaluational procedures that depend on such criteria are common presumptions in contemporary social policy-making. They are presumptions that inhibit the serendipitous discovery of new criteria. Experience should be used explicitly as an occasion for evaluating our values as well as our actions.

Fourth, we need a reconsideration of social accountability. Individual preferences and social action need to be consistent in some way. But the process of pursuing consistency is one in which both the preferences and the actions change over time. Imagination in social policy formation involves systematically adapting to and influencing preferences. It would be unfortunate if our theories of social action encouraged leaders to ignore their responsibilities for anticipating public preferences through action and for providing social experiences that modify individual expectations.

Fifth, we need to accept playfulness in social organizations. The design of organizations should attend to the problems of maintaining both playfulness and reason as aspects of intelligent choice. Since much of the literature on social design is concerned with strengthening the rationality of decision, managers are likely to overlook the importance of play. This is partly a matter of making the individuals within an organization more playful by encouraging the attitudes and skills of inconsistency. It is also a a matter of making organizational structure and organizational procedure more playful. Organizations can be playful even when the participants in them are not. The managerial devices for maintaining consistency can be varied. We encourage organizational play by permitting (and insisting on) some temporary relief from control, coordination, and communication.

Intelligence and Foolishness

Contemporary theories of decision-making and the technology of reason have considerably strengthened our capabilities for effective social action. The conversion of the simple ideas of choice into an extensive technology is a major achievement. It is, however, an achievement that has reinforced some biases in the underlying models of choice in individuals and groups. In particular, it has reinforced the uncritical acceptance of a static interpretation of human goals.

There is little magic in the world, and foolishness in people and organizations is one of the many things that fail to produce miracles. Under certain conditions, it is one of several ways in which some of the problems of our current theories of intelligence can be overcome. It may be a good way. It preserves the virtues of consistency while stimulating change. If we had a good technology of foolishness, it might (in combination with the technology of reason) help in a small way to develop the unusual combinations of attitudes and behaviors that describe the interesting people, interesting organizations, and interesting societies of the world.

13

Bounded rationality, ambiguity, and the engineering of choice

James G. March

Abstract

Rational choice involves two guesses, a guess about uncertain future consequences and a guess about uncertain future preferences. Partly as a result of behavioral studies of choice over a 20-year period, modifications in the way the theory deals with the first guess have become organized into conceptions of bounded rationality. Recently, behavioral studies of choice have examined the second guess, the way preferences are processed in choice behavior. These studies suggest possible modifications in standard assumptions about tastes and their role in choice. This paper examines some of those modifications, some possible approaches to working on them, and some complications.

The Engineering of Choice and Ordinary Choice Behavior

Recently I gave a lecture on elementary decision theory, an introduction to rational theories of choice. After the lecture, a student asked whether it was conceivable that the practical procedures for decision-making implicit in theories of choice might make actual human decisions worse rather than

---

This paper was first published in *The Bell Journal of Economics*, Vol. 9, No. 2, Autumn 1978. Prior to that it was presented at a conference on the new industrial organization at Carnegie–Mellon University, 14–15 October 1977. The conference was organized to honor the contributions of Herbert A. Simon to economics, and his contribution to this paper is obvious. In addition, the author has profited from comments by Richard M. Cyert, Jon Elster, Alexander L. George, Elisabeth Hansot, Nannerl O. Keohane, Robert O. Keohane, Tjalling Koopmans, Mancur Olson, Louis R. Pondy, Roy Radner, Giovanni Sartori, and Oliver E. Williamson. The research was supported by a grant from the Spencer Foundation.

better. What is the empirical evidence, he asked, that human choice is improved by knowledge of decision theory or by application of the various engineering forms of rational choice? I answered, I think correctly, that the case for the usefulness of decision-engineering rested primarily not on the kind of direct empirical confirmation that he sought, but on two other things: on a set of theorems proving the superiority of particular procedures in particular situations if the situations are correctly specified and the procedures correctly applied, and on the willingness of clients to purchase the services of experts with skills in decision sciences.

The answer may not have been reasonable, but the question clearly was. It articulated a classical challenge to the practice of rational choice, the possibility that processes of rationality might combine with properties of human beings to produce decisions that are less sensible than the unsystematized actions of an intelligent person, or at least that the way in which we might use rational procedures intelligently is not self-evident. Camus (1951) argued, in effect, that man was not smart enough to be rational, a point made in a different way at about the same time by Herbert A. Simon (1957). Twenty years later, tales of horror have become contemporary cliches of studies of rational analysis in organizations (Wildavsky, 1971; Wildavsky and Pressman, 1973; Warwick, 1975).

I do not share the view of some of my colleagues that microeconomics, decision science, management science, operations analysis, and the other forms of rational decision-engineering are mostly manufacturers of massive mischief when they are put into practice. It seems to me likely that these modern technologies of reason have, on balance, done more good than harm, and that students of organizations, politics, and history have been overly gleeful in their compilation of disasters. But I think there is good sense in asking how the practical implementation of theories of choice combines with the ways people behave when they make decisions, and whether our ideas about the engineering of choice might be improved by greater attention to our descriptions of choice behavior.

At first blush, pure models of rational choice seem obviously appropriate as guides to intelligent action, but more problematic for predicting behavior. In practice, the converse seems closer to the truth for much of economics. So long as we use individual choice models to predict the behavior of relatively large numbers of individuals or organizations, some potential problems are avoided by the familiar advantages of aggregation. Even a small signal stands out in a noisy message. On the other hand, if we choose to predict small numbers of individuals or organizations or give advice to a single individual or organization, the saving graces of aggregation are mostly lost. The engineering of choice depends on a relatively close articulation between choice as it is comprehended in the assumptions of the model and choice as it is made comprehensible to individual actors.

This relation is reflected in the historical development of the field. According to conventional dogma, there are two kinds of theories of human behavior; descriptive (or behavioral) theories that purport to describe actual behavior of individuals or social institutions, and prescriptive (or normative) theories that purport to prescribe optimal behavior. In many ways, the distinction leads to an intelligent and fruitful division of labor in social science, reflecting differences in techniques, objectives, and professional cultures. For a variety of historical and intellectual reasons, however, such a division has not characterized the development of the theory of choice. Whether one considers ideas about choice in economics, psychology, political science, sociology, or philosophy, behavioral and normative theories have developed as a dialectic rather than as separate domains. Most modern behavioral theories of choice take as their starting point some simple ideas about rational human behavior. As a result, new developments in normative theories of choice have quickly affected behavioral theories. Contemplate, for example, the impact of game theory, statistical decision theory, and information theory on behavioral theories of human problem-solving, political decision-making, bargaining, and organizational behavior (Rapoport, 1960; Vroom, 1964; Binkley, Bronaugh, and Marras, 1971; Tversky and Kahneman, 1974; Mayhew, 1974). It is equally obvious that prescriptive theories of choice have been affected by efforts to understand actual choice behavior. Engineers of artificial intelligence have modified their perceptions of efficient problem-solving procedures by studying the actual behavior of human problem solvers (Simon, 1969; Newell and Simon, 1972). Engineers of organizational decision-making have modified their models of rationality on the basis of studies of actual organizational behavior (Charnes and Cooper, 1963; Keen, 1977).

Modern students of human choice frequently assume, at least implicitly, that actual human choice behavior in some way or other is likely to make sense. It can be understood as being the behavior of an intelligent being or a group of intelligent beings. Much theoretical work searches for the intelligence in apparently anomalous human behavior. This process of discovering sense in human behavior is conservative with respect to the concept of rational man and to behavioral change. It preserves the axiom of rationality; and it preserves the idea that human behavior is intelligent, even when it is not obviously so. But it is not conservative with respect to prescriptive models of choice. For if there is sense in the choice behavior of individuals acting contrary to standard engineering procedures for rationality, then it seems reasonable to suspect that there may be something inadequate about our normative theory of choice or the procedures by which it is implemented.

Rational choice involves two kinds of guesses: guesses about future consequences of current actions and guesses about future preferences for those consequences (Savage, 1954; Thompson, 1967). We try to imagine what will happen in the future as a result of our actions and we try to imagine how we shall evaluate what will happen. Neither guess is necessarily easy. Anticipating future consequences of present decisions is often subject to substantial error. Anticipating future preferences is often confusing. Theories of rational choice are primarily theories of these two guesses and how we deal with their complications. Theories of choice under uncertainty emphasize the complications of guessing future consequences. Theories of choice under conflict or ambiguity emphasize the complications of guessing future preferences.

Students of decision-making under uncertainty have identified a number of ways in which a classical model of how alternatives are assessed in terms of their consequences is neither descriptive of behavior nor a good guide in choice situations. As a result of these efforts, some of our ideas about how the first guess is made and how it ought to be made have changed. Since the early writings of Herbert A. Simon (1957), for example, bounded rationality has come to be recognized widely, though not universally, both as an accurate portrayal of much choice behavior and as a normatively sensible adjustment to the costs and character of information gathering and processing by human beings (Radner, 1975a, 1975b; Radner and Rothschild, 1975; Connolly, 1977).

The second guess has been less considered. For the most part, theories of choice have assumed that future preferences are exogenous, stable, and known with adequate precision to make decisions unambiguous. The assumptions are obviously subject to question. In the case of collective decision-making, there is the problem of conflicting objectives representing the values of different participants (March, 1962; Olson, 1965; M. Taylor, 1975; Pfeffer, 1977). In addition, individual preferences often appear to be fuzzy and inconsistent, and preferences appear to change over time, at least in part as a consequence of actions taken. Recently, some students of choice have been examining the ways individuals and organizations confront the second guess under conditions of ambiguity (i.e., where goals are vague, problematic, inconsistent, unstable) (Cohen and March, 1974; Weick, 1976; March and Olsen, 1976; Crozier and Friedberg, 1977). Those efforts are fragmentary, but they suggest that ignoring the ambiguities involved in guessing future preferences leads both to misinterpreting choice behavior and to misstating the normative problem facing a decision-maker. The doubts are not novel; John Stuart Mill (1838) expressed many of them in his essay on Bentham. They are not devastating; the theory of choice is probably robust enough to cope with them. They are not esoteric; Hegel is relevant, but may not be absolutely essential.

Bounded Rationality

There is a history. A little over 20 years ago, Simon published two papers that became a basis for two decades of development in the theory of choice (1955, 1956). The first of these examined the informational and computational limits on rationality by human beings. The paper suggested a focus on stepfunction utility functions and a process of information-gathering that began with a desired outcome and worked back to a set of antecedent actions sufficient to produce it. The second paper explored the consequences of simple payoff functions and search rules in an uncertain environment. The two papers argued explicitly that descriptions of decision-making in terms of such ideas conformed more to actual human behavior than did descriptions built upon classical rationality, that available evidence designed to test such models against classical ones tended to support the alternative ideas.

Because subsequent developments were extensive, it is well to recall that the original argument was a narrow one. It started from the proposition that all intendedly rational behavior is behavior within constraints. Simon added the idea that the list of technical constraints on choice should include some properties of human beings as processors of information and as problem-solvers. The limitations were limitations of computational capability, the organization and utilization of memory, and the like. He suggested that human beings develop decision procedures that are sensible, given the constraints, even though they might not be sensible if the constraints were removed. As a short-hand label for such procedures, he coined the term 'satisficing'.

Developments in the field over the past 20 years have expanded and distorted Simon's original formulation. But they have retained some considerable flavor of his original tone. He emphasized the theoretical difficulty posed by self-evident empirical truths. He obscured a distinction one might make between individual and organizational decision-making, proposing for the most part the same general ideas for both. He obscured a possible distinction between behavioral and normative theories of choice, preferring to view differences between perfect rationality and bounded rationality as explicable consequences of constraints. Few of the individual scholars who followed had precisely the same interests or commitments as Simon, but the field has generally maintained the same tone. Theoretical puzzlement with respect to the simplicity of decision behavior has been extended to puzzlement with respect to decision inconsistencies and instability, and the extent to which individuals and organizations do things without apparent reason (March and Olsen, 1976). Recent books on decision-making move freely from studies of organizations to studies of individuals (Janis and Mann, 1977). And recent books on normative decision-making accept many standard forms of organizational behavior as sensible (Keen, 1977).

Twenty years later, it is clear that we do not have a single, widely-accepted, precise behavioral theory of choice. But I think it can be argued that the empirical and theoretical efforts of the past 20 years have brought us closer to understanding decision processes. The understanding is organized in a set of conceptual vignettes rather than a single, coherent structure; and the connections among the vignettes are tenuous. In effect, the effort has identified major aspects of some key processes that appear to be reflected in decision-making; but the ecology of those processes is not well captured by any current theory. For much of this development. Simon bears substantial intellectual responsibility.

Simon's contributions have been honored by subsumption, extension, elaboration, and transformation. Some writers have felt it important to show that aspiration level goals and goal-directed search can be viewed as special cases of other ideas, most commonly classical notions about rational behavior (Riker and Ordeshook, 1974). Others have taken ideas about individual human behavior and extended them to organizations (both business firms and public bureaucracies) and to other institutions, for example, universities (Bower, 1968; Allison, 1969; Steinbruner, 1974; Williamson, 1975). Simon's original precise commentary on specific difficulties in rational models has been expanded to a more general consideration of problems in the assumptions of rationality, particularly the problems of subjective understanding, perception, and conflict of interest (Cyert and March, 1963; Porat and Haas, 1969; Carter, 1971; R. N. Taylor, 1975; Slovic, Fischhoff, and Lichtenstein, 1977). The original articles suggested small modifications in a theory of economic behavior, the substitution of bounded rationality for omniscient rationality. But the ideas ultimately have led to an examination of the extent to which theories of choice might subordinate the idea of rationality altogether to less intentional conceptions of the causal determinants of action (March and Olsen, 1976).

Alternative Rationalities

The search for intelligence in decision-making is an effort to rationalize apparent anomalies in behavior. In a general way, that effort imputes either calculated or systemic rationality to observed choice behavior. Action is presumed to follow either from explicit calculation of its consequences in terms of objectives, or from rules of behavior that have evolved through processes that are sensible but which obscure from present knowledge full information on the rational justification for any specific rule.

Most efforts to rationalize observed behavior have attempted to place that behavior within a framework of calculated rationality. The usual argument is that a naïve rational model is inadequate either because it focuses on the wrong unit of analysis, or because it uses an inaccurate characterization of the preferences involved. As a result, we have developed ideas of limited rationality, contextual rationality, game rationality, and process rationality.

Ideas of *limited rationality* emphasize the extent to which individuals and groups simplify a decision problem because of the difficulties of anticipating or considering all alternatives and all information (March and Simon, 1958; Lindblom, 1959, 1965; Radner, 1975a, 1975b). They introduce, as reasonable responses, such things as step-function tastes, simple search rules, working backward, organizational slack, incrementalism and muddling through, uncertainty avoidance, and the host of elaborations of such ideas that are familiar to students of organizational choice and human problem-solving.

Ideas of *contextual rationality* emphasize the extent to which choice behavior is embedded in a complex of other claims on the attention of actors and other structures of social and cognitive relations (Long, 1958; Schelling, 1971; Cohen, March, and Olsen, 1972; Weiner, 1976; Sproull, Weiner, and Wolf, 1978). They focus on the way in which choice behavior in a particular situation is affected by the opportunity costs of attending to that situation and by the apparent tendency for people, problems, solutions, and choices to be joined by the relatively arbitrary accidents of their simultaneity rather than by their *prima facie* relevance to each other.

Ideas of *game rationality* emphasize the extent to which organizations and other social institutions consist of individuals who act in relation to each other intelligently to pursue individual objectives by means of individual calculations of self-interest (Farquharson, 1969; Harsanyi and Selten, 1972; Brams, 1975). The decision outcomes of the collectivity in some sense amalgamate those calculations, but they do so without imputing a super-goal to the collectivity or invoking collective rationality. These theories find reason in the process of coalition formation, sequential attention to goals, information bias and interpersonal gaming, and the development of mutual incentives.

Ideas of *process rationality* emphasize the extent to which decisions find their sense in attributes of the decision process, rather than in attributes of decision outcomes (Edelman, 1960; Cohen and March, 1974; Kreiner, 1976; Christensen, 1976). They explore those significant human pleasures (and pains) found in the ways we act while making decisions, and in the symbolic content of the idea and procedures of choice. Explicit outcomes are viewed as secondary and decision-making becomes sensible through the intelligence of the way it is orchestrated.

All of these kinds of ideas are theories of intelligent individuals making calculations of the consequences of actions for objectives, and acting sensibly to achieve those objectives. Action is presumed to be consequential, to be connected consciously and meaningfully to knowledge about personal goals and future outcomes, to be controlled by personal intention.

Although models of calculated rationality continue to be a dominant style, students of choice have also shown considerable interest in a quite different kind of intelligence, systemic rather than calculated. Suppose we imagine that knowledge, in the form of precepts of behavior, evolves over time within a system and accumulates across time, people, and organizations without complete current consciousness of its history. Then sensible action is taken by actors without comprehension of its full justification. This characterizes models of adaptive rationality, selected rationality, and posterior rationality.

Ideas of *adaptive rationality* emphasize experiential learning by individuals or collectivities (Cyert and March, 1963; Day and Groves, 1975). Most adaptive models have the property that if the world and preferences are stable and the experience prolonged enough, behavior will approach the behavior that would be chosen rationally on the basis of perfect knowledge. Moreover, the postulated learning functions normally have properties that permit sensible adaptation to drifts in environmental or taste attributes. By storing information on past experiences in some simple behavioral predilections, adaptive rationality permits the efficient management of considerable experiential information; but it is in a form that is not explicitly retrievable – particularly across individuals or long periods of time. As a result, it is a form of intelligence that tends to separate current reasons from current actions.

Ideas of *selected rationality* emphasize the process of selection among individuals or organizations through survival or growth (Winter, 1964, 1971, 1975; Nelson and Winter, 1973). Rules of behavior achieve intelligence not by virtue of conscious calculation of their rationality by current role players but by virtue of the survival and growth of social institutions in which such rules are followed and such roles are performed. Selection theories focus on the extent to which choice is dominated by standard operating procedures and the social regulation of social roles.

Ideas of *posterior rationality* emphasize the discovery of intentions as an interpretation of action rather than as a prior position (Hirschman, 1967; Weick, 1969; March, 1973). Actions are seen as being exogenous and as producing experiences that are organized into an evaluation after the fact. The valuation is in terms of preferences generated by the action and its consequences, and choices are justified by virtue of their posterior consistency with goals that have themselves been developed through a critical interpretation of the choice. Posterior rationality models maintain the idea that action should be consistent with preferences. but they conceive action as being antecedent to goals.

These explorations into elements of systemic rationality have, of course, a strong base in economics and behavioral science (Wilson, 1975; Becker, 1976); but they pose special problems for decision-engineering. On the one hand, systemic rationality is not intentional. That is, behavior is not understood as following from a calculation of consequences in terms of prior objectives. If such a calculation is asserted, it is assumed to be an interpretation of the behavior but not a good predictor of it. On the other hand, these models claim, often explicitly, that there is intelligence in the suspension of calculation. Alternatively, they suggest that whatever sense there is in calculated rationality is attested not by its formal properties but by its survival as a social rule of behavior, or as an experientially verified personal propensity.

In a general way, these explications of ordinary behavior as forms of rationality have considerably clarified and extended our understanding of choice. It is now routine to explore aspects of limited, contextual, game, process, adaptive, selected, and posterior rationality in the behavioral theory of choice. We use such ideas to discover and celebrate the intelligence of human behavior. At the same time, however, this discovery of intelligence in the ordinary behavior of individuals and social institutions is an implicit pressure for reconstruction of normative theories of choice, for much of the argument is not only that observed behavior is understandable as a human phenomenon, but that it is, in some important sense, intelligent. If behavior that apparently deviates from standard procedures of calculated rationality can be shown to be intelligent, then it can plausibly be argued that models of calculated rationality are deficient not only as descriptors of human behavior but also as guides to intelligent choice.

The Treatment of Tastes

Engineers of intelligent choice sensibly resist the imputation of intelligence to all human behavior. Traditionally, deviations of choice behavior from the style anticipated in classical models were treated normatively as errors, or correctable faults, as indeed many of them doubtless were. The objective was to transform subjective rationality into objective rationality by removing the needless informational, procedural, and judgmental constraints that limited the effectiveness of persons proceeding intelligently from false or incomplete informational premises (Ackoff and Sasieni, 1968). One of Simon's contributions to the theory of choice was his challenge of the self-evident proposition that choice behavior necessarily would be improved if it were made more like the normative model of rational choice. By asserting that certain limits on rationality stemmed from properties of the human organism, he emphasized the possibility that actual human choice behavior was more intelligent than it appeared.

Normative theories of choice have responded to the idea. Substantial parts of the economics of information and the economics of attention (or time) are tributes to the proposition that information-gathering, information-processing, and decision-making impose demands on the scarce resources of a finite capacity human organism (Stigler, 1961; Becker, 1965; McGuire and Radner, 1972; Marschak and Radner, 1972; Rothschild and Stiglitz, 1976). Aspiration levels, signals, incrementalism, and satisficing rules for decision-making have been described as sensible under fairly general circumstances (Hirschman and Lindblom, 1962; Spence, 1974; Radner, 1975a, 1975b; Radner and Rothschild, 1975).

These developments in the theory of rational choice acknowledge important aspects of the behavioral critique of classical procedures for guessing the future consequences of present action. Normative response to behavioral discussions of the second guess, the estimation of future preferences, has been similarly conservative but perceptible. That standard theories of choice and the engineering procedures associated with them have a conception of preferences that differs from observations of preferences has long been noted (Johnson, 1968). As in the case of the informational constraints on rational choice, the first reaction within decision-engineering was to treat deviations from well-defined, consistent preference functions as correctable faults. If individuals had deficient (i.e., inconsistent, incomplete) preference functions, they were to be induced to generate proper ones, perhaps through revealed preference techniques and education. If groups or organizations exhibited conflict, they were to be induced to resolve that conflict through prior discussion, prior side payments (e.g., an employment contract), or prior bargaining. If individuals or organizations exhibited instability in preferences over time, they were to be induced to minimize that instability by recognizing a more general specification of the preferences so that apparent changes became explicable as reflecting a single, unchanging function under changing conditions or changing resources.

Since the specific values involved in decision-making are irrelevant to formal models of choice, both process rationality and contextual rationality are, from such a perspective, versions of simple calculated rationality. The criterion function is changed, but the theory treats the criterion function as any arbitrary set of well-ordered preferences. So long as the preferences associated with the process of choice or the preferences involved in the broader context are well-defined and well-behaved, there is no deep theoretical difficulty. But, in practice, such elements of human preference functions have not filtered significantly into the engineering of choice.

The record with respect to problems of goal conflict, multiple, lexicographic goals, and loosely coupled systems is similar. Students of bureaucracies have argued that a normative theory of choice within a modern bureaucratic structure must recognize explicitly the continuing conflict in preferences among various actors (Tullock, 1965; Downs, 1967; Allison and Halperin, 1972; Halperin, 1974). Within such systems 'decisions' are probably better seen as strategic first-move interventions in a dynamic internal system than as choices in a classical sense. Decisions are not expected to be implemented, and actions that would be optimal if implemented are suboptimal as first moves. This links theories of choice to game-theoretic conceptions of politics, bargaining, and strategic actions in a productive way. Although in this way ideas about strategic choice in collectivities involving conflict of interest are well established in part of the choice literature (Elster, 1977a), they have had little impact on such obvious applied domains as bureaucratic decision-making or the design of organizational control systems. The engineering of choice has been more explicitly concerned with multiple criteria decision procedures for dealing with multiple, lexicographic, or political goals (Lee, 1972; Pattanaik, 1973). In some cases these efforts have considerably changed the spirit of decision analysis, moving it toward a role of exploring the implications of constraints and away from a conception of solution.

Behavioral inquiry into preferences has, however, gone beyond the problems of interpersonal conflict of interest in recent years and into the complications of ambiguity. The problems of ambiguity are partly problems of disagreement about goals among individuals, but they are more conspicuously problems of the relevance, priority, clarity, coherence, and stability of goals in both individual and organizational choice. Several recent treatments of organizational choice behavior record some major ways in which explicit goals seem neither particularly powerful predictors of outcomes nor particularly well-represented as either stable, consistent preference orders or well-defined political constraints (Cohen and March, 1974; Weick, 1976; March and Olsen, 1976; Sproull, Weiner, and Wolf, 1978).

It is possible, of course, that such portrayals of behavior are perverse. They may be perverse because they systematically misrepresent the actual behavior of human beings or they may be perverse because the human beings they describe are, in so far as the description applies, stupid. But it is also possible that the description is accurate and the behavior is intelligent, that the ambiguous way human beings sometimes deal with tastes is, in fact, sensible. If such a thing can be imagined, then its corollary may also be imaginable: Perhaps we treat tastes inadequately in our engineering of choice. When we start to discover intelligence in decision-making where goals are unstable, ill-defined, or apparently irrelevant, we are led to ask some different kinds of questions about our normative conceptions of choice and walk closely not only to some issues in economics but also to some classical and modern questions in literature and ethics, particularly the role of clear prior purpose in the ordering of human affairs.

Consider the following properties of tastes as they appear in standard prescriptive theories of choice:

1 Tastes are *absolute*. Normative theories of choice assume a formal posture of moral relativism. The theories insist on morality of action in terms of tastes; but they recognize neither discriminations among alternative tastes, nor the possibility that a person reasonably might view his own preferences and actions based on them as morally distressing.
2 Tastes are *relevant*. Normative theories of choice require that action be taken in terms of tastes, that decisions be consistent with preferences in the light of information about the probable consequences of alternatives for valued outcomes. Action is willful.
3 Tastes are *stable*. With few exceptions, normative theories of choice require that tastes be stable. Current action is taken in terms of current tastes. The implicit assumption is that tastes will be unchanged when the outcomes of current actions are realized.
4 Tastes are *consistent*. Normative theories of choice allow mutually inconsistent tastes only in so far as they can be made irrelevant by the absence of scarcity or reconcilable by the specification of trade-offs.
5 Tastes are *precise*. Normative theories of choice eliminate ambiguity about the extent to which a particular outcome will satisfy tastes, at least in so far as possible resolutions of that ambiguity might affect the choice.
6 Tastes are *exogenous*. Normative theories of choice presume that tastes, by whatever process they may be created, are not themselves affected by the choices they control.

Each of these features of tastes seems inconsistent with observations of choice behavior among individuals and social institutions. Not always, but often enough to be troublesome. Individuals commonly find it possible to express both a taste for something and a recognition that the taste is something that is repugnant to moral standards they accept. Choices are often made without respect to tastes. Human decision-makers routinely ignore their own, fully conscious, preferences in making decisions. They follow rules, traditions, hunches, and the advice or actions of others. Tastes change over time in such a way that predicting future tastes is often difficult. Tastes are inconsistent. Individuals and organizations are aware of the extent to which some of their preferences conflict with other of their preferences; yet they do nothing to resolve those inconsistencies.

Many preferences are stated in forms that lack precision. It is difficult to make them reliably operational in evaluating possible outcomes. While tastes are used to choose among actions, it is often also true that actions and experience with their consequences affect tastes. Tastes are determined partly endogenously.

Such differences between tastes as they are portrayed by our models and tastes as they appear in our experience produce ordinary behavioral phenomena that are not always well accommodated within the structure of our prescriptions.

We manage our preferences. We select actions now partly in terms of expectations about the effect of those actions upon future preferences. We do things now to modify our future tastes. Thus, we know that if we engage in some particularly tasty, but immoral, activity, we are likely to come to like it more. We know that if we develop competence in a particular skill, we shall often come to favor it. So we choose to pursue the competence, or not, engage in an activity, or not, depending on whether we wish to increase or decrease our taste for the competence or activity.

We construct our preferences. We choose preferences and actions jointly, in part, to discover – or construct – new preferences that are currently unknown. We deliberately specify our objectives in vague terms to develop an understanding of what we might like to become. We elaborate our tastes as interpretations of our behavior.

We treat our preferences strategically. We specify goals that are different from the outcomes we wish to achieve. We adopt preferences and rules of actions that if followed literally would lead us to outcomes we do not wish, because we believe that the final outcome will only partly reflect our initial intentions. In effect, we consider the choice of preferences as part of an infinite game with ourselves in which we attempt to deal with our propensities for acting badly by anticipating them and outsmarting ourselves. We use deadlines and make commitments.

We confound our preferences. Our deepest preferences tend often to be paired. We find the same outcome both attractive and repulsive, not in the sense that the two sentiments cancel each other and we remain indifferent, but precisely that we simultaneously want and do not want an outcome, experience it as both pleasure and pain, love and hate it (Catullus, 58 BC, 1.1).

We avoid our preferences. Our actions and our preferences are only partly linked. We are prepared to say that we want something, yet should not want it, or wish we did not want it. We are prepared to act in ways that are inconsistent with our preferences, and to maintain that inconsistency in the face of having it demonstrated. We do not believe that what we do must necessarily result from a desire to achieve preferred outcomes.

We expect change in our preferences. As we contemplate making choices that have consequences in the future, we know that our attitudes about possible outcomes will change in ways that are substantial but not entirely predictable. The subjective probability distribution over possible future preferences (like the subjective probability distribution over possible future consequences) increases its variance as the horizon is stretched. As a result, we have a tendency to want to take actions now that maintain future options for acting when future preferences are clearer.

We suppress our preferences. Consequential argument, the explicit linking of actions to desires, is a form of argument in which some people are better than others. Individuals who are less competent at consequential rationalization try to avoid it with others who are more competent, particularly others who may have a stake in persuading them to act in a particular way. We resist an explicit formulation of consistent desires to avoid manipulation of our choices by persons cleverer than we at that special form of argument called consistent rationality.

It is possible, on considering this set of contrasts between decision-making as we think it ought to occur and decision-making as we think it does occur to trivialize the issue into a 'definitional problem'. By suitably manipulating the concept of tastes, one can save classical theories of choice as 'explanations' of behavior in a formal sense, but probably only at the cost of stretching a good idea into a doubtful ideology (Stigler and Becker, 1977). More importantly from the present point of view, such a redefinition pays the cost of destroying the practical relevance of normative prescriptions for choice. For prescriptions are useful only if we see a difference between observed procedures and desirable procedures.

Alternatively, one can record all of the deviations from normative specifications as stupidity, errors that should be corrected; and undertake to transform the style of existing humans into the styles anticipated by the theory. This has, for the most part, been the strategy of operations and management analysis for the past 20 years; and it has had its successes. But it has also had failures.

It is clear that the human behavior I have described may, in any individual case, be a symptom of ignorance, obtuseness, or deviousness. But the fact that such patterns of behavior are fairly common among individuals and institutions suggests that they might be sensible under some general kinds of conditions – that goal ambiguity, like limited rationality, is not necessarily a fault in human choice to be corrected but often a form of intelligence to be refined by the technology of choice rather than ignored by it.

Uncertainty about future consequences and human limitations in dealing with them are relatively easily seen as intrinsic in the decision situation and the nature of the human organism. It is much harder to see in what way ambiguous preferences are a necessary property of human behavior. It seems meaningful in ordinary terms to assert that human decision-makers are driven to techniques of limited rationality by the exigencies of the situation in which they find themselves. But what drives them to ambiguous and changing goals? Part of the answer is directly analogous to the formulations of limited rationality. Limitations of memory organization and retrieval and of information capacity affect information processing about preferences just as they affect information processing about consequences (March and Simon, 1958; Cyert and March, 1963; Simon, 1973; March and Romalaer, 1976). Human beings have unstable, inconsistent, incompletely evoked, and imprecise goals at least in part because human abilities limit preference orderliness. If it were possible to be different at reasonable cost, we probably would want to be.

But viewing ambiguity as a necessary cost imposed by the information processing attributes of individuals fails to capture the extent to which similar styles in preferences would be sensible, even if the human organism were a more powerful computational system. We probably need to ask the more general question: Why might a person or institution choose to have ambiguous tastes? The answer, I believe, lies in several things, some related to ideas of bounded rationality, others more familiar to human understanding as it is portrayed in literature and philosophy than to our theories of choice.

1 Human beings recognize in their behavior that there are limits to personal and institutional integration in tastes. They know that no matter how much they may be pressured both by their own prejudices for integration and by the demands of others, they will be left with contradictory and intermittent desires partially ordered but imperfectly reconciled. As a result, they engage in activities designed to manage preferences or game preferences. These activities make little sense from the point of view of a conception of human choice that assumes people know what they want and will want, or a conception that assumes wants are morally equivalent. But ordinary human actors sense that they might come to want something that they should not, or that they might make unwise or inappropriate choices under the influence of fleeting, but powerful, desires, if they do not act now either to control the development of tastes or to buffer action from tastes (Elster, 1977b).

2 Human beings recognize implicitly the limitations of acting rationally on current guesses. By insisting that action, to be justified, must follow preferences and be consistent both with those preferences and with estimates of future states, we considerably exaggerate the relative power of a choice based consistently upon two guesses compared to a choice that is itself a guess. Human beings are both proponents

for preferences and observers of the process by which their preferences are developed and acted upon. As observers of the process by which their beliefs have been formed and consulted, they recognize the good sense in perceptual and moral modesty (Williams, 1973; Elster, 1977c).

3 Human beings recognize the extent to which tastes are constructed, or developed, through a more or less constant confrontation between preferences and actions that are inconsistent with them, and among conflicting preferences. As a result, they appear to be comfortable with an extraordinary array of unreconciled sources of legitimate wants. They maintain a lack of coherence both within and among personal desires, social demands, and moral codes. Though they seek some consistency, they appear to see inconsistency as a normal, and necessary, aspect of the development and clarification of tastes (March, 1973).

4 Human beings are conscious of the importance of preferences as beliefs independent of their immediate action consequences. They appear to find it possible to say, in effect, that they believe something is more important to good action than they are able (or willing) to make it in a specific case. They act as though some aspects of their beliefs are important to life without necessarily being consistent with actions, and important to the long-run quality of choice behavior without controlling it completely in the short run. They accept a degree of personal and social wisdom in ordinary hypocrisy (Chomsky, 1968; March, 1973; Pondy and Olson, 1977).

5 Human beings know that some people are better at rational argument than others, and that those skills are not particularly well correlated with either morality or sympathy. As a result, they recognize the political nature of argumentation more clearly, and more personally, than the theory of choice does. They are unwilling to gamble that God made clever people uniquely virtuous. They protect themselves from cleverness by obscuring the nature of their preferences; they exploit cleverness by asking others to construct reasons for actions they wish to take (Shakespeare, 1623).

Tastes and the Engineering of Choice

These characteristics of preference processing by individual human beings and social institutions seem to me to make sense under rather general circumstances. As a result, it seems likely to me that our engineering of choice behavior does not make so much sense as we sometimes attribute to it. The view of human tastes and their proper role in action that we exhibit in our normative theory of choice is at least as limiting to the engineering applicability of that theory as the perfect knowledge assumptions were to the original formulations.

Since it has taken us over 20 years to introduce modest elements of bounded rationality and conflict of interest into prescriptions about decision-making, there is no particular reason to be sanguine about the speed with which our engineering of choice will accept and refine the intelligence of ambiguity. But there is hope. The reconstruction involved is not extraordinary, and in some respects has already begun. For the doubts I have expressed about engineering models of choice to be translated into significant changes, they will have to be formulated a bit more precisely in terms that are comprehensible within such theories, even though they may not be consistent with the present form of the theories or the questions the theories currently address. I cannot accomplish such a task in any kind of complete way, but I think it is possible to identify a few conceptual problems that might plausibly be addressed by choice theorists and a few optimization problems that might plausibly be addressed by choice engineers.

The conceptual problems involve discovering interesting ways to reformulate some assumptions about tastes, particularly about the stability of tastes, their exogenous character, their priority, and their internal consistency.

Consider the problem of *intertemporal comparison* of preferences (Strotz, 1956; Koopmans, 1964; Bailey and Olson, 1977; Shefrin and Thaler, 1977). Suppose we assume that the preferences that will be held at every relevant future point in time are known. Suppose further that those preferences change over time but are, at any given time, consistent. If action is to be taken now in terms of its consequences over a period of time during which preferences change, we are faced with having to make intertemporal comparisons. As long as the changes are exogenous, we can avoid the problem if we choose to do so. If we can imagine an individual making a complete and transitive ordering over possible outcomes over time, then intertemporal comparisons are implicit in the preference orderings and cause no particular difficulty beyond the heroic character of the assumption about human capabilities. If, on the other hand, we think of the individual as having a distinct, complete, and consistent preference relation defined over the outcomes realized in a particular time period, and we imagine that those preferences change over time, then the problem of intertemporal comparisons is more difficult. The problem is technically indistinguishable from the problem of interpersonal comparison of utilities. When we compare the changing preferences of a single person over time to make trade-offs across time, we are, in the identical position as when we attempt to make comparisons across different individuals at a point in time. The fact that the problems are identical has the advantage of immediately bringing to bear on the problems of intertemporal comparisons the apparatus developed to deal with interpersonal comparisons (Mueller, 1976). It has the disadvantage that that apparatus allows a much weaker conception of solution than is possible within a single, unchanging set of preferences. We are left with the weak theorems of social welfare economics, but perhaps with a clearer recognition that there is no easy and useful way to escape the problem of incomparable preference functions by limiting our attention to a single individual, as long as tastes change over time and we think of tastes as being defined at a point in time.

Consider the problem of *endogenous change* in preferences (Von Weiszäcker, 1971; Olson, 1976). Suppose we know that future tastes will change in a predictable way as a consequence of actions taken now and the consequences of those actions realized over time. Then we are in the position of choosing now the preferences we shall have later. If there is risk involved, we are choosing now a probability distribution over future preferences. If we can imagine some 'super goal', the problem becomes tractable. We evaluate alternative preferences in terms of their costs and benefits for the 'super goal'. Such a strategy preserves the main spirit of normal choice theory but allows only a modest extension into endogenous change. This is the essential strategy adopted in some of the engineering examples below. In such cases desirable preferences cannot always be deduced from the 'super goal', but alternative preferences can be evaluated. In somewhat the same spirit, we can imagine adaptive preferences as a possible decision procedure and examine whether rules for a sequence of adaptations in tastes can be specified that lead to choice outcomes better in some easily recognized sense than those obtained through explicit calculated rationality at the start of the process. One possible place is the search for cooperative solutions in games in which calculated rationality is likely to lead to outcomes desired by no one (Cyert and de Groot, 1973; 1975). Also in the same general spirit, we might accept the strict morality position and attempt to select a strategy for choice that will minimize change in values. Or we might try to select a strategy that maximizes value change. All of these are possible explorations, but they are not fully attentive to the normative management of adaptation in tastes. The problem exceeds our present concepts: How do we act sensibly now to manage the development of preferences in the future when we do not have a criterion for evaluating future tastes that will not itself be affected by our actions? There may be some kind of fixed-point theorem answer to such a problem, but I suspect that a real conceptual confrontation with endogenous preferences will involve some reintroduction of moral philosophy into our understanding of choice (Friedman, 1967; Williams, 1973; Beck, 1975).

Consider the problem of *posterior preferences* (Schutz, 1967; Hirschman, 1967; Weick, 1969; Elster, 1976). The theory of choice is built on the idea of prior intentions. Suppose we relax the requirement of priority, allow preferences to rationalize action after the fact in our theories as well as our behavior. How do we act in such a way that we conclude, after the fact, that the action was intelligent, and also are led to an elaboration of our preferences that we find fruitful? Such a formulation seems closer to a correct representation of choice problems in politics, for example, than is conventional social welfare theory. We find meaning and merit in our actions after they are taken and the consequences are observed and interpreted. Deliberate efforts to manage posterior constructions of preferences are familiar to us. They include many elements of child-rearing, psychotherapy, consciousness-raising, and product advertising. The terms are somewhat different. We talk of development of character in child-rearing, of insight in psychotherapy, of recognition of objective reality in political, ethnic, or sexual consciousness-raising, and of elaboration of personal needs in advertising. But the technologies are more similar than their ideologies. These techniques for the construction (or excavation) of tastes include both encouraging a reinterpretation of experience and attempting to induce current behavior that will facilitate posterior elaboration of a new understanding of personal preferences. I have tried elsewhere to indicate some of the possibilities this suggests for intelligent foolishness and the role of ambiguity in sensible action (March, 1973). The problem is in many ways indistinguishable from the problem of poetry and the criticism of poetry (or art and art criticism). The poet attempts to write a poem that has meanings intrinsic in the poem but not necessarily explicit at the moment of composition (Ciardi, 1960). In this sense, at least, decisions, like poems, are open; and good decisions are those that enrich our preferences and their meanings. But to talk in such a manner is to talk the language of criticism and aesthetics, and it will probably be necessary for choice theory to engage that literature in some way (Eliot, 1933; Cavell, 1969; Steinberg, 1972; Rosenberg, 1975).

Finally, consider the problem of *inconsistency* in preferences (Elster, 1977c). From the point of view of ordinary human ideas about choice, as well as many philosophical and behavioral conceptions of choice, the most surprising thing about formal theories of choice is the tendency to treat such terms as values, goals, preferences, tastes, wants, and the like, as either equivalent or as reducible to a single objective function with properties of completeness and consistency. Suppose that instead of making such an assumption, we viewed the decision-maker as confronted simultaneously with several orderings of outcomes. We could give them names, calling one a moral code, another a social role, another a personal taste, or whatever. From the present point of view what would be critical would be that the several orderings were independent and irreducible. That is, they could not be deduced from each other, and they could not be combined into a single order. Then instead of taking the conventional step of imputing a preference order across these incomparables by some kind of revealed preference procedure, we treat them as truly incomparable and examine solutions to internal inconsistency that are more in the spirit of our efforts to provide intelligent guidance to collectivities in which we accept the incomparability of preferences across individuals. Then we could give better advice to individuals who want to treat their own preferences strategically, and perhaps move to a clearer recognition of the role of contradiction and paradox in human choice (Farber, 1976; Elster, 1977c). The strategic problems are amenable to relatively straightforward modifications of our views of choice under conflict of interest; the other problems probably require a deeper understanding of contradiction as it appears in philosophy and literature (Elster, 1977c).

Formulating the conceptual problems in these ways is deliberately conservative *vis-à-vis* the theory of choice. It assumes that thinking about human behavior in terms of choice on the basis of some conception of intention is useful, and that the tradition of struggle between normative theories of choice and behavioral theories of choice is a fruitful one. There are alternative paradigms for understanding human behavior that are in many situations likely to be more illuminating. But it is probably unwise to think that every paper should suggest a dramatic paradigm shift, particularly when the alternative is seen only dimly.

Such strictures become even more important when we turn to the engineering of choice. Choice theorists have often discussed complications in the usual abstract representation of tastes. But those concerns have had little impact on ideas about the engineering of choice, because they pose the problems at a level of philosophic complexity that is remote from decision-engineering. Thus, although I think the challenges that ambiguity makes to our models of choice are rather fundamental, my engineering instincts are to sacrifice purity to secure tractability. I suspect we should ask the engineers of choice not initially to reconstruct a philosophy of tastes but to re-examine, within a familiar framework, some presumptions of our craft, and to try to make the use of ambiguity somewhat less of a mystery, somewhat more of a technology. Consider, for example, the following elementary problems in engineering.

The Optimal Ambition Problem

The level of personal ambition is not a decision variable in most theories of choice; but as a result of the work by Simon and others on satisficing, there has been interest in optimal levels of aspiration. These efforts consider an aspiration level as a trigger that either begins or ends the search for new alternatives. The optimization problem is one of balancing the expected costs of additional search with the expected improvements to be realized from the effort (March and Simon, 1958).

But there is another, rather different, way of looking at the optimum ambition problem. Individuals and organizations form aspirations, goals, targets, or ambitions for achievement. These ambitions are usually assumed to be connected to outcomes in at least two ways: they affect search (either directly or through some variable like motivation) and thereby performance; they affect (jointly with performance) satisfaction (March and Simon, 1958). Suppose we wish to maximize some function of satisfaction over time by selecting among alternative ambitions over time, alternative initial ambitions, or alternatives defined by some other decision variable that affects ambition. Examples of the latter might be division of income between consumption and savings, tax policies, or choice among alternative payment schemes. In effect, we wish to select a preference function for achievement that will, after the various behavioral consequences of that selection are accounted for, make us feel that we have selected the best ambition. It is a problem much more familiar to the real world of personal and institutional choice than it is to the normative theory of choice, but it is something about which some things could be said.

The Optimal Clarity Problem

Conventional notions about intelligent choice often begin with the presumption that good decisions require clear goals, and that improving the clarity of goals unambiguously improves the quality of decision-making. In fact, greater precision in the statement of objectives and the measurement of performance with respect to them is often a mixed blessing. There are arguments for moderating an unrestrained enthusiasm for precise performance measures: Where contradiction and confusion are essential elements of the values, precision misrepresents them. The more precise the measure of performance, the greater the motivation to find ways of scoring well on the measurement index without regard to the underlying goals. And precision in objectives does not allow creative interpretation of what the goal might mean (March, 1978). Thus, the introduction of precision into the evaluation of performance involves a tradeoff between the gains in outcomes attributable to closer articulation between action and performance on an index of performance and the losses in outcomes attributable to misrepresentation of goals, reduced motivation to development of goals, and concentration of effort on irrelevant ways of beating the index. Whether one is considering developing a performance evaluation scheme for managers, a testing procedure for students, or an understanding of personal preferences, there is a problem of determining the optimum clarity in goals.

The Optimal Sin Problem

Standard notions of intelligent choice are theories of strict morality. That is, they presume that a person should do what he believes right and believe that what he does is right. Values and actions are to be consistent. Contrast that perspective with a view, somewhat more consistent with our behavior (as well as some theology), that there is such a thing as sin, that individuals and institutions sometimes do things even while recognizing that what they do is not what they wish they did, and that saints are a luxury to be encouraged only in small numbers. Or contrast a theory of strict morality with a view drawn from Nietzsche (1918) or Freud (1927) (see also Jones, 1926) of the complicated contradiction between conscience and self-interest. Although the issues involved are too subtle for brief treatment, a reasonably strong case can be made against strict morality and in favor of at least some sin, and therefore hypocrisy. One of the most effective ways of maintaining morality is through the remorse exhibited and felt at immoral action. Even if we are confident that our moral codes are correct, we may want to recognize human complexities. There will be occasions on which humans will be tempted by desires that they recognize as evil. If we insist that they maintain consistency between ethics and actions, the ethics will often be more likely to change than the actions. Hypocrisy is a long-run investment in morality made at some cost (the chance that, in fact, action might otherwise adjust to morals). To encourage people always to take responsibility for their actions is to encourage them to deny that bad things are bad – to make evil acceptable. At the same time, sin is an experiment with an alternative morality. By recognizing sin, we make it easier for persons to experiment with the possibility of having different tastes. Moral systems need those experiments, and regularly grant licenses to experiment to drunks, lovers, students, or sinners. These gains from sin are purchased by its costs. Thus, the optimization problem.

The Optimal Rationality Problem

Calculated rationality is a technique for making decisions. In standard versions of theories of choice it is the only legitimate form of intelligence. But it is obvious that it is, in fact, only one of several alternative forms of intelligence, each with claims to legitimacy. Learned behavior, with its claim to summarize an irretrievable but relevant personal history, or conventional behavior and rules, with their claims to capture the intelligence of survival over long histories of experience more relevant than that susceptible to immediate calculation, are clear alternative contenders. There are others: Revelation or intuition, by which we substitute one guess for two; or imitation, or expertise, by which we substitute the guess of someone else for our own. Among all of these, only calculated rationality really uses conscious preferences of a current actor as a major consideration in making decisions. It is easy to show that there exist situations in which any one of these alternative techniques will make better decisions than the independent calculation of rational behavior by ordinary individuals or institutions. The superiority of learned or conventional behavior depends, in general, on the amount of experience it summarizes and the similarity between the world in which the experience was accumulated and the current world. The superiority of imitation depends, in general, on the relative competence of actor and expert and the extent to which intelligent action is reproducible but not comprehendible. At the same time, each form of intelligence exposes an actor to the risks of corruption. Imitation risks a false confidence in the neutrality of the process of diffusion; calculated rationality risks a false confidence in the neutrality of rational argument; and so on. It is not hard to guess that the relative size of these risks vary from individual to individual, or institution to institution. What is harder to specify in any very precise way is the extent and occasions on which a sensible person would rely on calculated rationality rather than the alternatives.

A Romantic Vision

Prescriptive theories of choice are dedicated to perfecting the intelligence of human action by imagining that action stems from reason and by improving the technology of decision. Descriptive theories of choice are dedicated to perfecting the understanding of human action by imagining that action makes sense. Not all behavior makes sense; some of it is unreasonable. Not all decision-technology is intelligent; some of it is foolish. Over the past 20 years, the contradiction between the search for sense in behavior and the search for improvement in behavior has focused on our interpretation of the way information about future consequences is gathered and processed. The effort built considerably on the idea of bounded rationality and a conception of human decision-making as limited by the cognitive capabilities of human beings. Over the next 20 years. I suspect the contradiction will be increasingly concerned with an interpretation of how beliefs about future preferences are generated and utilized. The earlier confrontation led theories of choice to a slightly clearer understanding of information-processing and to some modest links with the technologies of computing inference, and subjective probability. So perhaps the newer confrontation will lead theories of choice to a slightly clearer understanding of the complexities of preference processing and to some modest links with the technologies of ethics, criticism, and aesthetics. The history of theories of choice and their engineering applications suggests that we might appropriately be pessimistic about immediate, major progress. The intelligent engineering of tastes involves questions that encourage despair over their difficulty (Savage, 1954). But though hope for minor progress is a romantic vision, it may not be entirely inappropriate for a theory built on a romantic view of human destiny.

References

Ackoff, R. L., and Sasieni, M. W. (1968) *Fundamentals of Operations Research*. New York: Wiley.

Allison, G. T. (1969) *Essence of Decision: Explaining the Cuban Missile Crisis.* Boston: Little, Brown.

Allison, G. T., and Halperin, M. H. (1972) Bureaucratic Politics: Paradigm and Some Policy Implications, in R. Tanter and R. H. Ullman (eds), *Theory and Policy in International Relations*. Princeton: Princeton University Press.

Bailey, M. J., and Olson M. (1977) Pure Time Preference, Revealed Marginal Utility, and Friedman-Savage Gambles. Unpublished manuscript.

Beck, L. W. (1975) *The Actor and the Spectator*. New Haven: Yale University Press.

Becker, G. S. (1965) A Theory of the Allocation of Time. *Economic Journal*, Vol. 75, 493–517.

Becker, G. S. (1976) Altruism, Egoism, and Genetic Fitness: Economics and Sociobiology. *Journal of Economic Literature*, Vol. 14, 718–26.

Binkley, R., Bronaugh, R., and Marras, A., (eds) (1971) *Agent, Action, and Reason*. Toronto: University of Toronto Press.

Bower, J. L. (1968) Descriptive Decision Theory from the 'Administrative Viewpoint', in R. A. Bauer and K. J. Gergen (eds), *The Study of Policy Formation*. New York: Free Press.

Brams, S. J. (1975) *Game Theory and Politics*. New York: Free Press.

Camus, A. (1951) *L'Homme Révolte*. Paris: Gallimard. (Published in English as *The Rebel.*)

Carter, E. E. (1971) The Behavioral Theory of the Firm and Top-Level Corporate Decisions. *Administrative Science Quarterly*, Vol. 16, 413–29.

Catallus, G. V. (58 BC) *Carmina*, 85. Rome.

Cavell, S. (1969) *Must We Mean What We Say?* New York: Scribner.

Charnes, A., and Cooper, W. W. (1963) Deterministic Equivalents for Optimizing and Satisficing under Chance Constraints. *Operations Research*, Vol. 11, 18–39.

Christensen, S. (1976) Decision Making and Socialization, in J. G. March and J. P. Olsen (eds) *Ambiguity and Choice in Organizations*, Bergen: Universitetsforlaget.

Chomsky, N. (1968) *Language and Mind*. New York: Harcourt, Brace, & World.

Ciardi, J. (1960) *How Does a Poem Mean?* Cambridge: Houghton Mifflin.

Cohen, M. D., and March, J. G. (1974) *Leadership and Ambiguity: The American College President.* New York: McGraw-Hill.

Cohen, M. D., and Olsen, J. P. (1972) A Garbage Can Model of Organizational Choice. *Administrative Science Quarterly*, Vol. 17, 1–25.

Connolly, T. (1977) Information Processing and Decision Making in Organizations, in B. M. Staw and G. R Salancik (eds), *New Directions in Organizational Behavior*, Chicago: St. Clair.

Crozier, M., and Friedberg, E. (1977) *L'Acteur et le Système*. Paris: Seuil.

Cyert, R. M., and De Groot, M. H. (1973) An Analysis of Cooperation and Learning in a Duopoly Context. *The American Economic Review*, Vol. 63, No. 1, 24–37.

Cyert, R. M., and De Groot, M. H. (1975) Adaptive Utility in R. H. Day and T. Groves (eds), *Adaptive Economic Models*, New York: Academic Press.

Cyert, R. M., and March, J. G. (1963) *A Behavioral Theory of the Firm.* Englewood Cliffs, NJ: Prentice-Hall.

Day, R. H., and Groves, T. (eds) (1975) *Adaptive Economic Models.* New York: Academic Press.

Downs, A. (1967) *Inside Bureaucracy.* Boston: Little, Brown.

Edelman, M. (1960) *The Symbolic Uses of Politics.* Champaign, Ill.: University of Illinois Press.

Eliot, T. S. (1933)*The Use of Poetry and the Use of Criticism.* Cambridge: Harvard University Press.

Elster, J. (1976) A Note on Hysteresis in the Social Sciences. *Synthese.* Vol. 33, pp.371–91.

Elster, J. (1977a) *Logic and Society.* London: Wiley.

Elster, J. (1977b) Ulysses and the Sirens: A Theory of Imperfect Rationality. *Social Science Information,* Vol. 16, No. 5, 469–526.

Elster, J. (1977c) Some Unresolved Problems in the Theory of Rational Behavior. Unpublished manuscript.

Farber, L. (1976) *Lying, Despair, Jealousy, Envy, Sex, Suicide, Drugs, and the Good Life.* New York: Basic Books.

Farquharson, R. (1969) *Theory of Voting.* New Haven: Yale University Press.

Freud, S. (1927) *The Ego and the Id.* London: Hogarth.

Friedman, M. (1967) *To Deny Our Nothingness: Contemporary Images of Man.* New York: Delacorte.

Halperin, M. H. (1974) *Bureaucratic Politics and Foreign Policy.* Washington, DC: The Brookings Institution.

Harsanyi, J. C., and Selten, R. (1972) A Generalized Nash Solution for Two-Person Bargaining Games with Incomplete Information. *Management Science*, Vol. 18, 80–106.

Hegel, G. W. F. (1832) *G. W. F. Hegel's Werke.* Berlin: Duncker und Humblot.

Hirschman, A. O. (1967) *Development Projects Observed.* Washington, DC: The Brookings Instituion.

Hirschman, A. O., and Lindblom, C. E. (1962) Economic Development, Research and Development, Policy Making: Some Converging Views, *Behavioral Science*, Vol. 7, 211–22.

Janis, I. L., and Mann, L. (1977) *Decision Making*, New York: Free Press.

Johnson, E. (1968) *Studies in Multiobjective Decision Models*. Lund: Studentlitteratur.

Jones, E. (1926) The Origin and Structure of the Superego. *International Journal of Psychoanalysis*. Vol. 7, 303–11.

Keen, P. G. W. (1977) The Evolving Concept of Optimality. *TIMS Studies in the Management Sciences,* Vol. 6, 31–57.

Koopmans, T. C. (1964) On Flexibility of Future Preferences, in M. W. Shelly and G. L. Bryan (eds), *Human Judgments and Optimality*, New York: Wiley.

Kreiner, K. (1976) Ideology and Management in a Garbage Can Situation, in J. G. March and J. P. Olsen (eds), *Ambiguity and Choice in Organizations*, Bergen: Universitetsforlaget.

Lee, S. M. (1972) *Goal Programming for Decision Analysis*. Philadelphia: Auerbach.

Lindblom, C. E. (1959) The Science of Muddling Through. *Public Administration Review*, Vol. 19, 79–88.

Lindblom, C. E. (1965) *The Intelligence of Democracy*. New York: Macmillan.

Long, N. E. (1958) The Local Community as an Ecology of Games. *American Journal of Sociology*, Vol. 44, 251–61.

Mao, T. T. (1952) *On Contradiction*. Published in English by Foreign Language Press. Peking.

March, J. G. (1962) The Business Firm As a Political Coalition. *Journal of Politics*, Vol. 24, 662–78.

March, J. G. (1973) Model Bias in Social Action. *Review of Educational Research,* Vol. 42, 413–29.

March, J. G. (1978) American Public School Administration: A Short Analysis. *School Review*, Vol. 86, 217–50.

March, J. G., and Olsen, J. P. (eds) (1976) *Ambiguity and Choice in Organizations*. Bergen: Universitetsforlaget.

March, J. G., and Romelaer, P. J. (1976) Position and Presence in the Drift of Decisions, in J. G. March and J. P. Olsen (eds) *Ambiguity and Choice in Organizations*, Bergen: Universitetsforlaget.

March, J. G., and Simon, H. A. (1958) *Organizations*. New York: Wiley.

Marschak, J. and Radner, R. (1972) *Economic Theory of Teams*. New Haven: Yale University Press.

Mayhew, D. R. (1974) *Congress: The Electoral Connection*. New Haven: Yale University Press.

McGuire, C. B., and Radner, R. (eds) (1972) *Decision and Organization*. Amsterdam: North-Holland.

Mills, J. S. (1838). (1950) *Bentham*. Reprinted in *Mill on Bentham and Coleridge*. London: Chatto and Windus.

Mueller, D. C. (1976) Public Choice: A Survey. *Journal of Economic Literature*, Vol. 14, 395–433.

Nelson, R. R., and Winter, S. G. (1973) Towards an Evolutionary Theory of Economic Capabilities. *The American Economic Review*, Vol. 63, 440–9.

Newell, A., and Simon, H. A. (1972) *Human Problem Solving*. Englewood Cliffs, NJ: Prentice-Hall.

Nietzsche, F. (1918) *The Geneology of Morals*. New York: Boni and Liveright.

Olson, M. (1965) *The Logic of Collective Action*. New York: Schocken.

Olson, M. (1976) Exchange, Integration, and Grants, in M. Pfaff, ed., *Essays in Honor of Kenneth Boulding*, Amsterdam: North-Holland, 1976.

Pattanaik, P. K. (1973) Group Choice with Lexicographic Individual Orderings. *Behavioral Science*, Vol. 18, 118–23.

Pfeffer, J. (1977) Power and Resource Allocation in Organizations, in B. M. Staw and G. R. Salancik (eds), *New Directions in Organizational Behavior*, Chicago: St. Clair.

Pondy, L. R., and Olson, M. L. (1977) Organization and Performance. Unpublished manuscript.

Porat, A. M., and Haas, J. A. (1969) Information Effects on Decision Making. *Behavioral Science*, Vol. 14, 98–104.

Radner, R. (Spring 1975a) A Behavioral Model of Cost Reduction. *The Bell Journal of Economics*, Vol. 6, No. 1, 196–215.

Radner, R. (1975b) Satisficing. *Journal of Mathematical Economics*, Vol. 2, 253–62.

Radner, R., and Rothschild, M. (1975) On the Allocation of Effort. *Journal of Economic Theory*, Vol. 10, 358–76.

Rapoport, A. (1960) *Fights, Games, and Debates*. Ann Arbor: University of Michigan Press.

Riker, W., and Ordeshook, P. (1974) *An Introduction to Positive Political Theory*. Englewood Cliffs, NJ: Prentice-Hall.

Rosenberg, H. (1975) *Art on the Edge: Creators and Situations*. New York: Macmillan.

Rothschild, M., and Stiglitz, J. (1976) Equilibrium in Competitive Insurance Markets: An Essay on the Economics of Imperfect Information. *Quarterly Journal of Economics*, Vol. 90, 629–49.

Savage, L. J. (1954) *Foundations of Statistics*. New York: Wiley.

Schelling, T. (1971) On the Ecology of Micro-Motives. *Public Interest*, Vol. 25, 59–98.

Schutz, A. (1967) *The Phenomenology of the Social World*. Evanston, Ill.: Northwestern.

Shakespeare, W. (1623) *Hamlet, Prince of Denmark*. Stratford-upon-Avon.

Shefrin, H. M., and Thaler, R. (1977) An Economic Theory of Self-Control. Unpublished manuscript.

Simon, H. A. (1955) A Behavioral Model of Rational Choice. *Quarterly Journal of Economics*, Vol. 69, 99–118.

Simon, H. A. (1956) Rational Choice and the Structure of the Environment. *Psychological Review*. Vol. 63, 129–38.

Simon, H. A. (1957) *Models of Man*. New York: Wiley.

Simon, H. A. (1969) *The Science of the Artificial*. Cambridge: MIT Press.

Simon, H. A. (1973) The Structure of Ill-Structured Problems. *Artificial Intelligence*, Vol. 4, 181–201.

Slovic, P., Fischhoff, B., and Lichtenstein, S. (1977) Behavioral Decision Theory. *Annual Review of Psychology*, Vol. 28, 1–39.

Spence, A. M. (1974) *Market Signalling*. Cambridge: Harvard University Press.

Sproull, L. S. Weiner, S. S., and Wolf, D. B. (1978) *Organizing an Anarchy*. Chicago: University of Chicago Press.

Steinbruner, J. D. (1974) *The Cybernetic Theory of Decision*. Princeton: Princeton University Press.

Steinberg, L. (1972) *Other Criteria: Confrontations with Twentieth Century Art*. New York: Oxford University Press.

Stigler, G. J. (1961) The Economics of Information. *Journal of Political Economy*, Vol. 69, 213–25.

Stigler, G. J., and Becker, G. S. (1977) *De Gustibus Non Est Disputandum. The American Economic Review*, Vol. 67, 76–90.

Strotz, R. H. (1956) Myopia and Inconsistency in Dynamic Utility Maximization. *Review of Economic Studies*, Vol. 23.

Taylor, M. (1975) The Theory of Collective Choice in F. I. Greenstein and N. W. Polsby (eds), *Handbook of Political Science*, Vol. 3, Reading, Mass.: Addison-Wesley.

Taylor, R. N. (1975) Psychological Determinants of Bounded Rationality: Implications for Decision-making Strategies. *Decision Sciences*, Vol. 6, 409–29.

Thompson, J. (1967) *Organizations in Action*. New York: McGraw-Hill.

Tullock, G. (1965) *The Politics of Bureaucracy*. Washington, DC: Public Affairs.

Tversky, A., and Kahneman, D. (1974) Judgment under Uncertainty: Heuristics and Biases. *Science*, Vol. 185, 1124–31.

Von Weiszäcker, C. C. (1971) Notes on Endogenous Change of Taste. *Journal of Economic Theory*, Vol. 3, 345–72.

Vroom, V. H. (1964) *Work and Motivation*. New York: Wiley.

Warwick, D. P. ((1975) *A Theory of Public Bureaucracy: Politics, Personality, and Organization in the State Department*. Cambridge: Harvard University Press.

Weick, K. E. (1969) *The Social Psychology of Organizing*. Reading, Mass.: Addison-Wesley.

Weick, K. E. (1976) Educational Organizations as Loosely Coupled Systems. *Administrative Science Quarterly*, Vol. 21, 1–18.

Weiner, S. S. (1976) Participation, Deadlines, and Choice, in J. G. March and J. P. Olsen (eds), *Ambiguity and Choice in Organizations*, Bergen: Universitetsforlaget.

Wildavsky, A. (1971) *Revolt Against the Masses and Other Essays on Politics and Public Policy*. New York: Basic Books.

Wildavsky, A., and Pressman, H. (1973) *Implementation*. Berkeley: University of California Press.

Williams, B. A. O. (1973) *Problems of the Self*. Cambridge: Cambridge University Press.

Williamson, O. E. (1975) *Markets and Hierarchies*. New York: Free Press.

Wilson, E. O. (1975) *Sociobiology*. Cambridge: Harvard University Press.

Winter, S. G. (1964) Economic 'Natural Selection' and the Theory of the Firm. *Yale Economic Essays*, Vol. 4, 225–72.

Winter, S. G. (1971) Satisficing, Selection, and the Innovating Remnant. *Quarterly Journal of Economics*, Vol. 85, 237–61.

Winter, S. G. (1975) Optimization and Evolution in the Theory of the Firm, in R. H. Day and T. Groves (eds), *Adaptive Economic Models*, New York: Academic Press.

14

A Garbage Can Model of Organizational Choice

Michael D. Cohen, James G. March, and Johan P. Olsen

Abstract

Organized anarchies are organizations characterized by problematic preferences, unclear technology, and fluid participation. Recent studies of universities, a familiar form of organized anarchy, suggest that such organizations can be viewed for some purposes as collections of choices looking for problems, issues and feelings looking for decision situations in which they might be aired, solutions looking for issues to which they might be an answer, and decision-makers looking for work. These ideas are translated into an explicit computer simulation model of a garbage can decision process. The general implications of such a model are described in terms of five major measures on the process. Possible applications of the model to more narrow predictions are illustrated by an examination of the model's predictions with respect to the effect of adversity on university decision-making.

Consider organized anarchies. These are organizations – or decision situations – characterized by three general properties.[1] The first is problematic preferences. In the organization it is difficult to impute a set of

---

1 This paper was first published in *Administrative Science Quarterly*, Vol. 17, No. 1, March 1972. The authors are indebted to Nancy Block, Hilary Cohen, and James Glenn for computational, editorial, and intellectual help; to the Institute of Sociology, University of Bergen, and the Institute of Organization and Industrial Sociology, Copenhagen School of Economics, for institutional hospitality and useful discussions of organizational behavior; and to the Ford Foundation for the financial support that made our collaboration feasible. We also wish to acknowledge the helpful comments and suggestions of Søren Christensen, James S. Coleman, Harald Enderud, Kåre Rommetveit, and William H. Starbuck.

preferences to the decision situation that satisfies the standard consistency requirements for a theory of choice. The organization operates on the basis of a variety of inconsistent and ill-defined preferences. It can be described better as a loose collection of ideas than as a coherent structure; it discovers preferences through action more than it acts on the basis of preferences.

The second property is unclear technology. Although the organization manages to survive and even produce, its own processes are not understood by its members. It operates on the basis of simple trial-and-error procedures, the residue of learning from the accidents of past experience, and pragmatic inventions of necessity. The third property is fluid participation. Participants vary in the amount of time and effort they devote to different domains; involvement varies from one time to another. As a result, the boundaries of the organization are uncertain and changing; the audiences and decision-makers for any particular kind of choice change capriciously.

These properties of organized anarchy have been identified often in studies of organizations. They are characteristic of any organization in part – part of the time. They are particularly conspicuous in public, educational, and illegitimate organizations. A theory of organized anarchy will describe a portion of almost any organization's activities, but will not describe all of them.

To build on current behavioral theories of organizations in order to accommodate the concept of organized anarchy, two major phenomena critical to an understanding of anarchy must be investigated. The first is the manner in which organizations make choices without consistent, shared goals. Situations of decision-making under goal ambiguity are common in complex organizations. Often problems are resolved without recourse to explicit bargaining or to an explicit price system market – two common processes for decision-making in the absence of consensus. The second phenomenon is the way members of an organization are activated. This entails the question of how occasional members become active and how attention is directed toward, or away from, a decision. It is important to understand the attention patterns within an organization, since not everyone is attending to everything all of the time.

Additional concepts are also needed in a normative theory of organizations dealing with organized anarchies. First, a normative theory of intelligent decision-making under ambiguous circumstances (namely, in situations in which goals are unclear or unknown) should be developed. Can we provide some meaning for intelligence which does not depend on relating current action to known goals? Second, a normative theory of attention is needed. Participants within an organization are constrained by the amount of time they can devote to the various things demanding attention. Since variations in behavior in organized anarchies are due largely to questions of who is attending to what, decisions concerning the allocation of attention are prime ones. Third, organized anarchies require a revised theory of management. Significant parts of contemporary theories of management introduce mechanisms for control and coordination which assume the existence of well-defined goals and a well-defined technology, as well as substantial participant involvement in the affairs of the organization. Where goals and technology are hazy and participation is fluid, many of the axioms and standard procedures of management collapse.

This article is directed to a behavioral theory of organized anarchy. On the basis of several recent studies, some elaborations and modifications of existing theories of choice are proposed. A model for describing decision-making within organized anarchies is developed and the impact of some aspects of organizational structure on the process of choice within such a model is examined.

The Basic Ideas

Decision opportunities are fundamentally ambiguous stimuli. This theme runs through several recent studies of organizational choice.[2] Although organizations can often be viewed conveniently as vehicles for solving well-defined problems or structures within which conflict is resolved through bargaining, they also provide sets of procedures through which participants arrive at an interpretation of what they are doing and what they have done while in the process of doing it. From this point of view, an organization is a collection of choices looking for problems, issues and feelings looking for decision situations in which they might be aired, solutions looking for issues to which they might be the answer, and decision-makers looking for work.

Such a view of organizational choice focuses attention on the way the meaning of a choice changes over time. It calls attention to the strategic effects of timing, through the introduction of choices and problems, the time pattern of available energy, and the impact of organizational structure.

To understand processes within organizations, one can view a choice opportunity as a garbage can into which various kinds of problems and solutions are dumped by participants as they are generated. The mix of garbage in a single can depends on the mix of cans available, on the labels

2 We have based the model heavily on seven recent studies of universities: Christensen (1971), Cohen and March (1974), Enderud (1971), Mood (1971), Olsen (1970, 1971), and Rommetveit (1971). The ideas, however, have a broader parentage. In particular, they obviously owe a debt to Allison (1969), Coleman (1957), Cyert and March (1963), Lindblom (1965), Long (1958), March and Simon (1958), Schilling (1968), Thompson (1967), and Vickers (1965)

attached to the alternative cans, on what garbage is currently being produced, and on the speed with which garbage is collected and removed from the scene.

Such a theory of organizational decision-making must concern itself with a relatively complicated interplay among the generation of problems in an organization, the deployment of personnel, the production of solutions, and the opportunities for choice. Although it may be convenient to imagine that choice opportunities lead first to the generation of decision alternatives, then to an examination of their consequences, then to an evaluation of those consequences in terms of objectives, and finally to a decision, this type of model is often a poor description of what actually happens. In the garbage can model, on the other hand, a decision is an outcome or interpretation of several relatively independent streams within an organization.

Attention is limited here to interrelations among four such streams.

Problems. Problems are the concern of people inside and outside the organization. They might arise over issues of lifestyle; family; frustrations of work; careers; group relations within the organization; distribution of status, jobs, and money; ideology; or current crises of mankind as interpreted by the mass media or the nextdoor neighbor. All of these require attention.

Solutions. A solution is somebody's product. A computer is not just a solution to a problem in payroll management, discovered when needed. It is an answer actively looking for a question. The creation of need is not a curiosity of the market in consumer products; it is a general phenomenon of processes of choice. Despite the dictum that you cannot find the answer until you have formulated the question well, you often do not know what the question is in organizational problem-solving until you know the answer.

Participants. Participants come and go. Since every entrance is an exit somewhere else, the distribution of 'entrances' depends on the attributes of the choice being left as much as it does on the attributes of the new choice. Substantial variation in participation stems from other demands on the participants' time (rather than from features of the decision under study).

Choice opportunities. These are occasions when an organization is expected to produce behavior that can be called a decision. Opportunities arise regularly and any organization has ways of declaring an occasion for choice. Contracts must be signed; people hired, promoted, or fired; money spent; and responsibilities allocated.

Although not completely independent of each other, each of the streams can be viewed as independent and exogenous to the system. Attention will be concentrated here on examining the consequences of different rates and patterns of flows in each of the streams and different procedures for relating them.

The Garbage Can

A simple simulation model can be specified in terms of the four streams and a set of garbage-processing assumptions. Four basic variables are considered; each is a function of time.

A stream of choices. Some fixed number, *m*, of choices is assumed. Each choice is characterized by (1) an entry time, the calendar time at which that choice is activated for decision; and (2) a decision structure, a list of participants eligible to participate in making that choice.

A stream of problems. Some number, *w*, of problems is assumed. Each problem is characterized by (1) an entry time, the calendar time at which the problem becomes visible, (2) an energy requirement, the energy required to resolve a choice to which the problem is attached (if the solution stream is as high as possible), and (3) an access structure, a list of choices to which the problem has access.

A rate of flow of solutions. The verbal theory assumes a stream of solutions and a matching of specific solutions with specific problems and choices. A simpler set of assumptions is made and focus is on the rate at which solutions are flowing into the system. It is assumed that either because of variations in the stream of solutions or because of variations in the efficiency of search procedures within the organization, different energies are required to solve the same problem at different times. It is further assumed that these variations are consistent for different problems. Thus, a solution coefficient, ranging between 0 and 1, which operates on the potential decision energies to determine the problem-solving output (effective energy) actually realized during any given time period is specified.

A stream of energy from participants. It is assumed that there is some number, *v*, of participants. Each participant is characterized by a time series of energy available for organizational decision-making. Thus, in each time period, each participant can provide some specified amount of potential energy to the organization.

Two varieties of organizational segmentation are reflected in the model. The first is the mapping of choices onto decision-makers, the decision structure. The decision structure of the organization is described by D, a v-by-m array in which d_{ij} is 1 if the ith participant is eligible to participate in the making of the jth choice. Otherwise, d_{ij} is 0. The second is the mapping of problems onto choices, the access structure. The access structure of the organization is described by A, a w-by-m array in which a_{ij} is 1 if the jth choice is accessible to the ith problem. Otherwise, a_{ij} is 0.

In order to connect these variables, three key behavioral assumptions are specified. The first is an assumption about the additivity of energy requirements, the second specifies the way in which energy is allocated to choices, and the third describes the way in which problems are attached to choices.

Energy additivity assumption. In order to be made, each choice requires as much effective energy as the sum of all requirements of the several problems attached to it. The effective energy devoted to a choice is the sum of the energies of decision-makers attached to that choice, deflated, in each time period, by the solution coefficient. As soon as the total effective energy that has been expended on a choice equals or exceeds the requirements at a particular point in time, a decision is made.

Energy allocation assumption. The energy of each participant is allocated to no more than one choice during each time period. Each participant allocates his energy among the choices for which he is eligible to the one closest to decision, that is the one with the smallest energy deficit at the end of the previous time period in terms of the energies contributed by other participants.

Problem allocation assumption. Each problem is attached to no more than one choice each time period, choosing from among those accessible by calculating the apparent energy deficits (in terms of the energy requirements of other problems) at the end of the previous time period and selecting the choice closest to decision. Except to the extent that priorities enter in the organizational structure, there is no priority ranking of problems.

These assumptions capture key features of the processes observed. They might be modified in a number of ways without doing violence to the empirical observations on which they are based. The consequences of these modifications, however, are not pursued here. Rather, attention is focused on the implications of the simple version described. The interaction of organizational structure and a garbage can form of choice will be examined.

Organizational Structure

Elements of organizational structure influence outcomes of a garbage can decision process (1) by affecting the time pattern of the arrival of problems, choices, solutions, or decision-makers, (2) by determining the allocation of energy by potential participants in the decision, and (3) by establishing linkages among the various streams.

The organizational factors to be considered are some that have real-world interpretations and implications and are applicable to the theory of organized anarchy. They are familar features of organizations, resulting from a mixture of deliberate managerial planning, individual and collective learning, and imitation. Organizational structure changes as a response to such factors as market demand for personnel and the heterogeneity of values, which are external to the model presented here. Attention will be limited to the comparative statics of the model, rather than to the dynamics produced by organizational learning.

To exercise the model, the following are specified:

1 a set of fixed parameters which do not change from one variation to another;
2 the entry times for choices;
3 the entry times for problems;
4 the net energy load on the organization;
5 the access structure of the organization;
6 the decision structure of the organization;
7 the energy distribution among decision-makers in the organization.

Some relatively pure structural variations will be defined in each and examples of how variations in such structures might be related systematically to key exogenous variables will be given. It will then be shown how such factors of organizational structure affect important characteristics of the decisions in a garbage can decision process.

Fixed Parameters

Within the variations reported, the following are fixed:

1 number of time periods – twenty;
2 number of choice opportunities – ten;
3 number of decision-makers – ten;

4 number of problems – twenty; and
5 the solution coefficients for the 20 time periods – 0.6 for each period.[3]

Entry Times

Two different randomly generated sequences of entry times for choices are considered. It is assumed that one choice enters per time period over the first ten time periods in one of the following orders: (a) 10, 7, 9, 5, 2, 3, 4, 1, 6, 8, or (b) 6, 5, 2, 10, 8, 9, 7, 4, 1, 3.

Similarly, two different randomly generated sequences of entry times for problems are considered. It is assumed that two problems enter per time period over the first ten time periods in one of the following orders: (a) 8, 20, 14, 16, 6, 7, 15, 17, 2, 13, 11, 19, 4, 9, 3, 12, 1, 10, 5, 18, or (b) 4, 14, 11, 20, 3, 5, 2, 12, 1, 6, 8, 19, 7, 15, 16, 17, 10, 18, 9, 13.

Net Energy Load

The total energy available to the organization in each time period is 5.5 units. Thus, the total energy available over twenty time periods is $20 \times 5.5 = 110$. This is reduced by the solution coefficients to 66. These figures hold across all other variations of the model. The net energy load on the organization is defined as the difference between the total energy required to solve all problems and the total effective energy available to the organization over all time periods. When this is negative, there is, in principle, enough energy available. Since the total effective energy available is fixed at 66, the net load is varied by varying the total energy requirements for problems. It is assumed that each problem has the same energy requirement under a given load. Three different energy load situations are considered.

Net energy load 0: light load. Under this condition the energy required to make a choice is 1.1 times the number of problems attached to that choice. That is, the energy required for each problem is 1.1. Thus, the minimum total effective energy required to resolve all problems is 22, and the net energy load is $22 - 66 = -44$.

Net energy load 1: moderate load. Under this condition, the energy required for each problem is 2.2. Thus, the energy required to make a

3 The model has also been exercised under conditions of a set of solution coefficients that varies over the time periods. Specifically, the following series has been used: 1, 0.9, 0.7, 0.3, 0.1, 0.1, 0.3, 0.7, 0.9, 1, 0.6, 0.6, 0.6, 0.6, 0.6, 0.6, 0.6, 0.6, 0.6, 0.6. This simulation, using only one combination of choice and problem entry times, gives results consistent with all of the conclusions reported in the present article.

choice is 2.2 times the number of problems attached to that choice, and the minimum effective energy required to resolve all problems is 44. The net energy load is $44 - 66 = -22$.

Net energy load 2: heavy load. Under this condition, each problem requires energy of 3.3. The energy required to make a choice is 3.3 times the number of problems attached to that choice. The minimum effective energy required to resolve all problems is 66, and the net energy load is $66 - 66 = 0$.

Although it is possible from the total energy point of view for all problems to be resolved in any load condition, the difficulty of accomplishing that result where the net energy load is zero – a heavy load – is obviously substantial.

Access Structure

Three pure types of organizational arrangements are considered in the access structure (the relation between problems and choices).

Access structure 0: unsegmented access. This structure is represented by an access array in which any active problem has access to any active choice.

$$A_0 = \begin{array}{c} 1111111111 \\ 1111111111 \\ 1111111111 \\ 1111111111 \\ 1111111111 \\ 1111111111 \\ 1111111111 \\ 1111111111 \\ 1111111111 \\ 1111111111 \\ 1111111111 \\ 1111111111 \\ 1111111111 \\ 1111111111 \\ 1111111111 \\ 1111111111 \\ 1111111111 \\ 1111111111 \\ 1111111111 \\ 1111111111 \end{array}$$

Access structure 1: hierarchical access. In this structure both choices and problems are arranged in a hierarchy such that important problems – those with relatively low numbers – have access to many choices, and important choices – those with relatively low numbers – are accessible only to important problems. The structure is represented by the following access array:

$$
A_1 = \begin{array}{l}
1111111111 \\
1111111111 \\
0111111111 \\
0111111111 \\
0011111111 \\
0011111111 \\
0001111111 \\
0001111111 \\
0000111111 \\
0000111111 \\
0000011111 \\
0000011111 \\
0000001111 \\
0000001111 \\
0000000111 \\
0000000111 \\
0000000011 \\
0000000011 \\
0000000001 \\
0000000001
\end{array}
$$

Access structure 2: specialized access. In this structure each problem has access to only one choice and each choice is accessible to only two problems, that is, choices specialize in the kinds of problems that can be associated to them. The structure is represented by the access array at the top of p. 304.

Actual organizations will exhibit a more complex mix of access rules. Any such combination could be represented by an appropriate access array. The three pure structures considered here represent three classic alternative approaches to the problem of organizing the legitimate access of problems to decision situations.

Decision Structure

Three similar pure types are considered in the decision structure (the relation between decision-makers and choices).

$$A_2 = \begin{array}{c}
1000000000 \\
1000000000 \\
0100000000 \\
0100000000 \\
0010000000 \\
0010000000 \\
0001000000 \\
0001000000 \\
0000100000 \\
0000100000 \\
0000010000 \\
0000010000 \\
0000001000 \\
0000001000 \\
0000000100 \\
0000000100 \\
0000000010 \\
0000000010 \\
0000000001 \\
0000000001
\end{array}$$

Decision structure 0: unsegmented decisions. In this structure any decision-maker can participate in any active choice opportunity. Thus, the structure is represented by the following array:

$$D_0 = \begin{array}{c}
1111111111 \\
1111111111 \\
1111111111 \\
1111111111 \\
1111111111 \\
1111111111 \\
1111111111 \\
1111111111 \\
1111111111 \\
1111111111
\end{array}$$

Decision structure 1: hierarchical decisions. In this structure both decision-makers and choices are arranged in a hierarchy such that important choices – low numbered choices – must be made by important decision-makers – low numbered decision-makers – and important decision-makers can participate in many choices. The structure is represented by the following array:

$$D_1 = \begin{matrix} 1111111111 \\ 0111111111 \\ 0011111111 \\ 0001111111 \\ 0000111111 \\ 0000011111 \\ 0000001111 \\ 0000000111 \\ 0000000011 \\ 0000000001 \end{matrix}$$

Decision structure 2: specialized decisions. In this structure each decision-maker is associated with a single choice and each choice has a single decision-maker. Decision-makers specialize in the choices to which they attend. Thus, we have the following array:

$$D_2 = \begin{matrix} 1000000000 \\ 0100000000 \\ 0010000000 \\ 0001000000 \\ 0000100000 \\ 0000010000 \\ 0000001000 \\ 0000000100 \\ 0000000010 \\ 0000000001 \end{matrix}$$

As in the case of the access structure, actual decision structures will require a more complicated array. Most organizations have a mix of rules for defining the legitimacy of participation in decisions. The three pure cases are, however, familiar models of such rules and can be used to understand some consequences of decision structure for decision processes.

Energy Distribution

The distribution of energy among decision-makers reflects possible variations in the amount of time spent on organizational problems by different decision-makers. The solution coefficients and variations in the energy requirement for problems affect the overall relation between energy available and energy required. Three different variations in the distribution of energy are considered.

Energy distribution 0: important people – less energy. In this distribution important people, that is people defined as important in a hierarchial decision structure, have less energy. This might reflect variations in the combination of outside demands and motivation to participate within the organization. The specific energy distribution is indicated as follows:

Decision-maker	Energy	
1	0.1	
2	0.2	
3	0.3	
4	0.4	
5	0.5	$= E_0$
6	0.6	
7	0.7	
8	0.8	
9	0.9	
10	1.0	

The total energy available to the organization each time period (before deflation by the solution coefficients) is 5.5.

Energy distribution 1: equal energy. In this distribution there is no internal differentiation among decision-makers with respect to energy. Each decision-maker has the same energy (0.55) each time period. Thus, there is the following distribution:

Decision-maker	Energy	
1	0.55	
2	0.55	
3	0.55	
4	0.55	
5	0.55	$= E_1$
6	0.55	
7	0.55	
8	0.55	
9	0.55	
10	0.55	

The total energy available to the organization each time period (before deflation by the solution coefficients) is 5.5.

Energy distribution 2: important people – more energy. In this distribution energy is distributed unequally but in a direction opposite to that in E_0. Here the people defined as important by the hierarchical decision structure have more energy. The distribution is indicated by the following:

Decision-maker	Energy	
1	1.0	
2	0.9	
3	0.8	
4	0.7	
5	0.6	$=E_2$
6	0.5	
7	0.4	
8	0.3	
9	0.2	
10	0.1	

As in the previous organizations, the total energy available to the organization each time period (before deflation by the solution coefficients) is 5.5.

Where the organization has a hierarchical decision structure, the distinction between important and unimportant decision-makers is clear. Where the decision structure is unsegmented or specialized, the variations in energy distribution are defined in terms of the same numbered decision-makers (lower numbers are more important than higher numbers) to reflect possible status differences which are not necessarily captured by the decision structure.

Simulation Design

The simulation design is simple. A Fortran version of the garbage can model is given in the appendix, along with documentation and an explanation. The $3^4=81$ types of organizational situations obtained by taking the possible combinations of the values of the four dimensions of an organization (access structure, decision structure, energy distribution, and net energy load) are studied here under the four combinations of choice and problem entry times. The result is 324 simulation situations.

Summary Statistics

The garbage can model operates under each of the possible organizational structures to assign problems and decision-makers to choices, to determine the energy required and effective energy applied to choices, to make such choices and resolve such problems as the assignments and energies indicate are feasible. It does this for each of the twenty time periods in a 20-period simulation of organizational decision-making.

For each of the 324 situations, some set of simple summary statistics on the process is required. These are limited to five.

Decision Style

Within the kind of organization postulated, decisions are made in three different ways:

By resolution. Some choices resolve problems after some period of working on them. The length of time may vary, depending on the number of problems. This is the familiar case that is implicit in most discussions of choice within organizations.

By oversight. If a choice is activated when problems are attached to other choices and if there is energy available to make the new choice quickly, it will be made without any attention to existing problems and with a minimum of time and energy.

By flight. In some cases choices are associated with problems (unsuccessfully) for some time until a choice more attractive to the problems comes along. The problems leave the choice, and thus it is now possible to make the decision. The decision resolves no problems; they having now attached themselves to a new choice.

Some choices involve both flight and resolution – some problems leave, the remainder are solved. These have been defined as resolution, thus slightly exaggerating the importance of that style. As a result of that convention, the three styles are mutually exclusive and exhaustive with respect to any one choice. The same organization, however, may use any one of them in different choices. Thus, the decision style of any particular variation of the model can be described by specifying the proportion of completed choices which are made in each of these three ways.

Problem Activity

Any measure of the degree to which problems are active within the organization should reflect the degree of conflict within the organization or the degree of articulation problems. Three closely-related statistics of problem activity are considered. The first is the total number of problems not solved at the end of the 20 time periods; the second is the total number of times that any problem shifts from one choice to another, while the third is the total number of time periods that a problem is active and attached to some choice, summed over all problems. These measures are strongly correlated with each other. The third is used as the measure of problem activity primarily because it has a relatively large variance; essentially the same results would have been obtained with either of the two other measures.

Problem Latency

A problem may be active, but not attached to any choice. The situation is one in which a problem is recognized and accepted by some part of the organization, but is not considered germane to any available choice. Presumably, an organization with relatively high problem latency will exhibit somewhat different symptoms from one with low latency. Problem latency has been measured by the total number of periods a problem is active, but not attached to a choice, summed over all problems.

Decision-Maker Activity

To measure the degree of decision-maker activity in the system, some measure which reflects decision-maker energy expenditure, movement, and persistence is required. Four are considered:

1 the total number of time periods a decision-maker is attached to a choice, summed over all decision-makers;
2 the total number of times that any decision-maker shifts from one choice to another;
3 the total amount of effective energy available and used;
4 the total effective energy used on choices in excess of that required to make them at the time they are made. These four measures are highly intercorrelated. The second was used primarily because of its relatively large variance; any of the others would have served as well.

Decision Difficulty

Because of the way in which decisions can be made in the system, decision difficulty is not the same as the level of problem activity. Two alternative measures are considered: the total number of choices not made by the end of the 20 time periods and the total number of periods that a choice is active, summed over all choices. These are highly correlated. The second is used, primarily because of its higher variance; the conclusions would be unchanged if the first were used.

Implications of the Model

An analysis of the individual histories of the simulations shows eight major properties of garbage can decision processes.

First, resolution of problems as a style for making decisions is not the most common style, except under conditions where flight is severely restricted (for instance, specialized access) or a few conditions under light load. Decision-making by flight and oversight is a major feature of the process in general. In each of the simulation trials there were twenty problems and ten choices. Although the mean number of choices not made was 1.0, the mean number of problems not solved was 12.3. The results are detailed in table 14.1. The behavioral and normative implications of a decision process which appears to make choices in large part by flight or by oversight must be examined. A possible explanation of the behavior of organizations that seem to make decisions without apparently making progress in resolving the problems that appear to be related to the decisions may be emerging.

Table 14.1 Proportion of choices that resolve problems under four conditions of choice and problem entry times, by load and access structure

		Access structure			
		All	*Unsegmented*	*Hierarchical*	*Specialized*
Load	Light	0.55	0.38	0.61	0.65
	Moderate	0.30	0.04	0.27	0.60
	Heavy	0.36	0.35	0.23	0.50
	All	0.40	0.26	0.37	0.58

Second, the process is quite thoroughly and quite generally sensitive to variations in load. As table 14.2 shows, an increase in the net energy load on the system generally increases problem activity, decision-maker activity, decision difficulty, and the uses of flight and oversight. Problems are less likely to be solved, decision-makers are likely to shift from one problem to another more frequently, choices are likely to take longer to make and are less likely to resolve problems. Although it is possible to specify an organization that is relatively stable with changes in load, it is not possible to have an organization that is stable in behavior and also has other desirable attributes. As load changes, an organization that has an unsegmented access structure with a specialized decision structure stays quite stable. It exhibits relatively low decision difficulty and decision-maker activity, very low problem latency, and maximum problem activity. It makes virtually all decisions placed before it, uses little energy from decision-makers, and solves virtually no problems.

Table 14.2 Effects of variations in load under four conditions of choice and problem entry times

		Mean problem activity	*Mean decision-maker activity*	*Mean decision difficulty*	*Proportion of choices by flight or oversight*
Load	Light	114.9	60.9	19.5	0.45
	Moderate	204.3	63.8	32.9	0.70
	Heavy	211.1	76.6	46.1	0.64

Third, a typical feature of the model is the tendency of decision-makers and problems to track each other through choices. Subject to structural restrictions on the tracking, decision-makers work on active problems in connection with active choices; both decision-makers and problems tend to move together from choice to choice. Thus, one would expect decision-makers who have a feeling that they are always working on the same problems in somewhat different contexts, mostly without results. Problems, in a similar fashion, meet the same people wherever they go with the same result.

Fourth, there are some important interconnections among three key aspects of the efficiency of the decision processes specified. The first is problem activity, the amount of time unresolved problems are actively attached to choice situations. Problem activity is a rough measure of the potential for decision conflict in the organization. The second aspect is problem latency, the amount of time problems spend activated but not linked to choices. The third aspect is decision time, the persistence of choices. Presumably, a good organizational structure would keep both problem activity and problem latency low through rapid problem solution in its choices. In the garbage can process such a result was never observed. Segmentation of the access structure tends to reduce the number of unresolved problems active in the organization but at the cost of increasing the latency period of problems and, in most cases the time devoted to reaching decisions. On the other hand, segmentation of the decision structure tends to result in decreasing problem latency, but at the cost of increasing problem activity and decision time.

Fifth, the process is frequently sharply interactive. Although some phenomena associated with the garbage can are regular and flow through nearly all of the cases, for example, the effect of overall load, other phenomena are much more dependent on the particular combination of structures involved. Although high segmentation of access structure generally produces slow decision time, for instance, a specialized access structure, in combination with an unsegmented decision structure, produces quick decisions.

Sixth, important problems are more likely to be solved than unimportant ones. Problems which appear early are more likely to be resolved than later ones. Considering only those cases involving access hierarchy where importance is defined for problems, the relation between resolution, problem importance and order of arrival is shown in table 14.3. The system, in effect, produces a queue of problems in terms of their importance, to the disadvantage of late-arriving, relatively unimportant problems, and particularly so when load is heavy. This queue is the result of the operation of the model. It was not imposed as a direct assumption.

Table 14.3 Proportion of problems resolved under four conditions of choice and problem entry times, by importance of problem and order of arrival of problem (for hierarchical access)

		Time of arrival of problem	
		Early, first 10	*Late, last 10*
Importance of problem	High first 10	0.46	0.44
	Low last 10	0.48	0.25

Seventh, important choices are less likely to resolve problems than unimportant choices. Important choices are made by oversight and flight. Unimportant choices are made by resolution. These differences are observed under both of the choice entry sequences but are sharpest where important choices enter relatively early. Table 14.4 show the results. This property of important choices in a garbage can decision process can be naturally and directly related to the phenomenon in complex organizations of important choices which often appear to just happen.

Eighth, although a large proportion of the choices are made, the choice failures that do occur are concentrated among the most important and least important choices. Choices of intermediate importance are virtually

Table 14.4 Proportion of choices that are made by flight or oversight under four conditions of choice and problem entry times, by time of arrival and importance of choice (for hierarchical access or decision structure)

		Time of arrival of choice	
		Early, first 5	*Late, last 5*
Importance of of choice	High first 5	0.86	0.65
	Low last 5	0.54	0.60

always made. The proportion of choice failures, under conditions of hierarchical access or decision structures is as follows:

Three most important choices	0.14
Four middle choices	0.05
Three least important choices	0.12

In a broad sense, these features of the process provide some clues to how organizations survive when they do not know what they are doing. Much of the process violates standard notions of how decisions ought to be made. But most of those notions are built on assumptions which cannot be met under the conditions specified. When objectives and technologies are unclear, organizations are charged to discover some alternative decision procedures which permit them to proceed without doing extraordinary violence to the domains of participants or to their model of what an organization should be. It is a hard charge, to which the process described is a partial response.

At the same time, the details of the outcomes clearly depend on features of the organizational structure. The same garbage can operation results in different behavioral symptoms under different levels of load on the system or different designs of the structure of the organization. Such differences raise the possibility of predicting variations in decision behavior in different organizations. One possible example of such use remains to be considered.

Garbage Cans and Universities

One class of organization which faces decision situations involving unclear goals, unclear technology, and fluid participants is the modern college or university. If the implications of the model are applicable anywhere, they are applicable to a university. Although there is great variation among colleges and universities, both between countries and within any country, the model has general relevance to decision-making in higher education.

General Implications

University decision-making frequently does not resolve problems. Choices are often made by flight or oversight. University decision processes are sensitive to increases in load. Active decision-makers and problem track one another through a series of choices without appreciable progress in solving problems. Important choices are not likely to solve problems.

Decisions whose interpretations continually change during the process of resolution appear both in the model and in actual observations of universities. Problems, choices, and decision-makers arrange and rearrange themselves. In the course of these arrangements the meaning of a choice can change several times, if this meaning is understood as the mix of problems discussed in the context of that choice.

Problems are often solved, but rarely by the choice to which they are first attached. A choice that might, under some circumstances, be made with little effort becomes an arena for many problems. The choice becomes almost impossible to make, until the problems drift off to another arena. The matching of problems, choices, and decision-makers is partly controlled by attributes of content, relevance, and competence; but it is also quite sensitive to attributes of timing, the particular combinations of current garbage cans, and the overall load on the system.

Universities and Adversity

In establishing connections between the hypothetical attributes of organizational structure in the model and some features of contemporary universities, the more detailed implications of the model can be used to explore features of university decision-making. In particular, the model can examine the events associated with one kind of adversity within organizations, the reduction of organizational slack.

Slack is the difference between the resources of the organization and the combination of demands made on it. Thus, it is sensitive to two major factors: (1) money and other resources provided to the organization by the external environment; and (2) the internal consistency of the demands made on the organization by participants. It is commonly believed that organizational slack has been reduced substantially within American colleges and universities over the past few years. The consequences of slack reduction in a garbage can decision process can be shown by establishing possible relations between changes in organizational slack and the key structural variables within the model.

Net energy load. The net energy load is the difference between the energy required within an organization and the effective energy available. It is affected by anything that alters either the amount of energy available to the organization or the amount required to find or generate problem solutions. The energy available to the organization is partly a function of the overall strength of exit opportunities for decision-makers. For example, when there is a shortage of faculty, administrators, or students in the market for participants, the net energy load on a university is heavier than it would be when there is no shortage. The energy required to find solutions depends on the flow of possible problem solutions. For example, when the environment of the organization is relatively rich, solutions are easier to find and the net energy is reduced. Finally, the comparative attractiveness and permeability of the organization to problems affects the energy demands on it. The more attractive, the more demands. The more permeable, the more demands. Universities with slack and with relatively easy access, compared to other alternative arenas for problem carriers, will attract a relatively large number of problems.

Access structure. The access structure in an organization would be expected to be affected by deliberate efforts to derive the advantages of delegation and specialization. Those efforts, in turn, depend on some general characteristics of the organizational situation, task, and personnel. For example, the access structure would be expected to be systematically related to two features of the organization: (1) the degree of technical and value heterogeneity; and (2) the amount of organizational slack. Slack, by providing resource buffers between parts of the organization, is essentially a substitute for technical and value homogeneity. As heterogeneity increases, holding slack constant, the access structure shifts from an unsegmented to a specialized to a hierarchical structure. Similarly, as slack decreases, holding heterogeneity constant, the access structure shifts from an unsegmented to a specialized to a hierarchical structure. The combined picture is shown in figure 14.1.

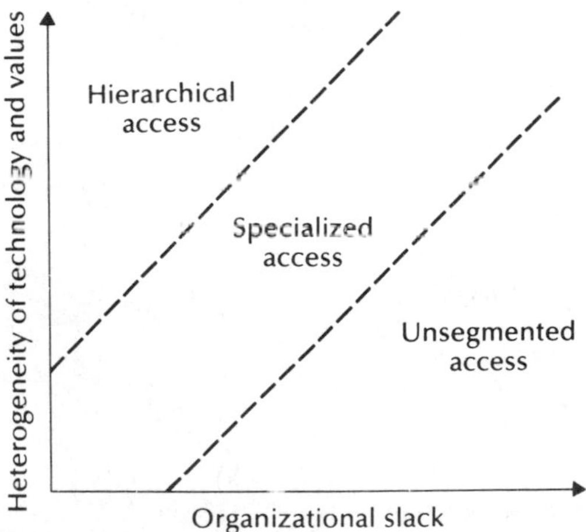

Figure 14.1. Hypothesized relationship between slack, heterogeneity and the access structure of an organization.

Decision structure. Like the access structure, the decision structure is partly a planned system for the organization and partly a result of learning and negotiation within the organization. It could be expected to be systematically related to the technology, to attributes of participants and problems, and to the external conditions under which the organization operates. For example, there are joint effects of two factors: (1) relative administrative power within the system, the extent to which the formal administrators are conceded substantial authority; and (2) the average degree of perceived interrelation among problems. It is assumed that high administrative power or high interrelation of problems will lead to hierarchical decision structure, that moderate power and low interrelation of problems leads to specialized decision structures, and that relatively low administrative power, combined with moderate problem interrelation, leads to unsegmented decision structures. The hypothetical relations are shown in figure 14.2.

Energy distribution. Some of the key factors affecting the energy distribution within an organization are associated with the alternative opportunities decision-makers have for investing their time. The extent to which there is an active external demand for attention affects the extent to which decision-makers will have energy available for use within the organization. The stronger the relative outside demand on important people in the organization, the less time they will spend within the organization relative to others. Note that the energy distribution refers only to the relation between the energy available from important people and less important people. Thus, the energy distribution variable is a

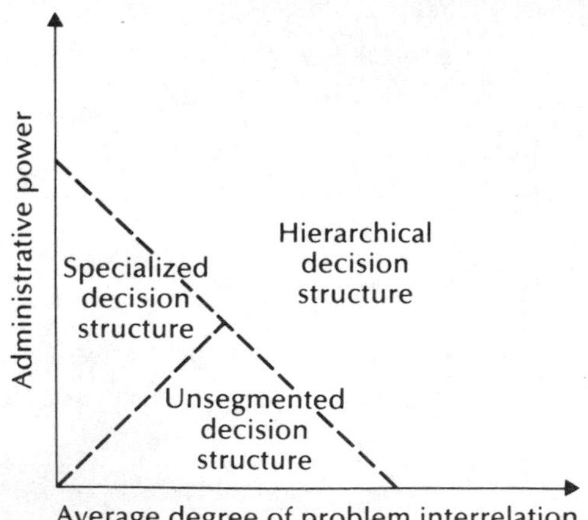

Figure 14.2. Hypothesized relationship between administrative power, interrelation of problems, and the decision structure of an organization

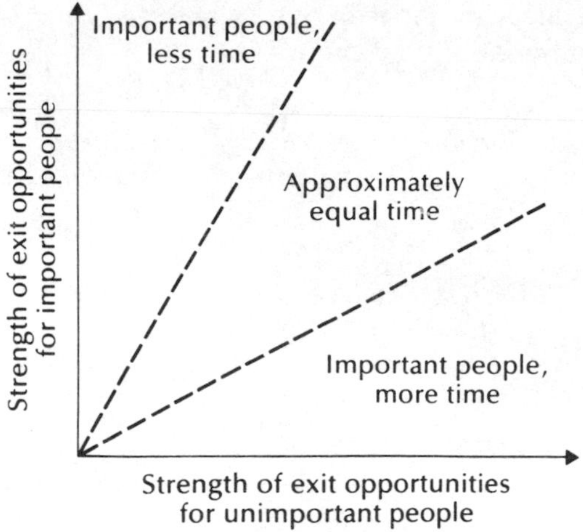

Figure 14.3. Hypothesized relationship between exit opportunities and the distribution of energy within an organization

function of the relative strength of the outside demand for different people, as shown in figure 14.3.

Within a university setting it is not hard to imagine circumstances in which exit opportunities are different for different decision-makers. Tenure, for example, strengthens the exit opportunities for older faculty members. Money strengthens the exit opportunities for students and faculty members, though more for the former than the latter. A rapidly changing technology tends to strengthen the exit opportunities for young faculty members.

Against this background four types of colleges and universities are considered:

1 large, rich universities;
2 large, poor universities;
3 small, rich colleges;
4 small, poor colleges.

Important variations in the organizational variables among these schools can be expected. Much of that variation is likely to be within-class variation. Assumptions about these variables, however, can be used to generate some assumptions about the predominant attributes of the four classes, under conditions of prosperity.

Under such conditions a relatively rich school would be expected to have a light energy load, a relatively poor school a moderate energy load. With respect to access structure, decision structure, and the internal distribution of energy, the appropriate position of each of the four types of schools is is marked with a circular symbol on figures 14.4, 14.5, and 14.6. The result is the pattern of variations indicated below:

	Load	*Access structure*	*Decision structure*	*Energy distribution*
Large, rich	Light 0	Specialized 2	Unsegmented 0	Less 0
Large, poor	Moderate 1	Hierarchical 1	Hierarchical 1	More 2
Small, rich	Light 0	Unsegmented 0	Unsegmented 0	More 2
Small, poor	Moderate 1	Specialized 2	Specialized 2	Equal 1

With this specification, the garbage can model can be used to predict the differences expected among the several types of school. The results are found in table 14.5. They suggest that under conditions of prosperity, overt conflict (problem activity) will be substantially higher in poor schools than in rich ones, and decision time will be substantially longer. Large, rich schools will be characterized by a high degree of problem latency. Most decisions will resolve some problems.

What happens to this group of schools under conditions of adversity – when slack is reduced? According to earlier arguments, slack could be expected to affect each of the organizational variables. It first increases net energy load, as resources become shorter and thus problems require a larger share of available energy to solve, but this effect is later compensated by the reduction in market demand for personnel and in the relative attractiveness of the school as an arena for problems. The market effects also reduce the differences in market demand for important and unimportant people. The expected results of these shifts are shown by the positions of the square symbols in figure 14.6.

At the same time, adversity affects both access structure and decision structure. Adversity can be expected to bring a reduction in slack and an increase in the average interrelation among problems. The resulting hypothesized shifts in access and decision structures are shown in figures 14.4 and 14.5.

Table 14.5 shows the effects of adversity on the four types of schools according to the previous assumptions and the garbage can model. By examining the first stage of adversity, some possible reasons for discontent among presidents of large, rich schools can be seen. In relation to other schools they are not seriously disadvantaged. The large, rich schools have a moderate level of problem activity, a moderate level of decision by

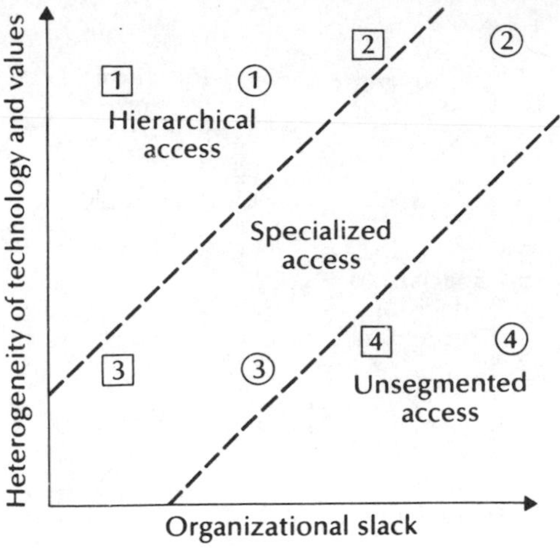

① Large, poor school, good times
② Large, rich school, good times
③ Small, poor school, good times
④ Small, rich school, good times

[1] Large, poor school, bad times
[2] Large, rich school, bad times
[3] Small, poor school, bad times
[4] Small, rich school, bad times

Figure 14.4. Hypothesized location of different schools in terms of slack and heterogeneity

resolution. In relation to their earlier state, however, large, rich schools are certainly deprived. Problem activity and decision time have increased greatly; the proportion of decisions which resolve problems has decreased from 68 per cent to 21 per cent; administrators are less able to move around from one decision to another. In all these terms, the relative deprivation of the presidents of large, rich schools is much greater, in the early stages of adversity, than that of administrators in other schools.

The large, poor schools are in the worst absolute position under adversity. They have a high level of problem activity, a substantial decision time, a low level of decision-maker mobility, and a low proportion of decisions being made by resolution. But along most of these dimensions, the change has been less for them.

The small rich schools experience a large increase in problem activity, an increase in decision time, and a decrease in the proportion of decisions by resolution as adversity begins. The small, poor schools seem to move

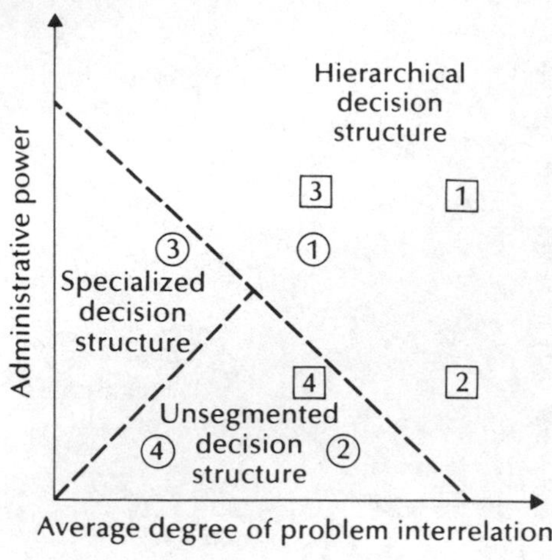

① Large, poor school, good times
② Large, rich school, good times
③ Small, poor school, good times
④ Small, rich school, good times

[1] Large, poor school, bad times
[2] Large, rich school, bad times
[3] Small, poor school, bad times
[4] Small, rich school, bad times

Figure 14.5. Hypothesized location of different schools in terms of administrative power and perceived interrelation of problems

in a direction counter to the trends in the other three groups. Decision style is little affected by the onset of slack reduction, problem activity, and decision time decline, and decision-maker mobility increases. Presidents of such organizations might feel a sense of success in their efforts to tighten up the organization in response to resource contraction.

The application of the model to this particular situation among American colleges and universities clearly depends upon a large number of assumptions. Other assumptions would lead to other interpretations of the impact of adversity within a garbage can decision process. Nevertheless, the derivations from the model have some face validity as a description of some aspects of recent life in American higher education.

The model also makes some predictions of future developments. As adversity continues, the model predicts that all schools, and particularly rich schools, will experience improvement in their position. Among large, rich schools decision by resolution triples, problem activity is cut by almost

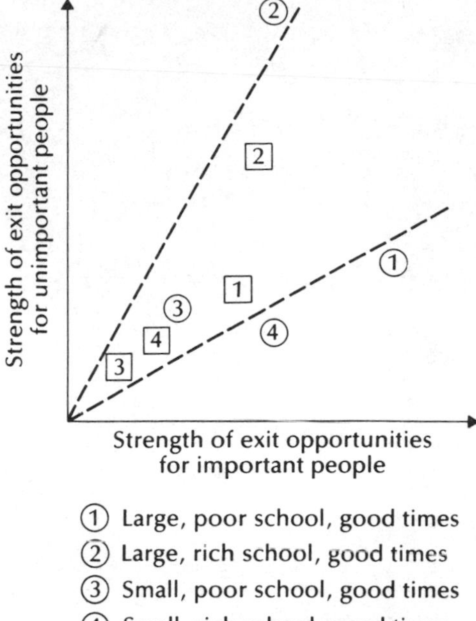

Figure 14.6. Hypothesized location of different schools in terms of text opportunties

three-quarters, and decision time is cut more than one-half. If the model has validity, a series of articles in the magazines of the next decade detailing how President *X* assumed the presidency of large, rich university *Y* and guided it to 'peace' and 'progress' (short decision time, decisions without problems, low problem activity) can be expected.

Conclusion

A set of observations made in the study of some university organizations has been translated into a model of decision-making in organized anarchies, that is, in situations which do not meet the conditions for more classical models of decision-making in some or all of three important ways: preferences are problematic, technology is unclear, or participation is fluid. The garbage can process is one in which problems, solutions, and

Table 14.5 Effect of adversity on four types of colleges and universities operating within a garbage can decision process

		Outcome				
Type of school/ type of situation	*Organizational type*	*Decision style proportion resolution*	*Problem activity*	*Problem latency*	*Decision-maker activity*	*Decision time*
Large, rich universities						
Good times	0200	0.68	0	154	100	0
Bad times, early	1110	0.21	210	23	58	34
Bad times, late	0111	0.65	57	60	66	14
Large, poor universities						
Good times	1112	0.38	210	25	66	31
Bad times, early	2112	0.24	248	32	55	38
Bad times, late	1111	0.31	200	30	58	28
Small, rich colleges						
Good times	0002	1.0	0	0	100	0
Bad times, early	1002	0	310	0	90	20
Bad times, late	0001	1.0	0	0	100	0
Small, poor colleges						
Good times	1221	0.54	158	127	15	83
Bad times, early	2211	0.61	101	148	73	52
Bad times, late	1211	0.62	78	151	76	39

participants move from one choice opportunity to another in such a way that the nature of the choice, the time it takes, and the problems it solves all depend on a relatively complicated intermeshing of elements. These include the mix of choices available at any one time, the mix of problems that have access to the organization, the mix of solutions looking for problems, and the outside demands on the decision-makers.

A major feature of the garbage can process is the partial uncoupling of problems and choices. Although decision-making is thought of as a process for solving problems, that is often not what happens. Problems are worked upon in the context of some choice, but choices are made only when the shifting combinations of problems, solutions, and decision-makers happen to make action possible. Quite commonly this is after problems have left a given choice arena or before they have discovered it (decisions by flight or oversight).

Four factors were specified which could be expected to have substantial effects on the operation of the garbage can process: the organization's net energy load and energy distribution, its decision structure, and problem access structure. Though the specifications are quite simple their interaction is extremely complex, so that investigation of the probable behavior of a system fully characterized by the garbage can process and previous specifications requires computer simulation. No real system can be fully characterized in this way. None the less, the simulated organization exhibits behaviors which can be observed some of the time in almost all organizations and frequently in some, such as universities. The garbage can model is a first step toward seeing the systematic interrelatedness of organizational phenomena which are familiar, even common, but which have previously been regarded as isolated and pathological. Measured against a conventional normative model of rational choice, the garbage can process does appear pathological, but such standards are not really appropriate. The process occurs precisely when the preconditions of more normal rational models are not met.

It is clear that the garbage can process does not resolve problems well. But it does enable choices to be made and problems resolved, even when the organization is plagued with goal ambiguity and conflict, with poorly-understood problems that wander in and out of the system, with a variable environment, and with decision-makers who may have other things on their minds.

There is a large class of significant situations in which the preconditions of the garbage can process cannot be eliminated. In some, such as pure research, or the family, they should not be eliminated. The great advantage of trying to model garbage can phenomena is the possibility that that process can be understood, that organizational design and decision-making can take account of its existence and that, to some extent, it can be managed.

Appendix

Version five of the Fortran program for the garbage can model reads in entry times for choices, solution coefficients, entry times for problems, and two control variables. *NA* and *IO*. *NA* controls various combinations of freedom of movement for decision-makers and problems. All results are based on runs in which *NA* is 1. Comment cards included in the program describe other possibilities. The latter variable, *IO*, controls output. At the value 1, only summary statistics are printed. At the value 2, full histories of the decision process are printed for each organizational variant.

The following are ten summary statistics:

1 (*KT*) Problem persistence, the total number of time periods a problem is activated and attached to a choice, summed over all problems.
2 (*KU*) Problem latency, the total number of time periods a problem is activated, but not attached to a choice, summed over all problems.
3 (*KV*)Problem velocity, the total number of times any problem shifts from one choice to another.
4 (*KW*) Problem failures, the total number of problems not solved at the end of the twenty time periods.
5 (*KX*) Decision-maker velocity, the total number of times any decision-maker shifts from one choice to another.
6 (*KS*) Decision-maker inactivity, the total number of time periods a decision-maker is not attached to a choice, summed over all decision makers.
7 (*KY*) Choice persistence, the total number of time periods a choice is activated, summed over all choices.
8 (*KZ*) Choice failures, the total number of choices not made by the end of the twenty time periods.
9 (*XR*) Energy reserve, the total amount of effective energy available to the system but not used because decision makers are not attached to any choice.
10 (*XS*) Energy wastage, the total effective energy used on choices in excess of that required to make them at the time they are made.

In its current form the program generates both the problem access structure and the decision structure internally. In order to examine the performance of the model under other structures, modification of the code or its elimination in favor of Read statements to take the structures from cards will be necessary.

Under *IO*=2, total output will be about ninety pages. Running time is about two minutes under a Watfor compiler.

Appendix Table: Fortran Program for Garbage Can Model; Version Five

```
C  THE GARBAGE CAN MODEL. VERSION 5
C  ***
C  IO IS 1 FOR SUMMARY STATISTICS ONLY
C  IO IS 2 FOR SUMMARY STATISTICS PLUS HISTORIES
C  ***
C  NA IS 1 WHEN PROBS AND DMKRS BOTH MOVE
C  NA IS 2 WHEN DMKRS ONLY MOVE
C  NA IS 3 WHEN PROBS ONLY MOVE
C  NA IS 4 WHEN NEITHER PROBS NOR DMKRS MOVE
C  ***
C  IL IS A FACTOR DETERMINING PROB ENERGY REQ
C  ***
C  VARIABLES
C  ***
C  NUMBERS
C   COUNTERS UPPER LIMITS NAME
C   ***
C   I          NCH          CHOICES
C   J          NPR          PROBLEM
C   K          NDM          DECMKRS
C   LT         NTP          TIME
C  ***
C  ARRAYS
C   CODE       DIMEN        NAME
C   * * *
C   ICH        NCH          CHOICE ENTRY TIME
C   ICS        NCH          CHOICE STATUS
C   JET        NPR          PROB. ENTRY TIME
C   JF         NPR          PROB. ATT. CHOICE
C   JFF        NPR          WORKING COPY JF
C   JPS        NPR          PROB. STATUS
C   KDC        NDM          DMKR. ATT. CHOICE
C   KDCW       NDM          WORKING COPY KDC
C   XEF        MCH          ENERGY EXPENDED
C   XERC       NCH          CHOICE EN. REQT.
C   XERP       NPR          PROB. EN. REQT.
C   XSC        NTP          SOLUTION COEFFICIENT
C  ***
C  2-DIMENSIONAL ARRAYS
```

```
C  ***
C  CODE       DIMEN        NAME
C  ***
C  IKA        NCH,NDM      DECISION STRUCTURE
C  JIA        NPR,NCH      ACCESS STRUCTURE
C  XEA        NDM,NTP      ENERGY MATRIX
C  ***
C  ***
C  ***
C  ***
C  SUMMARY STATISTICS FOR EACH VARIANT
C     COL 1: KZ: TOTAL DECISIONS NOT MADE
C     COL 2: KY: TOTAL NUMBER ACTIVE CHOICE PERIODS
C     COL 3: KX: TOTAL NUMBER CHANGES BY DECISION
      MAKERS
C     COL 4: KW: TOTAL PROBLEMS NOT SOLVED
C     COL 5: KV: TOTAL NUMBER CHANGES BY PROBLEMS
C     COL 6: KU: TOTAL NUMBER LATENT PROBLEM PERIODS
C     COL 7: KT: TOTAL NUMBER ATTACHED PROBLEM PERIODS
C     COL 8: KS: TOTAL NUMBER PERIODS DMKRS RESTING
C     COL 9: XR: TOTAL AMOUNT OF UNUSED ENERGY
C     COL 10:XS: TOTAL AMOUNT OF WASTED ENERGY
C  ***
C  INPUT BLOCK. READ-IN AND INITIALIZATIONS.
     DIMENSION ICH(20),JF(20),XERC(20),XEE(20),XSC(20),JFF(20),
    XERP(20),JET(20),JPS(20),ICS(20),KDC(20),KDCW(20),JIA(20,
    20),IKA(20,20),CXEA(20,20),KABC(20,20),KBBC(20,20),KCBC(20,20)
1001  FORMAT(5(I3,1X))
1002  FORMAT(10(I3,1X))
1003  FORMAT(25(I1,1X))
1004  FORMAT(10F4.2)
      NTP=20
      NCH=10
      NPR=20
      NDM=10
8   READ(5,1002)(ICH(I),I=1,NCH)
    READ(5,1004)(XSC(LT),LT=1,NTP)
    READ(5,1002)(JET(J),J=1,NPR)
    READ(5,1003) NA,IO
    WRITE(6,1050) NA
1050  FORMAT('1   DEC.MAKER MOVEMENT CONDITION (NA)
      IS ',I1/)
      DO 998 IL=1.3
```

```
      IB=IL-1
      DO 997 JAB=1,3
      JA=JAB-1
      DO 996 JDB=1,3
      JD=JDB-1
      DO 995 JEB=1,3
      JE=JEB-1
      XR=0.0
      XS=0.0
      KS=0
      DO 10 I=1,NCH
      XERC(I)=1.1
      XEE(I)=0.0
10    ICS(I)=0
      DO 20 K=1,NDM
      KDC(K)=0
20    KDCW(K)=KDC(K)
      DO 40 J=1,NPR
      XERP(J)=IL*1.1
      JF(J)=0
      JFF(J)=0
40    JPS(J)=0
C     SETTING UP THE DECISION MAKERS ACCESS TO CHOICES.
      DO 520 I=1,NCH
      DO 510 J=1,NDM
      IKA(I,J)=1
      IF(JD.EQ.1) GO TO 502
      IF(JD.EQ.2) GO TO 504
      GO TO 510
502   IF(I.GE.J) GO TO 510
      IKA(I,J)=0
      GO TO 510
504   IF(J.EQ.) GO TO 510
      IKA(I,J)=0
510   CONTINUE
520   CONTINUE
C     SETTING UP THE PROBLEMS ACCESS TO CHOICES.
      DO 560 I=1,NPR
      DO 550 J=1,NCH
      JIA(I,J)=0
      IF(JA.EQ.1) GO TO 532
      IF(JA.EQ.2) GO TO 534
      JIA(I,J)=1
```

```
      GO TO 550
532   IF ((I - J).GT.(1/2)) GO TO 550
      JIA(I,J) = !
      GO TO 550
534   IF(I.NE.(2*J)) GO TO 550
      JIA(I,J) = 1
      JIA(I - 1,J) = 1
550   CONTINUE
560   CONTINUE
      DO 590 I = 1,NDM
      DO 580 J = 1,NTP
      XEA(I,J) = 0.55
      IF(JF.EQ.1)GO TO 580
      XXA = I
      IF(JE.EQ.0)GO TO 570
      XEA(I,J) = (11.0 - XXA)/10.0
      GO TO 580
570   XEA(I,J) = XXA/10.0
580   CONTINUE
590   CONTINUE
C     *** FINISH READ INITIALIZATION
      DO 994 LT = 1,NTP
1006  FORMAT(2X.6HCHOICE,2X,I3,2X.6HACTIVE )
C     CHOICE ACTIVATION
      DO 101 I = 1,NCH
      IF(ICH(I).NE.LT)GO TO 101
      ICS(I) = 1
101   CONTINUE
C     PROB. ACTIVATION
      DO 110 J = 1,NPR
      IF(JET(J).NE.LT)GO TO 110
      JPS(J) = 1
110   CONTINUE
C     FIND MOST ATTRACTIVE CHOICE FOR PROBLEM J
      DO 120 J = 1,NPR
      IF (JPS(J).NE.1) GO TO 120
      IF(NA.EQ.2)GO TO 125
      IF(NA.EQ.4)GO TO 125
      GO TO 126
125   IF(JF(J).NE.0)GO TO 127
126   S = 1000000
      DO 121 I = 1,NCH
      IF (ICS(I).NE.1) GO TO 121
```

```
      IF(JIA(J.I).EQ.0)GO TO 121
      IF(JF(J).EQ.0)GO TO 122
      IF(JF(J).EQ.I)GO TO 122
      IF((XERP(J)+XERC(I)-XEE(I)).GE.S)GO TO 121
      GO TO 123
122   IF((XERC(I)-XEE(I)).GE.S)GO TO 121
      S=XERC(I)-XEE(I)
      GO TO 124
123   S=XERP(J)+XERC(I)-XEE(I)
124   JFF(J)=I
121   CONTINUE
      GO TO 120
127   JFF(J)=JF(J)
120   CONTINUE
      DO 130 J=1,NPR
131   JF(J)=JFF(J)
130   JFF(J)=0
      LTT=LT-1
      IF(LT.EQ.1)LTT=1
C     FIND MOST ATTRACTIVE CHOICE FOR DMKR K
      DO 140 K=1,NDM
      IF(NA.EQ.3)GO TO 145
      IF(NA.EQ.4) GO TO 145
      GO TO 146
145   IF(KDC(K).NE.0)GO TO 147
146   S=1000000
      DO 141 I=1,NCH
      IF (ICS(I).NE.1) GO TO 141
      IF(IKA(I.K).EQ.0)GO TO 141
      IF(KDC(K).EQ.0)GO TO 142
      IF(KDC(K).EQ.I)GO TO 142
148   IF((XFRC(I)-XEE(I)-(XEA(K,LTT)*XSC(LTT))).GE.S)GO
      TO 141
      GO TO 143
142   IF((XERC(I)-XEE(I)).GE.S)GO TO 141
      S=XERC(I)-XEE(I)
      GO TO 144
143   S=XERC(I)-XEE(I)-XEA(K,LTT)*XSC(LTT)
144   KDCW(K)=I
141   CONTINUE
      GO TO 140
147   KDCW(K)=KDC(K)
140   CONTINUE
```

```
      DO 150 K = 1,NDM
151   KDC(K) = KDCW(K)
      IF(KDC(K).NE.0)GO TO 150
      XR = XR + (XEA(K,LT)*XSC(LT))
      KS = KS + 1
150   KDCW(K) = 0
C     ESTABLISHING THE ENERGY REQUIRED TO MAKE EACH
      CHOICE.
      DO 199 I = 1,NCH
      IF(ICS(I).EQ.0)GO TO 199
      XERC(I) = 0.0
      DO 160 J = 1,NPR
      IF (JPS(J).NE.1) GO TO 160
      IF(JF(J).NE.I)GO TO 160
      XERC(I) = XERC(I) + XERP(J)
160   CONTINUE
      DO 170 K = 1,NDM
      IF(IKA(I.K).EQ.0)GO TO 170
      IF(KDC(K).NE.I)GO TO 170
      XEE(I) = XEE(I) + XSC(LT)*XEA(K,LT)
170   CONTINUE
199   CONTINUE
C     MAKING DECISIONS
      DO 299 I = 1,NCH
      IF (ICS(I).NE.1) GO TO 299
      IF(XERC(I).GT.XEE(I)GO TO 299
      XS = XS = XEE(I) – XERC(I)
      ICS(I) = 2
      DO 250 J = 1,NPR
      IF(JF(J).NE.I)GO TO 250
      JPS(J) = 2
250   CONTINUE
      IF(NA.EQ.3)GO TO 261
      IF(NA.EQ.4)go to 261
      GO TO 299
261   DO 262 K = 1,NDM
      IF(KDC(K).NE.1)GO TO 262
      KDCW(K) = 1
262   CONTINUE
299   CONTINUE
      DO 200 I = 1,NCH
200   KABC(LT.I) = ICS(I)
      DO 210 K = 1,NDM
```

```
      KBBC(LT,K)=KDC(K)
      IF(KDCW(K).EQ.0)GO TO 210
      KDC(K)=0
210   KDCW(K)=0
      DO 220 J=1,NPR
      KCBC(LT,J)=JF(J)
      IF(JPS(J).EQ.0) GO TO 230
      IF(JPS(J).EQ.1) GO TO 220
      KCBC(LT,J)=1000
      GO TO 220
230   KCBC(LT,J)=-1
220   CONTINUE
992   CONTINUE
C     FINISH TIME PERIOD LOOP. BEGIN ACCUMULATION OF
      10 SUMMARY STATISTICS.
      KZ=0
      KY=0
      KX=0
      KW=0
      KV=0
      KU=0
      KT=0
      DO 310 I=1,NTP
      DO 320 J=1,NCH
      IF(KABC(I,J).NE.1)GO TO 320
      KY=KY+1
      IF(I.NE.NTP)GO TO 320
      KZ=KZ+1
320   CONTINUE
310   CONTINUE
      DO 330 I=2,NTP
      DO 340 J=1,NDM
      IF(KBBC(I,J).EQ.KBBC(I-1,J))GO TO 340
      KX=KX+1
340   CONTINUE
330   CONTINUE
      DO 350 I=1,NTP
      DO 360 J=1,NPR
      IF(KCBC(I.J).EQ.0)GO TO 351
      IF(KCBC(I.J).EQ.-1) GO TO 360
      IF(KCBC(I.J).EQ.1000) GO TO 352
      KT=KT+1
      GO TO 360
```

```
351   KU=KU+1
      GO TO 360
352   IF(I.NE.NTP)GO TO 360
      KW=KW+1
360   CONTINUE
350   CONTINUE
      KW=NPR=KW
      DO 370 I=2,NTP
      DO 380 J=1,NPR
      IF(KCBC(I,J).EQ.KCBC(I-1,J))GO TO 380
      KV=KV+1
380   CONTINUE
370   CONTINUE
C     BEGIN WRITEOUT OF MATERIALS FOR THIS ORGANIZA-
      TIONAL VARIANT.
1000  FORMAT(1H1)
1019  FORMAT(2X,'LOAD=',I1,'PR.ACC.=',I1,'DEC.STR.=',I1'.
      'EN.DIST.='.BI1,2X,'STATS I-10',3X,8I5,1X,2F6.2/)
      WRITE(6,1019)IB,JA,JD,JE,KZ,KY,KX,KW,KV,KY,KT,KS,ZR,
      XS
      IF(IO.EQ.1) GO TO 995
2000  FORMAT(' CHOICE ACTIVATION HISTORY',34X,'DEC.
      MAKER ACTIVITY HISTOR BY'/'20 TIME PERIODS,10
      CHOICES',33X,'20 TIME PERIODS,10 DEC. MAKE CRS
      '/' 0=INACTIVE,1=ACTIVE,2=MADE',33X,'0=INACTIVE,
      X=WORKING ON CHOICE X'//9X,' 1 2 3 4 5 6 7 8 9 10',
      30X,'1 2 3 4 5 6 7 8 9 10'/)
      WRITE(6,2000)
2001  FORMAT( 5X,I2,3X,10I2,25X,12,3X,10I2)
      WRITE(6,2001)(LT,(KABC(LT,J),J=1,NCH).LT.( KBBC(LT,J),
      J=1,NDM), LT=1,NTP )
2002  FORMAT(/' PROBLEM HISTORY:ROWS=TIME,COLS=
      PROBS., -1=NOT ENTERED,, O=UNATTACHED,X=
      ATT.TO CH.X,**=SOLVED'/1OX.
      ' 1 2 3 4 5 6 7 8 9 10 11 12 13 14 15 16 17 18 19 20'/)
      WRITE(6,2002)
2003   FORMAT(20(5X,I2,3X,20(1X,I2)/))
      WRITE(6,2003)(LT,(KCBC(LT,J),J=1,NPR),LT=1,NTP)
      WRITE(6,1000)
995   CONTINUE
996   CONTINUE
997   CONTINUE
998   CONTINUE
```

```
      STOP
      END

******* DATA AS FOLLOWS (AFTER GUIDE CARDS) ***********

0        1         2         3         4
1234567890123456789012345678901234567890
         5         6         7         8
1234567890123456789012345678901234567890

008.005.006.007.004.009.002.010.003.001
1.000.900.700.300.100.100.300.700.901.00
0.600.600.600.600.600.600.600.600.600.60
009.005.008.007.010.003.003.001.007.009
006.008.005.002.004.002.004.010.006.001
1 2
```

References

Allison, Graham T. (1969) Conceptual models and the Cuban missile crises. *American Political Science Review,* 63, 689–718.

Christensen, Søren (1971) *Institut og laboratorieorganisation på Danmarks tekniske Højskole*. Copenhagen: Copenhagen School of Economics.

Cohen, Michael D., and James G. March (1974) *The American College President*. New York: McGraw-Hill, Carnegie Commission on the Future of Higher Education.

Coleman, James S. (1957) *Community Conflict*. Glencoe: Free Press.

Cyert, Richard M., and James G. March (1963) *Behavioral Theory of the Firm*. Englewood Cliffs: Prentice-Hall.

Enderud, Harald (1971) *Rektoratet og den centrale administration på Danmarks tekniske Højskole*. Copenhagen: Copenhagen School of Economics.

Lindblom, Charles E. (1965) *The Intelligence of Democracy*. New York: Macmillan.

Long, Norton (1958) The local community as an ecology of games. *American Journal of Sociology*, 44, 251–61.

March, James G., and Herbert A. Simon (1958) *Organizations*. New York: John Wiley.

Mood, Alexander (ed.) (1971) *More Scholars for the Dollar*. New York: McGraw-Hill, Carnegie Commission on the Future of Higher Education.

Olsen, Johan P. (1970) *A Study of Choice in an Academic Organization*. Bergen: University of Bergen.

Olsen, Johan P. (1971) *The Reorganization of Authority in an Academic Organization*. Bergen: University of Bergen.

Rommetveit, Kåre (1971) *Framveksten av det medisinske fakultet ved Universitet i Tromsø*. Bergen: University of Bergen.

Schilling, Warner R. (1968) The H-bomb decision: how to decide without actually choosing. In W. R. Nelson (ed.), *The Politics of Science*. London: Oxford University Press.

Thompson, James D. (1967) *Organizations in Action*. New York: McGraw-Hill.

Vickers, Geoffrey (1965) *The Art of Judgment*. New York: Basic Books.

15

The Uncertainty of the Past: Organizational Learning under Ambiguity

James G. March and Johan P. Olsen

Abstract

Classical theories of omniscient rationality in organizational decision-making have largely been replaced by a view of limited rationality, but no similar concern has been reflected in the analysis of organizational learning. There has been a tendency to model a simple complete cycle of learning from unambiguous experience and to ignore cognitive and evaluative limits on learning in organizations. This paper examines some theoretical possibilities for assuming that individuals in organizations modify their understanding in a way that is intendedly adaptive even though faced with ambiguity about what happened, and whether it is good. To develop a theory of learning under such conditions, we probably require ideas about information exposure, memory, and retrieval; learning incentives; belief structures; and the micro-development of belief in organizations. We exhibit one example by specifying a structural theory of the relations among liking, seeing, trusting, contact, and integration in an organization. The argument is made that some understanding of factors affecting learning from experience will not only be important to the improvement of policy-making in an organizational context, but also a necessary part of a theory of organizational choice.

This paper was first published in the *European Journal of Political Research*, 3, 1975, 147–71. It is a revised version of a paper read at the ECPR workshop on 'Models and Cases in Administrative Decision-Making', Strasbourg, 29 March – 2 April, 1974. The authors have profited considerably from their discussions with Søren Christensen, Michael D. Cohen, James R. Glenn, Kristian Kreiner, Kåre Rommetveit, Per Stava, Harald Sætren, and Stephen S. Weiner.

Organizational intelligence, like individual intelligence, is built on two fundamental processes. The first of these is rational calculation, by which expectations about future consequences are used to choose among current alternatives. Rationality in policy-making is typified by planning, analysis, forecasting and the paraphernalia of decision theory and management science; it is the logic of most recent efforts to improve the quality of decision-making in public policy (as well as in non-public organizations).

The second process is learning from experience. Through learning, feedback from previous experience is used to choose among present alternatives. Learning in policy-making is typified by experimentation, evaluation, assessment, and the paraphernalia of experimental design and control theory; it is the logic of an increasing number of efforts to improve policy-making, particularly in areas such as education, social welfare, and social organization.

In the last two decades there has been considerable examination of the cognitive and evaluative limitations on rationality. Although presumptions of rationality both as an objective and as a reality are still common, the literature is full of attempts to develop the major implications of limitations on the awareness of alternatives, on the precision of information about consequences, and on the clarity and consistency of goals (Simon, 1955; March and Simon, 1958; Cyert and March, 1963; Lindblom, 1965). There is no longer general acceptance of a model of superhuman organizational omniscience in the service of rationality. Instead, there is an inclination to accept the proposition that while organizations are intendedly rational, they frequently act on incomplete or incorrect information and without being aware of all of their alternatives. Similarly, there is no longer general acceptance of a simple view of a well-defined organizational preference function. Instead, there is an effort to accommodate in the theory the frequent observations of inconsistent and conflicting organizational objectives.

Little comparable effort has been devoted to assessing the cognitive and evaluative limitations on organizational learning. As a result, learning is ordinarily understood in terms of a model of simple rational adaptation.[1] Policy makers may have limited abilities to predict consequences or control events, but they are presumed to be able to see what happens and understand why. They can distinguish success from failure. If organizations

1 A recent exception is Axelrod (1973); Cohen and March (1974) discuss the relevance of superstitious learning as an organizational phenomenon; see also Weick (1969). Olsen (1970) shows that a decision-making process is a process of interpretation as well as a process of choice. Thompson (1967) has a very interesting discussion of how organizations keep score: 'Even if we concede that organizations sometimes maximize, the organizational question is whether the organization has any way of knowing that it has done so. And how does it assess itself on the ultimate question, its fitness for the future' (p. 84).

fail to improve, the explanation is found in various forms of organizational rigidities that inhibit the adoption of changes even though clearly indicated by experience, or in lack of motivation, or in some other inexplicable failure of the organization to learn.

We wish to examine some limitations on learning from experience. We will assume that organizations adapt their behavior in terms of their experience, but that experience requires interpretation. They learn under conditions in which goals (and therefore 'success' and 'failure') are ambiguous or in conflict, in which what happened is unclear, and in which the causality of events is difficult to untangle. People in organizations come to believe what happened, why it happened, and whether it was good; but the process by which those beliefs are established in the face of a quite problematic 'objective' world affects systematically what is learned.

Such a focus does not suggest that organizations are conspicuously foolish in their learning, any more than that idea of limited rationality suggests that they are conspicuously foolish in their rational calculations. Both notions recognize some constraints on human action and some utility in theories of organizational intelligence that consider those constraints.

The Complete Cycle of Choice

Consider what might be called the complete cycle of organizational choice. It is a familiar conception, and a useful one:

> At a certain point in time some participants see a discrepancy between what they think the world ought to be (given present possibilities and constraints) and what the world actually is. This discrepancy produces individual behavior, which is aggregated into collective (organizational) action or choices. The outside world then 'responds' to this choice in some way that affects individual assessments both of the state of the world and of the efficacy of the actions.

This conception of choice assumes a closed cycle of connections (figure 15.1):

1 The cognitions and preferences held by individuals affect their behavior.
2 The behavior (including participation) of individuals affects organizational choices.
3 Organizational choices affect environmental acts (responses).
4 Environmental acts affect individual cognitions and preferences.

These basic ideas are fundamental to much of our understanding of decisions in organizations. The ideas are implicit in most ordinary conversations about organizations and about important events of policy-making. They are the basis for many theoretical treatments, including our own. While we think this conception of choice illuminates choice situations significantly, we want to modify the details of that perspective and explore some specific limitations in a theory based on the closed sequence shown in figure 15.1. The limitations we will consider are of considerable significance under some situations, of little significance under others. The limitations are particularly important when the cycle is incomplete, when one or more of the connections are broken or confounded by exogenous factors.

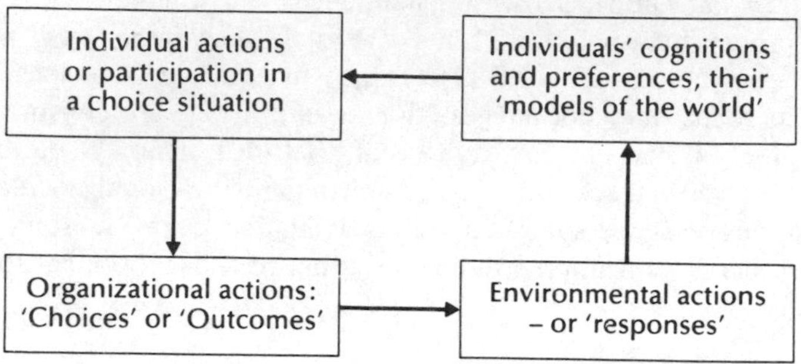

Figure 15.1. The complete cycle of choice

Limitations in the Complete Cycle

The complete cycle of organizational choice assumes four simple relations. Each of those relations is obviously more complex than the closed cycle represents it to be. More importantly, those relations are more complex in ways that lead to systematic limitations in the theory.

Individual Beliefs and Individual Action

Most organization theory is purposive. It assumes that behavior and attention[2] follow belief and attitude. Beliefs and attitudes, in turn, are stable enough so that attention is stable over the course of a choice; and differential levels of attention are predictable from the content of the decision. Decision-making activity thus stems from self-interest and is generally attractive so long as the resources being allocated are significant.

2 The concept of attention is deliberately broad. We will use it with reference to activities like searching information, discussing, proselytising, attending meetings, voting, making speeches, campaigning and competing for offices, with no references to the motivation for or the effect of the activities.

Our observations suggest a modification of this view.[3] Instead of a stable activity level we find that people move in and out of choice situations. There is considerable variation among individuals, and over time for the same individual, in terms of the degree and form of attention to decision problems. A step toward understanding this flow of attention, and its connection to individual beliefs and attitudes, is to note that time and energy are scarce resources.

Involvement in decisions is not attractive for everyone in all relevant choice situations, all the time. The capacity for beliefs, attitudes, and concerns is larger than the capacity for action. A choice situation may be perceived as relevant, but the individual may not have any time or energy for action. Under such circumstances, we will observe beliefs and values without behavioral implications. Even given the time and energy, there are alternative choice situations where an individual can present his concerns. The flow of attention will not depend on the content of a single choice alone, but upon the collection of choice situations available. We should not expect that a set of beliefs and preferences will have behavioral implications in any specific choice situation independent of the available claims on attention.

A theory that recognizes time as a scarce resource (Becker, 1965; Linder, 1970) makes attention contextual, subject to resource constraints and alternative 'consumption' possibilities. Such a conception assumes some hierarchy of beliefs and preferences, and some hierarchy of choice situations in terms of attractiveness. Individuals are seen to allocate available energy by attending to choice situations with the highest expected return. They do not act in one arena because they are acting in another. Although it clarifies some aspects of decision involvement, even this contextual version of the connection between values and action is problematic in an organization. It ignores the importance of roles, duties, and standard operating procedures for determining behavior; and it underestimates the ambiguity of self-interest.

3 Modifications have been suggested by a rather broad range of people. Weick (1969, p. 29) notes that the assumption in organization theory 'that once the perceptions or organization members are affected, action consistent with these perceptions will follow automatically' has not been affected by recent work by psychologists interested in how beliefs and values get translated into action. Both Weick (1969) and Bem (1970) argue for theories assuming that cognition follows action. The primacy of behavior or praxis over ideas or theory is a classical theme in Marxist theory. Often the point of departure is Marx's statement that life is not determined by consciousness, but consciousness by life (Marx, 1962). However, the debate between Marxists and non-Marxists has to some degree detracted attention from the debate among Marxists on the role of ideas as a driving force in history. Ibsen reflected some of the complexity when he had Peer Gynt state (on observing a man chopping off a finger to avoid being drafted): 'The thought, perhaps – the wish – the will. Those I could understand, but really to do the deed! Ah, no – that astounds me'.

Any complex social structure has considerable capability for weakening the connection between individual behavior and individual beliefs and preferences. The potential has produced some affective ambivalence. It has been celebrated as an important device in fighting personal favoritism and establishing equity and equality. It has been portrayed as a major source of organizational inertia preventing progress. Here we are not primarily concerned with a normative evaluation, but with the simple fact that roles, duties, and obligations are behaviorally important to involvement. People attend to decisions not only because they have an interest at stake, but because they are expected to or obliged to. They act according to rules.

Even when they act in self-interest terms, participants in organizations do not appear to act in a way fully anticipated by self-interest theories. They have an abundance of preferences and beliefs. The complexity increases as one moves from interest in immediate, substantive outcomes to long-term effects and to various side agendas (e.g., status) involved in a decision situation. The architecture of these values does not easily lend itself to description in terms of well-behaved preference functions. The behavior apparently stemming from the values proceeds without concern about those values. Not all values are attended to at the same time; attention focus, rather than utility, seems to explain much of the behavior (Cyert and March, 1963). At the same time, beliefs and preferences appear to be the results of behavior as much as they are the determinants of it. Motives and intentions are discovered *post factum* (March, 1972).

We require a theory that takes into consideration the possibility that there may be attitudes and beliefs without behavioral implications, that there may be behavior without any basis in individual preferences, and that there may be an interplay between behavior and the definition (and redefinition) of 'self-interest'.

Individual Action and Organizational Choice

Organizational choices are ordinarily viewed as derivative of individual actions. A decision process transforms the behavior of individuals into something that could be called organizational action. Explorations into the nature of this 'visible hand' comprise much of the literature; and most of the theoretical issues are questions of suitable metaphors for characterizing the process. It is sometimes captured by metaphors of deduction (organizational goals, sub-goals, efficiency); sometimes by metaphors of implicit conflict (markets, bureaucracy); sometimes by metaphors of explicit conflict (bargaining, political processes, power). Each of these metaphors accepts the basic notion that organizational choice is understandable as some consequence of individual action. They interpret organizations as instruments of individuals.

Our observations suggest that the connection between individual action and organizational action is sometimes quite loose. Sometimes we observe that the (internal) decision-making process is not strongly related to the organizational action, i.e., the policy selected, the price set, the man hired. Rather it is connected to the definition of truth and virtue in the organization, to the allocation of status, to the maintenance or change of friendship, goodwill, loyalty, and legitimacy; to the definition and redefinition of 'group interest'. In short, the formal decision-making process sometimes is directly connected to the maintenance or change of the organization as a social unit, as well as to the accomplishment of making collective decisions and producing substantive results. A theory of organizational choice probably should attend to the interplay between two aspects of the internal process.

Sometimes we observe a considerable impact on the process of the temporal flow of autonomous actions. We need a theory that considers the timing of different individual actions, and the changing context of each act. Most theories imply the importance of the context of an act. Typically, however, they have assumed that this context has stable properties that allow unconditional predictions. We observe a much more interactive, branching, and contextual set of connections among the participants, problems, and solutions in an organization.

Sometimes we observe an internal process swamped by external events or factors. Organizational action is conspicuously independent of internal process. The dramatic version – where some external actor intervenes directly, or where some external event completely changes the conditions under which the organization is operating – is well-known. In a similar way, macro-theorists of social process rarely feel required to consider the details of organizational phenomena. Theories of the market or long-run social movements have identified important characteristics of the deep structure in which organizational phenomena occur; and it would be foolish for a theory of organizational choice situations not to recognize the extent to which the decision process is part of a broader stream of events. We need a theory of choice that articulates the connections between the environmental context of organizations and their actions in such a way that neither is simply the residual unexplained variance for the other.

In general, we need a theory of organizational choice that considers the connection between individual actions and organizational actions as sometimes variable. Organizational action may be determined, or strongly constrained, by external forces. Internal process may be related to other phenomena than the organizational choice (i.e., allocating status, defining organizational truth and virtue). The structure of the internal process may be highly time-dependent; changing contexts of the individual acts may produce organizational actions not anticipated or desired by anyone.

Organizational Choice and Environmental Response

The complete cycle of choice assumes a connection between organizational actions and environmental actions. The latter are treated as *responses* to the choices made in the organization.[4] The notion is a simple one. We assume that there is an environment with a schedule of responses to alternative actions on the part of the organization. Voters respond to party platforms or candidate images. Consumers respond to produce quality and price. Competitors respond to challenges. Students respond to curricula. Citizens respond to social experiments. Out of such a paradigm come many of our ideas about organizational learning and natural selection (Cohen and March, 1974; Winter, 1964).

We need a theory of the environment which is less organization-centered, a theory where the actions and events in the environment sometimes may have little to do with what the organization does. Environmental acts frequently have to be understood in terms of relationships among events, actors, and structures in the environment, not as responses to what the organization does. As a result the same organizational action will have different responses at different times; different organizational actions will have the same response. The world of the absurd is sometimes more relevant for our understanding of organizational phenomena than is the idea of a tight connection between action and response.

The independence of action and response is accentuated by our tendency to attempt to explain fine gradations in both. Organizations act within environmentally constrained boundaries. On the rare occasions on which they violate those constraints, the environment is likely to react unambiguously. Most of the time, however, the range of behavior is relatively small; and within that range very little of the variation in response is attributable to variations in the action. In so far as we wish to explain variations in organizational behavior within the range in which we observe it, we will require a theory that recognizes only a modest connection between environmental response and organizational decision.[5]

4 There are two versions of the theory: The strong organization making the environment adapt to its decisions, and the weak organization being 'conditioned' by the environment.

5 Participants in an organization are likely, under a variety of circumstances, to see the connection between action and response as tighter than it is. As a result, one of the major phenomena that we will need to comprehend is superstitious learning within organizations; the way in which the subjective experience of learning can be compelling without any learning taking place.

Environmental Response and Individual Beliefs

Classical theory offers two alternative versions on how environmental actions and events are connected to individual cognition. In the first version, the problem is assumed away. Organizational decision-makers are equipped with perfect information about alternatives and consequences. Since the full cycle is well understood ahead of any individual action there is no learning in the system. In the second version, the connection is understood in terms of a model of individual, rational adaption. Beliefs and models of the world are tied to reality through experience. Events are observed; the individual changes his beliefs on the basis of his experience; he improves his behavior on the basis of this feedback.

Our observations suggest a modification of this view. There is a need for introducing ideas about the process by which beliefs are constructed in an organizational setting. In many contexts the interpretation of an organizational choice process is as important as the immediate, substantive action we commonly consider.[6] Individuals, as well as organizations or nations, develop myths, fictions, legends, and illusions. They develop conflicts over myths and ideology. We need models of the development of belief which do not assume necessary domination by events or 'objective reality'.

Environmental actions and events frequently are ambiguous. It is not clear what happened, or why it happened. Ambiguity may be inherent in the events, or be caused by the difficulties participants have in observing them. The complexity of, and change in, the environment often overpower our cognitive capacity. Furthermore, our interpretations are seldom based only on our own observations; they rely heavily on the interpretations offered by others. Our trust in the interpretations is clearly dependent on our trust in the interpreters. The degree of ambiguity will be strongly dependent upon the efficiency of the channels through which interpretations are transmitted.

The elaboration of such a theory is particularly germane to the study of organizations. Much of what we know, or believe we know, is based on our interpretation of reports from participants. When we ask a participant to report what happened, we solicit his model of events. When we ask a participant to assess the relative power of various individuals or groups, we ask him to carry out a complex theoretical analysis (March, 1966). It is often true that participants differ in significant ways among

6 Vickers (1965, p. 15) is interested in both these two outcomes of choices: 'events' and 'ideas'. He views the Royal Commissions as units which seldom are supposed to make direct choices, but to affect opinions and conceptions or 'the appreciative setting' of a certain phenomenon.

themselves or differ in significant ways from the interpretations that we, as outside observers, report. In order to sort out the complications of developing an understanding of participant reports, we need to understand the development of belief structures in an organization under conditions of ambiguity.

Implications for Theories of Choice Situations

We remain in the tradition of viewing organizational participants as problem solvers and decision-makers. However, we assume that individuals find themselves in a more complex, less stable, and less understood world than standard theories of organizational choice suppose; they are placed in a world over which they often have only modest control. Nevertheless, we assume organizational participants will try to understand what is going on, to activate themselves and their resources in order to solve their problems and move the world in desired directions. These attempts will have a less heroic character than assumed in the perfect cycle theories, but they will be real.

We have argued that any of the connections in the basic cycle of choice can be broken or changed so significantly as to modify the implications of the whole system. Intention does not control behavior precisely. Participation is not a stable consequence of properties of the choice situation or individual preferences. Outcomes are not a direct consequence of process. Environmental response is not always attributable to organizational action. Belief is not always a result of experience.

In addition, the cycle is frequently touched by exogenous factors outside the control of the internal process. The process is embedded in a larger system. Under relatively easily realized situations, any one of the connections may be overwhelmed by exogenous effects. External factors may dictate individual action without regard to individual learning, organizational action without regard to individual action, environmental action without regard to organizational action, or individual learning without regard to environmental action.

In order to respond to such concerns in a theory of organizations, we require three clusters of interrelated theoretical ideas:

First, we need a modified theory of organizational choice. Such a theory will need to be contextual in the sense that it reflects the ways in which the linkages in the complete cycle of choice are affected by exogenous events, by the timing of events, by the varieties of ways in which the participants wander onto and off the stage. It will need to be structural in the sense that it reflects ways in which stabilities can arise in a highly contextual system. We have tried to suggest the basis for such a theory elsewhere (Cohen, March and Olsen, 1972).

Second, we need a theory of organizational attention. Such a theory should treat the allocation of attention by potential participants as problematic. Where will they appear? What are the structural limits on their decision-activity? How do they allocate time within those limits? Such a theory must attend to the elements of rational choice in attention allocation, to the importance of learning to the modification of attention rules, and to the norms of obligation that affect individual attention to alternative organizational concerns. We have attempted to indicate an outline to such a theory elsewhere (March and Olsen, 1976).

Third, we need a theory of learning under conditions of organizational ambiguity. The complete cycle is implicitly a theory of learning. What happens when the cycle is incomplete? What is a possible perspective on the development and change of belief structures? The present paper is directed to an understanding of these issues of learning in the face of ambiguity.

Learning under Ambiguity

Choice situations provide occasions for argumentation and interpretation as well as decision-making. The ideas, beliefs and attitudes that participants come to hold are themselves important outcomes of the process. Interpretations of the ways in which meanings arise, the ways in which participants in an organization come to 'know' or 'believe', build on a set of simple theoretical ideas about rational adaptation. Beliefs are modified on the basis of experience. These ideas, however, seem inadequate for understanding some familiar phenomena. For example, we have been impressed by the regularities in the ways in which different individuals develop different interpretations of their common experience in a decison situation, with the ways in which organizations rewrite their histories and facilitate retrospective learning, with the ease with which participants come to have impressions of the power distribution within an organization, and with the importance for leadership in organizations of managing historical interpretation and the formation of belief. All these observations signal the significance and complexity of learning and the construction of belief to an understanding of organizational behavior.

Our general focus is on experimental learning within organizations. We ask how individuals and organizations make sense of their experience and modify behavior in terms of their interpretations of events. Our attempts are in the tradition of efforts to understand organizational behavior in terms of adaptive rationality. That tradition assumes a simple logic of experiential learning: an action is taken; there is some response from the environment; and then a new action is taken reflecting the impact of the sequence. A basic presumption in the literature is that as an organization gains experience, it learns more and more about coping with its environment and with its internal problems. Normally it is argued that organizations try to perpetuate the fruits of their learning by formalizing them (Starbuck, 1965, p.480). There is a belief that 'when the problem is solved, mass productions begins' (Perrow, 1970, p. 68).

The situation is familiar and has been portrayed in figure 15.1. It captures some important domains of behavior in organizations. There is a rather large family of models designed to interpret behavior within such a situation. The ideas of the complete cycle are made explicit in the following model by Cyert and March (1963, p. 99):

1 There exist a number of states of the system (organization). At any point in time, the system in some sense 'prefers' some of these states to others.
2 There exists an external source of disturbance or shock to the system. These shocks cannot be controlled.
3 There exist a number of decision variables internal to the system. These variables are manipulated according to some decision-rules.
4 Each combination of external shocks and decision variables in the system changes the state of the system. Thus, given an existing state, an external shock, and a decision, the next state is determined.
5 Any decision-rule that leads to a preferred state at one point is more likely to be used in the future than it was in the past.

We wish to examine what happens when the cycle is incomplete; in particular, to consider the development of belief under conditions of ambiguity.

Incomplete Learning Cycles

Some of the more interesting phenomena in organizations occur when the learning cycle is not complete, when one or more of the connections is attenuated. As we have indicated above, there are a number of ways in which the cycle may be broken. Although it is not necessarily true that the cycle is broken at only one place, we can illustrate the study of incomplete cycles by considering the four incomplete cycles involving only one missing link. The first situation is *role-constrained* experiential learning. In this situation, everything proceeds in the same manner as in the complete cycle except that individual learning has little or no effect on individual behavior. The circle is broken by constraints of role-definition and standard operating procedures (see figure 15.2).

The situation is one that reflects some important dynamics of organizational behavior. One of the conspicuous things about complex organizations

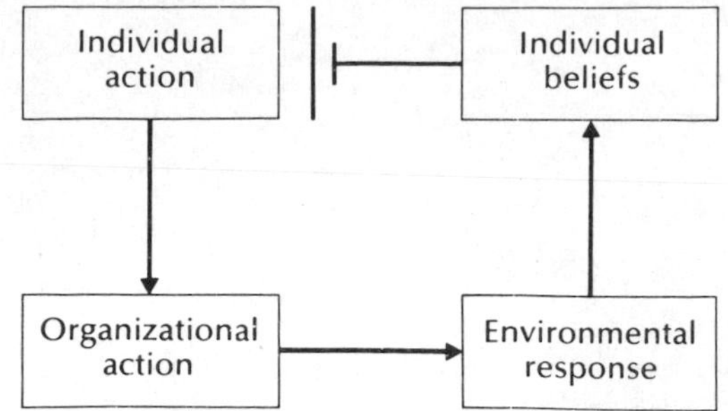

Figure 15.2. Role-constrained experiential learning

(or any complex social structure) is their ability to inhibit the modification of individual behavior on the basis of individual learning. The complication has formed the basis of a number of studies of organizations, most commonly in treatments of organizational inertia; but we do not have a systematic theory of the implications (for the time path of organizational behavior) of a separation of knowledge from action.

The second incomplete cycle is *superstitious* experiential learning. In this situation we assume that individuals within an organization take action, that action produces organizational behavior, that individuals learn from the apparent environmental response, and that subsequent action is modified in what appears to be an appropriate fashion. The critical feature is that the connection between organizational action and environmental response is severed. Learning proceeds. Inferences are made and action is changed. Organizational behavior is modified as a result of an interpretation of the consequences, but the behavior does not affect the consequences significantly. Although superstitious learning in organizations has not received as much attention as it deserves, some discussion of it can be found in Cohen and March (1974) and Lave and March (1975). As Hill (1971, p. 75) observes: 'Many of man's beliefs, not only in charms and magic, but also in medicine, mechanical skills, and administrative techniques probably depend on such superstitious learning' (see figure 15.3).

The third situation is *audience* experiential learning. In this situation the connection between individual action and organizational action becomes problematic. The individual no longer affects (at least in an unambiguous way) organizational action. What he learns cannot affect subsequent behavior by the organization. Learning occurs, but adaptation does not (necessarily). Much of our understanding of learning within politics or research falls within this situation, although it has not received much attention within modern organization theory, except in conjunction with the fourth situation below, when adaptation through interpretation becomes conspicuous as an alternative.

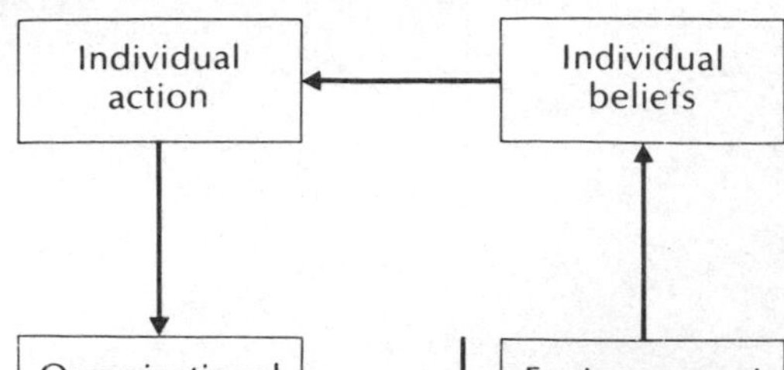

Figure 15.3. Superstitious experiential learning

Thus, the final incomplete cycle is one of experiential learning under *ambiguity*. In this situation it is not clear what happened or why it happened.[7] The individual tries to learn and to modify his behavior on the basis of his learning. In the simple situation, he affects organizational action and that action affects the environment; but subsequent events are seen only dimly, and causal connections among events have to be inferred (see figure 15.5). Learning takes place and behavior changes; but a model of the process requires some ideas about the imputation of meaning and structure to events. Such ideas have had little role in the organizational literature.

Information, Incentives, Cognitive Structures and Micro-Development

The problems of ambiguity in organizations are conspicuous. Nevertheless, the literature on organizational learning is rarely uncoupled from the idea that learning is adaptive. Experience is viewed as producing wisdom and

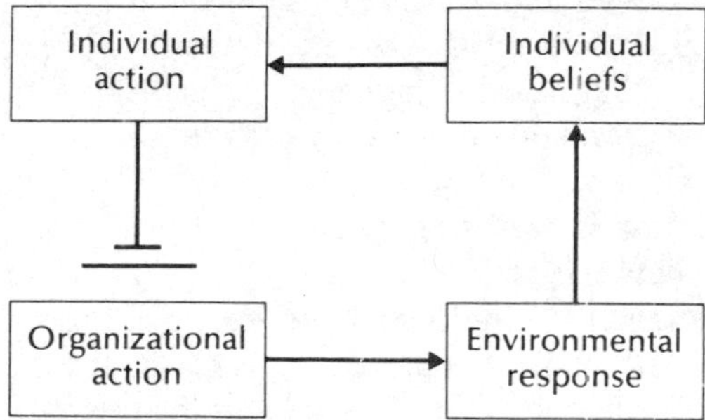

Figure 15.4. Audience experiential learning

7 Ambiguity here refers to an 'objective' assessment of the situation (in practice the assessment of the researcher). The individual participants may view the situation as quite unambiguous, though they disagree about the content of that interpretation

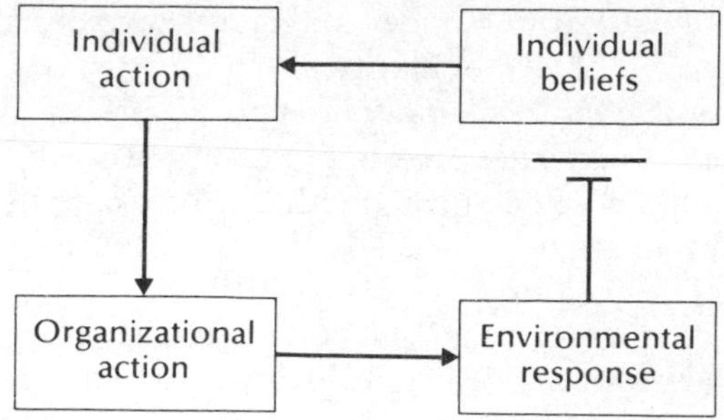

Figure 15.5. Experiential learning under ambiguity

improved behavior. For purposes of studying experiential learning under ambiguity it is necessary to relax such an assumption. Modern organizations develop myths, fictions, legends, folklore, and illusions. They develop conflict over myths. The connection between environmental response to organizational action and individual and organizational interpretation of that response is often weak.

We relax the presumption of improvement but not the presumption of a process of learning. We assume that individuals modify their understandings in a way that is intendedly adaptive. They are, however, operating under conditions in which (a) what happened is not immediately obvious; (b) why it happened is obscure; and (c) whether what happened is good is unclear.

A theory of adaptation under conditions of ambiguity might reasonably include four broad categories of ideas:

1 Some ideas of information exposure, memory, and retrieval. Organizations have communication structures through which individuals and parts of the organization 'see' different worlds. The occasions for seeking information, as well as where information is searched for, are presumably not random, but vary with both organizational and environmental factors. Organizations have records and other ways of recording history. These records are more or less accurate, more or less complete, more or less shared, and more or less retrievable at some future date. How organizational memory functions and how it functions differently at different times and for different parts of the organization are questions that considerably affect the pattern of organizational beliefs. The tendency to use or activate different parts of an organizational memory will vary across individuals as well as organizational subunits.

2 Some ideas about learning incentives. Incentives in learning are usually associated with 'motivation', some measure of factors that influence an inclination to accept information and modify behavior.

In organizational learning under ambiguity, we confront a different form of incentive. If lack of clarity in the situation or in the feedback makes several alternative interpretations possible, what are the incentives that might lead a particular person, or part of the organization, to select one interpretation rather than another. For example, what are the incentives for an evaluator of a social experiment to find it a success? Or a failure?

3 Some ideas about belief structures. The development of beliefs under conditions of ambiguity probably accentuates the significance of a pre-existing structure of related values and cognitions. Understandings of events are connected to previous understandings, to the understandings of other people, and to social linkages of friendship and trust. Learning is a form of attitude formation.

4 Some ideas about the micro-development of belief. It is reasonable to suspect that beliefs, like decisions, are sensitive to the fine detail of the timing, order, and context of information. Suppose, for example, that we think of one process that determines the current degrees of salience of various elements of organizational information and another process that relates new information to the structure of existing information. Then modifications in response to experience will depend importantly on the interleaving of the two processes. Similarly, suppose that the elaboration of the meaning of experience is a claim (for time or energy) on a limited capacity system. Then learning will be affected by the characteristics of the other demands on the system.

We do not propose here to specify a theory of audience learning under ambiguity that deals with all of these clusters of ideas. We can, however, illustrate the kinds of considerations that are important by elaborating one version of the ideas about structure – that associated with various notions of consistency or balance in belief and perception. The spirit of the effort is strongly in the tradition of Heider (1958), Newcomb (1959), and Abelson (1968).

An Example – Seeing, Liking and Trusting

We assume that organizational participants generally try to make sense of ongoing events and processes. They discover or impose order, attribute meanings, and provide explanations. We wish to identify a simple set of ideas about the ways in which persons in organizations come to learn from experience, how they come to believe what they believe. We are not primarily interested in the ultimate validity of different beliefs. Our focus is on the process by which conceptions of reality are affected by experience in an organizational setting. We do not attempt to specify all of the detail of that process.

For expository purposes, a distinction is made between beliefs about what a person 'sees' and beliefs about what a person 'likes'. The beliefs about what a person sees include the ways in which the individual defines actions and outcomes, the theories he has about the world, and his interpretations of those theories. The beliefs about what a person likes include the affective sentiments he has, his values, and his tastes. By making this distinction, we will be able to link our ideas to ordinary discourse about fact and value; but it should be clear as we proceed that we do not postulate a fundamentally different process for coming to believe that something exists or is true from a process for coming to believe that something is desirable.

The tightness of the connection between environmental response and individual learning hinges on the extent to which the interpretation of events is controlled by six presumptions of ordinary life in unambiguous systems:

He sees what is to be seen.
He likes what is to be liked.
He sees what he expects to see.
He likes what he expects to like.
He sees what he is expected to see.
He likes what he is expected to like.

The first two presumptions reflect the extent to which the processes of perception and preference are effectively self-evident. The second two reflect the intra-personal limitations on perceptions and preferences. The last reflect the role of social norms. By presenting the six as distinct, we mean to suggest some possible utility in avoiding the dictum that all knowledge is necessarily 'social'.

An organizational participant sees what is to be seen. There is an ordinary process of perceiving reality. The process is normatively well-defined. Through it, an individual establishes reliably what has happened in the phenomenal world. He is able to relate observed events to their future consequences, and to their more stable underlying causes. A correct link can be established between his past choices and subsequent states of the world (i.e., it is possible to disentangle the effects of own choices and the effects of external factors). There exist some criteria for determining what choice situations are similar. Although much of what we want to discuss relates to other factors, we wish to acknowledge the possibility, and frequent dominance, of what is usually called objective reality.

An organizational participant likes what is to be liked. There are objective interests in the sense that given an individual's position in society (or organization) it is possible to assert that some things are in his interest and others are not, even if that is not his own present awareness. Although such a conception of interest is uncommon in modern social science, we consider it a defensible assumption of a theory that intends to predict actual behavior over time. Indeed, it is the basis of much effective prediction in social behavior.

An organizational participant sees what he expects to see. We assume that an individual approaches any perceptual situation with expectations. Those expectations may come from experience; they may come from the structure of his beliefs about the world. In either case, the expectations help to control their own realization.

An organizational participant likes what he likes. Individuals come to any particular choice situation with a set of values, attitudes, and opinions. These values are substantially fixed. Changes that occur within a relatively brief time period must attend to problems of consistency with the pre-existing attitude structure. In some cases, the restrictions imposed by this presumption will dominate the behavior.

An organizational participant sees what he is expected to see and likes what he is expected to like. The role of social norms in facilitating the interpretation of events and attitudes is a familiar theme in the analyses of social behavior. Among the best-known examples of social provision of precision are the studies of strongly ideological, religious, and political messianistic movements (e.g., Festinger et al., 1956). The phenomenon extends well beyond such cases, however.

In many cases, seeing and liking are controlled by the elemental exogenous forces of objective reality, attitude structures, social reality, and social norms. In the rest of this paper, however, we wish to examine situations in which the six elementary presumptions of seeing and liking do not completely determine the interpretations of events, where there is some degree of contextual ambiguity. Under such conditions a different set of assumptions becomes important and some attributes of organizations have significant impact on the development of belief and the process of learning.

Situations of ambiguity are common. The patterns of exposure to events and the channels for diffusing observations and interpretations often obscure the events. In situations where interpretations and explanations are called forth some time after the events, the organizational 'memory' (e.g., files, budgets, statistics, etc.) and the retrieval-system will affect the degrees to which different participants can use past events, promises, goals, assumptions, behavior, etc. in different ways. Pluralism, decentralization, mobility and volatility in attention all tend to produce perceptual and attitudinal ambiguity in interpreting events.

Despite ambiguity and uncertainty, organizational participants interpret and try to make sense out of their lives. They try to find meaning in happenings and provide or invent explanations. These explanations and their development over time are our primary focus.

For the present purposes an organization is considered to consist of individuals characterized by:

1 Varying *patterns of interaction* with each other. The frequency and duration of contacts between any two people may vary. In part this may reflect choice; in part it may be a consequence of organizational structure.
2 Varying *degrees of trust* in each other. The belief in another person's ability and strength, together with the confidence in his motives, varies.
3 Varying *degrees of integration* into the organization. A person is integrated to the extent to which he accepts responsibility for the organization and feels that the actions of the organization are fundamentally his actions or the actions of those he trusts. The converse relation with the organization is alienation. We will view an individual as alienated from the organization to the extent to which he does not accept responsibility for it and feels that the actions of the organization are neither his actions nor the actions of others whom he trusts.
4 Varying *orientations to events* in the phenomenal world. These orientations have four key dimensions: (a) the extent to which the event is *seen*; (b) the extent to which the event is *liked*; (c) the extent to which the event is *relevant* to different interpersonal relations; (d) the extent to which an event is seen as *controlled* by different individuals.

We assume that the individuals in an organization develop their interpretations of events in a way broadly consistent with some hypotheses of cognitive consistency. In a general way, we assume that there are clear interdependencies between cognitive organization (i.e., perceiving someone as causing something, owning something, being close, etc.) and attitudinal organization (i.e., liking or disliking something or someone). The interdependencies with which we will concern ourselves reflect various tendencies toward consistency. We believe that such tendencies capture important aspects of the formation of beliefs in organizations. At the same time, however, it should be obvious that we do not anticipate that the attitude structures we will observe in organizations will exhibit a high degree of consistency on some absolute scale. Ambiguity in the environment, short attention spans, and considerable human tolerance for inconsistency (Bem, 1970) conspire to maintain a high level of incongruence at any one point of time even in a process in which there are substantial efforts toward cognitive structure.

To focus on a simple set of ideas about movement toward cognitive consistency, we make four propositions about seeing and liking:

Proposition 1: An organizational participant will – to the extent to which he is integrated into the organization – see what he likes. To the extent to which he is alienated from the organization he will see what he dislikes.

Thus we assume that the elementary screening devices used by the individual in looking at the world tend to obscure those elements of reality that are not consonant with his attitudes. To the extent possible, the individual sees what he wants to see. The result of such wishful thinking is highly dependent upon his integration into the organization. If he is alienated from the organization, he will see evidence confirming his alienation.

Proposition 2: An organizational participant will – to the degree he is integrated into the organization – like what he sees. To the extent to which he is alienated from the organization he will dislike what he sees.

Not only does the individual modify his perceptions to accommodate his attitudes, he also modifies his attitudes to accommodate his perceptions. We assume that individuals discover pleasures in the outcomes arising from worlds into which they are integrated relatively independent of what those outcomes are; and displeasures from worlds from which they are alienated.

Proposition 3: An organizational participant will – to the extent to which he trusts others with whom he has contact – like what they like. To the extent to which he distrusts others with whom he has contact, he will dislike what they like.

Most organizational participants most of the time will not be eye-witnesses to most relevant events. Both what they 'see' and what they 'like' will be dependent upon available sources of information, which of the sources available they are exposed to, which of those they are exposed to they trust. Learning under such conditions becomes dependent both upon processes like discussions and persuasion, and upon relationships like trust and antagonism. We assume that sentiments diffuse through the contact network characterized by variations in trust. They spread positively across trust relationships, negatively across distrust relationships.

The frequency of interaction will be especially important when different trusted people hold different likes. We assume that an organizational participant under such conditions will tend to like what those whom he most frequently interacts with, like.

Proposition 4: An organizational participant will – to the degree he trusts others with whom he has contact – see what they see. To the extent to which he distrusts others with whom he has contact, he will not see what they see.

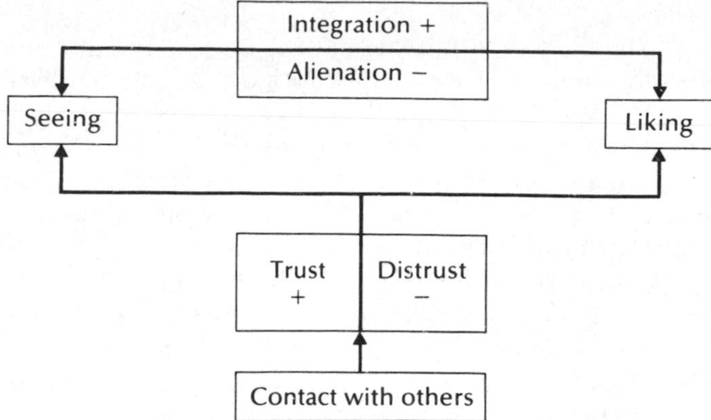

Figure 15.6. Seeing, liking, and trusting

Perceptions also diffuse through the contact network, mediated by the trust structure. Individuals (most of the time) have difficulties in seeing things different from what a unanimous group of trusted people see.

This elementary set of propositions results in a simple system for coming to believe what one believes, as portrayed in figure 15.6.

Finally we need to complete the basic system by adding six propositions that reflect the dynamics of balancing within the organizations of life for each participant:

Proposition 5: An organizational participant will come to trust others whom he sees as producing relevant events that he likes and preventing relevant events that he dislikes.

Proposition 6: An organizational participant will come to believe that people he trusts cause events he likes and that people he distrusts cause events he dislikes.

Proposition 7: An organizational participant will come to believe that events are relevant if he agrees about them with people he trusts and disagrees about them with people he distrusts.

Proposition 8: An organizational participant will be active to the extent to which his seeing, liking, and trusting are unambiguous.

Proposition 9: An organizational participant will – to the extent to which the organizational structure and his activity level permit – seek contact with people he trusts and avoid contact with people he distrusts.

Proposition 10: An organizational participant will feel integrated into an organization to the extent to which he likes the relevant events that he sees.

Taken together these propositions suggest a view of reality forming that emphasizes the impact of interpersonal connections within the organization and the affective connection between the organization and the participant on the development of belief, as well as the interaction between seeing and liking. In keeping with the balance ideas, the propositions emphasize the organization of belief as vital to the substance of belief, and accept a particular form of consistency as an organizing device.

The propositions appear to fit the observations in some case studies. They also seem to fit some more casual observations of organizational life. Their ultimate utility, however, hinges heavily on the extent to which the dynamics they postulate can be used to interpret more subtle aspects of changes in beliefs over time.

Conclusion

Organizations, and the people in them, learn from their experience. They act, observe the consequences of their action, make inferences about those consequences, and draw implications for future action. The process is adaptively rational. If the information is accurate, the goals clear and unchanging, the inferences correct, the behavior modification appropriate, and the environment stable, the process will result in improvement over time.

As we have come to recognize the limitations on rational calculation, planning, and forecasting as bases for intelligence in many organizations, interest in the potential for organizational learning has increased. That interest, however, tends to underestimate the extent to which adaptive rationality is limited by characteristics of human actors and organizations. The problems are similar to, and probably as profound as, the limits on calculated rationality. We have tried to suggest a few of the complications involved in assuming that organizations 'improve' through learning, particularly under conditions of ambiguity.

Despite the difficulties, it is important to study the process of learning in organizations. Individuals try to make sense of their experience, even when that experience is ambiguous or misleading and even when that learning does not affect organizational actions. They impose order, attribute meaning, and provide explanations. We have outlined an application of one set of ideas about cognitive consistency to the question of how ambiguous events in organizations are interpreted, and thus how people in an organization come to believe what they believe.

Some significant understanding of the factors affecting learning from experience will not only be important to the improvement of policy-making in an organizational context. It will also be a necessary part of a theory of the full cycle of organizational choice and of the consequences that accrue from breaking the cycle in different ways under different circumstances. Policy analysts interested in designing organizations that can learn intelligently and organization theorists interested in understanding the dynamics of organizational choice share the need for an effective model of organizational learning under conditions of uncertainty about what events happened, why they happened, and whether they were good or bad. Such situations are common in a wide variety of organizations; they are conspicuous in most public organizations, somewhat more concealed in business organizations.

References

Abelson, R., et al (1968) *Theories of Cognitive Consistency: A Sourcebook*. Chicago: Rand McNally.

Axelrod, R. (1973) Schema Theory: An Information Processing Model of Perception and Cognition. *The American Political Science Review,* Vol. 57, 1248–66.

Becker, G. S. (1965) A Theory of the Allocation of Time. *Economic Journal,* Vol. 75, 493–517.

Bem, D. J. (1970) *Beliefs, Attitudes and Human Affairs.* Belmont: Brooks/Cole.

Cohen, R. M., and March, J. G. (1974) *Leadership and Ambiguity*. New York: McGraw-Hill.

Cohen, M. D., March, J. G., and Olsen, J. P. (1972) A Garbage Can Model of Organizational Choice. *Administrative Science Quarterly*, Vol. 17, 1–25.

Cyert, R. M., and March, J. G. (1963) *A Behavioral Theory of the Firm.* Englewood Cliffs: Prentice Hall.

Festinger, L. et al. (1956) *When Prophecy Fails.* Minneapolis: University of Minnesota Press.

Heider, F. (1958) *The Psychology of Interpersonal Relations.* New York: John Wiley.

Hill, W. F. (1971) *Learning* (revised edn). Scranton: Chandler.

Lave, C. A., and March, J. G. (1975) *Introduction to Models in the Social Sciences.* New York: Harper and Row.

Lindblom, C. E. (1965) *The Intelligence of Democracy.* New York: The Free Press.

Linder, S. (1970) *The Harried Leisure Class.* New York: Columbia University Press.

March, J. G. (1966) The Power of Power, in D. Easton, *Varieties of Political Theories.* Englewood Cliffs: Prentice Hall.

March, J. G. (1972) Model Bias in Social Action. *Review of Educational Research,* Vol. 42, 413–29.

March, J. G., and Olsen, J. P. (1976) *Ambiguity and Choice in Organizations.* Bergen: Universitetsforlaget.

March, J. G., and Simon, H. A. (1958) *Organizations.* New York: John Wiley & Sons.

Marx, K., and Engels, F. (1962) *Die Deutsche Ideologie.* Marx Engels Werk Band 3, Berlin: Dietz Verlag.

Olsen, J. P. (1970) 'A Study of Choice in an Academic Organization', Bergen (mimeo).

Newcomb, T. M. (1959) Individual Systems of Orientation in Koch, *Psychology: A Study of Science.* New York: McGraw Hill.

Perrow, C. (1970) *Organizational Analysis: A Sociological View.* London: Tavistock Publications.

Simon, H. A. (1955) A Behavioral Model of Rational Choice *Quarterly Journal of Economics,* Vol. 69. Reprinted in H. A. Simon (1957), *Models of Man*. New York: John Wiley.

Starbuck, W. H. (1967) Organizational Growth and Development, in March, *Handbook of Organizations.* Chicago: Rand McNally.

Thompson, J. D. (1967) *Organizations in Action.* New York: McGraw Hill.

Vickers, G. (1965) *The Art of Judgement.* London: Chapman and Hall.

Weick, K. (1969) *The Social Psychology of Organizing*. Reading: Addison, Wesley.

16

Performance Sampling in Social Matches

James C. March and James G. March

Abstract

Many social structures can be viewed as collections of interconnected voluntary social pairings, for example, matches between jobholders and jobs, husbands and wives, or residents and neighborhoods. A general performance sampling model is suggested as a framework for exploring how mutual evaluation within such matches affects their continuation, and thus the structure of matches involved. The model treats continuation in a pairing as a decision made under conditions of imperfect information. It emphasizes the sampling errors involved in using small samples of observations to form judgments about matches. There are indications that the sampling characteristics of the process will often be robust enough to obscure other effects. The specific implications of one version of the model are shown to agree well with general observations from social mobility studies and more specific data from Wisconsin school superintendents. The implications of performance sampling for understanding careers in organizations and social pairings more generally are discussed. In contrast to an earlier paper, which explored major features of the gross structure of matches between superintendencies and superintendents, the present paper looks at the fine structure of the ways in which individuals leave jobs. The attempt is both to illuminate how a particular system of careers might arise from a series of elementary decisions with respect to job exits, and to connect a theory of organizational careers more explicitly with theories of other social pairings.

This paper was first published in the *Administrative Science Quarterly*, Vol. 25, no. 3, September 1978. The research was supported by grants from the Ford Foundation and the Spencer Foundation. The Ford Foundation grant was made through the National Academy of Education. The paper has profited from comments by Louis R. Pondy, Aage Sørensen, and Nancy B. Tuma.

Many social linkages can be viewed as voluntary pairings. The relation between husband and wife, resident and residence, job and jobholder, teacher and student, product and buyer are all examples of social matches that are voluntary in the sense that we imagine them to require some form of mutual consent.[1] Interconnected changes in pairings produce social structures of marriages, residences, careers, consumption patterns , and other matches. Associated with such structures are theoretical ideas about social mobility, specifically market theories of pairings (Stigler, 1961; Edwards, 1969; Becker, 1973) and Markovian and semi-Markovian models of movement (Blumen, Kogan, and McCarthy, 1955; White, 1970; Singer and Spilerman, 1974; Tuma, 1975). Although there are manifest differences between a social structure of careers and structures of marriages, residences, consumption, or other matches, there are broad similarities in mobility data taken from these apparently different domains. As a result, there is some reason to look for simple explanations of matching processes that are general enough to apply to different kinds of social pairings.

An earlier paper on Wisconsin school superintendents (March and March, 1977) showed how major features of the structure of matches between high-level management jobs and managers (Wisconsin school superintendents) could be approximated by assuming random matches between indistinguishable individuals and indistinguishable jobs. Such an approximation seems adequate for many ordinary forecasting and decision purposes and suggests some important features of careers in top management positions. In particular, it was argued that a nearly random career structure was produced by the increasing difficulty of making reliable discriminations among individuals and jobs for the higher positions in a career structure. Such an explanation, however, does not tie the gross structure of movement within a career system tightly to the fine structure of how individuals leave jobs. Nor does it link the process of job matching to a broader conception of social matches. The present paper is an effort in both directions. We elaborate a simple, baseline model of performance assessment in social matches. The model describes how important features of data on social mobility, including the key deviations from randomness observed in the data on Wisconsin school superintendents (March and March, 1977) may be attributed to statistical consequences of forming estimates of attributes

1 A more conservative listing might have pairings between resident and neighbors, employer and employee, and seller and buyer; and we will occasionally use such language. We believe, however, that it is a mistake to limit the metaphor of choice to individuals, and wish to question our conventional theological and linguistic preferences for such a limitation. Similarly, in using terms like 'voluntary' and 'consent' to describe behavior, we do not intend to suggest that the behavior is unconstrained, that the relation is without coercion, or that consent is necessarily informed consent. The terms are used as a plain language interpretation of social pairings that are terminated by withdrawal of either party.

on the basis of samples of performances. The main focus for much of the paper is on top managerial careers, but the intention is to describe a general framework for looking at any kind of voluntary pairing.

Imperfect Information and Performance Sampling

The most common theoretical notions about formation and dissolution of pairings treat them as a result of some kind of rational calculation. A pairing is formed when, for each partner, there is no other available partnership that would be better. It is terminated when that condition does not hold. The formation and continuation of a match depend on its attractiveness relative to alternatives. Matches are assumed to be stable if, for each partner, the advantages of the existing pairing over alternative pairings continue or are augmented over time. For example, for marriage formation the world is viewed as consisting of a pool of men and a pool of women. Each man and each woman has certain attributes that are valued by potential partners. Men and women marry, divorce, and remarry until no one can do better through voluntary pairing. Similarly, the world of work is viewed as consisting of a pool of workers and a pool of jobs. Each worker and each job has certain attributes that are valued by potential partners. The pairings of jobs and workers are such that neither workers nor jobs can do better through voluntary pairing.

Assumptions of rationality in the formation of social pairings, like assumptions of rationality in other domains of human behavior, seem to require substantial qualification to fit observed patterns of pairing. For example, there are legal and social constraints on the formation and dissolution of social pairings. At most, the rationality of pair-formation is rationality subject to constraints.

In addition, two familiar complications in rationality affect rational theories of social pairings:

Imperfect Information. In order to make rational pairings, potential partners must assess all relevant attributes of all possible partners, or at least gather as much of that information as is justified by the costs of obtaining it. The information available for some kinds of pairings in which we are interested (e.g., marriage, jobs) is generally incomplete. As a result, it may be necessary to make assumptions about how information is obtained, inferences are formed, and decisons made without complete information.

Endogenous changes. In simple theories of rationality it is assumed that attributes of goods and the preference functions of actors for them are exogenous to decisions based on them. Similarly, stationary Markov models assume exogenous rates of movement. But there is considerable indication that both attributes and preferences change as a result of actions. It may be necessary to make some assumptions about how attributes of partners or values associated with attributes change as a consequence of a match (Scitovsky, 1976; March, 1978).

Such limitations of simple rational models have generated theories of imperfect information, of the economics of information, and of the impact of decisions on cognitions, and mutual learning. In this paper we describe an imperfect information model as a possible interpretation of the process of forming and breaking voluntary matches.

Most studies seem to indicate that duration of a match increases the likelihood of its future continuation (Bartholomew, 1973). A frequent explanation is to view the outcome as the consequence of differential retention within a heterogenous population. If each pairing has some chance of persisting from one year to the next, and this chance is constant over time for each pair but varies among pairs, the collection of enduring pairs will include a smaller and smaller representation of low persistence pairs as time passes. As a result of this social sorting, the average chance of continuation will increase with length of match, even though no pair changes.

Alternative explanations relate increases in the likelihood of continuation with duration of a match to changes in the probabilities associated with individual pairs. For the most part, these explanations emphasize the transformation of the strength of the pairing through mutual adaptation of the partners. It is possible to imagine that experience in a pairing will lead partners to become more strongly attached to each other. That is, husbands and wives, or workers and jobs, increase their competence for dealing with each other, or the rewards they provide each other, at the cost of more generalized competences or rewards relevant to the whole pool of pairings (March and Simon, 1958; Tuma, 1976; Hannan, Tuma, and Groeneveld, 1977). Alternatively, the changes can be seen as changes in preferences. Husbands and wives, or workers and jobs, modify their preferences for attributes so as to increase their mutual attractiveness relative to the attraction each has for outsiders. This bilateral specialization of competences, rewards, or affections will generally reduce the chance that either partner will want to end the pairing.

Social sorting and adaptation theories posit similar effects on the propensities of both partners. Some other theories of change over time predict that the propensities should move in opposite directions. An unanticipated decrease in the wealth of a husband should, according to some theories, increase his interest in maintaining his present marriage, but reduce his wife's interest. An increase in general competence of a worker should (according to some theories) decrease the attractiveness of the current job to the worker, but increase the worker's attractiveness to the job. According to such theories, the rates of voluntary and involuntary departures from a job will move in opposite directions over time. Since many forms of mobility data do not permit disaggregation of voluntary and involuntary exits, it has not always been easy to use empirical data to test the alternative theoretical ideas unambiguously.

The model in this paper also considers the effect of duration of a match on future continuation of the match. Like models of social sorting and adaptation, the present model treats the attributes of partners as controlling the process. However, it emphasizes the informational consequences of performance sampling. The core idea is that matches are formed on the basis of imperfect information. Additional information is provided by experience in the match. As information is accumulated, estimates of partner attributes change in a way that is (on average) predictable. Longer duration of a match leads (on average) to better information about the partners. Although the model is a social sorting model, it emphasizes the sampling errors involved in sorting on the basis of small samples of performances (Deutsch and Madow, 1961; White, 1963; Tversky and Kahneman, 1971).

As students of the economics of information have noted, consumers secure information about products through various forms of prior signals (e.g., price) and through consumption (Nelson, 1970; Spence, 1974; Rosener, 1976). Similar comments can be made about information used in other social pairings. Workers use signals such as wages; employers use signals such as education; and both supplement such signals with experience in the employment relation. Men and women use premarital signals to assess the attractiveness of a potential marriage, and they supplement that information with actual experience in a marriage.

Performance sampling is the experiential observation of partners in a match. Two partners observe each other and themselves to gain information about their attributes, capabilities, and feelings. The information gained through experience affects subsequent assessments of the attractiveness of the match. Although it would be possible to imagine the deliberate design of a performance sample by one or both partners, the emphasis here is on the natural experiments that life provides.

Information gathering through performance sampling is complicated by the ways individuals observe and assess events in significant social relations. It seems obvious that inference and belief are subject to predictable systematic biases that would affect the duration of pairs. It seems likely that information on attributes often induces efforts (perhaps successful) to change those attributes. No attempt to include such complications is made here. The present intent is to describe a simple model structure that shows the central ideas of performance sampling in the hope that others will elaborate those ideas in ways that more adequately reflect the subtlety of our knowledge about how individuals form estimates of each other on the basis of observations. For purposes of the present discussion, it is assumed that observation is made without error, that attributes do not change as a result of information about them, and that only very simple beliefs are formed.

In this elementary version of performance sampling, performance of one of the partners provides information about some attribute of that partner to both members of the pair. The information may support each partner's intentions to remain in the match; it may encourage one or the other (or possibly both) to look elsewhere. For example, information on the capabilities of a husband as a lover may lead either husband or wife to revise prior estimates of the attractiveness of the match. As those observations continue over time, the relevant estimates may reach a point at which withdrawal by one of the partners is precipitated.

Performance Sampling in Managerial Careers

Although performance sampling is relevant to any form of social pairing, both the data and the specific models to be used here are specific to the process by which individual managers and specific managerial positions are joined. The focus allows both the models and their implications to be made more specific, and to be related to some empirical data. It has the usual costs of limiting generality.

The structure of a performance sampling career system is built into the procedures of most formal organizations and forms the basis for the model of the process. In a general way, it is assumed that individuals enter an organization with some performance capabilities. These capabilities may reflect factors that do not change (e.g., ability, prior training), factors that change as a career develops (e.g., job experience, reputation), or factors related to the difficulty of the job. Jobs provide opportunities for exhibiting the capabilities of an individual. As a result of being observed exercising capabilities when given opportunities, an individual accumulates a record of performance. That record is a history of the outcomes attributed to an individual's behavior. The record is translated into the reputation of an individual by memory and recall. Careers are produced by vacancies and reputations. When vacancies occur, workers with good reputations progress in their careers, workers with moderate reputations do not progress, and workers with poor reputations are fired, and thus create new vacancies.

In such a description, careers are produced by organizations making distinctions among individuals (as indeed they appear to try to do). At the same time, individuals make distinctions among jobs and organizations. Jobs have capabilities for satisfying demands of jobholders and accumulate records and reputations based on those capabilities. Better jobs have lower turnover than poorer jobs, and careers are produced by the sequential selection of jobs. The duality of matches, the fact that they involve mutual choice, is easily obscured by a metaphor of careers.

The mutuality of choice may be particularly important in considering careers in top managerial positions. At least in some cases (March and March, 1977), social sorting in executive careers appears to be characterized by more enduring differentiation among jobs than among jobholders. Because individuals are ordinarily more likely to disappear from a top management career system than are jobs (positions), a system of dual social sorting on jobs and jobholders leaves greater heterogeneity among jobs than among jobholders. As a result, it is easier to distinguish among jobs than among executives.

This description of the process has the virtue of conforming to the apparent procedures of most formal organizations and to conventional terminology of careers. The one-sidedness of the description can be moderated by viewing promotion as an occasion on which a match is broken by the individual and exit as an occasion on which it is broken by the job, by considering performance to be a joint consequence of individual and job capabilities, and by remembering that both individuals and jobs develop reputations over a series of matches.

Performance-based sorting systems are a standard feature not only of organizations but of social life more generally. Such systems have been subject to numerous critiques in recent years, questioning many aspects of the meaning, measurement, and moral significance of merit as exhibited through performance sampling. Our interest is much narrower. It emphasizes how important features of career systems can be understood as arising from the problems of imperfect information in the evaluation of performance and the use of experience as a source of information.

Careers, of course, are both produced by vacancies and produce vacancies (White, 1970). Net aggregate rates of movement are connected by some simple accounting equations. In a relatively large, relatively stable system of jobs, however, fluctuations in vacancies are small enough that they can probably be ignored; and the movement of individuals through careers can be considered as a process in which vacancies will exist for individuals who qualify for promotion and the rates of movement will be in balance. In such a system of jobs, it is possible to treat the world as evaluating administrators and trying to promote good ones and remove bad ones, subject to limitations of information.

Such a description of the process conforms to most casual efforts to understand how managers get ahead, or don't, in executive careers. It assumes that things are, in some sense, what they appear to be. It remains to ask whether, if things are what they appear to be, the process would produce the pattern of careers that we observe.

Data and Results

Data from a career system in educational administration were used to explore the model. A career in educational administration can be seen as consisting of a period of experience before becoming a school superintendent, a series of appointments to superintendencies, and a period after leaving the last superintendency. It may also include interruptions of various lengths between appointments to superintendencies. The present study considers careers as superintendents for all persons who held at least one school superintendency in Wisconsin during the period 1940–72 (March and March, 1977). The data were gathered from the records of the Wisconsin State Department of Public Instruction, standard biographies, records of the University of Wisconsin School of Education, and personal interviews.[2] A record of Wisconsin superintendency careers that was essentially complete for the 33-year period was constructed. The restriction to a single state introduces some error produced by individuals whose careers as superintendents involved crossing state boundaries. Previous studies have indicated that the error is small (Knezevich, 1971), since almost all careers in educational administration are limited to a single state. The data involved 1,528 individuals and 454 school districts.[3] Appointments of individuals to superintendencies generated 2,516 pairings. Data on superintendency matches formed during the period are complete. Data on attributes of individuals are less complete. For example, we know the ages of individuals in 60 per cent of all cases, and 95 per cent of the cases of individuals beginning careers after 1949.

The main interest is in understanding variations in the age-and-tenure-specific promotion and exit rates. The promotion rate is the rate at which superintendents of given age, length of service in their present superintendency, and number of previous superintendencies go to new superintendencies. The exit rate is the rate at which they go to other jobs or retirement.

2 Special acknowledgment is due H. Thomas James, who initiated the collection of the data while he was Assistant State Superintendent of Public Instruction in Wisconsin and who supervised its completion for this study; and Mary E. James and Louise Morrisey for their work in filling the holes in the data.

3 Separate elementary districts are excluded from the data. The number of such districts varies over time but consisted of 54 districts in 1972.

The data on Wisconsin superintendents from 1940 through 1972 were used to determine the promotion and exit rates specific to a particular age, tenure, and number of previous superintendencies.[4] In an earlier paper (March and March, 1977) we discussed the extent to which the careers of these superintendents could be approximated by the simplest of random models in which the chance of going to another superintendency and the chance of leaving the ranks of superintendents in any year was the same for all years and all superintendents. A strict random model assumes only chance variations from constant rates of promotion or exit. The observed surfaces show some systematic deviations from such expectations.[5]

1 As superintendents approach retirement age (i.e., from about age fifty-eight onward), the promotion rate declines to a value very close to zero, and the exit rate rises very rapidly.
2 Before age fifty-eight, both the promotion rate and the exit rate show a similar pattern as a function of tenure (controlling for age and number of superintendencies). The rates are relatively low the first year, rise to a peak about the second, third, or fourth year, and decline thereafter. The exit rate appears to peak a year or two later than the promotion rate.
2 Before age fifty-eight, the relative magnitudes of the promotion rate and the exit rate change as a function of the number of superintendencies served. Promotion rate becomes relatively larger with each additional superintendency.
4 Before age fifty-eight, promotion rate decreases as age increases (controlling for length of tenure and number of superintendencies). This effect is small and subject to relatively large fluctuations.

The retirement effect seems largely irrelevant to other processes that lead to dissolution of a match, and is used only to justify limiting our attention to data on superintendents younger than fifty-eight. The other features of the deviations from strictly constant departures are generally consistent with previous studies of the duration of jobs (Lane and Andrew, 1955; Bartholomew, 1973; Tuma, 1976). Duration of matches in employment can often be approximated by distributions (e.g., the lognormal) characterized by a long right-side tail and a mode near, but not at, the left extreme point.

4 For a discussion of such career surfaces and an examination of them for the American college presidency, see Cohen and March (1974).

5 In the present paper only those deviations that are associated with duration of the match, number of matches, and age of superintendents are considered. Another source of deviation from the career patterns predicted by a pure chance model is heterogeneity among school districts (jobs) in their attractiveness. Jobs are graded by the size and location of the districts. This heterogeneity among jobs is clearer than is any grading among individual superintendents by their individual characteristics.

Performance Sampling Models

In a career system in which managerial performance is sampled, individual managers are sorted (i.e., fired, retained, or promoted) on the basis of estimates about their capabilities formed from observations of their performances. Such a system is describable in terms of the attributes of individuals that affect their performances (individual capabilities), sampling procedures by which performances are observed (observation rules), the inferences that transform a specific history of observations into a reputation (estimation rules), and the procedures by which a reputation is converted into a career through personal mobility (decision-rules).

In the models to be explored, the following assumptions are made:

Capabilities. Individual capabilities are assumed to be summarized by the probability that a particular individual will execute a successful performance at a particular time.

Observation. Opportunities for performances are assumed to occur at a fixed rate over time and a random sample of those performances is assumed to be observed. The observations are assumed to be without error. The history of observations of a particular individual is a record of successes and failures, each with a time subscript.

Estimation. Once a minimum number of observations is recorded, reputation is assumed to be a moving average of the proportion of observed performances that are successes. The relative importance of past performances declines with distance from the present, where distance is measured in terms of both time and job changes.[6]

Decision. Decisions are assumed to be dictated by a retention band defined on the range of possible reputations. Reputations higher than the band lead to promotion; reputations lower than the band lead to exit.

Thus, managers are assumed to bring some skills to their jobs. They and the world form estimates of those skills by sampling outcomes

6 A moving average accommodates reasonably well some standard observations about the greater impact of recent observations, i.e., recency effects; it does not accommodate observations about the differential impact of early observations, i.e., primacy effects. Adding primacy effects would have two modest consequences: (1) it would accentuate sampling error; and (2) it would reduce slightly the exit rate from a job after the first few performances. Neither of these affects the general implications drawn, though such a modification might be useful in a specific case. A more fundamental modification, in which the outcome of one performance affects the probability of success on a subsequent performance, is more complicated and has not been investigated.

determined (probabilistically) by the skills. On the basis of these estimates, managers are promoted, retained, or removed. A career is produced by a sequence of observed performances, their outcomes, and the resultant promotions or exits. Except for sampling error, variations in managerial careers will reflect variations in managerial skill. Better managers will be promoted faster and to better jobs than poorer managers.

Performance sampling models are essentially acceptance inspection schemes, in which a manager's performances over time are seen as a sample drawn from the universe of all possible performances. Decisions are made to accept (i.e., promote), reject (i.e., fire), or continue sampling (i.e., retain) a manager on the basis of the number of observations and the number of those observations in which the performances are judged to be failures.

Acceptance inspection plans usually seek a minimal cost procedure ensuring both that the probability of rejecting a lot does not exceed some fixed level, α, whenever the true proportion of failures is less than some number, p_0; and that the probability of accepting a lot does not exceed another fixed level, β, whenever the true proportion of failures is greater than another number, p_1. This leads to a continuation band defined by two parallel lines on an inspection chart, and is the basis for an extensive literature (Wald, 1947; Shiriaev, 1973).

The focus is reversed when performance sampling is considered as an organizational phenomenon. Instead of deriving decision-rules from prior objectives, we examine consequences arising from given decision-rules.

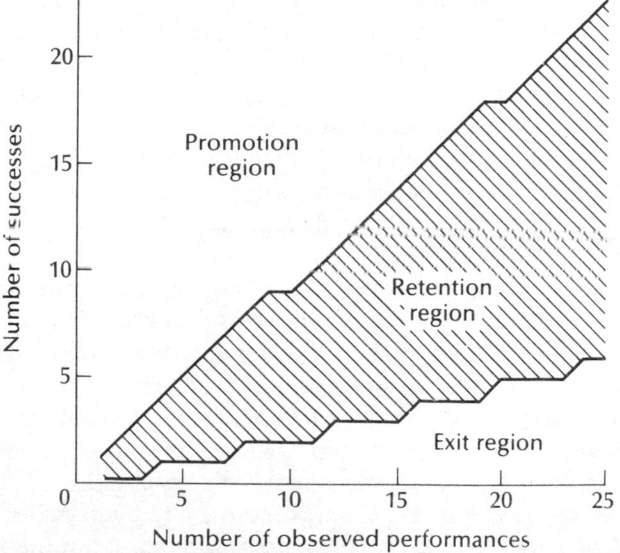

Figure 16.1. Acceptance graph for performance sample ($S = 0.90, F = 0.25$)

Decision-rules are assumed to be specified in terms of a fixed proportion of successes for promotion and some other fixed proportion of successes for exit. The resulting retention region is defined by two diverging lines on an inspection chart, as shown in figure 16.1. A manager's record of successes and failures can be plotted on this chart. Each observed performance leads to movement of one unit on the horizontal axis. If that performance is a success, it leads to movement of one unit on the vertical axis. The objective here is not to design a better performance sampling procedure but to understand the implications for careers of following such procedures.

The record of an individual is a sequential sample of successes and failures determined probabilistically by the rate of performances, the chance of success, and the chance of observation. Part of the variation in records will be due to differences in individual capabilities. Highly capable individuals will have, on average, better records than less capable individuals. Part of the variation in records, however, will be due to probabilistic variation in success and observation. Even if the chance of success in any particular performance were the same for all managers, there would be variation among managers in the proportion of successes. Even if the sampling proportion of observations were the same for all managers, there would be variation among managers in the actual number of observations taken, per unit time. In combination, these sources of random variation will produce differences in records of managerial performance that are not due to underlying differences in capabilities.

The number and magnitude of such sampling errors depend on the number of observed performances of individuals (a joint product of the performance rate, the sampling rate, and time), the capability of the individuals, and the total number of individuals on whom records are kept. If there are a relatively small number of observations, capabilities that are neither almost zero nor almost one, and a large number of individuals, there will be a nontrivial number of records that deviate considerably from the true capabilities they are intended to describe.

In addition, performance sampling involves record sorting. That is, managers with good records are promoted; managers with bad records exit. Regardless of the underlying capabilities of managers, records held by managers remaining in a job are those showing proportions of successes within the retention region. If reputations carry over to new jobs, then the mix of reputations involved at the start of each better job is affected by the decision-rules. This sorting of record leads to a changing mix of records even when there is no change in either the underlying capabilities of individual managers or in the mix of capabilities represented by managers in jobs.

These effects are explored initially here by looking at how performance sampling yields a distribution of records and thus a distribution of promotions and exits under conditions in which all individuals have the same capabilities. That is, variations in careers are due to chance fluctuations in a probabilistic process of gathering performance information about managers. First, a simplified form of performance sampling is considered, in which the relevance of past performance does not decay with time or change of job.

If it is assumed that each individual has the same, unchanging capability and that estimation procedures treat every observation as equally valid (i.e., there is no loss of memory or relevance for observed performance over time), exit and promotion rates per performance depend on:

P = the probability that a performance will be successful,
R = the probability that a performance will be observed,
F = the minimum acceptable proportion of observed performances that are successes (the exit level),
S = the maximum acceptable proportion of observed performances that are successes (the promotion level), and
L = the minimum number of observations required before decision.

Exit and promotion rates per unit time depend, in addition, on the performance rate over time.

The procedures described make promotion and exit a compound result of two stochastic processes: sampling and performance. The performance process generates a distribution of successes and failures. The sampling process selects a sample of those performances. If sampling and success rates are fixed and independent, they yield a fixed probability of an observed success for each period. These processes are, however, further affected by the delay in first judgment and the sequential decision process. Delay in the first judgment generates a distribution of first judgment times (from the sampling rate). The decision process sequentially chops the tails off the distribution of successes and failures and fills the next jobs with individuals who have records in the successful tail of the distribution.

Performance sampling generates a record of performance outcomes. A record has as its numerator the number of observed successes, K, and as its denominator the number of observations, J. Exit and promotion rates depend on the relation between this record and the retention region, (F,S), at a series of decision points beginning at $J=L$ and continuing through $J=L+1$, $J=L+2$, and so on.

If we ignore the optional stopping produced by the decision-rules, it is clear that K/J approaches P as J becomes indefinitely large, and that the variance of K/J around P is approximately $P(1-P)/J$. Thus, exit or promotion 'errors' at the first decision point will become smaller as L becomes larger. If P lies within the retention region, exit and promotion rates at the first decision point will decline monotonically with L.

First decision points will be distributed across individuals. The performance, H, at which the Lth observation will be made is distributed as the negative binomial:

$$\text{Probability } (H=h) = \binom{h-1}{L-1} R^L (1-R)^{h-L}, \tag{1}$$

where $h \geq L$. For any number of observations, J, it is possible to determine U_J, the highest integer value for K that makes $K/J < S$; and W_J, the lowest integer value for K that makes $K/J > F$. U_J and W_J correspond to the acceptance and rejection numbers of acceptance sampling, a_m and r_m, in Wald's notation. At the first decision point, $J = L$, the probability that a record will lie within the retention region is given by

$$\text{Probability } (U_L \geq K \geq W_L) = \sum_{i=W_L}^{U_L} \left[\binom{L}{i} P^i (1-P)^{L-i} \right]; \tag{2}$$

therefore, D_1, the performance immediately preceding a first decision departure is distributed according to

$$\text{Probability } (D_1 = h) = \binom{h-1}{L-1} R^L (1-R)^{h-L} \left\{ 1 - \sum_{i=W_L}^{U_L} \left[\binom{L}{i} P^i (1-P)^{L-i} \right] \right\} \tag{3}$$

Although this fairly simple expression for first decision departures over time can be generated, nth decision departures are more complicated. In particular, the probability that K/J will be in the retention region for $J = T$ is not independent of the value of K/J at $T-1$, and thus the effect of the decision truncation of the distribution when $T > L$ cannot be ignored. For any particular set of values for the parameters, calculating the result is frequently not overly complicated, but a general analytical expression for the distribution of all departures over time is relatively cumbersome to write and involves a cascade of conditional probabilities. However, it is possible to show the results for selected cases. This is done for promotion probabilities in figure 16.2.

The distributions shown in figure 16.2 are plotted across performances in the first job. Converting a performance axis to a time axis requires specifying the rate of performance over time. Extending the analysis to subsequent jobs is not so simple, but the general character of the outcomes can be derived. Individuals entering their first jobs are assumed in the model to have no records. In second and subsequent jobs, they bring with them a record in which $K/J \geq S$. As a result, it is clear that departures in the

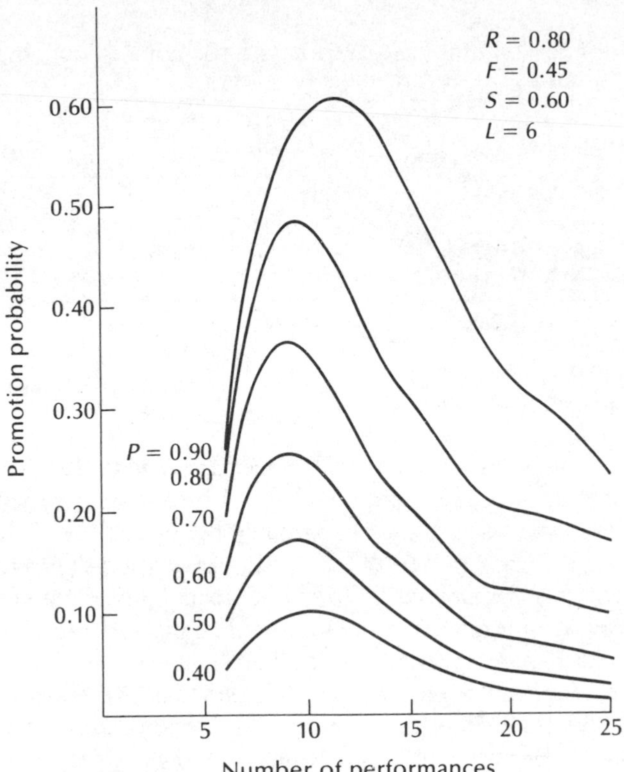

Figure 16.2. Promotion probability as a function of number of performances for various capabilities (*P*)

second job will have a higher proportion of promotions (rather than exits) than will departures in the first job. This assumes that the only individuals who have a second job are promoted directly from a first. Among the Wisconsin superintendents, the analysis is complicated by some people exiting from a first job and subsequently (after an interruption of one or more years) returning to a second. This moderates, but does not change the effect, as long as the numbers of such people are fairly small. It is also possible, of course, that the record accumulated during the interruption brings such superintendents back with starting records in which $K/J \geq S$. In the third and subsequent jobs, starting values for K/J are not systematically different from those on entering the previous job (if the retention region is the same for all jobs), but J becomes systematically larger from one job to the next. As a result, it is also clear that each subsequent job will have a higher proportion of all departures that are promotions. Some results for selected values are shown in table 16.1

Table 16.1 Proportion of departures that are promotions, by job and value of *P*, first 12 observed performances on each job[a]

	Value of P								
	0.10	*0.20*	*0.30*	*0.40*	*0.50*	*0.60*	*0.70*	*0.80*	*0.90*
Job									
1	0.001	0.020	0.088	0.230	0.442	0.674	0.861	0.964	0.997
2	0.004	0.047	0.201	0.495	0.787	0.940	0.990	0.999	1.000
3	0.015	0.131	0.493	0.849	0.972	0.996	1.000	1.000	1.000

[a] R-probability of observing a performance = 0.80
F-exit level = 0.45
S-promotion level = 0.60
L-minimum number of observations = 6

In the discussion thus far not only has it been assumed that each individual has the same unchanging capability, but also that all observations are equally relevant across time and changes in jobs. The original assumptions were different. They reflected the ordinary expectation that relevance of past performance for estimating individual capabilities in a current job would decay with distance in time and with changes in jobs. Estimators act as though they assume that capabilities change over time, and that capabilities required by one job are not necessarily the same as those required by another. Thus, more recent observations are treated as more relevant than older ones, and observations from the current job are treated as more relevant than observations from previous ones. The consequence of this is to increase sampling error and thus (if *P* lies within the retention region) to reduce the rate of change in departure rates as a function of tenure in a match and number of previous matches. The weighting of recent experiences more heavily than distant ones increases sampling error, if *P* is constant across individuals and time. It reflects the fact that such weighting schemes surrender some precision in estimating *P*, if it is constant, in order to protect against the possibility that it is not. Departure rates will decline over duration of a match and across a sequence of matches, but the decline will be slower than would be observed if all outcomes were counted without regard to their recency. The magnitude of the difference depends on the specific estimation function assumed, but the data from Wisconsin suggest a relatively high discount rate on the relevance of past successes to current reputation.

Performance sampling models predict the basic qualitative features of data on the length of Wisconsin superintendencies, as well as other data on job duration. For reasonable parameters, they will produce promotion and exit rates that rise briefly at the beginning of a match and then decline with duration, and they predict that the ratio of promotion rates to exit rates will increase over a sequence of jobs. These qualitative characteristics are not unique properties of performance sampling models. Theories of social sorting and mutual adaptation in social matches both predict that promotion and exit rates will decline with increased duration of a match. Although neither theory predicts the relatively low level of departure rates in the early years of a match, it is not hard to graft a distribution of first decision times onto either in such a way as to produce a 'honeymoon'. The changing ratio of promotions to exits is easily accommodated within a social sorting theory, less easily within a mutual adaptation theory.

A potential advantage of a performance sampling model is that it conforms to ordinary descriptions of performance evaluation and does not require either that there be heterogeneity in the capabilities of individuals or that their capabilities be changing over time. If the population of managers varies in fit to a match, either across individuals or across duration of the match, performance sampling will (under fairly general conditions) produce the same basic results. But even if they do not vary, or if they improve not their fit to the match but their capabilities for promotion, performance sampling will still yield the same pattern. This last property of performance sampling can be exhibited by considering three variations of the models and comparing them to the observed pattern of promotions and exits from Wisconsin superintendencies.[7] The three versions posit different basic ideas about superintendents:

7 When the models were compared with the Wisconsin data, the same parameters were used for all three cases, except for the assumptions about individual capabilities. Some effort was made to find a set of parameters that fit Wisconsin data reasonably well, but the search was not exhaustive through the parameter space. The acceptance region was set at (0.25, 0.95) for all jobs, the sampling rate at 0.30, and the first decision point after two observations. In addition, it was necessary to specify the rate at which performances occurred over time (4 per year) and the reputation function that made the relative importance of past successes and failures decline with the passage of time and change of jobs, an exponentially weighted moving average. After n observations, of which m were successes, the reputation of an individual manager was given by:

$$\sum_{k=1}^{m} 1.1^{D(k)} \Big/ \sum_{j=1}^{n} 1.1^{D(j)}$$

where $D(k)$ is the distance from the start of a career to the kth success, and $D(j)$ is the distance from the start of a career to the jth observation, and where distance is simply the number of performances observed thus far in a career plus eight times the number of job changes. Thus, a job change is treated as reducing the relevance of past successes and failures by the same amount as the instantaneous passage of the time required for eight observations. Since only superintendents who were less than 58 years old were considered, some assumptions were required about the entering ages of individuals. Superintendents were assumed to begin their last pre-superintendency job at ages uniformly distributed from age twenty-six to forty. Finally some superintendents were assumed to have had interruptions in their careers. That is, they left a superintendency to go to some other job and subsequently returned to a superintendency. This accounts for a minority of the cases; but in the model, superintendents

Version 1: Heterogeneity. The pool of potential superintendents has a distribution of individual capabilities.[8] Those capabilities remain constant for any one individual, but the average capability of the group of remaining superintendents can change over time.
Version 2: Learning. The pool consists of individuals who initially have the same capabilities. However, an individual's capability improves with each observed performance. Learning rates are the same for each individual, but the history of experiences may differ.[9]
Version 3: Homogeneity. The pool consists of individuals, each of whom has the same capability. Those capabilities remain constant throughout their experience.[10]

The three versions are different. In the first, individuals differ but do not change over time (although the mix does); in the second, individuals are initially the same but change over time as a result of their experiences; in the third, individuals are indistinguishable in capabilities and do not change with experience. Superimposed on these differences is a performances sampling process. In each case, individuals accumulate records on the basis of experience and are promoted or exit on the basis of their reputations.

Each version of a performance sampling model predicts annual rates of promotion, exit, and arrival at age fifty-eight across complete histories of three (or fewer) consecutive appointments to superintendencies, including the effects of interruptions in careers between jobs. More precisely, each version predicts a distribution of such histories.[11] The

---

who exited returned to a new superintendency after some number of years (during which they aged and changed the relevance of past reputation by the equivalent of one additional job change) at a rate determined by parameters estimated in an earlier paper (March and March, 1977).

8 The initial pool of potential superintendents is assumed to include individuals with a uniform distribution of capabilities ranging from $P=0.30$ to $P=0.60$.

9 The initial capability is the same for all potential superintendents ($P_0=0.45$). Whenever a performance is observed, the individual manager involved learns. If P_J is the probability of success on the *J*th observed performances, the probability of success on the next performance will be $P_J+0.003(1-P_J)$.

10 The capability is fixed at $P=0.50$.

11 The results discussed are based on monte carlo simulations of the models. The models take individuals from the start of their final pre-superintendency jobs and follow them through their careers until they become fifty-eight, or leave the ranks of superintendents permanently. The predictions from the models are compared with the observed data through 1972 for Wisconsin superintendents who began their careers between 1940 and 1972. From either the data or the models we can obtain the age-and-tenure-specific rates of promotion to another superintendency and exit for first, second, and subsequent superintendencies. The analyses reported are based on comparing these outcomes. In some cases, the report is in terms of the departure rate (the sum of promotion and exit rates) or the continuation rate (1-departure rate).

versions can be compared with each other and with the data in a number of ways, but the interpretation must be cautious. The number of parameters is relatively large, and the observed data on age-and-tenure-specific departure rates are, in many cases, based on only a few observations. No attempt was made to find the best-fitting estimates for the parameters of the models, and the comments that follow are limited to those that are relatively insensitive to changes in parameters.

Three things can be said with modest confidence about these three versions of a performance sampling model. First, performance sampling generates the same basic pattern of predictions under any of the versions specified. The correlations across the predicted career surfaces of pairs in the versions are 0.47, 0.36, and 0.33;[12] and the general character of the surfaces is the same in each case.

The specific quantitative predictions are not, of course, independent of the specific assumptions, about the magnitudes and character of distributions of capabilities (as well as other parameters). In particular, it should be noted that the version in which variation among individuals is assumed yields a different pattern of departures during the (early) pre-superintendency phase of careers. Specifically, exit rates are higher than in the other models. These exits reduce skill heterogeneity among individuals who are promoted to a first superintendency. Since performance sampling will obscure moderate variations among individuals, but not large ones, the closer you come to the top of a career chain, the less the variation, and the more version 1 and version 3 become indistinguishable. Similarly, version 2 in which learning is assumed, will not produce the same qualitative results as the others under all conditions. If learning is rapid or the learning experience prolonged, there should be a tendency for promotion rates to rise while exit rates decline. What is significant here is that such a clear long-run implication of a model is not seen in the short run.

The similarities among results under a wide range of assumptions about the attributes of individuals suggest that sampling phenomena associated with performance evaluation can become significant enough to mask variations in the underlying attributes of individuals, even in cases in which those underlying attributes are known to affect job performance. If the world were a performance sampling world of the kind described, it would

12 All of the correlations across career surfaces reported in this section consider the 170 points in the first two superintendencies of careers for which an estimate of the age-and-tenure-specific departure rate was based on at least 12 cases in the observed data. 104 of the points involve the first superintendency, and 66 involve the second. The correlations compared estimates of departure rates generated by the model with estimates obtained from the data. Because of the relatively high attrition rate, most of the points are concentrated in the early tenures and ages between thirty and forty-nine.

be difficult, on the basis of observing the structure of careers, to tell whether managers differed considerably or were truly indistinguishable.

Second, all of the versions improve on simple Markov models of the process, but none of them is a very precise predictor of observed rates. When observed continuation rates associated with duration of match and age of superintendent are correlated with the predicted rates of each version of the model, the correlations are consistently greater than zero. The correlations are not high, ranging from 0.26 to 0.17.

The process shows significant sampling variation in the estimates of age-and-tenure-specific departure rates when the cohort size is the same as is found in the Wisconsin data. When several probabilistically identical Monte Carlo simulations of the same version of the model are correlated with each other, using cohorts of the same approximate size as the data cohort, correlations across replications of the same model are only slightly higher than those found in comparing such simulations with the data. This indicates that the models would be unlikely to fit the data much better than they do, even if the theory precisely captured reality; but one should perhaps be conservative about using such a result as a basis for confidence in a theory.

Third, each of the models captures the qualitative features already noted as characteristics of the data. In the models, as in the data, both promotion rate and exit rate show a similar pattern as a function of tenure, controlling for age and number of superintendencies. The rates are relatively low the first year, rise to a peak about the second, third, or fourth year, and decline irregularly thereafter. The exit rate appears to peak a little later than the promotion rate. Before age fifty-eight, the relative magnitudes of promotion rate and exit rate change as a function of the number of superintendencies served. Promotion rates become relatively larger from one superintendency to the next. Before age fifty-eight, promotion rates decrease as age increases, controlling for length of match and number of superintendencies. This effect is small and subject to relatively large fluctuations. In all these respects, the models match the data.

The consistency of the models with the data suggests performance sampling explanations for some phenomena that have more commonly been interpreted otherwise. In addition, it is possible to suggest some reasons why promotion rates decline with age and why exit rates peak later than promotion rates. Since age does not enter explicitly into the models, any predicted age effect is spurious. Within the models, promotion rate decreases as age increases, controlling for length of match and number of superintendencies, apparently because age is related to differences in the past records of superintendents that are not controlled by length of match and number of earlier superintendencies, specifically such things as whether arrival at the present superintendency has followed directly upon departure from a previous one and the length of the record in earlier jobs.

Similarly, the fact that exit rates in the model (as in the data) peak slightly later in the duration of a match than promotion rates has a natural performance sampling interpretation. Exit rates peak later because of record sorting. Individuals beginning a job tend to have good records. That is how they were promoted to the job. Over time, some of them will accumulate enough new performance failures to reach the exit point, but on the average it will take longer to reach that point than the promotion point, given that they begin with a successful record.

Within the limitations of the data and the character of the models, these specific performance sampling models predict patterns of movement through careers that are consistent with the Wisconsin data. Personnel evaluation and promotion procedures having the basic characteristics of performance sampling can be expected to produce outcomes similar to those observed in Wisconsin even under circumstances that deviate considerably (as in the case of version 3) from the rationale of those procedures and common interpretations of those outcomes. If managers get ahead because they do well, and the procedures by which they are evaluated involve performance sampling, about the same pattern of careers should be expected regardless of moderate heterogeneity among them in their abilities to perform successfully on the job, or to learn over the course of the job.

Discussion

The formation of a match between an individual and a job in an administrative or career hierarchy is based on imperfect information gathered partly through the observation of performances. On the basis of such observations, organizations sort individual managers into reputational categories. People come to be viewed as incompetent, and are fired; as exceptionally qualified, and are promoted; or as adequate, and are retained. Similarly, managers sort organizations into reputational categories. Organizations come to be viewed as unmanageable, and are avoided; as outstanding, and are sought; or as adequate, and are neither avoided nor pursued.

Since performance sampling is subject to sampling variation, at least some of the sorting among individuals and organizations and the variations in careers and turnover they produce could be due to sampling error, rather than to individual differences in administrative competence or organizational differences in manageability. This seems particularly likely near the top levels in an administrative career hierarchy, where the samples of performance are comparatively small, their evaluation comparatively difficult, and the variation among individuals at the end of a series of evaluations comparatively small.

Performance sampling processes show properties that are independent of their details and are of some importance for appreciating how careers can yield subjectively compelling impressions of causal determinacy, as in the following specific examples.

1 *False record effect*. A group of managers of identical (moderate) ability will show considerable variation in their performance records in the short run. Some will be found at one end of the distribution and will be viewed as ineffective. The longer a manager stays in a job, the less the probable difference between the observed record of performance and actual ability. Time on the job increases the expected sample of observations, reduces expected sampling error, and thus reduces the chance that the manager (of moderate ability) will either be promoted or exit.

2 *Hero effect*. Within a group of managers of varying abilities, the faster the rate of promotion, the less likely it is to be justified. Performance records are produced by a combination of underlying ability and sampling variation. Managers who have good records are more likely to have high ability than managers who have poor records, but the reliability of the differentiation is small when records are short.

3 *Disappointment effect*. On the average, new managers will be a disappointment. The performance records by which managers are evaluated are subject to sampling error. Since a manager is promoted to a new job on the basis of a good previous record, the proportion of promoted managers whose past records are better than their abilities will be greater than the proportion whose past records are poorer. As a result, on the average, managers will do less well in their new jobs than they did in their old ones, and observers will come to believe that higher level jobs are more difficult than lower level ones, even if they are not.

The generality of such characteristics of performance sampling is supported by the present examination of three alternative variants of a performance sampling model. Although the three variants are quite different and make different assumptions about individual managers, they all yield results similar to each other, and they all capture the major features of data on a 33-year record of careers in educational administration in Wisconsin. Apparently, the general behavior of these models is due less to assumptions about managers than to assumptions about the process of evaluating success and failure in management. Specifically, if managers are evaluated on the basis of critical incidents that are infrequent (but not rare) and accumulate reputations based on those evaluations, aggregate career results will be dominated by chance variations in sample observations, and patterns in top administrative careers will not be much affected either by variations in initial skill among entrants into the pool of administrators or by learning on the job.

There are reasons for anticipating nearly random careers among top administrators in educational organizations (March and March, 1977). The social sorting that takes place on the way to the career and during it, the ambiguity of judgment within educational organizations, and the stability of educational activities often seem to operate to make superintendents indistinguishable. The present results reinforce the idea that indistinguishability among managers is a joint property of the individuals being evaluated and the process by which they are evaluated. Performance sampling models show how careers may be the consequence of erroneous interpretations of varitions in performances produced by equivalent managers. But they also indicate that the same pattern of careers could be the consequence of unreliable evaluation of managers who do, in fact, differ, or of managers who do, in fact, learn over the course of their experience.

The role of performance sampling in other organizations or matches is unclear, but there is reason to suspect that the model may be applicable in other settings. For example, a key assumption of the performance sampling model is that promotion and retention decisions depend only on the proportion of successes observed and not on the total number of observations on which that proportion is based, once the first decision point is reached. Since such an assumption ignores the unreliability of estimates based on small samples, it might be questioned as improbable, or perhaps listed as unique to educational organizations. In fact, the assumption is consistent with experimental studies of individual decision behavior. Tversky and Kahneman, as well as others (Tversky and Kahneman, 1971; Kahneman and Tversky, 1972; Tversky and Kahneman, 1974; Slovic, Fischhoff, and Lichtenstein, 1977), have cited considerable evidence that individuals confronted with problems requiring the estimation of proportions act as though sample size were substantially irrelevant to the reliability of their estimates. The present analysis can be viewed as an extension of those studies as well as some indirect confirmation of the generality of their results.

The plausibility of the process suggests that other social pairings should be expected to show patterns attributable to the ways in which performance sampling generates reputations not necessarily identical to the underlying distribution of qualities. Husbands and wives, buyers and sellers, landlords and tenants, students and teachers all resolve some elements of uncertainty about their choices through the sampling of performance in a match. Where the variation in qualities is modest, as it often is in a socially-controlled system of matches, the opportunities for evaluation infrequent, and the memory (or presumed relevance) of previous experience declines over time, many of the details of a system of matches among those individuals, institutions, or goods permitted to enter the pool of eligibles will be explicable in terms of sampling variation in performance evaluation. If there are differences in individual attributes, these differences will not translate reliably into differences in reputations. If there are no differences in attributes, there will nevertheless appear to be some; and those appearances will be nearly as compelling as they would be if the true differences were substantial.

References

Bartholomew, David J. (1973) *Stochastic Models for Social Processes*, 2nd edn London: Wiley.

Becker, Gary S. (1973) A theory of marriage: part I. *Journal of Political Economy*, 81: 813–46.

Blumen, Isadore, Marvin Kogan, and Philip J. McCarthy (1955) *The Industrial Mobility of Labor as a Probability Process*. Ithaca, NY: Cornell University Press.

Deutsch, Karl W., and William G. Madow (1961) A note on the appearance of wisdom in large bureacratic organizations. *Behavioral Science*, 6: 72–8.

Edwards, John N. (1969) Familial behavior as social exchange. *Journal of Marriage and the Family*, 31: 518–26.

Hannan, Michael T., Nancy B. Tuma, and Lyle P. Groenveld (1977) Income and marital events: evidence from an income maintenance experiment. *American Journal of Sociology*, 82: 1186–211.

Kahneman, Daniel, and Amos Tversky (1972) Subjective probability: a judgment of representativeness. *Cognitive Psychology*, 3: 430–54.

Knezevich, Steven (ed.), (1971) *The American School Superintendent*. Washington: American Association of School Administrators.

Lane, K. F., and J. E. Andrew (1955) A method of labour turnover analysis. *Journal of the Royal Statistical Society*, A118: 296–323.

March, James C., and James G. March (1977) Almost random careers: the Wisconsin school superintendency, 1940–1972. *Administrative Science Quarterly*, 22: 377–409.

March, James G. (1978) Bounded rationality, ambiguity, and the engineering of choice. *Bell Journal of Economics* 9: 587–608.

March, James G., and Herbert A. Simon (1958) *Organizations*. New York: Wiley.

Nelson, Phillip (1970) Information and consumer behavior. *Journal of Political Economy*, 78: 311–29.

Rosener, Lynn (1975) 'Identification of problems associated with household pre- and post-purchase information behavior'. Unpublished honors thesis, Department of Economics, Stanford University.

Scitovsky, Tibor (1976) *The Joyless Economy*. New York: Oxford University Press.

Shiriaev, Albert N. (1973) *Statistical Sequential Analysis: Optimal Stopping Rules*. Lisa and Judah Rosenblatt (trans.), Providence, RI: American Mathematical Society.

Singer, Burton, and Seymour Spilerman (1974) Social mobility models for heterogeneous populations. In Herbert L. Costner (ed.), *Sociological Methodology* 1973–4: 356–401. San Francisco: Jossey-Bass.

Slovic, Paul, Baruch Fischhoff, and Sarah Lichtenstein (1977) Behavioral decision theory. *Annual Review of Psychology*, 28: 1–39.

Spence, A. Michael (1974) *Market Signalling*. Cambridge, MA: Harvard University Press.

Stigler, George (1961) The economics of information. *Journal of Political Economy*, 69: 213–25.

Tuma, Nancy B. (1976) Rewards, resources, and the rate of mobility: a nonstationary multivariate stochastic model. *American Sociological Review*, 41: 338–60.

Tversky, Amos, and Daniel Kahneman (1971) The belief in the law of small numbers. *Psychological Bulletin,* 76: 105–10.

Tversky, Amos, and Daniel Kahneman (1974) Judgment under uncertainty: heuristics and biases. *Science*, 185: 1124–31.

White, Harrison C. (1963) Uses of mathematics in sociology. In James C. Charlesworth (ed.), *Mathematics and the Social Sciences:* Philadelphia: American Academy of Political and Social Science, pp. 77–94.

White, Harrison C. (1970) *Chains of Opportunity: System Models of Mobility in Organizations*. Cambridge, MA: Harvard University Press.

Wald, Abraham (1947) *Sequential Analysis*. New York: Wiley.

17

Ambiguity and Accounting: The Elusive Link between Information and Decision-Making

James G. March

Abstract

This paper argues that theories of choice, as reflected in microeconomics, n-person game theory, or statistical decision theory, are incomplete and potentially misleading bases for thinking about and modifying the design of information systems, including accounting systems. The argument stems from recent behavioral research on the ambiguities surrounding individual and organizational decision-making. It is developed around four simple assertions:

1 Contemporary ideas about information engineering tie strategies for seeking, organizing, and utilizing information to ideas of anticipatory, consequential choice as pictured in decision theory.
2 Behavioral studies of decision-making in organizations indicate that the portrayal of decision-making and information found in decision theory ignores or significantly underestimates the ambiguities of choice.
3 Analysis of discrepancies between the actual behavior of decision-makers and the recommendations of decision theory shows that the behavior often

This paper was first published in *Accounting, Organizations and Society* 12 (1987) 153–168. It is an extension and elaboration of an address given at the annual meetings of the American Accounting Association, New York, 22 August 1986. It is based on research supported by grants from the Spencer Foundation, the Stanford Graduate School of Business, and the Hoover Institution. The author is grateful for the comments of Robert H. Aston, Gary C. Biddle, Robert A. Burgelman, George Foster, Anthony G. Hopwood, Charles T. Horngren, Maureen F. McNichols, Johan P. Olsen, James M. Patell, Jeffrey Pfeffer, Allyn Romanow, Robert J. Swieringa, Eugene J. Webb and Mark A. Wolfson.

introduces elements of good sense not routinely recognized within the theory, so an information system that is closely articulated with choices in the way anticipated by decision theory is often incomplete.

4 As a result, the engineering of information might profit from conceptions of decision-making and information that blend the traditions of theories of choice with an understanding of the traditions of history, culture and literature.

Introduction

The history of information engineering can be written as a story of the search for a theory, a conception of information that might, in principle, be used to justify or improve the information processing instruments and procedures used in accounting and other information systems (Horngren, 1981; Tinker, Merino and Neimark, 1982; Davis, Menon and Morgan, 1982). The intention in this paper is not to write such a history but to examine contemporary information doctrine. The argument is that efforts to embed information engineering in theories of choice, as reflected in microeconomics, n-person game theory, or statistical decision theory, are clearly useful; but they are incomplete and potentially misleading for thinking about and modifying the design of information systems.

The argument stems, in part, from recent behavioral research on individual and organizational decison-making. It is developed around four simple assertions:

1 Contemporary ideas about information engineering tie strategies for seeking, organizing, and utilizing information to ideas of anticipatory, consequential choice as pictured in decision theory.
2 Behavioral studies of decision-making in organizations indicate that the portrayal of decision-making and information found in decision theory ignores or significantly underestimates the ambiguities of choice.
3 Analysis of discrepancies between the actual behavior of decision-makers and the recommendations of decision theory shows that the behavior often introduces elements of good sense not routinely recognized within the theory, so an information system that is closely articulated with choices in the way anticipated by decision theory is often incomplete.
4 As a result, the engineering of information might profit from conceptions of decision-making and information that blend the traditions of theories of choice with the traditions of history, culture, and literature.

Information and Decision-Making

Most recent writing on information in organizations links it to decision-making. Information systems, such as accounting, are seen as part of a decision-support system for managers, financial analysts, stockholders, or others with a stake in the organization (Keen and Scott Morton, 1978; Demski, 1980; Sprague and Carlson, 1982). The axiomatic foundations are found in statistical decision theory, n-person game theory, and microeconomics. The main uncertainty in decision-making is portrayed as ignorance about future consequences of possible current actions, including ignorance about the knowledge possessed by others and their probable actions, and the main rationale for information is its role in reducing that uncertainty.

Rather early in the development of information engineering, these connections to choice led to concern with problems of estimation and inference (Trueblood and Cyert, 1957; Morgenstern, 1963). It is not trivial for an organization to assure that the events observed are representative of the universe, that they are observed accurately and consistently, and that models for analysis of data are specified so as to lead to valid estimates and inferences. For example, in classical sampling theory, where observations are assumed to be independent, the accuracy (i.e., the standard error) of an estimate depends on the variability in the universe and the number of observations (sample size). This leads to an emphasis on increasing accuracy through increasing sample size. In organizational life, however, the independence of observations cannot be assumed, so sample size declines in (relative) importance, and some of the more powerful strategies for improving the accuracy of information involve increasing the independence of observations rather than simply increasing their numbers.

Contemporary theories of decision-making, however, are less inclined to highlight biases in estimation and inference, and more inclined to focus on two additional complications in the use of information for making decisions in organizations: those of limited rationality and conflict of interest. The fundamental idea of *limited rationality* is that not everything can be known, that decision-making is based on incomplete information about alternatives and their consequences. There are costs associated with gathering, organizing, and retrieving information (Simon, 1955; March and Simon, 1958). From the point of view of rational choice, therefore, expected costs of information must be justified by expected benefits. The expected benefits from an information source are well specified in single-person, single-period decision theory. They are equal to the expected value of a choice situation if the information were available (taking into account its expectation) minus the expected value of the situation without the information (Lindley, 1971). The formulation yields some precise calculations in well-defined specific cases. It also yields some familiar caveats of information: Don't pay good money for bad data; don't ask a question if you already know the answer. Extensions to multi-person, multi-period decisions are more complicated, less completely understood, and a major focus of contemporary work (Hilton, 1981).

The fundamental idea of *conflict of interest* is that an organization is a coalition of individuals and groups pursuing different objectives (March, 1962; Cyert and March, 1963). As a result, information in organizations is not innocent. Accounting and accounting standards are arenas of power politics (Horngren, 1984). Information providers try to shape decisions through judicious management of the information under their control (Akerlof, 1970; Rothschild, 1973). Unless an organization can ensure that information providers will not lie or withhold information that should be valuable to a decision-maker, classical statistics loses some of its force. Interest in designing cost-effective incentives that induce rational, self-interested agents to be honest in their reports is a major theme of contemporary theories of agency (Ross, 1973; Hirshleifer and Riley, 1979; Fama, 1980; Milgrom, 1981; Levinthal, 1984).

To a student of organizations, the flowering of information economics and agency theory as bases for microeconomics and information engineering is a gratifying reminder that empirical research can affect theoretical conceptions. Twenty to thirty years ago, behavioral students of organizations criticized theories of the firm for ignoring limited rationality and conflict of interest in decision-making (March and Simon, 1958; Cyert and March, 1963). Although one may question whether contemporary information economics attends to these problems with all the delicacy and grace that they deserve, they have certainly captured the attention of many economists, including applied economists concerned with accounting (Demski, 1980; Verrecchia, 1982).

Ambiguities in the Link between Information and Decision-Making

Without denying the importance of contributions made from a perspective build around limited rationality and conflict of interest, more recent research on decision-making in organizations indicates that such a frame may provide an incomplete representation of the problems of decision-making, thus possibly also of information engineering. These additional qualifications can be summarized in terms of four observations about the ambiguities of organizational decision-making:

> Observation 1: the ambiguities of preferences. The preferences of organizations, their owners, and their managers are frequently less clear than is assumed in theories of rational choice. Preferences are often vague or contradictory. The develop over time, changing as a result of experience and the decision process.

The conception of choice enshrined in the axioms of contemporary decision theory and microeconomics assumes optimization over given alternatives on the basis of two guesses: The first guess is about the uncertain future consequences that will follow from alternative actions that might be taken. The second guess is about the uncertain future preferences the decision-maker will have with respect to those consequences when they are realized.

The first guess has received most of the attention from students of decision-making. Much of modern management science, microeconomics, and operations research is devoted either to improving the optimization calculations involved in complex choices, or to improving the procedures for estimating the probability distribution over future consequences conditional on an action. No comparable effort has been devoted to understanding or improving either the generation of alternatives or the guess about future preferences (Von Weizsacker, 1971; Winston, 1980). For the most part, both alternatives and preferences are taken as given. In practice, of course, management science and decision theoretic techniques are often used by skillful decision-makers to help discover alternatives and clarify objectives (Lindley, 1971); but decision theory yields little assistance in that effort. It treats the preferences as controlling choice but excludes their development from consideration.

The usual justification for exempting preferences from engineering is a commitment to value neutrality. Whereas one can claim that a particular optimization technique has certain unambiguously admirable qualities, or that a particular treatment of data has certain attractive properties of statistical efficiency, no comparable claim is thought to be possible with respect to procedures for preference engineering. The argument can be faulted both for ignoring the ways in which any decision calculus favors preferences measurable within that calculus over preferences that are not, and for failing to recall that the classic trinity is one of truth, beauty, and justice, rather than truth alone. But it is not the intent here to doubt the virtues of decision-engineering that is, as nearly as possible, independent of the specific value premises that a decision-maker may wish to entertain.

The argument being made is narrower and more technical than that. It is that the preferences assumed in decision theory differ in important ways from the preferences of human decision-makers.[1] Within the theory, preferences are assumed either to be consistent, stable, and exogenous, or to be beneficially convertible to preferences that are. Such assumptions are clearly deficient as a description of actual human preferences. Both individuals and organizations regularly have inconsistent preferences, wanting things that are conflicting, yet doing little to resolve the inconsistency. Preferences change over time, and predicting future preferences is not easy.[2] And while preferences are expected to control actions and often do, experience with actions and their consequences affects preferences at the same time. That is, preferences are endogenous to a decision process.

Each of these features of preferences complicates decision theory (March, 1978; Elster, 1979; 1983). The theory deals awkwardly with inconsistent preferences that cannot be reconciled through utility trade-offs. Since preferences change over time and the preferences relevant to a decision are the uncertain future preferences that will be held when the consequences of current action are realized, the usefulness of a theory that assumes stable preferences is in doubt. And when preferences are endogenous, decision-making cannot be decomposed into separable problems of defining prior preferences and taking subsequent actions, thereby compromising the basic framework of conventional expected utility decision theory. Although it is possible that the theory may be suitably robust against such difficulties, the assumptions of consistency, stability, and exogeneity are *prima facie* suspect.

It might be imagined that the problems posed by ambiguous preferences could be avoided by training human decision-makers to have the desired consistent, stable and exogenous preferences; but such an approach requires more confidence in the virtues of unambiguous preferences than our experience supports. It is not hard to specify conditions under which poorer decisions will be made by specifying explicit trade-offs than by struggling with inconsistent desires. For example, Camus (1951) argues that simple rules against killing, though they clearly cannot be sustained as absolute against the claims of other values, consistently lead to more moral action than do efforts to place an explicit value on life and calculate net benefits (March, 1979). It is not hard to specify conditions under which an intelligent decision-maker would prefer to have or anticipate changing preferences (Kreps, 1979). For example, it is not clear why we should want to value jogging or eating the same at all times (Winston, 1980; 1985).

1 Throughout this paper, a conception of preferences is assumed in which preferences are taken to exist independent of choices. The same problems exist, but in slightly different form, in a 'revealed preference' theory.

2 For a contrary opinion, see Stigler and Becker (1977).

And it is not hard to specify conditions under which the construction of preferences in the course of making choices is more appropriately encouraged than avoided. For example, parents routinely require children to attend cultural events they would otherwise not attend in order to help them develop a taste for fine music or art (March, 1971). In short, the ambiguous preferences observed in actual human decision-makers often are more intelligent than are the kinds of preferences normally specified in decision theory (March, 1978).

These complications in preferences have led to suggestions that decision-engineers might well spend more time understanding the implications of intertemporal comparisons of preferences, endogenous changes in preferences, and the problem of optimal inconsistency among preferences and between preferences and actions – sometimes called the optimal sin problem. A similar set of conclusions could be extended to information engineering in the service of decision-making. Information systems contribute to the construction of preferences as well as to their implementation, to their complication as well as to their simplification (Follett, 1930).

> Observation 2: The ambiguities of relevance. Organizational decision-making often has less coherence than decision theory attributes to it. Problems, solutions, and actions are frequently only loosely coupled, or connected by their simultaneity rather than their consequentiality. Information strategies are relatively independent of specific anticipated decisions.

In decision-theoretic treatments, information strategies are consciously designed to resolve uncertainties about future states of the world that are relevant to choice. Actual information behavior in organizations in general and more specifically in decision-making often does not fit such a characterization very well. Information seems to be gathered and processed with scant regard for its relevance to specific decisions. In general, empirical studies of organizational decision-making indicate that most theories of choice overestimate the coherence of decision processes (Cohen, March and Olsen, 1972; Cohen and March, 1986). Organizations seem to be loosely coupled systems in which the connections between problems and solutions are obscure, as are the connections between means and ends, between action today and action yesterday, and between action in one part of the organization and action in another part (March and Olsen, 1976; Weick, 1976). People, problems, solutions, and choice opportunities seem to be combined in confusing ways that make predicting agenda and outcomes difficult (Kingdon, 1984; March and Olsen, 1986).

Observations such as these have led some people to describe decision processes in organizations as completely without order. Others, however, have tried to specify alternative conceptions of order that might be used to understand the process. One example of the latter is the garbage can model of organizational choice (Cohen, March and Olsen, 1972). Garbage can models substitute a temporal order for a consequential order among solutions, problems and decision-makers. In a garbage can decision process, the explicit intentions of actors and the consequential coherence of choices are often lost in context dependent flows of problems, solutions, people, and choices. Solutions are linked to problems, and decision-makers to choices, primarily by their simultaneity (March and Olsen, 1986).

Studies of the uses of information in policy-making suggest a similar disconnection of information strategies from decision strategies. Policy-analysis offices are disconnected from policy makers, yet continue to produce policy papers (Feldman, 1986). Research reports produce diffuse changes in world-views, rather than direct effects on decisions (Weiss, 1977). The generation and elaboration of information about problems and solutions is sustained more by professional and sub-culture norms than by anticipation of a direct contribution to decisions.

There are a number of possible rationalizations for the divorce of an information structure from the decision structure in organizations. It is probably true, for example, that tight linkages between information and its uses increase the vulnerability of decision-makers to manipulation by information providers (Feldman and March, 1981). It is also probably true that future decision options are sufficiently obscure as to make the possible benefits from different information strategies almost indistinguishable. In such circumstances, cost/benefit calculations over alternative information strategies are sensitive primarily to relative costs, and choice of an information strategy does not depend significantly on the decision structure that it serves (March and Sevón, 1984). The rationalizations are, however, less significant here than the facts they seek to rationalize. The structure of relevance in an organization is more complicated and less articulated to decisions than decision theory anticipates. An information system designed to link information with a set of well-defined decisions will not necessarily be useful in decision-making where attention and consequential connections between problems and solutions are ambiguous.

Observation 3: The ambiguities of intelligence in complex ecologies. Although individual actors within organizations often try to act intelligently by calculating the expected consequences of possible actions, such a basis for action is typically supplemented by, or subordinated to, the following of rules that encode historical lessons learned within a complex ecology of nested organizations.

Modern theories of interactive decision-making and competition are theories of calculated cleverness in the interest of self. We imagine a world of self-interested decision-makers nested within organizations that are, in turn, nested within markets, communities and political institutions. Each of the actors within this world attempts to make and influence decisions in a way that advances his or her self-interest as he or she calculates it by considering alternatives in terms of their expected consequences. These considerations pervade the decision process and the production of information involved in decisions.

Consider, for example, the production of income statements. There are ample signs that managers, investors, and workers attend to income statements. Because income statements matter, many clever people try to make the statements say what they would like them to say (Greenhouse, 1986). Clever managers try to outwit clever accountants and clever analysts, who are at the same time trying to outwit them. Clever investors and clever public officials try to interpret the information provided through this culture of cleverness. And clever economists try to develop theories specifying the equilibria of clever processes, that is processes involving multiple interacting clever people and the pervasive cleverness of calculation.

The literature on clever processes describes a kind of morality play in three acts:

> In the beginning God created innocents and sophisticates. Sophisticates are clever; innocents are not. Cleverness pursues self-interest with as much guile and imagination as possible. Information is an instrument in the service of the clever, and competition rewards people in proportion to their relative cleverness with information instruments. This is the creed of numerous articles on how to exploit information to further self-interest. If reports in the *Wall Street Journal* or *New York Times* are to be given credence, much of modern management and finance is based on a belief that it is frequently easier and more rewarding to manage the accounts of organizations than it is to manage the activities and processes of which they are accounts.
>
> Before long: Competition destroys innocence. Less clever people are eliminated from the competition, either by losing their innocence or by losing their livelihood. Once the innocent are gone, variations in cleverness are small and the effects of cleverness on the distribution of winnings is nil. Everyone in the game is clever (or can hire someone who is). This is the argument of numerous theories of competition in politics, ecology, and economics, the most prominent recent reincarnations being ideas of rational expectations and efficient markets in economics. The assumptions that adaptation is relatively fast, that there is no exogenous replenishment of innocents, and that adequate supplies of cleverness are readily available are,

> of course, questionable, but they may perhaps be glossed over in a simple story. The key conclusion is that the cleverness of competitors makes cleverness necessary but insignificant in affecting distributional outcomes. Since only very clever people survive, no one outwits anyone else – though everyone tries.
>
> But ultimately: Sophistication loses both victims and competitive advantage. The elimination of innocents reduces the competitive value of the kinds of cleverness that eliminated them. However, it is in the interest of each surviving participant to continue being clever as long as the others do, even though the effect of clever behavior on the relative competitve strength of survivors is nil when all engage in it. The energy devoted to cleverness is not devoted to other things, thereby making all of the clever participants vulnerable to new kinds of predation from outside. Thus, a clever system of account management is likely to be destroyed by the depletion of innocents to exploit and the specialization of managerial competence to skills that are irrelevant to new threats.

This story is an old one, hardly unique to information engineering. It calls attention to, but underestimates the complexity of, the problems in understanding the evolution of ecologies of competition (Aldrich, 1979; Gould, 1982; Axelrod, 1984; Arthur, 1985). When competition takes place over long periods of time, at several nested levels of organization, and in a changing world, exclusive reliance on cleverness – the conscious calculation of guileful strategies by self-interested individuals – is by no means guaranteed to evolve as a dominant style of behavior.

The ecological difficulty with calculated self-interest and cleverness is not that they are immoral in the usual sense, but that they are forms of incompetence. Recent efforts to improve cleverness are instructive in this regard. It is not an accident that modern students of competition have discovered the significance of trust relations, reputations, and conventions of behavior for success in games played repetitively over long periods of time (Kreps and Wilson, 1982; Milgrom and Roberts, 1982; Wilson, 1983; Wolfson, 1985). Nor is it surprising that behavioral students of decision have discovered that the rules individuals follow in forming inferences from data and making decisions often (though not always) seem to be wiser than the decision theory and statistical canons they violate (March and Shapira, 1982; 1987; Einhorn, 1986).

The recognition of intelligence in rules encourages hope that ultimately we may be able to rationalize the information content of rules by solving analytically the complicated problem of fitness that is addressed (imperfectly) by historical processes. For example, rules of thumb for dealing with moral hazard or adverse selection have been assessed and probably improved. In general, however, such efforts reflect a hope, not a guarantee. The history is one of repeated revelations of inadequate analyses. The intelligence of rules is found not in their ability to solve problems that are recognized and understood correctly, but in their treatment of the many problems that are incompletely understood, misunderstood, or not seen at all. Recognition of such implicit capabilities in rules might suggest more effort to understand and improve history-dependent processes, rather than assume they can be replaced.

In information engineering, the primary manifestations of history-dependent rules are the professional standards of accountants, statisticians, and other dealers in information. These rules of appropriate behavior have evolved from experience. They are codified through discussion and debate, and sanctified through the creation of a profession with attendant educational institutions. Clearly, such professional standards interfere with the free competition of cleverness and are unwarranted if it is possible to claim the unlimited efficacy of such competition, just as restrictions on physical assault are unwarranted if the unlimited efficacy of physical competition can be demonstrated. The standards of information engineering are, from this point of view, cultural standards of decency. They encompass experience with limitations (and advantages) of calculated intelligence that cannot be retrieved explicitly by an individual actor operating within a framework of cleverness. As a result, their claims to intelligence are real.

In the contemporary competition between reason and tradition, as has been true since Aristotle, there are victories for each; but the difficult questions associated with specifying the likely conditions for each remain largely unanswered. The evolution of tradition is affected by several complications of ecological complexity: the environment is an endogenously changing one; maximizing the likelihood of the survival of an ecology of rules and institutions is different from maximizing the survival of its components; a system may have multiple stable equilibria, and the optimality of any particular one is not assured; history can branch dramatically thus making outcomes sensitive to near random events at critical times; and the adaptive processes involved are typically too slow to reach an equilibrium before conditions change.

Because of these complexities, history-dependent processes of experiential learning and evolution, like processes of rational calculation, have traps that no theory of intelligence can ignore. These include tendencies toward superstitious and self-serving learning (March and Olsen, 1975); but perhaps the most significant restrictions on learning or evolution as devices for intelligence are connected to their dependence on experimentation (Herriott, Levinthal and March, 1985; Lounamaa and March, 1987). Without experimentation, history-dependent adaptation tends to become obsolescent (Kaplan, 1984). Nevertheless, as we study the standard rules and roles of organizational life, we discover elements of intelligence in them (Axelrod, 1984). Those artifacts of history store lessons of experience that appear to be unattractive or inaccessible to individual actors, thus supplement and caution conscious self-interested calculation (March, 1981a; 1981b).

> Observation 4: The ambiguities of meaning. Most information in organizations is collected and recorded not primarily to aid decision-making directly, but as a basis for interpretations that allow coherent histories to be told. As a structure of meaning evolves from information and from the process of decision-making, specific decisions are fitted into it.

Theories of rational choice obscure the extent to which information handling and decision-making contribute, largely independently, to the development of meaning. Decisions are not so much made in organizations as they develop within a context of meaning. Organizational information processing seems to be driven less by uncertainty about the consequences of specific decision alternatives than by lack of clarity about how to talk about the world – what alternatives there are and how they related to stories we think we understand, how we describe history and how we interpret it (March and Feldman, 1981; March and Sevón, 1984). Information shapes the meaning of a decision situation, thus normally changes both the structure of alternatives and the preferences being pursued. Through the processing of information and the unfolding of decisions, the meanings of shared experience are elaborated and modified: foolish recklessness is redefined as creative independence (or vice versa), and elegant argument is redefined as sophistry (or vice versa).

Standard accounts are part of the social language by which organizations comprehend what they are doing, why they are doing it, and how they might do it better. New accounting instruments stimulate interest in new dimensions of organizational description and redefine decision alternatives (Burchell, Clubb and Hopwood, 1986; Hopwood, 1986). And information that is generated for decision-irrelevant reasons becomes a topic of conversation, and ultimately contributes to redefining the way we think about decision strategies. As a result, a good information strategy is not so much one that removes uncertainty from a prestructured array of decision alternatives connected to a predetermined array of preferences, as it is one that moves the whole apparatus of information, desires, and options in a productive direction, simultaneously developing ideas of what is 'productive' and instruments for achieving it.

Similarly, decision processes are not simply ways to choose among alternatives. Indeed, they seem to be only imperfectly understood as being concerned with substantive decisions at all. As March and Olsen (1986, pp. 16–17) report:

> It has been observed that individuals fight for the right to participate in decision-making, then do not exercise that right with any vigor (Olsen, 1976); that organizations ignore formation they have, ask for more information, then ignore the new information when it is available (Feldman and March, 1981; March and Sevón, 1984); that organizations buffer processes of thought from processes of action (Brunsson, 1982; 1985); that managers spend substantial amounts of time in activities that appear to have few consequences beyond acknowledging the importance of others, as well as themselves (Cohen and March, 1986); that minor issues create a governmental crisis and unexpected patterns of political activation, then drift away again (Olsen, 1983: chapter 3); that organizational participants contend acrimoniously over adoption of a policy, but once the policy is adopted, the same contenders appear to be largely indifferent to its implementation, or lack of it (Christensen, 1976; Sætren, 1983; Baier, March and Sætren, 1986).

In short, decision-making is a sacred ritual involving highly symbolic activities. It celebrates central values of a society, in particular the ideas that life is under intentional human control and that control is exercised through individual and collective choices based on an explicit anticipation of alternatives and their probable consequences (Feldman and March, 1981; March and Olsen, 1984). It reinforces the legitimacy of existing authorities, and at the same time provides a basis for interpreting their downfall as appropriate. These sacred values are interpreted and reinforced through the information systems and decision processes of organizations. Individuals establish their reputations for virtue; an interpretation of history is developed, shared, and enforced; dissent is nurtured and contained; new ideas are grafted to old ones or disassociated from them; alliances are developed, tested, and displayed; the young are socialized.

The processes of choice in organization are also processes through which participants become committed to action (Hedberg, Nystrom and Starbuck, 1976; Swieringa and Weick, 1986). They organize arguments and information to create and sustain a belief in the wisdom of the action chosen, thus in the enthusiasm required to implement it. Where the process fails to do this, implementation is compromised (Brunsson, 1982; 1985; Baier, March and Sætren, 1986). Where it does this too well, decisions are ill-considered and their consequences poorly evaluated (Janis and Manns, 1977; George, 1980). The extensive postdecision elaboration of the reasons for action already chosen, including the development of information to support it (Feldman and March, 1981), and the avoidance of postdecision evaluation (Meyer and Rowan, 1977; Harrison and March, 1984), can be seen as part of this process of commitment. Postdecision justification of choices already made reflects an awareness that, as Salancik has observed (Pfeffer, 1986), we spend more time living with our decisions than we do in anticipating or making them.

These ritual, symbolic, and affirmative components of decisions and decision processes are not unfortunate manifestations of an irrational culture. They are important aspects of the way organizations develop the common culture and vision that become primary mechanisms for effective action, control and innovation. As a result, information strategies are as much strategies for managing interpretations and creating visions as they are strategies for clarifying decisions. And if this sometimes seems perverse, it may be well to remind ourselves that human life is, in many ways, less a collection of choices than a mosaic of interpretations. It involves both discovering reality and constructing it.

Implications for Information-Engineering

These observations about the ambiguities surrounding decision-making in organizations are persistent themes of recent behavioral research. If they are true, or partly true, they have implications for thinking about information systems. The implications stem in part from the fact that an information system that is to be used by humans in an organization must be attentive to properties of individuals and organizations, even when those properties are disconcerting. And they stem in part from the fact that, even if there were no individuals or organizations involved, the model of choice that is used in current thinking about information would be incomplete.

Attending to Problems with Human Decision-Makers

There are three classical engineering approaches to dealing with apparent deficiencies in human beings. The first is to adapt the system to observed characteristics of human beings (George, 1980; Newman, 1980). Rather than having a decision-support system that is unconnected to the world as seen by decision-makers and that they do not use, the system can be designed to provide information in a form familiar and useful to decision-makers. For example, if decision-makers feel more comfortable with multiple financial ratios, even though the information contained in them is redundant, the ratios should be provided. If the main information of interest is information on the conventions of behavior observed by others, the system should provide that. If corporate directors can deal with pie charts but not with regression equations or confidence intervals, they should have pie charts.

Under this approach to engineering, the major problem is understanding the decision questions of particular users and shaping the system to their wishes. Such an approach is not as easy as it appears. Although it is frequently observed that the language of organizational discourse seems only partly consonant with the language of accounts, or rudely forced into that language, careful information about the ways in which decision-makers use information and make decisions is scarce. There are remarkably few analyses of what managers actually do with their time, or what information they use or might use. Moreover, a system of accounts and reports that is useful for one decision-maker is not guaranteed to be useful for another. For example, an information system designed to help solve the decision problems of stock speculators will be of interest and concern to a corporate manager and will stimulate efforts to control the reports generated within it; but such a system will not necessarily be of much use to management of the productive or service activities in a firm (Johnson and Kaplan, 1987). Conversely, a system of accounts useful to a manager will not necessarily be of much use to the person to whom the manager is accountable (Ijiri, 1975).

The second engineering strategy for coping with human characteristics is to change the ways in which human decision-makers make decisions and think about information. In over 30 years of education and consultation, the technology of management science and operations research has made important changes in decision-making in modern organizations. More recently, research on decision behavior of human beings has been associated with strategies for improving the capabilities of human information processors to deal with human biases (Fischhoff, 1982; Nisbett, et al., 1982). Decades of trying to make human decision-makers behave more in keeping with the precepts of decision theory indicate, however, that the task is not trivial, that the biases, prejudices, and wisdom of decision-makers are resistant to profound corruption in the name of decision theory and modern statistics (Nisbett and Ross, 1980; Kahneman, Slovik and Tversky, 1982).

The third strategy is to replace human beings with machines, in this case primarily with computers and the software associated with them. The substitution of electronic information processing for human information processing is now commonplace, as are phrases such as 'artificial intelligence', 'knowledge-engineering', and 'expert systems'. Although the rate at which machines will replace humans in complex decision-making has been persistently and spectacularly exaggerated, progress has been made in situations where problems are decomposable into hierarchical structures (Simon, 1969; Cohen, 1986), and where the availability of patently relevant information exceeds the retrieval capabilities of human memory. The prospects for improving human decision-making through some form of computer-based program appear to be substantial where a decision involves storing and retrieving large amounts of data, or modeling complex processes, and where the organizational structure is conducive to the effort (Kunreuther and Schoemaker, 1981). Information retrieval systems with large data bases have been shown to be useful in coping with such things as historical financial data, medical diagnosis where the main difficulty in diagnosis is the organization and recovery of available information, estimating future personnel flows or loan losses, and the details of internal audit review.

It should also be observed that the capabilities of computer-based information systems for storing and retrieving data would appear to have reduced substantially the classical advantages of carefully conceived data collection. Contemporary work in data-handling seems to suggest that the trade-offs between careful prior formulation of information needs and the exploratory analysis of data collected without much anticipation of possible uses may be shifting considerably in the favor of the latter. This would appear to lend some credence to an argument that the computer-based information system of the future will not draw its model from ideas that emphasize a close linkage between information gathering and anticipations of information use.

Attending to Problems in the Theory of Decision-Making

Research on decision-making not only describes individuals and organizations as making decisions in a way that violates the recommendations of decision theory; it also suggests that the differences between the ways humans use information and make decisions, and the ways our theories say they should do so, are partly attributable to limitations in the theories, rather than limitations in the behavior. In particular, a close articulation of decisions and information is of little use in ambiguous situations where preferences, causal structures and meanings are unclear and changing. As has been observed above, those situations are not unusual (March, 1984; March and Olsen, 1986). Thus, although many decision problems in contemporary organizations will fall comfortably within the domain of decision theory and yield gracefully to its dictates, many of the more interesting ones will not.

The complications introduced by the ambiguities of preferences, relevance, intelligence and meaning can be illustrated by considering some common theoretical aphorisms about information and decision-making:

> Look before you leap! As long as you operate within the framework of anticipatory, consequential rationality, it is important to know what you want before you act. But it is clear that intelligent decision-makers frequently act as though they do not believe in absolute conformity to such a dictum. They recognize action as a way of discovering and developing preferences, as well as acting on them.

Don't act if you don't understand! It is an axiom of ideas of rational choice that actions are justified by understanding and anticipating their consequences. Although less than complete understanding of consequences is often recommended, the magnitude of optimal ignorance is calibrated by its expected consequences. But it is clear that it is possible to act intelligently without an explicit comprehension of the consequential reasons for the actions. By following intuitions, rules, duties, and the advice of others, intelligent decision-makers act without conscious understanding.

Don't ask a question if the answer can't affect a decision! Within decision theory conceptions, the value of information lies in its ability to reduce uncertainties that affect choices. Yet, most of the information gathered, purchased, or communicated has no such direct decision relevance. It develops a context of knowledge and meaning for unknown possible actions and for talking about experience. Human actors understand the significance of information gathering as an investment in an inventory of knowledge and as an aid to defining preferences and alternatives as well as choosing among them.

Know what you want to say before you speak! Some treatments of communication assume that a message must be fully comprehended by a sender and then transmitted as precisely as possible to a receiver. But much of the most effective communication in organizations, as in the rest of life, is quite different, using ambiguous formulations to evoke responses that interpret and elaborate possible meanings.

The conclusion is simple: one can design an information system around a precise, static decision structure, and for many elementary decision problems in organizations that is a good idea. But the more difficult and more important task for information engineering involves the design of a system for an imprecise, changing decision structure. The relevant question is: How do you construct an account when you do not know when that account is going to be used, or by whom, or for what purpose, or in what context (Marshall, 1972; Hedberg and Jönsson, 1978; Mitroff and Mason, 1983)? The problem is fundamentally different in spirit from that of specifying an optimal set of accounts within a well-defined decision structure. In some cases, it can be reduced to a variant of the standard problem by assuming that the probability distribution over possible future uses and users is known or can be estimated; but such a contrivance is ordinarily of limited use. Quite aside from the fact that an explicit solution to the expanded problem is several orders of magnitude more difficult than the standard one, it does not really address the deeper problems of ambiguity.

These more general issues have been discussed, but not really solved, in institutions associated with knowledge systems of an educated culture. At least in principle, it is possible to imagine designing a system for knowledge generation and dissemination that explicitly identifies the probable decisions to be made, prior knowledge about them, and the marginal expected return from various alternative knowledge instruments, given that structure. Such an approach has been proposed from time to time for making allocation decisions within such familiar knowledge systems as those of science, journalism, and education. In each of these cases, however, it is clear that the *ex ante* linkages among the expected uses of information in making decisions, its generation and its actual uses are rather loose.

This is not simply because the people involved in science, journalism, and education have been powerful enough to resist intrusions into their fiefdoms. Within limits and with sporadic doubts, the rest of society seems to accept the propostion that such independence makes sense. Scientific research institutions, particularly the best of them, are traditionally buffered from anticipation of their uses. Funding arrangements, security of tenure, and an ideology of serendipity conspire to make those information systems remarkably independent of the decision systems they presumably serve. Journalism generates accounts of daily events intended to be sold to readers, ostensibly because they find the accounts worthy of their attention. From a decision point of view, however, most of the information generated by journalism is gossip as far as most readers are concerned (March and Sevón, 1984). It resolves no immediate decision problems (save perhaps what TV shows are available). And this feature is particularly true of those newspapers that cost the most and have the highest reputations. Educational curricula are sometimes designed around a specification of the particular uses, ordinarily employment uses, that will be made of the knowledge learned. But such curricula seem to be systematically less characteristic of educational programs that command a higher price and greater demand.

Suppose we see the relation between organizational accounts and the users of those accounts as similar to the relation between science and the users of science, or journalism and the readers of journalism, or education and the users of education. From this perspective, the structure of accounts should be rather independent of the *ex ante* intentions or desires of its users or the existing decision structure. The organizational implications of seeing information in this way are not novel, but they are somewhat different from proposals to link information and decision-making closely. They call for the relative autonomy of information gatherers, a loose articulation of information activities and decision activities, rather than a close articulation. Buffers to articulation are provided by professional standards and the development of legitimacy in sub-cultures that create their own conceptions of relevant and interesting information.

More generally, we note that preferences are developed in the course of solving problems and constructing interpretations (March, 1978). We ask whether that development can be made more intelligent (March, 1971; Cohen and Axelrod, 1984). We note that rules store the implications of otherwise irretrievable historical experience (March and Olsen, 1987). We ask how we can assess or augment the probable information value of specific inexplicable rules (Lounamaa and March, 1987). We note that ambiguous problems are often best approached through less structured, exploratory problem-solving (Lindblom, 1959; 1979). We ask how that can be implemented within modern information technology (Vancil, 1979; Sheil, 1983). We note that meaning evolves through the evocative exploration of the deep structure of language. We ask how information engineering can contribute to that evolution (Weick, 1979).

Many of these considerations can be folded into conventional theoretic models with suitable will and ingenuity. The paradigm is impressively flexible. The perspective outlined here also suggests, however, that information engineering – like research, journalism, and education – might well find part of its character grounded in theories of history, language, culture, art, and criticism. The writing of good history is the exploration of possible histories. It is also the exploration of the efficiencies and inefficiencies of the accumulation of history in tradition and belief. Theories of language engage questions of the way in which the use of properly chosen language exploits the structure of language to capture and impart meaning that is not fully comprehended. Theories of culture explore the ways cultural development reflects adaptation to, and enactment of, a changing environment. Theories of art and criticism permit us to see good information engineering not as a passive or manipulative activity in a decision scheme, but as an instrument of interpretation (March, 1976; Broms, 1985).

Thus, a system of accounts can be judged in terms of its evocativeness, its power to provide not just confirmation of familiar orders but also suggestions of alternative orders, not just communication of what is known but the transformation of what is knowable. Portraying information engineers as poets is a form of romanticism that glorifies each unconscionably. Yet, it is not without a certain charm. When he was a young man, T. S. Eliot wrote a tribute to the complexities of aging, called 'The Love Song of J. Alfred Prufrock'. Later, on reading the comments of a critic (Joseph Margolis) about 'Prufrock', Eliot wrote (1961, pp. 125–6) that the analysis of 'Prufrock': 'was an attempt to find out what the poem really meant – whether that was what I had meant it to mean or not. And for that I was grateful'. To Eliot, apparently, the essence of poetry lay in providing stimuli to the elaboration of meaning, rather than in providing unequivocal texts. Toward that end, he created ambiguous, textured accounts and invited others to find greater meaning in them than he had consciously created.

It is, perhaps, a strange vision of information engineering to say that an accounting report should be a form of poetry, using the language of numbers, ledgers, and ratios to extend our horizons and expand our comprehensions, rather than simply fill in the unknowns on a decision tree. But it is not an entirely unworthy vision of professionals to say that their accounts and reports can be richer in meaning than they are aware or intend, and that they can enrich our senses of purpose and enlarge our interpretations of our lives. And it may not be entirely ludicrous to imagine a day when professional students of accounting will discuss the aesthetics and evocative power of ambiguity in a proposed accounting procedure with as much fervor as they exhibit in debating its impact on tax liability.

References

Akerlof, George (1970) The market for 'lemons': qualitative uncertainty and the market mechanism, *Quarterly Journal of Economics*, 89, 488–500.

Aldrich, Howard E. (1979) *Organizations and Environments*. Englewood Cliffs, NJ: Prentice-Hall.

Arthur, W. Brian (1985) Competing technologies and lock-in by historical small events: The dynamics of allocation under increasing returns. Unpublished ms., Stanford University.

Axelrod, Robert (1984) *The Evolution of Cooperation*. New York, NJ: Basic Books.

Baier, Vicki Eaton, James G. March, and Harald Sætren (1986) Implementation and ambiguity, *Scandinavian Journal of Management Studies*, forthcoming.

Broms, Henri (1985) Mantras that look like plans, *Scandinavian Journal of Management Studies*, 1, 257–70.

Brunsson, Nils (1982) The irrationality of action and action rationality: decisions, ideologies and organizational actions, *Journal of Management Studies*, 19, 29–44.

Brunsson, Nils (1985) *The Irrational Organization: Irrationality as a Basis for Organizational Action and Change*. Chichester, UK: Wiley.

Burchell, Stuart, Colin Clubb, and Anthony G. Hopwood (1985) Accounting in its social context: towards a history of value added in the United Kingdom. *Accounting, Organizations, and Society*, 11.

Camus, Albert (1951) *L'Homme Révolté*. Paris: Gallimard.

Christensen, Søren (1976) Decision making and socialization. In James G. March and Johan P. Olsen, *Ambiguity and Choice in Organizations*, 351–85. Bergen, Norway: Universitetsforlaget.

Cohen, Michael D. (1986) Artificial intelligence and the dynamic performance of organizational design. In James G. March and Roger Weissinger-Baylon (eds), *Ambiguity and Command: Organizational Perspectives on Military Decision Making*, 53–71. Cambridge, MA: Ballinger.

Cohen, Michael D., and Robert Axelrod (1984) Coping with complexity: the adaptive value of changing utility. *American Economic Review*, 74, 30–42.

Cohen, Michael D., and James G. March (1986) *Leadership and Ambiguity*, 2nd ed. Boston, MA: Harvard Business School Press.

Cohen, Michael D., James G. March, and Johan P. Olsen (1972) A garbage can model of organizational choice, *Administrative Science Quarterly*, 17, 1–25.

Cyert, Richard M., and James G. March (1983) *A Behavioral Theory of the Firm*. New York, NY: Prentice-Hall.

Davis, Stanley W., Krishnagopal Menon, and Gareth Morgan (1982) The images that have shaped accounting theory, *Accounting, Organizations and Society*, 7, 307–18.

Demski, Joel (1980) *Information Analysis*, Reading, MA: Addison Wesley.

Einhorn, Hillel (1986) Accepting error to make less error, *Journal of Personality Assessment*, in press.

Eliot, T. S. (1961) *On Poetry and Poets*. New York, NY: Noonday Press.

Elster, Jon (1979) *Ulysses and the Sirens*. Cambridge: Cambridge University Press.

Elster, Jon (1983) *Sour Grapes: Studies in the Subversion of Rationality*. Cambridge, UK: Cambridge University Press.

Fama, Eugene F. (1980) Agency problems and the theory of the firm, *Journal of Political Economy*, 88, 288–307.

Feldman, Martha S. (1986) The invisible mind: order without design. Unpublished ms., University of Michigan.

Feldman, Martha S., and James G. March (1981) Information as signal and symbol, *Administrative Science Quarterly*, 26, 171–86.

Fischhoff, Baruch (1982) Debiasing. In Daniel Kahneman, Paul Slovic, and Amos Tversky (eds), *Judgment under Uncertainty: Heuristics and Biases*. Cambridge: Cambridge University Press, pp. 422–44.

Follett, Mary Parker (1930) *Creative Experience*. New York, NY: Longman, Green and Co.

George, Alexander L. (1980) *Presidential Decision making in Foreign Policy: The Effective Use of Information and Advice*. Boulder, CO: Westview Press.

Gould, Stephen Jay (1982) Darwinism and the expansion of evolutionary theory, *Science*, 216, 380–7.

Greenhouse, Steven (1986) The folly of inflating quarterly profits, *New York Times*, 2 March.

Harrison, J. Richard, and James G. March (1984) Decision making and postdecision surprises, *Administrative Science Quarterly*, 25, 26–42.

Hedberg, Bo L. T., and Sten Jönsson (1978) Designing semi-confusing information systems for organizations in changing environments, *Accounting Organizations, and Society*, 3, 47–64.

Hedberg, Bo L. T., Paul C. Nystrom, and William H. Starbuck (1976) Camping on seesaws: prescriptions for a self-designing organization, *Administrative Science Quarterly*, 21, 41–65.

Herriott, Scott R., Daniel Levinthal, and James G. March (1985) Learning from experience in organizations, *American Economic Review*, 75, 298–302.

Hilton, Ronald W. (1981) The determinants of information value: synthesizing some general results, *Management Science*, 27, 57–64.

Hirshleifer, J., and John G. Riley (1979) The analytics of uncertainty and information – an expository survey, *Journal of Economic Literature*, 17, 1375–421.

Hopwood, Anthony G. (1986) The archaeology of accounting systems, *Accounting, Organizations, and Society*, 11, in press.

Horngren, Charles T. (1981) Uses and limitations of a conceptual framework, *Journal of Accountancy*, 151, 88–95.

Horngren, Charles T. (1984) Institutional alternatives for regulating financial reporting. Unpublished ms., Stanford University.

Ijiri, Yuji (1975) *Theory of Accounting Measurement*. Sarasota, FL: American Accounting Association.

Janis, Irving L., and L. Mann (1977) *Decision-Making: A Psychological Analysis of Conflict, Choice and Commitment*. New York, NY: Free Press.

Johnson, H. Thomas, and Robert S. Kaplan (1987) *Relevance Lost: The Rise and Fall of Management Accounting*. Boston, MA: Harvard Business School Press.

Kahneman, Daniel, Paul Slovik, and Amos Tversky (1982) *Judgment under Uncertainty: Heuristics and Biases*. Cambridge: Cambridge University Press.

Kaplan, Robert S. (1984) The evolution of management accounting, *Accounting Review*, 59, 390–418.

Keen, Peter G. W., and Michael S. Scott Morton (1978) *Decision Support Systems: An Organizational Perspective*. Reading, MA: Addison-Wesley.

Kingdon, John W. (1984) *Agendas, Alternatives, and Public Policies*. Boston, MA: Little, Brown.

Kreps, David M. (1979) A representation theorem for 'preference for flexibility', *Econometrica*, 47, 565–77.

Kreps, David M., and Robert Wilson (1982) Reputation and imperfect information, *Journal of Economic Theory*, 27, 253–79.

Kunreuther, Howard C., and Paul J. H. Schoemaker (1981) Decision analysis for complex systems: integrating descriptive and prescriptive components, *Knowledge*, 3, 389–412.

Levinthal, Daniel (1984) A survey of agency models of organizations. Technical Report Number 443, Institute for Mathematical Studies in the Social Sciences, Stanford University.

Lindblom, Charles E. (1959) The science of 'muddling through', *Public Administration Review*, 19, 79–88.

Lindblom, Charles E. (1979) Still muddling, not yet through, *Public Administration Review*, 39, 517–26.

Lindley, D. V. (1970) *Making Decisions*. London: Wiley.

Lounamaa, Pertti, and James G. March (1987) Adaptive coordination of a learning team. *Management Science*, 33, 107–123.

March, James G. (1962) The business firm as a political coalition, *Journal of Politics*, 24, 662–78.

March, James G. (1971) The technology of foolishness, *Civiløkonomen*, 18(4), 4–12.

March, James G. (1976) Susan Sontag and heteroscedasticity. Unpublished address to the American Education Research Association.

March, James G. (1975) Bounded rationality, ambiguity, and the engineering of choice, *Bell Journal of Economics*, 9, 587–608.

March, James G. (1979) Science, politics and Mrs Gruenberg. In *The National Research Council in 1979*, 27–36. Washington, DC: National Academy of Science.

March, James G. (1981a) Decisions in organizations and theories of choice. In Andrew Van de Ven and William Joyce (eds), *Assessing Organizational Design and Performance*. New York: Wiley, 205–44.

March, James G. (1981b) Footnotes to organizational change, *Administrative Science Quarterly*, 26, 563–77.

March, James G. (1984) How we talk and how we act: administrative theory and administrative life. In Thomas J. Sergiovanni and John E. Corbally (eds), *Leadership and Organizational Culture*. Urbana, IL: University of Illinois Press, 18–35.

March, James G., and Johan P. Olsen (1975) The uncertainty of the past: organizational learning under ambiguity, *European Journal of Political Research*, 3, 147–71.

March, James G., and Johan P. Olsen (1976) *Ambiguity and Choice in Organizations*. Bergen, Norway: Universitetsforlaget.

March, James G., and Johan P. Olsen (1984) The new institutionalism: organizational factors in political life, *American Political Science Review*, 78, 734–49.

March, James G., and Johan P. Olsen (1986) Garbage can models of decision making in organizations. In James G. March and Roger Weissinger-Baylon (eds), *Ambiguity and Command: Organizational Perspectives on Military Decision Making*. Cambridge, MA: Ballinger, 11–35.

March, James G., and Johan P. Olsen (1987) Popular sovereignty and the search for appropriate institutions, *Journal of Public Policy*, in press.

March, James G., and Guje Sevón (1984) Gossip, information, and decision making. In Lee S. Sproull and J. Patrick Crecine (eds), *Advances in Information Processing in Organizations*, Vol. I, 95–107. Greenwich, CT: JAI Press.

March, James G., and Zur Shapira (1982) Behavioral decision theory and organizational decision theory. In Gerardo R. Ungson and Daniel N. Braunstein (eds), *Decision Making: An Interdisciplinary Inquiry*, 92–115. Boston, MA: Kent Publishing.

March, James G., and Zur Shapira (1987) Managerial perspectives on risk and risk taking, *Management Science*, in press.

March, James G., and Herbert A. Simon (1958) *Organizations*. New York, NY: Wiley.

Marshall, Ronald M. (1972) Determining an optimal accounting system for an unidentified user, *Journal of Accounting Research*, 10, 286–307.

Meyer, John W., and Brian Rowan (1977) Institutionalized organizations: formal structure as myth and ceremony, *American Journal of Sociology*, 83, 340–60.

Milgrom, Paul (1981) Good news and bad news: representation theorems and applications, *Bell Journal of Economics*, 12, 380–91.

Milgrom, Paul, and John Roberts (1982) Predation, reputation, and entry deterrence, *Journal of Economic Theory*, 27, 280–312.

Mitroff, Ian, and R. O. Mason (1983) Can we design systems for managing messes? Why so many management information systems are uninformative, *Accounting, Organizations, and Society*, 8, 195–203.

Morgenstern, Oskar (1963) *On the Accuracy of Economic Observations*, 2nd edn, Princeton, NJ: Princeton University Press.

Newman, D. Paul (1980) Prospect theory: implications for information evaluation, *Accounting, Organizations, and Society*, 5, 217–30.

Nisbett, Richard E., David H. Krantz, Christopher Jepson, and Geoffrey T. Fong (1982) Improving inductive inference. In Daniel Kahneman, Paul Slovic, and Amos Tversky (eds), *Judgment under Uncertainty: Heuristics and Biases*. Cambridge: Cambridge University Press, pp. 445–59.

Nisbett, Richard, and Lee Ross (1980) *Human Inference: Strategies and Shortcomings in Social Judgment*. Englewood Cliffs, NJ: Prentice-Hall.

Olsen, Johan P. (1976) University governance: non-participation as exclusion or choice. In James G. March and Johan P. Olsen, *Ambiguity and Choice in Organizations*, 277–313. Bergen, Norway: Universitetsforlaget.

Olsen, Johan P. (1983) *Organized Democracy*. Bergen, Norway: Universitetsforlaget.

Pfeffer, Jeffrey (1986) Personal communication.

Ross, Stephen A. (1973) The economic theory of agency: the principal's problem, *American Economic Review*, 63, 134–9.

Rothschild, M. (1973) Models of market organization with imperfect information: a survey, *Journal of Political Economy*, 81, 1283–308.

Sætren, Harald (1983) *Iverksetting av Offentlig Politikk: Utflytting av Statsinstitusjoner fra Oslo*. Bergen, Norway: Universitetsforlaget.

Sheil, Beau (1983) Power tools for programmers, *Datamation*, February, 131–43.

Simon, Herbert A. (1955) A behavioral model of rational choice, *Quarterly Journal of Economics*, 69, 99–118.

Simon, Herbert A. (1969) *The Sciences of the Artificial*. Cambridge, MA: MIT Press.

Sprague, Ralph H., Jr, and Eric Carlson (1982) *Building Effective Decision Support Systems*. Englewood Cliffs, NJ: Prentice-Hall.

Stigler, George J., and Gary S. Becker (1977) De gustibus non est disputandum, *American Economic Review*, 67, 76–90.

Swieringa, Robert J., and Karl E. Weick (1986) Action rationality in managerial accounting, *Accounting, Organizations, and Society*, 11.

Tinker, Anthony M., Barbara D. Merino, and Marilyn Dale Neimark (1982) The normative origins of positive theories: ideology and accounting thought, *Accounting, Organizations and Society*, 7, 167–200.

Trueblood, Robert M., and Richard M. Cyert (1957) *Sampling Techniques in Accounting*. Englewood Cliffs, NJ: Prentice-Hall.

Vancil, Richard F. (1979) *Decentralization: Managerial Ambiguity by Design*. Homewood, IL: Dow-Jones-Irwin.

Verrecchia, Robert E. (1982) Use of mathematical models in financial accounting, *Journal of Accounting Research*, 20, supplement 1–42.

von Weizsacker, C. C. (1971) Notes on endogenous changes of tastes, *Journal of Economic Theory*, 3, 345–72.

Weick, Karl E. (1976) Educational organizations as loosely coupled systems, *Administrative Science Quarterly*, 21, 1–19.

Weick, Karl E. (1979) *The Social Psychology of Organizing*, 2nd edn. Reading, MA: Addison-Wesley.

Weiss, Carol H. (1977) Research for policy's sake: the enlightenment function of social science research, *Policy Analysis*, 3, 531–45.

Wilson, Robert (1983) Auditing: perspectives from multiperson decision theory, *Accounting Review*, 58, 305–18.

Winston, Gordon C. (1980) Addiction and backsliding: a theory of compulsive consumption, *Journal of Economic Behavior and Organization*, 1, 295–324.

Winston, Gordon C. (1985) The reasons for being of two minds: a comment on Shelling's 'Enforcing rules on oneself', *Journal of Law, Economics, and Organization*, 1, 375–9.

Wolfson, Mark A. (1985) Empirical evidence of incentive problems and their mitigation in oil and gas tax shelter programs. In John W. Pratt and Richard J. Zeckhauser (eds), *Principals and Agents: The Structure of Business*. Cambridge, MA: Harvard Business School Press.

18

Information in Organizations as Signal and Symbol

Martha S. Feldman and James G. March

Abstract

Formal theories of rational choice suggest that information about the possible consequences of alternative actions will be sought and used only if the precision, relevance, and reliability of the information are compatible with its cost. Empirical studies of information in organizations portray a pattern that is hard to rationalize in such terms. In particular, organizations systematically gather more information than they use, yet continue to ask for more. We suggest that this behavior is a consequence of some ways in which organizational settings for information use differ from those anticipated in a simple decision-theory vision. In particular, the use of information is embedded in social norms that make it highly symbolic. Some of the implications of such a pattern of information use are discussed.

Introduction

Organizations are consumers, managers, and purveyors of information. Rules for gathering, storing, communicating, and using information are essential elements of organizational operating procedures. The technologies associated with using and managing information are the bases for several major growth industries, most notably computing and consulting.

This paper was first published in the *Administrative Science Quarterly*, 26, 1981, 171–86. The authors are grateful for the comments of Kenneth Arrow, Kennette Benedict, Robert Biller, David Brereton, Louise Comfort, Jerry Feldman, Victor Fuchs, Anne Miner, J. Rounds, Alan Saltzstein, Guje Sevón, and J. Serge Taylor; for the assistance of Julia Ball; and for grants from the Spencer Foundation, Brookings Institution, Hoover Institution, and National Institute of Education.

Reputations for organizational intelligence are built on capabilities for securing, analyzing, and retrieving information in a timely and intelligent manner. This practical consciousness of the importance of information is mirrored by research intended to understand and improve the uses of information by human beings. Information-processing interpretations of cognition, economic theories of information, and cybernetic perspectives on adaptation all build on the idea that the processing of information is a vital aspect of human behavior.

The study of information in organizations, like the study of choice with which it is often closely allied, involves a dialectic between students of information behavior on one hand and information engineers (or economists) on the other. Information engineers hope to design information systems with some clear elements of sensibility in them, or, in the best of all worlds, to design optimal systems (Kanter, 1972; Keen, 1977; Henderson and Nutt, 1978). For students of behavior, the problem is to understand actual human encounters with information. They focus on such things as the ways in which individuals and organizations deal with information on environmental uncertainty and risk (Tversky and Kahneman, 1974; Janis and Mann, 1977; Slovic, Fischhoff, and Lichtenstein, 1977; Nisbett and Ross, 1980), the ways in which individuals and organizations initiate and discontinue search activities (March and Simon, 1958; Cyert and March, 1963; Staw and Szwajkowski, 1975; Sabatier, 1978), and the ways in which organizational biases are reflected in information processing (Cyert, March and Starbuck, 1961; Wilensky, 1967; Allen, 1969; Adelman, Stewart and Hammond, 1975).

The dialogue between information engineers and students of information processing is most direct when differences between actual human behavior and apparently optimal information behavior are observed. Engineers characteristically seek to improve behavior, to instruct human actors in techniques for making better use of information. Students of information behavior characteristically suspect that some strange human behavior may contain a coding of intelligence that is not adequately reflected in engineering models. This paper follows the latter tradition. It recounts some familiar observations about information in organizations that are difficult to make consistent with simple notions of the value of information in making decisions; and it attempts to identify ways in which the behavior might make sense if placed in a somewhat broader frame.

Information and Organizational Choice

The classic representation of organizational choice is a simple extension of decision theory visions of individual choice. In particular, decisions are seen as derived from an estimate of uncertain consequences of possible actions and an estimate of uncertain future preferences for those consequences (Luce and Raiffa, 1957; Taylor, 1975). Both estimates are problematic. They depend on information that is imperfect in a number of obvious ways. Organizations make explicit and implicit decisions about seeking and using information that might improve estimates of future consequences and future preferences. These decisions are, of course, also presumed to be based on estimates of the expected benefits and costs of particular information, information strategies, or information structures.

Within this basic framework, search behavior, investments in information, and the management of information are driven by the desire to improve decisions. The value of information depends in a well-defined way on the information's relevance to the decision to be made, and on its precision, cost, and reliability. Information has value if it can be expected to affect choice. It is a good investment if its marginal expected return in improving decisions exceeds its marginal cost. The calculation of information value in a particular case is likely to be quite difficult. The framework, however, is simple and the idea is appealing (Raiffa, 1968; Marschak and Radner, 1972). This perspective on decision-making leads to some simple expectations for information utilization. For example, relevant information will be gathered and analyzed prior to decision-making; information gathered for use in a decision will be used in making that decision; available information will be examined before more information is requested or gathered; needs for information will be determined prior to requesting information; information that is irrelevant to a decision will not be gathered.

Studies of the uses of information in organizations, however, reveal a somewhat different picture. Organizations seem to deal with information in a different way from that anticipated from a simple reading of decision theory. The following three stories of decision-making in organizations illustrate the contrasts. These stories provide a contextual description of the relation between information and decision-making. The three episodes are not exceptional. They are taken from studies by Merewitz and Sosnick (1971), Bower (1970), and Hägg (1977). Others could easily have been used. They include examples taken from private and public, profit and non-profit, American and foreign, and large and small organizations. None of the studies was primarily concerned with the information focus of the present paper. Rather, each study portrays a typical, minor example of the process of problem-solving and decision-making in an undramatic situation. The descriptions here are brief and incomplete, but we have tried to retain the flavor of the use of information reported in the original studies.

Illustration 1: Supersonic Transport

Consider decision-making within the American national government regarding governmental support for the development of a commercial supersonic aircraft (Merewitz and Sosnick, 1971). In 1961, Congress appropriated funds for exploratory research on supersonic transports. Earlier studies had been commissioned by both the air force and the Federal Aviation Agency. These studies indicated that aircraft manufacturers were unlikely to undertake construction of a supersonic aircraft without government support. The FAA feasibility study commissioned in 1960 was available in 1963. It found 'no economic justification for the SST' (Merewitz and Sosnick, 1971, p. 252). In 1963, after Pan American Airways took options on six Concordes (the British–French SST), President Kennedy committed the United States to developing a supersonic transport in partnership with private industry. By 1966, construction of a prototype was underway. In 1967, the FAA found the supersonic transport to be 'viable as a public investment' (Merewitz and Sosnick, 1971, p. 254). The same year, Congress voted to continue prototype construction. In 1970, Congress rejected a $290 million appropriation for the project, finally approving (in 1971) only $85 million. This meant an end to the development, at least for the near future.

Illustration 2: A New Manufacturing Facility

Consider this standard example of corporate planning and capital investment (Bower, 1970). The case involved a project that originally developed as a sideline at one plant of a manufacturing company. As the project expanded, it outgrew existing facilities, and proposals were made either to expand the plant or to build a new facility for the project. Between February 1966 and April 1967, repeated analyses and forecasts about the project were made. In April 1966, the project was losing more than had been forecast. The loss was attributed to low sales and high development costs. By October 1966 the project was showing increasingly poor operating results, lower than predicted by the forecasts. This was interpreted as having been caused by marketing problems; no change in the project was considered. Initial proposals to modify an existing plant by building a new warehouse were expanded to include building a whole new facility as well. As the plans for capital investment went forward, estimates of the projected performance were adjusted downward several times to make the proposal more believable.

Illustration 3: New Equipment

Consider the *post hoc* review of a project involving buying and installing packaging equipment in the manufacturing department of a Swedish firm (Hägg, 1977). The project was seen as a way to reduce personnel and thereby avoid production delays attributable to absenteeism. The investment proposal was submitted and approved in September 1973. By mid-1974, the equipment had been bought and installed and was in operation. In December 1974, a review report was written. The review showed that the project had, in fact, reduced the number of personnel by two. However, it also showed that the resetting times had been longer than expected and that installation problems had delayed the achievement of normal working conditions beyond the projected date. These problems produced the types of delays that the reduction in the number of personnel was supposed to eliminate. No action was taken as a result of the review. Installation problems were attributed to 'the supplier who had given wrong information and who had not supplied the needed expert service' (Hägg, 1977, p. 81), and the longer resetting times were seen as a result of inadequately trained mechanics. The review was seen as a good idea, nevertheless.

These case studies show a relation between information and decision-making that is rather distant from the one anticipated by classical conceptions drawn from decision theory. Considerable information was gathered by the organizations involved in the decisions. Considerable information was sometimes volunteered by other organizations. There was little systematic relation between the time of receiving the results of a study and the time of making a decision. There was no obvious consistent relation between the findings of studies and the decision made. Information was gathered. More information was sought. Information was considered. But the link between decisions and information was weak.

Similar stories are told repeatedly in the research literature. Their number could be increased almost at will.[1] The literature reports phenomena that can be summarized by six observations about the gathering and use of information in organizations. The observations are consistent with the research literature yet close enough to personal experience to be almost self-evident:

1 For example, Lindblom (1959); Wohlstetter (1962, 1965); Cyert and March (1963); Wilensky (1967); Olsen (1970); Allison (1971); Beneviste (1972); Cohen and March (1974); Eliasson (1974); Halperin (1974); Lucas and Dawson (1974); Steinbruner (1974); Lynch (1975); Graham (1976); Kreiner (1976); March and Olsen (1976); Meltsner (1976); Tietenberg and Toureille (1976); Weiss (1977); Estler (1978); Sabatier (1978); Sproull, Weiner, and Wolf (1978); Clark and Shrode (1979); Krieger (1979).

1 Much of the information that is gathered and communicated by individuals and organizations has little decision relevance.
2 Much of the information that is used to justify a decision is collected and interpreted after the decision has been made, or substantially made.
3 Much of the information gathered in response to requests for information is not considered in the making of decisions for which it was requested.
4 Regardless of the information available at the time a decision is first considered, more information is requested.
5 Complaints that an organization does not have enough information to make a decision occur while available information is ignored.
6 The relevance of the information provided in the decision-making process to the decision being made is less conspicuous than is the insistence on information. In short, most organizations and individuals often collect more information than they use or can reasonably expect to use in the making of decisions. At the same time, they appear to be constantly needing or requesting more information, or complaining about inadequacies in information.

It is possible, on considering these phenomena, to conclude that organizations are systematically stupid. There is no question that organizational processes are sometimes misguided and that organizational procedures are sometimes incomprehensibly inattentive to relevant information. Nevertheless, it is possible to try to discover why reasonably successful and reasonably adaptive organizations might exhibit the kinds of information behaviors that have been reported. Perhaps the stories of information perversity tell us less about the weaknesses of organizations than about the limitations of our ideas about information.

Information Incentives, Gossip, and Misrepresentation

There are several elementary instrumental reasons why information use in organizations deviates from a standard decision theory vision. At the outset two relatively conventional explanations should be noted. First, organizations may be unable, because of organizational or human limitations, to process the information they have. They experience an information glut as a shortage. Indeed, it is possible that the overload contributes to the breakdown in processing capabilities (Wohlstetter, 1962; Miller, 1977). The second explanation is that the information available to organizations is sytematically the wrong kind of information. Limitations of analytical skill or coordination lead decision-makers to collect information that cannot be used. Thus, although there is a great deal of information, there is not enough relevant information (Janis and Mann, 1977). These interpretations certainly have bases in what we know about the uses of information in organizations, but they seem to be limited by their implicit acceptance of the standard formulation of the decision problem in an organization.

There are three other conspicuous features affecting the instrumental use of information in organizations. First, ordinary organizational procedures provide positive incentives for underestimating the costs of information relative to its benefits. Second, much of the information in an organization is gathered in a surveillance mode rather than in a decision mode. Third, much of the information used in organizational life is subject to strategic misrepresentation.

Information Incentives

Organizations provide incentives for gathering more information than is optimal from a strict decision perspective (Bobrow, 1973; Handel, 1977; Chan, 1979). Consider, for example, two simple speculations about systematic bias in estimating the benefits and costs of information. First, the costs and benefits of information are not all incurred at the same place in the organization. Decisions about information are often made in parts of the organization that can transfer the costs to other parts of the organization while retaining the benefits. Suppose having too much information (i.e., having an information overload) increases the risk of being unable either to comprehend the information or to use it effectively in a decision. Since the information-gathering functions are typically separated from the information-using functions of organizations, incentives are modest for gatherers to avoid overloading users. The user of information invites a bias by accepting responsibility for the utilization of information while delegating responsibility for its availability.

Second, *post hoc* accountability is often required of both individual decision-makers and organizations. An intelligent decision-maker knows that a decision made in the face of uncertainty will almost always be different from the choice that would have been made if the future had been precisely and accurately predicted. As a consequence, a decision-maker must anticipate two *post hoc* criticisms of information-gathering behavior: (1) that the likelihoods of events that in fact subsequently occurred were, on the average, underestimated, and thus that less information about these events was secured than should have been; and (2) that the likelihoods of events that in fact subsequently did not occur were, on average, overestimated, and thus that *more* information about them was secured than should have been. If, as seems very likely, the first criticism is more likely to be voiced than the second, it is better from the decision-maker's point of view to have information that is not needed than not to have information that might be needed. The asymmetry in *post hoc* assessment leads directly to an incentive for gathering too much information.

Information as Surveillance

Organizations, as well as individuals, collect gossip (Aguilar, 1967; Mintzberg, 1972). They gather information that has no apparent immediate decision consequences. As a result, the information seems substantially worthless within a decision theory perspective. The perspective is misleading. Instead of seeing an organization as seeking information in order to choose among given alternatives in terms of prior preferences, we can see an organization as monitoring its environment for surprises (or for reassurances that there are none). The surprises may be new alternatives, new possible preferences, or new significant changes in the world. The processes are more inductive than deductive. The analysis is more exploratory data analysis than estimation of unknown parameters or hypothesis-testing.

The surveillance metaphor suggests either a prior calculation of needed information or a kind of thermostatic linkage between observations and actions. In this metaphor, systems for surveillance are justified in terms of the expected decisions and environments to be faced. Systems for surveillance are connected to decision-rules in such a way that the relatively long lead times required for information-gathering can be linked to relatively short decision times. This vision, however, can easily become overly heroic if it presumes explicit calculations by the organization. Such calculations are made in organizations, but they do not seem to account for much of what we observe. Organizations gather gossip – news that might contain something relevant but usually does not – in situations in which relevance cannot be specified precisely in advance.

Strategic Information

Many studies of human information-processing involve situations in which experimental subjects are asked to respond to information known by the experimenter to be reasonable, neutral information. Very few situations in the real world of organizations are of that sort. Most information that is generated and processed in an organization is subject to misrepresentation. Information is gathered and communicated in a context of conflict of interest and with consciousness of potential decision consequences. Often information is produced in order to persuade someone to do something. It is obvious that information can be an instrument of power, and substantial recent efforts to refine the economics of information and the economics of agency focus on managing the problems of strategic unreliability in information (Crozier, 1964; Rothschild and Stiglitz, 1976; Hirshleifer and Riley, 1979).

When strategic misrepresentation is common, the value of information to a decision-maker is compromised. Strategic misrepresentation also stimulates the oversupply of information. Competition among contending liars turns persuasion into a contest in (mostly unreliable) information. If most received information is confounded by unknown misrepresentations reflecting a complicated game played under conditions of conflicting interests, a decision-maker would be curiously unwise to consider information as though it were innocent. The modest analyses of simplified versions of this problem suggest the difficulty of devising incentive schemes that yield unambiguously usable information (Mirrlees, 1976; Demski and Feltham, 1978). Yet organizations somehow survive and even succeed. Individuals develop rules for dealing with information under conditions of conflict. Decision-makers discount much of the information that is generated. Not all information is ignored, however, and inferences are made. Decision-makers learn not to trust overly clever people, and smart people learn not to be overly clever (March, 1979).

The significant organizational incentives for gathering information, the gathering of information in a surveillance mode rather than a decision mode, and the strategic misrepresentation of information in organizations all contribute to the information phenomena that have been noted in organizations and provide reasons for decoupling information from decisions. Rational, sensible individuals in organizations, pursuing intelligent behavior, will often gather more information than would be expected in the absence of such considerations and will attend to information less. Such instrumental complications affecting information behavior in organizations are, however, not the only explanations for the anomalies we observe. In fact, they are probably less important than a more profound linkage between decision behavior and the normative context within which it occurs. Information is a symbol and a signal.

Information as Symbol and Signal

Information as Symbol

Organizational decisions allocate scarce resources and are thereby of considerable social and individual importance. But decision-making in organizations is more important than the outcomes it produces. It is an arena for exercising social values, for displaying authority, and for exhibiting proper behavior and attitudes with respect to a central ideological construct of modern Western civilization: the concept of intelligent choice.[2] Bureaucratic organizations are edifices built on ideas of rationality. The cornerstones of rationality are values regarding decision-making (Weber, 1947). There are no values closer to the core of Western ideology than these ideas of intelligent choice, and there is no institution more prototypically committed to the systematic application of information to decisions than the modern bureaucratic organization.

The gathering of information provides a ritualistic assurance that appropriate attitudes about decision-making exist. Within such a scenario of performance, information is not simply a basis for action. It is a representation of competence and a reaffirmation of social virtue. Command of information and information sources enhances perceived competence and inspires confidence. The belief that more information characterizes better decisions engenders a belief that having information, in itself, is good and that a person or organization with more information is better than a person or organization with less. Thus the gathering and use of information in an organization is part of the performance of a decision-maker or an organization trying to make decisions intelligently in a situation in which the verification of intelligence is heavily procedural and normative. A good decision-maker is one who makes decisions in the way a good decision-maker does, and decision-makers and organizations establish their legitimacy by their use of information.

Observable features of information use become particularly important in this scenario. When there is no reliable alternative for assessing a decision-maker's knowledge, visible aspects of information gathering and storage are used as implicit measures of the quality of information possessed and used. For example, being the first to have information and having more and different information indicate the proximity of an individual or organization to important information sources. Similarly, the resources expended on gathering, processing, and displaying information indicate the quantity and quality of information an individual or organization is likely to have. Displaying information and being able to explain decisions or ideas in terms of information indicate an ability to use information easily and appropriately.

These symbols of competence are simultaneously symbols of social efficacy, and they secure part of their justification there. Belief in the appropriateness of decisions, the process by which they are made, and the roles played by the various actors involved is a key part of a social structure. It is important not only to decision-makers that they be viewed as legitimate; it is also vital to society. Ritual acknowledgement of important

2 For more general discussion of the role of symbols in decision-making, see Edelman (1964, 1977); March and Olsen (1976); Pfeffer (1980).

values celebrates a shared interpretation of reality (Berger and Luckman, 1966). Thus, requesting information and assembling it are ways of making social life meaningful and acceptable.

Standard decision theory views of choice seem to underestimate these symbolic importances of information and the use of information in decision-making. Because the acts of seeking and using information in decisions have important symbolic value to the actors and to the society, individuals and organizations will consistently gather more information that can be justified in conventional decision theory terms. Decisions are orchestrated so as to ensure that decision-makers and observers come to believe that the decisions are reasonable – or even intelligent. Using information, asking for information, and justifying decisions in terms of information have all come to be significant ways in which we symbolize that the process is legitimate, that we are good decision-makers, and that our organizations are well managed.

Information as Signal

When legitimacy is a necessary property of effective decisions, conspicuous consumption of information is a sensible strategy for decision-makers. The strategy need not be chosen deliberately. It will accompany processes that work. Decisions that are viewed as legitimate will tend to be information-intensive. Decision-makers who are persuasive in securing acceptance of decisions will request information, gather information, and cite information. The behavior is a representation of appropriate decision-making.

From this point of view, we can examine information-gathering and requesting as the kind of signal familiar to the economics of information (Spence, 1974; Nelson, 1974; Meyer, 1979). It is possible that the signal is a valid one. This would be true if organizations that generally produce better decisions are also able to gather and exhibit information at lower cost than those who produce poorer decisions. Even if information contributes nothing directly to the quality of decisions, better decision-makers would invest more in information, and decision-maker quality could be estimated accurately by monitoring information practice.

A strategy of legitimation through the use of information cannot, however, be chosen at will. The arbitrary symbolic use of information is subject to limits imposed by competition for legitimacy and variations in the costs of exhibiting information consumption. Since organizations compete for legitimacy, no single organization can control its own relative reputation by its own actions, and the comparative positions of different organizations depend critically on differences in the costs to organizations of maintaining an information posture.

The price of securing information is the value of foregone opportunities. The cost calculation depends not only on the usual considerations of efficiency but also on the kinds of alternative investments that are available. If, for example, the quality of decisions is automatically reflected in costless performance measures, the net returns from further signaling would be negatively correlated with decision quality. As a result, the signal would not be a valid one. By this analysis, information use is more likely to be a valid signal when performance criteria are obscure than when they are clear. Indeed, when the intrinsic quality of decisions is exceptionally difficult to assess, the signaling process may itself affect quality. Suppose, for example, that belief in the legitimacy of a decision is encouraged by the conspicuous utilization of information, and that the legitimacy of a decision, in turn, affects its implementation (an element of quality). Then those organizations that have relatively low signaling costs (or that for other reasons invest in information) will ultimately become better decision-makers. The signal will, by this mechanism, become a valid one.

When benefits from information use are approximately equal among organizations, and costs of maintaining an information system are less for good decision-makers than for others, conspicuous consumption of information is neither organizationally nor socially foolish. The behavior is an effective signal. It is, of course, possible that an alternative signaling system might be devised that would be less costly for organizations and for society and would still provide equally reliable information. In particular, a system that dampened the competition for legitimacy homogeneously across organizations might be preferred. But the signal that exists appears to have some of the properties associated with signaling validity and cannot be casually discarded.

The information economics perspective is instructive, particularly in its focus on conditions for signal validity and stability in a signaling system. But that perspective is not essential to an appreciation of the symbolic significance of information posturing. Reason, rationality, and intelligence are central values in modern industrial societies. Within such societies, life is choice; choice is appropriately informed when the best available information about possible future consequences of present actions is sought. In a society committed to intelligent choice, requests for information and the gathering of information will generally be rewarded by observers; less systematic procedures are common, but they tend to be less reliably rewarded. Whether we think of simple learning, of some ideas about role-taking, or of socialization into basic values, we develop a similar conclusion. The pattern of information-gathering and utilization that characterizes such a society must be as much a part of ordinary experience as the most elementary social values of honesty, autonomy, and self-reliance.

The Dynamics of Symbols

This paper has presented some possible reasons for certain apparently peculiar information behavior in organizations. The reasons suggested above emphasize the strategic and symbolic incentives for gathering information. Such reasons are, however, only an introduction to understanding the process. In particular, there is no reason to assume that organizational behavior with respect to information is stable, that the process is in equilibrium. Consider, for example, the classic dynamics of symbolic life: I learn French to symbolize my commitment to a cultured life, but having learned French I discover ways in which it is useful; I buy a car to symbolize my affluence, but having the car leads me to discover the pleasures of automobile travel; I work for a political candidate to symbolize civic duty and solidarity, but in the process I discover opportunities for political power. When organizations establish information systems, however symbolic or strategic the initial reasons may be, they create a dynamic that reveals new justifications as the organizational process unfolds.

The analytical problem is similar to the problem of understanding hypocrisy in individual behavior. The hypocrite presumably adopts the assertion of a value as a symbolic substitute for action. In the short run, hypocrisy is both a social acknowledgement of the importance of a value and an evasion of the value. In the long run, however, proclamation of social values, particularly when associated with opportunities for social approbation, changes the action. The changes are not necessarily intentional. It is not easy to be a stable hypocrite. Similarly, it is hard to find stable symbols or tactics in organizations. Each creates a dynamic by which it is transformed.

At the individual level, symbols produce belief and belief stimulates the discovery of new realities. For example, suppose that individuals in organizations are inclined to attribute successes, but not failures, to factors they control (Davis and Davis, 1972; Miller and Ross, 1975) and suppose that information-gathering decisions are something that successful decision-makers feel they control. Then successful decision-makers would come to believe that the information rituals they control are, in fact, important to decision-making. If they then act to make information important to decision-making, and discover new ways of making these tools indispensable, the circle is complete. Tactical uses of information are transformed into belief, and thence into functional necessity.

The process at the organizational level is similar, though the mechanisms are slightly different. An example is the creation of a special office symbolizing a newly important value (e.g., environmental protection, affirmative action). The office may have been established as a symbolic alternative to more substantial action (Edelman, 1964, 1977). New offices, however, are not passive. They affect their own functions. Consider the dynamics of flak-catching (Wolfe, 1970). Organizations create flak-catching offices – special offices to display their concern for outside complaints, pressures, and the like. But flak-catchers, who are commissioned to protect an organization from flak and to symbolize a commitment to deal appropriately with flak, quickly learn to enhance the importance of flak. The mechanisms are familiar. Partly, flak-catchers are chosen because of some willingness to deal with outsiders, perhaps because of prior affinity to them. Partly, they learn from their association with outsiders to identify with them. Partly, they discover that their importance in the organizations depends on the existence of flak (Taylor, 1980).

These dynamics apply to almost any specialized function in an organization. Individuals and organizations gathering, storing, and analyzing information are likely to behave in this way. Organizational departments assigned information-processing responsibilities are unlikely to remain neutral with respect to the uses of information. Partly, people who gather and use information will tend to be people who believe that information gathering is important. Individuals who discover they are good at solving problems using information will discover more ways for making it sensible to do so. Partly, people who gather and use information will associate with other information gatherers and users and will come to identify with them. As a class, they will generate belief in their importance. Partly, people who gather and use information will try to convince others of its importance as a natural way of ensuring their own importance. People who prepare reports are likely to try to persuade others to read them. Individuals who use information because it serves a particular purpose are likely to come to believe information is useful in a more general way. Individuals who request information are likely occasionally to find it useful, even to come to believe in the general utility of information-gathering.

Although it is easy to observe that arbitrary actions induce instrumental interpretations and become effective practical instruments under fairly general conditions, it is clear that the process does not always proceed rapidly and rarely goes to the limit. Exploring such dynamics significantly is beyond the scope of the present paper. These dynamics are, however, important to its spirit. We have tried to describe some ways in which apparently anomalous behavior is sensible and have explored particularly the symbolic significance of information use. In the process, we have suggested that simple decision theory visions of information and its value do not match the ways in which information is used in organizations as we observe them. The argument has been made in a form that might suggest a stable separation of symbolic and instrumental action. But organizations as we observe them are not stable. They change, and they change in a way that weaves the symbolic and instrumental aspects of life together, not in the sense that everything is both (though that is true enough) but in the sense that interpretations of life affect life. If there is substantial decision value in information, the present pattern of investment in information may be a good strategy for discovering that value. Symbolic investments in information are likely to convert to more instrumental investments.

A strategy of using symbolic investments in information as an instrument of change is dependent on a corresponding ideology. The symbolic value of information is a function of the social norms of a society and of a belief in rational decision processes of a particular kind. It is not hard to imagine a society in which requests for information, and insistence on reports and analyses, would be signs of indecisiveness or lack of faith. Even within the rational traditions of the enlightenment, decision theory perspectives on intelligence have competitors. Suppose that interpretations of decision-making that emphasize loose coupling rather than organizational structure, ambiguity rather than precision, and limited rather than complete rationality succeed in changing the normal conception of organizational life. Then the symbolic value of information will be compromised. Organizations will be less inclined to treat information gathering as a precious manifestation of their virtue. Information will be a less effective signal of their competence.

Conclusion

From a classical decision theory point of view, information is gathered and used because it helps make a choice. Investments in information are made up to the point at which marginal expected cost equals marginal expected return. Observations of organizations are not easy to reconcile with such a picture. Individuals and organizations invest in information and information systems, but their investments do not seem to make decision theory sense. Organizational participants seem to find value in information that has no great decision relevance. They gather information and do not use it. They ask for reports and do not read them. They act first and receive requested information later.

It is possible, on considering these phenomena, to conclude that organizations and the people in them lack intelligence. We prefer to be somewhat more cautious. We have argued that the information behavior observed in organizations is not, in general, perverse. We have suggested four broad explanations for the conspicuous over-consumption of information. First, organizations provide incentives for gathering extra information. These incentives are buried in conventional rules for organizing (e.g., the division of labor between information gathering and information using) and for evaluating decisions. Second, much of the information in organizations is gathered and treated in a surveillance mode rather than a decision mode. Organizations scan the environment for surprises as much as they try to clarify uncertainties. Third, much of the information in organizations is subject to strategic misrepresentation. It is collected and used in a context that makes the innocence of information problematic. Fourth, information use symbolizes a commitment to rational choice. Displaying the symbol reaffirms the importance of this social value and signals personal and organizational competence.

These factors seem important enough to a affect organizational information behavior significantly. They can influence organizational behavior through any of the usual mechanisms of adaptation. To some extent, individuals and organizations calculate the alternatives and decide to buy information (or use information). Such conscious decisions, if taken sensibly with knowledge of the factors we have discussed, will lead to an information strategy that is more like what is observed than what is expected from a simple model of information investment. Even without conscious calculation, organizations will learn from experience to follow strategies that generate information without using it. Strategies developed from calculation or learning could spread through a population of organizations by imitation. Alternatively, some process of natural selection among procedural rules can be seen as selecting rules that encourage considerable investment in information. In such cases, the intelligence of the behavior is buried in the rules and is not easily retrieved (or expressed) by individuals within the organization. Learning, imitation, and selection tend to hide the intelligence of behavior within rules and rule-following. Understanding fully the ways in which particular kinds of experience are coded into particular kinds of rules requires a precise specification of the adaptive mechanisms. For present purposes, however, all that is needed is to note that the factors identified here need not necessarily affect behavior by inducing incentives, conscious calculation, and intentionally strategic action. The mechanisms may be considerably more indirect than that, yet retain the same essential effect.

These general ideas have some obvious research implications. The factors we have identified are not homogeneously relevant across organizations, decision situations, and time. We should observe some systematic variation in the information behavior of organizations and the individuals in them. That is not to say that the phenomena are limited to a small number of organizations. On the contrary, they are very general. Nevertheless, we might expect investment in information to be particularly sensitive to variations in the symbolic requirements and signaling opportunities of the organization.

The kinds of information behavior noted here should be more common in situations in which decision criteria are ambiguous than in situations in which they are clear, more common where performance measures are vague than where they are precise, more common when decision quality requires a long period to establish than when there is quick feedback, more common where the success of a decision depends on other decisions that cannot be predicted or controlled than where a decision can be evaluated autonomously, more common where other legitimating myths (e.g., tradition or faith) are not important than where they are, more common in institutions and occasions closely linked to rational ideologies than in those that are distant from such ideologies. Thus, we might reasonably predict that the phenomena are more conspicuous in policy-making than in engineering, more conspicuous in the public sector than in the private, more conspicuous at the top of an organization than at the bottom, more conspicuous in business than in the church or family, more conspicuous in universities than in football teams. To list such speculations is not to claim their correctness. Indeed, casual evidence seems unsupportive of one or two of them. Nor is the present paper a good occasion for attempting to assess the ideas empirically. Such pleasures are left, in the grand tradition of such things, to the reader.

A static analysis of information use, however, is likely to be misleading. The symbolic significance of any activity depends on the social norms within which it is undertaken. Information is significant symbolically because of a particular set of beliefs in a particular set of cultures. These beliefs include broad commitments to reason and to rational discourse, as well as to the modern variants that are more specifically linked to decision theory perspectives on the nature of life. As social norms change, the relevance of information as a symbol, or signal, changes with them. At the same time, symbolic actions reveal more instrumental consequences. Like other behavior, symbolic behavior explores possible alternative interpretations of itself and creates its own necessity. Thus, it is possible that norms that are changing will be simultaneously losing symbolic significance and gaining instrumental importance. An elegant manifestation of the process would occur should values shift enough to leave information and information-based analysis as the true basis of organizational action that is legitimized by symbols of ambiguity and intuition.

References

Adelman, Leonard, Thomas R. Stewart, and Kenneth R. Hammond (1975) A case history of the application of social judgment to policy information, *Policy Sciences*, 6: 137–59.

Aguilar, Francis Joseph (1967) *Scanning the Business Environment*. New York: Macmillan.

Allen, Thomas J. (1969) The differential performance of information channels in the transfer of technology. In W. H. Gruber and D. G. Marquis (eds), *Factors in the Transfer of Technology*. Cambridge, MA: MIT Press.

Allison, Graham T. (1971) *Essence of Decision: Explaining the Cuban Missile Crisis*. Boston: Little, Brown.

Beneviste, Guy (1972) *The Politics of Expertise*. Berkeley, CA: Glendessary Press.

Berger, Peter L., and Thomas Luckman (1966) *The Social Construction of Reality: A Treatise in the Sociology of Knowledge*. New York: Doubleday.

Bobrow, David B. (1973) Analysis and foreign policy choice, *Policy Sciences*, 4: 437–51.

Bower, Joseph L. (1970) *Managing the Resource Allocation Process: A Study of Corporate Planning and Investment*. Boston: Harvard School of Business Administration.

Chan, Steve (1979) The intelligence of stupidity: Understanding failures in strategic warning, *American Political Science Review*, 73: 171–80.

Clark, Thomas D., Jr, and William A. Shrode (1979) Public sector decision structures: An empirically based description, *Public Administration Review*, 39: 343–54.

Cohen, Michael D., and James G. March (1974) *Leadership and Ambiguity: The American College President*. New York: McGraw-Hill.

Crozier, Michel (1964) *The Bureaucratic Phenomenon*. Chicago: University of Chicago Press.

Cyert, Richard M., and James G. March (1963) *A Behavioral Theory of the Firm*. Englewood Cliffs, NJ: Prentice-Hall.

Cyert, Richard M., James G. March, and William H. Starbuck (1961) Two experiments on bias and conflict in organizational estimation. *Management Science*, 8: 254–64.

Davis, William L., and D. Elaine Davis (1972) Internal–external control and attribution of responsibility for success and failure. *Journal of Personality*, 40: 123–36.

Demski, Joel S., and Gerald A. Feltham (1978) Economic incentives in budgetary control systems. *The Accounting Review*, 53: 336–59.

Edelman, Murray (1964) *The Symbolic Uses of Politics*. Urbana: University of Illinois Press.

Edelman, Murray (1977) *Political Language: Words that Succeed and Policies that Fail*. New York: Academic Press.

Eliasson, Gunnar (1974) *Corporate Planning – Theory, Practice, Comparison*. Stockholm: Federation of Swedish Industries.

Estler, Suzanne (1978) Rationality, Politics and Values: Systematic Analysis and the Management of Sexual Equity in the University. Unpublished PhD dissertation, Stanford University.

Graham, Otis L. Jr (1976) *Toward a Planned Society: From Roosevelt to Nixon*. New York: Oxford University Press.

Hägg, Ingemund (1977) *Review of Capital Investments*. Uppsala, Sweden: University of Uppsala, Department of Business Administration.

Halperin, Morton H. (1974) *Bureaucratic Politics and Foreign Policy*. Washington, DC: Brookings Institution.

Handel, Michael I. (1977) The Yom Kippur War and the inevitability of surprise. *International Studies Quarterly*. 21: 461–502.

Henderson, John D., and Paul C. Nutt (1978) On the design of planning information systems, *Academy of Management Review*, 3: 774–85.

Hirshleifer, J., and John C. Riley (1979) The analytics of uncertainty and information - an expository survey, *Journal of Economic Literature*, 17: 1375–421.

Janis, Irving L., and Leon Mann (1977) *Decision Making*. New York: Free Press.

Kanter, Jerome (1972) *Management-Oriented Management Information Systems*. Englewood Cliffs, NJ: Prentice-Hall.

Keen, Peter G. W. (1977) The evolving concept of optimality. TIMS *Studies in the Management Sciences*, 6: 31–57.

Kreiner, Kristian (1976) *The Site Organization*. Copenhagen: Technical University of Denmark.

Krieger, Susan (1979) *Hip Capitalism*. Beverly Hills, CA: Sage Publications.

Lindblom, Charles E. (1959) The science of muddling through, *Public Administration Review*, 19: 79–88.

Lucas, William A., and R. H. Dawson (1974) *The Organizational Politics of Defense*. Washington, DC: The International Studies Association.

Luce, R. Duncan, and Howard Raiffa (1957) *Games and Decisions*. New York: Wiley.

Lynch, Thomas D. (1975) *Policy Analysis in Public Policymaking*. Lexington, MA: Lexington Books, D. C. Heath.

March, James G. (1979) Science, politics, and Mrs. Gruenberg. In the *National Research Council in 1979*. Washington, DC: National Academy of Sciences.

March, James G., and Johan P. Olsen (1976) *Ambiguity and Choice in Organizations*. Bergen, Norway: Universitetsforlaget.

March, James G., and Herbert A. Simon (1958) *Organizations*. New York: Wiley.

Marschak, Jacob, and Roy Radner (1972) *Economic Theory of Teams*. New Haven: Yale University Press.

Meltsner, Arnold J. (1976) *Policy Analysis in the Bureaucracy*. Berkeley, CA: University of California Press.

Merewitz, Leonard, and Stephen H. Sosnick (1971) *The Budget's New Clothes*. Chicago: Rand McNally.

Meyer, Marshall W. (1979) Organizational structure as signaling. *Pacific Sociological Review*, 22: 481–500.

Miller, Dale T., and Michael Ross (1975) Self-serving biases in the attribution of causality. *Psychological Bulletin*, 82: 213–25.

Miller, James G. (1977) *Living Systems*. New York: McGraw-Hill.

Mintzberg, Henry (1972) The myth of MIS. *California Management Review*, 15: 92–7.

Mirrlees, James A. (1976) The optimal structure of incentives and authority within an organization, *Bell Journal of Economics*, 7: 105–31.

Nelson, Phillip (1974) Advertising as information *Journal of Political Economy*. 82: 729–54.

Nisbett, Richard, and Lee Ross (1980) *Human Inference: Strategies and Shortcomings of Social Judgment*. Englewood Cliffs, NJ: Prentice-Hall.

Olsen, Johan (1970) *A Study of Choice in an Academic Organization*. Bergen, Norway: Institute of Sociology, University of Bergen.

Pfeffer, Jeffrey (1980) Management as symbolic action: The creation and maintenance of organizational paradigms. Unpublished manuscript, Graduate School of Business Administration, Stanford University.

Raiffa, Howard (1968) *Decision Analysis: Introductory Lectures on Choices under Uncertainty*. Reading, MA: Addison-Wesley.

Rothschild, Michael, and Joseph Stiglitz (1976) Equilibrium in competitive insurance markets: An essay on the economics of imperfect information, *Quarterly Journal of Economics*, 90: 629–49.

Sabatier, Paul (1978) The acquisition and utilization of technical information by administrative agencies, *Administrative Science Quarterly*, 23: 396–417.

Slovic, Paul, Baruch Fischhoff, and Sarah Lichtenstein (1977) Behavioral decision theory, *Annual Review of Psychology*. 23: 1–39.

Spence, Michael (1974) *Market Signaling*. Cambridge, MA: Harvard University Press.

Sproull, Lee S., Stephen Weiner, and David Wolf (1978) *Organizing an Anarchy*. Chicago: University of Chicago Press.

Staw, Barry M., and Eugene Szwajkowski (1975) The scarcity-munificence component of organizational environments and the commission of illegal acts, *Administrative Science Quarterly*, 20: 345–54.

Steinbruner, John D. (1974) *The Cybernetic Theory of Decision*. Princeton: Princeton University Press.

Taylor, J. Serge (1980) Environmentalists in the bureaucracy. Unpublished manuscript, Graduate School of Business Administration, Stanford University.

Taylor, Michael (1975) The theory of collective choice. In Fred L. Greenstein and Nelson W. Polsby (eds), *Handbook of Political Science*, 3: 413–81. Reading, MA: Addison-Wesley.

Tietenberg, Thomas H., with Pierre Toureille (1976) *Energy Planning and Policy:* The Political Economy of Project Independence. Lexington, MA: Lexington Books, D. C. Heath.

Tversky, Amos, and Daniel Kahneman (1974) Judgment under uncertainty: Heuristics and biases, *Science*, 185: 1124–31.

Weber, Max (1947) *The Theory of Social and Economic Organization*. A. M. Henderson and T. Parsons (trans.) Oxford: Oxford University Press.

Weiss, Carol H. (ed.) (1977) *Using Social Research in Public Policy Making*. Lexington, MA: Lexington Books, D. C. Heath.

Wilensky, Harold L. (1967) *Organizational Intelligence*. New York: Basic Books.

Wohlstetter, Roberta (1962) *Pearl Habor: Warning and Decision*. Stanford, CA: Stanford University Press.

Wohlstetter, Roberta (1965) Cuba and Pearl Harbor: Hindsight and foresight. *Foreign Affairs*, 43: 691–707.

Wolfe, Tom (1970) *Radical Chic and Mau-Mauing the Flak Catchers*. New York: Farrar, Straus and Giroux.

19

Gossip, Information and Decision-Making

James G. March and Guje Sevón

Abstract

This paper examines the relation between information and decision-making, particularly in organizations. We observe that much of the information that human beings seek and receive is gossip, that is, information without decision relevance. We ask two general questions: Why do we observe so much idle talk in life? And what are the implications for understanding organizational decison-making and the design of management information systems? We conclude that the prevalence of idle talk stems from some systematic ways in which ordinary life, including ordinary managerial life, differs from the life anticipated by a focus on decision-making, and that information engineering may, as a result, be somewhat less informed by decision theory than we sometimes expect and somewhat more informed by literary criticism and the philosophy of education.

Introduction

In discussions of the design of information systems in organizations, the value of information is ordinarily linked to management in a simple way. We imagine that management is primarily a matter of making decisions and that a decision-maker chooses among several alternatives on the basis of information about consequences and preferences that are conditional on

---

This paper was first published in Lee S. Sproull and J. Patrick Crecine (eds), *Advances in Information Processing in Organizations*, Vol. 1, 1984, pp. 95–107. It was prepared for a symposium on information in organizations, at Carnegie-Mellon University, 16–17 October 1981. The authors are grateful for the comments of Nelly de Camargo, Omar El Sawy and Johan Olsen.

a choice. Additional information has value to the extent to which it can be expected to affect the choice. Thus, a prediction of snow in Helsinki has no value to a road maintenance crew in New York, as does a prediction of snow in New York in July. In the first case, the information is irrelevant to any decision; in the second it is redundant with prior information.

Within a decision theory frame, investments in information sources are made up to the point at which the marginal expected cost of the source equals the marginal expected improvement in decisions; and information systems are designed to assure that scarce resources of money and attention are allocated efficiently from such a point of view. The value of information depends on the decisions to be made, the precision and reliability of the information, and the availability of alternative sources (Marschak and Radner, 1972; Hirschleifer and Riley, 1979). Although calculating the relevant expected costs and returns is rarely trivial, the framework suggests some very useful rules of thumb: Don't pay for information that cannot affect choices you are making. Don't pay for information if the same information will be freely available anyway before you have to make a decision for which it is relevant. Don't pay for information that confirms something you already know. In general, we are led to an entirely plausible stress on the proposition that allocation of resources to information gathering or to information systems should depend on a clear idea of how potential information might affect decisions. Who needs the information and how is it relevant?

Actual investments in information and information sources appear to deviate considerably from these conventional canons of information management. Consider, for example, the daily newspaper. Significant numbers of individuals and institutions, including many located a considerable distance from New York, purchase and read the *New York Times*. The newspaper provides some information that is potentially relevant to some decisions faced by its readers: schedules of events, advertisements, reviews of books and various performances, market information, betting odds, etc. But what is the likely decision relevance of the information on sporting events? Or of the news from Washington, London, and Tokyo? Much of the political news we devour, like much of the news from Hollywood, is essentially gossip. It may have relevance to some decisions made by major political actors, but it is hard to see any analysis of the decision situations of professors in Palo Alto that would lead to an investment in the political or sports news of the *New York Times*, or indeed to much of the other content if the primary reason for such an investment were information value in standard decision terms (Simon, 1967).

The daily newspaper is only a mundane illustration of a more general phenomenon. Even in job situations with a good deal of task specificity, we devote substantial time to gathering and transmitting information that has no obvious connection to the immediate decisions we contemplate. Individual and organizational consumers of information invest in decision-support systems and patronize reports and conversations with little apparent attention to their decision relevance. Studies of the use of research in the public sector identify little connection between the research information that agencies seek and the decisions they make (Rich, 1977; Weiss, 1977; Deshpande, 1981). Business firms, armies, hospitals, and other organizations we observe systematically, gather, store, and display information that they do not, indeed could not, use; they invest in large information systems and in irrelevant forecasts (Swanson, 1978; Feldman and March, 1981). Although there is no question that individuals and organizations invest in decision-relevant information under many circumstances, much of the information that is gathered and reported makes little direct contribution to resolving choices. In that sense at least, it is essentially idle talk.

Understanding Idle Talk

The persistence and pervasiveness of idle talk makes it relevant not only to understanding everyday life but also to improving managerial behavior and to designing management information systems. Gossip cannot easily be ignored. It is either an inefficiency in information or a symptom of inadequacy in our ways of thinking about information. Without denying the former possibility, we wish to explore the latter. The information investments of individuals and organizations seem to suggest that the connection between information and action is more subtle than we have made it, or that our focus on choice as the central metaphor of life is misleading. We want to argue that both things are true and that they have implications for understanding and improving the uses of information in organizations.

Research on gossip is primarily concerned with information, with or without a known basis in fact, about the personal affairs of individuals (Hannertz, 1967; Rosnow and Fine, 1976). Gossip is sometimes seen as a simple source of entertainment (Rosnow and Fine, 1976). However, much of the research portrays gossip as contributing to system maintenance more than to decision-making. It is seen as a way to communicate rules, values, and morals – usually by pointing at failures to satisfy them. It facilitates the diffusion of community traditions and history (Lumley, 1925; Gluckman, 1968; Haviland, 1977), and the maintenance of exclusivity (Gluckman, 1963). Gossip is a way of making friends (Rosnow and Fine, 1976), a way of protecting personal interests (Paine, 1976; 1970), and a way of legitimizing collective action, such as a riot (Mitchell, 1956). Though it often reinforces existing beliefs by providing an interpretation of ambiguous experience that is consistent with them (Allport and Postman, 1965), and offering a guide to existing social structure (Hannertz, 1967), gossip is also a vehicle for social change. It is a mechanism for a collective reconstruction of reality in which existing explanations of the nature of things are modified and new sensibilities and ideas emerge and are elaborated (Shibutani, 1966).

It is clear that such research on gossip can hope to provide only indirect clues to the analysis of idle talk in organizations, but it suggests that there may be somewhat more intelligence in the social processing of decision-irrelevant information than a decision theoretic analysis would indicate. Although our search for reasons for idle talk will extend beyond the relatively narrow focus of gossip research, it is in the same general spirit. We will argue that an exclusive focus on the role of information in well-defined decisions is likely to lead to an inadequate characterization of the information investment problem and thus to inadequacies in the design of management information systems. In particular, we will argue that:

1 Information systems need to be exercised in slack times in order to be useful when needed. Information is processed, in part, to maintain the system rather than to use it.
2 Human action is often less a matter of choice than a matter of imitating the actions of others, learning from experience, and matching rules and situations on the basis of appropriateness.
3 Decisions are often made in situations that are quite distant from the situations implicit in ideas of rational choice. Neither the precise decisions, the alternatives, the objectives, nor the causal structures are clear.
4 Information is often as much dedicated to developing interpretations, explanations, understandings, and enjoyments of the events of life as it is to resolving specific choices.

Gossip as System Maintenance

Idle talk is a way an information system is kept effective. On the one hand, it smooths interpersonal and inter-group strains introduced by organizational life. People engage in idle talk in order to exhibit their reasonability and legitimacy, to exchange sentiments of solidarity, to reduce the risks of misunderstanding, and to make it easier to arrange the minor flexibilities that allow an organization to function (Frankenberg, 1957; Gluckman, 1963; Rosnow and Fine, 1976). Arguments that Finnish business organizations need the sauna in order to thrive, or that American businesses need the three-martini lunch, may be as fatuous as they appear; but coordination in families, neighborhoods, societies, and organizations is facilitated by the gossip that fills such institutions. This integrating and catalytic consequence of talk is hard to link concretely to specific actions or specific consequences, but it appears to almost all observers of social systems to be relatively fundamental.

Moreover, a communication system may need irrelevant exercise to maintain effectiveness. Individuals, organizations, and species risk developing specializations that reflect optimal short-run allocations of effort and ignore long-run investments in capabilities for dealing with infrequent or unlikely situations of importance. From this perspective, the specific content of talk is largely irrelevant. Gossip maintains links among people, for example in a neighborhood or between organizations, during those long periods when communication is unneeded, so that the communication links will be easily available should they be needed. Similarly, an organization may find that idle talk has the consequence of maintaining connections among parts of the organization that require few regular connections. Idle talk of this sort is an inexpensive substitute for emergency drills. From such a point of view, the justification for idle talk comes not from some subtle relevance but directly from its irrelevance. If it is desirable to maintain links among parts of an organization that are, under normal conditions, quite sensibly not connected, the decision irrelevance of gossip has the admirable property of producing contact between parts of an organization having no current need for coordination.

Information and Alternative Concepts of Action

The idea of choice and the idea of expected value maximization with which it is joined in contemporary decision theory are possible metaphors for thinking about action in organizations, but they are not the only possible metaphors. The idea of decision-making implies an anticipatory, consequential logic. That is, it assumes that action results from two guesses about the future: a guess about the uncertain future consequences of taking one action or another, and a guess about the uncertain future feelings a decision-maker will have about those consequences when they are realized. Such a vision seems often to be a useful one for understanding some parts of organizational action, but students of organizations generally note several other ways in which organizational actions might be interpreted (March, 1981).

It is possible to see action as reflecting *experiential learning* in which propensities for doing one thing or another change as a result of simple behavioral reinforcement. In such a view, action is history dependent rather than expectational; the relevant information is information on contemporaneous events or past experiences rather than forecasts of the future. It is possible to see action as reflecting *contagion*, as spreading through a population of actors like measles through a population of children. In such a view, action diffuses on the basis of exposure and susceptibility; the relevant information is information on what other people are doing. It is possible to see action as *rule-following*, as the matching of rules, procedures and routines to appropriate situations. The routines may be seen as having evolved or been learned. Experiential history is stored in the rules and cannot easily be retrieved in encoded form. As a consequence, the logic of routine action is classificatory rather than consequential or anticipatory. It is filled with calculations of appropriateness and the relevant information is information that maps a set of rules for action onto a situation.

These alternative metaphors for action have been used extensively in interpreting individual and organizational behavior. They imply a different conception of relevant information than that based on a conception of anticipatory choice. In general, the information requirements for learning, diffusion, and for rule, procedure, and routine following place a greater emphasis on knowing what has been happening in the past, or is happening now, than do the requirements for decision-making, and a lesser emphasis on forecasting the future. The cognitive questions they ask involve description and classification more than they do chains of conditional consequences. The dominant vision is one that sees an organization as monitoring the environment for surprises (threats or opportunities) rather than assessing alternatives. Some information that looks like idle talk within the frame of intentional, anticipatory choice is more relevant to action when it is seen within these other metaphors.

The Decision Context of Information

Some decisions in organizations are readily amenable to a tight linkage between flows of specific information and the making of specific decisions. The chatter between an aircraft pilot and an air traffic controller, for example, normally contains very little idle talk. Information is precoded in decision-relevant form. Similar situations are common throughout modern organizations, as are successful efforts to design and maintain sensible information inventories. An optimal information inventory can be determined as long as it is possible to make reliable and precise predictions of future decision deadlines and information requirements. In a stable, uncomplicated environment, such forecasts will often be accurate enough to connect the collection of specific information to specific future decisions. We would expect an optimal decision-support system to develop an inventory of information that has, relative to its cost, a reasonable chance of being useful in future decisions.

There are, however, other kinds of decision contexts and it seems at least possible that the pervasiveness of gossip is due, in part, to the ways some decision contexts lead to loose linkages between specific current decisions and specific current information. First, there is no necessary reason to expect that decision deadlines will be consistent with the timing of information. One reason for an organization to gather information that is irrelevant to immediate choices is the disparity between the time (or other resources) required to obtain the information and the time that will be available when a decision using the information has to be made. If it takes a relatively long time to assemble and interpret information, it may be necessary to invest in information inventories in anticipation of the future stream of decisions. Decisions in modern warfare are an obvious example of a situation in which the real time demand for decisions in battle may easily overload an army's information gathering capabilities unless substantial information inventories are developed in advance. Planning for emergencies in general involves building inventories of information and routines whose relevance depends on a possibly unlikely contingency. Similarly, the work of collecting and organizing information about customers, competitors, friends, and enemies often cannot reasonably be postponed until the specific decisions involved are immediate.

Under such circumstances, it is possible that the 'irrelevance' of many investments in information is a *post hoc* illusion. Normally, we commit ourselves to attending to a source with only an estimate of what will be said; we invest in a spy system with only an estimate of what it will produce; we buy an econometric forecasting service with only an estimate of what information it will generate. If only a few possible signals are important to decision, but they are very important and very unlikely, most of the information actually received from a decision-relevant source will appear to be decision-irrelevant.

Second, where the future stream of decisions is unclear and future preferences are ambiguous, the selection of an information inventory is likely to be difficult. Returns in terms of improved future decisions are hard to assess when the long-run decision stream is not well specified. We do not know what we might need to know. This ambiguity tends to make the collection of information more dependent on properties of the information available than on predictions of possible future decision contexts and leads to the accumulation of knowledge of unknown decision relevance. Since estimates of the costs of gathering and storing information are less affected by decision uncertainties than are estimates of the benefits, calculations of the net return from alternative information strategies are likely to be primarily sensitive to variations in costs. For example, organizations are likely to gather considerable information of dubious benefit to decision-makers when it is possible to transfer the costs of gathering it to another budget, as in the case of government agencies that require others to collect data for them or the case of central office functionaries in dealing with district offices. If information inventory decisions are primarily a function of the costs of information gathering and processing, idle talk is likely to be an attractive information system for many organizations and many individuals. It provides information in a timely and inexpensive way. The information may or may not turn out to be relevant in the long run, but future decisions are sufficiently unclear as to make such uncertainties characteristic of almost any information that is available.

Third, a loose link between decisions and information can be strategic. It is common in talking about the design of information systems to disregard conflicts of interest between information sources and decision-makers, or to assume such conflicts are managed through explicit principal-agent contracts that assure jointly consistent behavior. In this way, strategic manipulation of information can be ignored. Where such contracts are difficult to specify or conclude, however, innocent information sources cannot be assumed. A request by a decision-maker for information is a signal of decision relevance and thereby an invitation for information sources to try to manipulate the content or increase the implicit price of information. Consequently, it may be useful for a decision-maker to obscure information relevance, to encourage the free flow of mostly irrelevant information in order to reduce the precision with which decision consequences can be anticipated by information sources. Such a strategy does not reduce the incentive toward lying by information sources, but it limits the potential for lying effectively and increases the innocence of the unwittingly relevant information that is provided.

Information and Interpretation

At most, the *New York Times* is relevant to only a few decisions most of us can expect to make in the foreseeable future. It is filled with gossip about politics, sports, art and finance that is distant from choices that we face. Yet, we think it possible that the *New York Times* is, nonetheless, useful to our lives. It provides the storyline for our pretenses and the content of our conversations. To see life or management as decision-making is to see it inadequately; and one of the reasons that much of the information that is communicated in organizations, as in life, is not obviously relevant to decision-making is that choice is not as compelling a metaphor for managers or other individuals as it is for students for choice. From many points of view, individual and organizational life is better seen as dedicated to developing interpretations of events and understandings of history than as making choices.

Intelligent choice often presumes understanding, of course, and it is possible to see the interpretation of history as instrumental to the action (choices) by which we seek to control our fate. It can, however, be seen as more fundamental than that. Perhaps interpretation is more a primary feature of human behavior than a servant of choice. From such a perspective, information is sought and considered because it contributes to understanding what is going on in life; and understanding what is going on is important independent of any purpose to which the knowledge might be put. Perhaps we can better understand the uses of information in organizations if we see information, and decision-making, as part of an effort to comprehend and appreciate human existence, as driven by elementary curiosity as much as by a hope for instrumental advantage. Information is not gathered in preparation for life. Gathering information *is* life. Moreover, this process of appreciation, of discovering, elaborating, and communicating interpretations of events, is a pleasure. Individuals and organizations are entertained by exchanging information and constructing what might be imagined to be true or just imagined. Fantasy is a part of understanding and idle talk is fun.

Such a viewpoint is not novel. It is familiar to literature, as well as anthropology and sociology, less familiar to economics. We can see organizations as having been designed (or evolved) around some problems of developing, enjoying, and sharing interpretations of reality; communication in organizations as tied to the discovery, clarification, and elaboration of meaning, and the process of decision-making in organizations as a performance within which individuals and groups construct an interpretation of experience that can be shared meaningfully and enjoyably.

Because understanding what is going on is important, people who understand what is going on are viewed as people of importance. People who know what is going on are eager to exhibit that fact and the exchange of information is the exchange of signals about power, position and competence. Note that from this perspective what makes information a source of power is not any added capabilities for effective action that knowledge provides, but rather the simple possession of a scarce and valued resource and the capability for signaling individual and organizational significance. Information is exchanged for other information (or other goods); it is exhibited as testimony to worth, much the way a plutocrat exhibits wealth.

If we see decisions as being somewhat less central to life than they are to decision theory, it should not be surprising that a theory of information *for decision-making* finds parts of information life irrelevant, and if the purpose of a formal information system is to strengthen the information base of current decision-making, it may not be necessary to be overly concerned with these 'irrelevant' considerations. If management can be seen as decision-making in a decision theory mode, then there is no substantial difference between the idea of a good management information system and the idea of a good decision-support system. Designing the former consists in designing the latter.

However, if we take a more general perspective on management, the design implications of these other factors may not be trivial. If we relax the presumption that the primary interpretive theme of management is choice and, thus, that the quality of management is determined primarily by the intelligence of the managerial decision-making, we may conclude that we have been excluding some important things in thinking about information in organizations. If management is seen as involving discovering new objectives, developing myths and interpretations of life, and modifying the diffuse beliefs and cultural understandings that make organizational events comprehensible and life enjoyable (March, 1973; 1978; 1984; Jönsson and Lundin, 1977; Feldman and March, 1981), then it is not obvious that the best management information system is a decision-support system. Intelligent managers might pay more for, and attend more to, something different.

Management Information Systems and Education

If the arguments made in the preceding section have merit, then it is not hard to see why the gathering and the processing of information in organizations would involve a significant amount of idle talk. At the same time, there seems little reason to assume that the chorus of idle talk that we hear in organizations is optimal. We require some way of approaching the design of information systems that is sensitive to the sensibility of idle talk, yet seeks to improve the quality of information available. We have tried to argue that a decision-oriented view of information, however valuable within the context of decision-making, may sometimes be misleading as a more general base for understanding and improving a management information system. If the innocence of information cannot be assumed, or if the future stream of decisions cannot be anticipated well, or if action is based on matching behavioral rules to appropriate situations, or if the point of information is the elaboration of a system of meaning, organizational engineers need a somewhat different set of models for designing information systems.

As always, it is easier to see the limitations of a decision perspective on information than to develop a clear alternative. One major problem, of course, is that the several complications we have identified do not immediately suggest a common remedy. If we focus on the complexities of the information context of decision-making while still retaining a general decision theory frame, we can generate a set of suggestions that emphasize exploiting reductions in the costs (or improvements in the speed) of gathering, storing, and retrieving information, working on reducing response time and retrieval time rather than anticipating specific needs. If we focus on alternative ideas for examining action, we generate a set of suggestions that emphasize monitoring the environment for critical signals and surprises, working on our capabilities for timely notice of environmental events rather than analytical or expectational capabilities. If we focus on the uses of information in the construction of meaning, we generate a set of suggestions that emphasize the ways in which meaningful stories are constructed and shared and the understanding of experience, working on the flexibility and imagination of the system for creating and articulating interpretations.

These different ideas lead to different implications, not obviously mutually consistent and not trivial to accomplish. It would appear that we require some notion of the value of alternative information sources that is less tied to a prior specification of a decision (or class of decisions) than to a wide spectrum of possible decisions impossible to anticipate in the absence of the information; less likely to show the consequences of known alternatives for existing goals than to suggest new alternatives and new objectives; less likely to test old ideas than to provoke new ones; less pointed toward anticipating uncertain futures than toward interpreting ambiguous pasts. The requirements considerably exceed our capabilities. We neither understand idle talk well enough nor are rash enough to propose a precise alternative model for the design of information systems in organizations. Our objective is more timid, to propose some caution in treating the problems of organizational information as problems in improving decision-making and to suggest that alternative perspectives are not completely alien to our intellectual traditions.

In fact, a view of information and life not far from the one we have sketched is a quite traditional one, associated classically with literature, art and education; and if there are appropriate models for a management information system of this sort, perhaps they lie in discussions of the nature and design of education rather than in modern theories of decision. Perhaps management information designers could profit from some attention to the ancient and modern discussions of the linkage between education and life, the arguments over the relevance of 'relevance' in thinking about a curriculum, and the efforts of art and literary criticism to explicate the expression of meaning.

To be sure, there are differences between an organization and a society and between managers and educators or artists. Many of those differences involve the relative specificity of activities and objectives in organizations, compared with the relative diffuseness of broader social relations. The differences make the leap from the analysis of education to the analysis of organizational information a large and possibly treacherous one, but not entirely foolish. As we discover the elements of loose coupling and ambiguity in organizations, the role of symbols in decision-making and information processing, the place of myths, stories and rituals in management and the significance of beliefs in the transformation of organizations (March and Olsen, 1976; Sproull, 1981), some of the distances between the properties of organizations and the properties of other social systems seem to grow smaller.

Proposing education as a possible alternative model for the design of information systems is undoubtedly disquieting. It seems possible that we know less about designing an education than we know about almost anything. At least, our confidence about it is gone. Discussions of curriculum cycle endlessly through questions of relevance without apparent resolution and educational philosophers seem hardly less confused than we. Indeed, some recent proposals for educational reform seem to be dedicated to thinking of education as a decision-support system and to tying educational activities and information rather tightly to their relevance for individual actions. It has become common to justify elements of a curriculum in terms of the improvement they provide in some specifiable activities that students will face in the future; some choices they will make.

That is not the philosophy of education – or of life – that we have in mind. We recall another long tradition in education and literature, one that views both education and poetry as linked loosely to a variety of ill-perceived possible future worlds and to understanding the confusions of life (Eliot, 1961; Freire, 1973). Such a vision sees education and literature as elegant forms of idle talk, as ways in which we gain appreciation of our existence and develop our sensitivity. To describe organizational management in such terms is, of course, to glorify it. It suggests that office memoranda might be viewed as forms of poetry and staff meetings as forms of theater and we may perhaps wonder whether it would be better to admit a distinction between a divisional sales chart and a Picasso painting – if only to assure that each may achieve its unique qualities. The dangers are real, but to a glorified view of idle talk and memoranda, we will add a romantic view of the possibilities for artistry in organizational engineering. Perhaps, with a little imagination here and there, educational philosophy and literary criticism could be used to point management information systems in the direction of a useful quality of irrelevance.

References

Allport, G. W., and L. Postman (1965) *The Psychology of Rumor*. New York: Henry Holt.

Deshpande, R. (1981) Action and enlightenment functions of research: comparing private- and public-sector perspectives. *Knowledge: Creation, Diffusion, Utilization,* 2: 317–30.

Eliot, T. S. (1961) *On Poetry and Poets*. New York: Noonday.

Feldman, M. S., and J. G. March (1981) Information in organizations as signal and symbol, *Administrative Science Quarterly*, 26: 171–86.

Frankenberg, R. (1957) *Village on the Border*. London: Cohen and West.

Freire, P. (1973) *Education for Critical Consciousness*. New York: Seabury.

Gluckman, M. (1963) Gossip and scandal. *Current Anthropology,* 4: 307–16.

Gluckman, M. (1968) Psychological, sociological and anthropological explanations of witchcraft and gossip: a clarification, *Man* 3, (n.s.), 20–34.

Hannertz, U. (1967), Gossip, networks and culture in a black American ghetto, *Ethnos*, 32: 35–60.

Haviland, J. B. (1977) *Gossip, Reputation, and Knowledge in Zinacantan*. Chicago: University of Chicago Press.

Hirshleifer, J., and J. G. Riley (1979) The analytics of uncertainty and information: an expository survey, *Journal of Economic Literature*, 17: 1375–417.

Jönsson, S. A., and R. A. Lundin (1977) Myths and wishful thinking as management tools. In Paul C. Nystrom and William H. Starbuck (eds), *Prescriptive Models of Organizations*. Amsterdam: North-Holland, pp. 151–70.

Lumley, F. E. (1925) *Means of Social Control*. New York: Century.

March, J. G. (1973) Model bias in social action, *Review of Educational Research*, 42, 413–29.

March, J. G. (1978) American public school administration: a short analysis, *School Review*, 82: 217–50.

March, J. G. (1984) How we talk and how we act: administrative theory and administrative life. In T. J. Sergiovanni and J. E. Corbally (eds), *Leadership and Organizational Culture*, Urbana, Ill: University of Illinois Press, pp. 18–35.

March, J. G. (1981) Footnotes to organizational change, *Administrative Science Quarterly,* 26: 563–77.

March, J. G., and J. P. Olsen (1976) *Ambiguity and Choice in Organizations*. Bergen: Universitetsforlaget.

Marschak, J., and R. Radner (1972) *Economic Theory of Teams*. New Haven: Yale.

Mitchell, J. C. (1956) *The Yao Village*. Manchester: Manchester University Press.

Paine, R. (1967) What is gossip about: an alternative hypothesis, *Man* 2 (n.s.), 278–85.

Paine, R. (1970) Information communication and information management, *The Canadian Review of Sociology and Anthropology*, 7: 172–88.

Rich, P. F. (1977) Uses of social science information by federal bureaucrats: knowledge for action versus knowledge for understanding. In Carol H. Weiss (ed.), *Using Social Research in Public Policy Making*. Lexington: Heath.

Rosnow, R. L., and G. A. Fine (1976) *Rumor and Gossip: The Social Psychology of Hearsay*. New York: Elsevier.

Shibutani, T. (1966) *Improvised News: A Sociological Study of Rumor*. Indianapolis: Bobbs-Merill.

Simon, H. A. (1967) Information can be managed, *Think*, December, 7–11.

Sproull, L. S. (1981) Beliefs in organizations. In Paul C. Nystrom and William H. Starbuck (eds), *Handbook of Organizational Design*. New York: Oxford, pp. 203–24.

Swanson, E. B. (1978) The two faces of organizational information, *Accounting, Organizations and Society*, 3: 237–46.

Weiss, C. H. (1977) Research for policy's sake: the enlightenment function of social research, *Policy Analysis*, 3: 531–46.

Index